IN THE KITCHEN

IN THE KITCHEN

MONICA ALI

Doubleday

LONDON • TORONTO • SYDNEY • AUCKLAND • JOHANNESBURG

This novel is a work of fiction. All characters, names of places and descriptions of events are the product of the author's imagination and any resemblance to actual persons or places is entirely coincidental.

TRANSWORLD PUBLISHERS
61–63 Uxbridge Road, London W5 5SA
A Random House Group Company
www.rbooks.co.uk

First published in Great Britain
in 2009 by Doubleday
an imprint of Transworld Publishers

A CIP catalogue record for this book
is available from the British Library.

ISBN 9780385614573 (cased)
ISBN 9780385614580 (tpb)

Addresses for Random House Group Ltd companies outside the UK
can be found at: www.randomhouse.co.uk
The Random House Group Ltd Reg. No. 954009

The Random House Group Limited supports The Forest Stewardship
Council (FSC), the leading international forest-certification organization. All our
titles that are printed on Greenpeace-approved FSC-certified paper carry the FSC logo.
Our paper procurement policy can be found at
www.rbooks.co.uk/environment

Typeset in 11.5/15pt Bembo by
Falcon Oast Graphic Art Ltd.
Printed and bound in Great Britain by
Clays Limited, Bungay, Suffolk

2 4 6 8 10 9 7 5 3 1

Mixed Sources
Product group from well-managed
forests and other controlled sources
www.fsc.org Cert no. TT-COC-2139
© 1996 Forest Stewardship Council
FSC

For Kim

CHAPTER ONE

WHEN HE LOOKED BACK, HE FELT THAT THE DEATH OF THE UKRAINIAN was the point at which things began to fall apart. He could not say that it was the cause, could not say, even, that it was a cause, because the events which followed seemed to be both inevitable and entirely random, and although he could piece together a narrative sequence and take a kind of comfort in that, he had changed sufficiently by then to realize that it was only a story he could tell, and that stories were not, on the whole, to be trusted. Nevertheless, he fixed the beginning at the day of the Ukrainian's death, when it was the following day on which, if a life can be said to have a turning point, his own began to spin.

On that morning in late October, Gleeson, the restaurant manager, sat down with Gabriel for their regular meeting. He had mislaid, so it seemed, his oily professional charm.

'You do realize it's on your patch,' said Gleeson. 'You realize that, yes?'

It was the first time that Gabe had seen him slip out of character. And the night porter certainly was on Gabe's 'patch'. What, in that case, was worrying Gleeson? In this business, until you could see all the angles, it was better to keep your mouth shut. Gabe tapped the neck of the crystal vase that sat on the table between them. 'Plastic flowers,' he said, 'are for Happy Eaters and funeral parlours.'

Gleeson scratched his scalp and fleetingly examined his fingernails.

'Yes or no, Chef? Yes or no?' His eyes were pale blue and disreputably alert. His hair, by contrast, he wore with a sharp side parting and a fervid rectitude, as if all his phoney honour depended on it.

Gabe looked across the empty restaurant, over the pink-tinged table linen and leather-backed chairs, the silver that here and there glinted in the shreds of autumn sun, the chandelier, ugly as a bejewelled dowager, the polished oak bar that, without a single elbow propped upon it, was too dark and infected with loneliness to look at for very long. In the circumstances, he decided, it was unwise to concede anything at all. 'The food and beverage meeting, three months ago at least. You agreed, no more plastic flowers.'

'They're silk,' said Gleeson smartly. 'Silk, please. I have never had plastic in my restaurant.'

'Now I think about it,' said Gabe, 'there were some other things . . .'

'Chef.' Gleeson laced his fingers together. 'You are a straight talker. I am a straight talker. Let's not beat about the bush.' He tilted his head and sieved the words through a smile. It was how he greeted diners, gliding in with hands clasped and head cocked. 'A dead body *on the premises*. This is hardly the time to be discussing pepper pots.' His tone was both ingratiating and contemptuous, the one reserved for the pre-theatre crowd, tourists and anyone – easily identified by the way they kept looking around – who had been saving up.

'For God's sake, Stanley. They took him away.'

'Really?' said Gleeson. 'Really? They took him away? Well. That settles everything. How stupid of me to waste your time.' He got up. 'I'm telling you, Chef . . . listen . . .' He stared at Gabe and then shook his head. 'Shit.' He adjusted his cufflinks and stalked off, muttering, quivering like a cat's tail.

Gabe went back to his office and pulled out the banqueting file. He shuffled the papers, and found the sheet he wanted. Sirovsky Product Launch. Under the 'Menu' heading, Oona had written 'Canapés: spring rolls, smoked salmon, quiche squares, guacamole, vol-au-vents (prawn), mini choc mousses.' Her handwriting was maddeningly childish. To look at it made you think of her sucking the end of her pencil. He put a thick black line through the list. He checked the per-head budget, staff resource and comments sections. 'Let's put out all the flags on this one.' Mr Maddox was taking a special interest. Put out all the flags. What did that mean? Caviar and truffle oil? Stuff the profit and loss? Gabe sighed. Whatever it meant, it wasn't quiche squares and prawn vol-au-vents.

The office was a white stud-walled cubicle in the corner of the kitchen, with a surfeit of air-conditioning ducts and a window over the battlefield. Apart from Gabe's desk and chair, the filing cabinet and a stand for the printer, there was room for one other plastic seat, squeezed in between desk and door. Sometimes, if he was busy completing order forms or logging timesheets, Gabe let his phone ring until it beeped and played the message. *You have reached the office of Gabriel Lightfoot, executive chef of the Imperial Hotel, London. Please leave your name and number after the tone and he will call you back as soon as possible.* To listen to it you'd think the office was something else, that he was someone else, altogether.

Looking up, he saw Suleiman working steadily at his mise-en-place, chopping shallots and, with a clean sweep of the broad knife blade, loading them into a plastic box. Victor came round from the larder section carrying a baguette. He stood behind Suleiman, clamped the bread between his thighs and, holding on to Suleiman's shoulders, aimed the baguette at his buttocks. In every kitchen there had to be one. There had to be a clown. Suleiman put down his knife. He grabbed the baguette and tried to stuff it down Victor's throat.

Even yesterday, after Benny had gone down to the catacombs to look for rat poison and returned with the news; after Gabe had seen Yuri for himself, after the police had arrived, after Mr Maddox had come down personally to announce that the restaurant would be closed and to speak to everyone about their responsibilities for the day; even after all that, Victor had to be the clown. He sidled up to Gabe, smiling and winking, a red flush to his schoolboy cheeks, as if a death were a small and welcome distraction like catching an eyeful of cleavage or the flash of a stocking top. 'So, he was naked, old Yuri.' Victor tittered and then made the sign of the cross. 'I think he was waiting for his girlfriend. You think so, Chef, eh, do you think?'

★

Naturally, the first thing Gabe had done was call the general manager, but he got through to Maddox's deputy instead. Mr James insisted on seeing for himself, arriving with a clipboard shielding his chest. He disappeared into the basement and Gabe thought, this could go on for ever. How many sightings of a dead body were required before it became an established fact? No one said it was the Loch Ness monster down there. He smiled to himself. The next moment he was swept by a watery surge of panic. What if Yuri was not dead? Benny had told him with a calm and unquestionable certainty that Yuri was dead. But what if he was still alive? There was a pool of blood around his head and he didn't look like a living thing because his legs, his chest, were blue, but who wouldn't be cold, stretched out naked and bleeding on the icy catacomb floor? Gabe should have checked for a pulse, he should have put something soft beneath Yuri's head, at the very least he should have called for an ambulance. *I should have sent you a doctor, Yuri, not Mr James with his bloody Montblanc fountain pen and his executive leather pad.*

The deputy manager was taking his time. Gabe stood in the kitchen with his chefs. The trainees, gathered round an open dustbin brimming with peelings, chewed their tongues, scratched their noses or fiddled with their pimples. Damian, the youngest, a straggly seventeen, trailed his hand in the bin as though contemplating diving in and hiding his sorry carcass under the rotting mound. Stand up straight, thought Gabriel. At another time he might have said it out loud. It occurred to him that Damian was the only other English person who worked in the kitchen. *Don't let the side down, lad.* It was a ridiculous thought. The kind of thing his father might say. Gabriel looked at Damian until Damian could not help looking back at him. Gabe smiled and nodded, as though to provide some kind of stiffening for those rubbery seventeen-year-old bones. The boy began flapping his hand inside the bin and the tic in his right eye started up. Jesus Christ, thought Gabe, and walked round to the sauce section to get the boy out of his sight.

The chefs de partie, Benny, Suleiman and Victor, lined up against the worktop with their arms folded across their chests, as if staging a wild-cat strike. Beyond them, Ivan was still working, cooking off lamb shanks that would later be braised. Ivan was the grill man. His station, at the front of the kitchen, close to the pass, encompassed a huge salamander, a triple-burner char grill, four-ring hob and double griddle. He kept them at full blaze. Around his forehead he wore a bandanna that soaked up some, though by no means all, of the sweat. He took pride in the amount of blood he managed to wipe from his fingers on to his apron. He worked split shifts, lunch and dinner six days a week, and apart from the crew who came in at five in the morning to grill sausages and fry eggs for the buffet breakfast, no one was allowed to venture into Ivan's domain. Gabriel liked to rotate his chefs between the sections, Benny on cold starters and desserts one month, Suleiman the next, but Ivan was implacable. 'Nobody else knowing about steaks like me, Chef. Don't put me chopping rabbit leaves.' He had a cauliflower ear, sharp Slavic cheekbones and an even sharper accent, the consonants jangling together like loose change. Gabe had decided straight away to move him but he had not done it yet.

Filling suddenly with impatience, Gabe walked towards the base-ment door. He slowed and finally halted by the chill cabinet of soft drinks and dairy desserts. If Yuri wasn't really dead then the deputy manager would be giving first aid and questioning him closely, doing all the things that Gabriel should have done, before going upstairs to report to Mr Maddox about all the things that Gabriel had failed to do. Gabe was aghast at the enormity of his managerial lapse. He was here not because he wanted to be, but only to prove himself. Show us, said the would-be backers for his own restaurant, manage a kitchen on that scale and we'll put up the money; work there for a year and turn that place around. They'd get word, of course. Everyone in this whole stinking business would know. And what would he say to Mr Maddox? How would he explain? To report, say, a side of salmon as missing, suspected stolen, only to have it turn up in the wrong store-room, that would be bad enough, but to report the death of an employee and to have the employee turn up alive if not exactly well, that was ineptitude of an altogether different order. Damn that Benny and his idiotic certainty. What made him an expert on death? Gabe touched the crown of his head where a little wormhole of baldness

11

had recently appeared. Damn that Yuri as well. He leaned against the chill cabinet, grimacing and swallowing, as if worry were something that had to be kept low down, somewhere in the intestinal tract.

When the deputy manager came through the door, Gabe scanned him quickly for signs. Mr James's fingers trembled as he punched numbers into his mobile phone and his face was unnaturally white, as if he too had bled out on the concrete floor. Thank God, thought Gabriel, preparing to act with authority. He tried to feel sorry for cursing Yuri but all he could feel was relief.

The ambulance and two policemen, a local foot patrol, arrived simultaneously. The paramedics pronounced the porter dead, but for a while all else was confusion. The foot patrol radioed a sergeant who in turn called in the Homicide Assessment Team. By the time Maddox got in from his meeting there were half a dozen coppers in his kitchen.

'What the hell is going on?' he said, as if he held Gabriel personally responsible.

'Get that back door locked,' said the sergeant. 'The fire exit too. I've just found someone trying to slip off.'

One of the plain-clothes guys – Gabriel had quickly lost track of who was who – rapped a work surface with a slotted spoon. 'Everyone needs to stay put. We'll be talking to you all individually. And I'm not interested in your papers. I'm not here for that.'

Mr James did his best to look authoritative, drawing himself up to full height. 'Every one of our employees has a national insurance number. I can vouch for it personally. That is a fact.'

The policeman ignored him. 'How you got here is no concern of mine. We're here to do a job. Those of you worrying about your papers can stop right now. Because *we* are not worried about *you*. Clear? We just want to know what you know. Everyone clear on that?'

'What the bloody hell is going on?' said Maddox.

There was no chatter in the kitchen now, only a row of watchful faces. One of the policemen emerged from the basement and asked Maddox and Gabriel to step into Gabe's office. 'Parks,' he said. 'I'm the senior investigating officer on this case.'

'Case?' said Maddox. 'What case?'

Parks smiled thinly. 'Duty officer – that's the sergeant there – didn't like the look of it. Soon as someone calls it sus, you're dealing with a crime scene, incident log's up and running.'

'Did he fall or was he pushed?' said Maddox, simmering. 'Do me a favour.'

'Matter of fact,' said Parks, 'I agree with you. Looks like your chap fell. Tell you what's caused the confusion. There's cast-off on the floor and a spot on the wall as well.'

'Meaning?' said Gabe.

Parks yawned. 'Apart from the blood pooled by the head there's some splashes around the place – like you might get if someone had been hit on the back of the head, for instance.'

'You're not saying . . .' began Maddox.

'I'm not. The CSM's taken a sample. Crime scene manager. We do like our acronyms.'

'And the splashes?' said Gabe.

'Bit of a boozer, was he? Few empties down there. Probably what's happened is he slipped over, cut his head, got up and staggered around a bit, and fell back down. I don't blame the duty officer for calling it, but when I can get a BPA expert down there – should be someone on his way now . . .' He checked his watch. 'Blood pattern analysis. When I get my BPA guy down there, hundred to one that's what he'll say.'

'So all this is a formality,' said Maddox.

'No sign of robbery or anything like that. His things don't seem to have been disturbed. Of course we'll be thorough. Once you set the ball rolling, you see, you've got to work it through to the end.'

'Can we open again tomorrow?' said Maddox.

The detective stuck his hands in his trouser pockets. He looked, Gabriel thought, somehow disappointing in his brown chinos and oatmeal sports jacket. 'Don't see why not,' said Parks. 'Should have the body out of there soon. The CSM's got to bag the head and hands and then it can go for the post mortem. That area will stay cordoned off for the time being.'

'The post mortem's the end of it?' said the general manager.

'The coroner will give his initial findings – injuries consistent with a fall, that kind of thing, open an inquest and adjourn it awaiting the final police report.'

'And the post-mortem results you get back when?'

'Unless the BPA throws up any surprises it won't go through on a rush job. We can get it done in forty-eight hours if there's cause, otherwise it's more like five or six days. Ah, looks like my blood man's arrived. I take it you've called environmental health?'

'Oh yes,' said Mr Maddox grimly. 'We've called in the council. We've called in Health and Safety. We've not called in the navy yet, but we've called everyone else.'

Gabe checked the time. Nearly ten thirty. He had been sitting in his office over half an hour without getting a single thing done. He tried to remember the last time he'd spoken to the Ukrainian. A conversation about the grease on the extractor hoods, but that was about a month ago. 'Yes, Chef,' Yuri would have said. 'I'll see to it, Chef.' Something like that. There wasn't much call for an executive chef to speak to a night porter unless he was giving trouble and Yuri, until yesterday, had been no trouble at all.

Oona knocked and entered the office, all in one bustling move. She squashed her backside into the orange plastic seat. 'I been keepin' up the spirits out there with a little bitta prayer.' Her voice was invariably strangled, as though she was just about managing not to laugh or cry or shout. She leaned her elbows on the desk and rested her chin on her hands.

We're not here for tea and bloody buns, thought Gabe. There was something about Oona that infuriated him. It wasn't the fact that she was so often late for work, it wasn't the inefficient manner in which she worked, it wasn't that her idea of fine dining was stew and dumplings *with a sprig of parsley on top*, and it wasn't even the fact that she couldn't cook so much as a fish finger without managing to cock it up. He had worked with lazier cooks, stupider cooks, cooks who would serve up a bowl of sick if they thought they could get away with it. What offended him about Oona was simply this: her domesticity. When she blew into his office and sat down it was as if she had just got home with the shopping, looking forward to a cuppa and a chat. The way she talked, the way she walked, the way she pressed her bosom when she was thinking, all of it, at core, was irreducibly and inescapably domestic. In Gabe's experience, women who worked in kitchens – and there were a few – worked the hardest, swore the loudest and told the dirtiest jokes. It wasn't about being one of the boys, not necessarily – they could flirt like hell too – but it showed that they knew the rules. The professional kitchen was not the same as the domestic kitchen. The two were worlds apart. Only Oona – who by staying on the spot for the best or worst part of two decades had risen to the rank of executive sous-chef – seemed unaware of the distinction.

He reached in his desk drawer for the staff rota, noticing yet again the way the Formica was beginning to split and the notches carved in the plywood base, put there it was said by the previous chef who was counting the days spent sober on the job (a total of nine), and when he turned back to Oona he sat very straight and correct as if that might dissuade her from melting all over his desk.

'There's a lot of different religions in here, Oona. You want to watch out you don't offend someone.'

'Hoo-ee,' said Oona, showing her gold tooth. 'The good Lord don' mind 'bout the words. As long as he hear the prayer.'

'It wasn't him I was thinking about,' said Gabe, wondering, not for the first time, if he should get rid of her or if it would be more trouble than it was worth.

'Well, darlin',' said Oona, 'that is the problem right there.'

Give me strength, thought Gabe. 'Right,' he said briskly, 'difficult day today. Can you call the agency and get some cover for Yuri? For Benny too. He's at home, getting over the . . . the shock.' Benny, in fact, had not wanted to take a day off but Gabe had ordered it, knowing HR would otherwise look askance.

'Poor, poor ting,' said Oona. The words formed little explosions on her lips so it seemed they had been forced from her body by a series of blows to the chest. She rolled her eyes up to heaven.

'Yes,' said Gabe, though why Benny had been roaming the subterranean corridors – 'the catacombs' as they were known – way past the dry-goods and freezer rooms, way past where any stores were kept, had yet to be explained. It occurred to Gabriel that, but for Benny, Yuri might not have been found, not for a long time at least. Stupid, how stupid, he thought, without knowing quite what he meant.

'My day off,' said Oona. 'Of course it all happen on my day off.'

Gabe considered this for a moment. If she had not been off, Oona seemed to be saying, everything would have been OK. Or perhaps she was simply regretting missing out on the drama. 'We have to keep our minds on the job,' he said.

'Yes, Chef,' said Oona. She smiled, crinkling her almond-shaped eyes. Her face was much younger than her fifty-five years, smooth-skinned and plump with a scattering of girlish freckles across the bridge of her nose. There was no trace of grey in her hair which she wore cropped high above her little ears. She kept diamanté hairclips fastened to her chef's coat and, presumably, fixed them either side of her head after work. She was fat but somehow the fat added to her youthfulness, as though it was something she would outgrow. 'Yuri,' she said, 'that poor ting, living down there like a little old rat. How long you tink he been down there, mmm?'

'Oona,' said Gabe, searching for a way to keep the conversation on the straight and narrow, 'the police are looking into all that.'

Oona slipped off a shoe and reached down to massage her instep. Her feet, it seemed, belonged to her age. They were so broad they were practically square, and the black flats she wore to work strained at the seams. 'They going to interview me this afternoon. Mr Maddox say so this mornin'. Lord,' she said, cramming her foot back into the shoe, 'Lord only know what happen.'

'It's pretty clear, actually,' said Gabe. Parks looked like a pen-pusher but he clearly knew his job. The 'crime scene' forensics had borne out his theory, and there'd be no rush with the post mortem. 'Yuri was living in the basement. He had a mattress down there and everything, the other side of the rubbish chutes, in what used to be the old facilities office. He took a shower in the waiters' locker room, he'd probably been drinking, he was going back to his room, he slipped, he banged his head, he died. Tragic, yes. Mysterious, no, not at all.'

'Lord only know,' repeated Oona.

Gabe picked up a pen, clicked the top to release the nib and clicked again to retract it. He wondered what it was that Gleeson could not come out and say about Yuri. He was sure Gleeson was involved in some way. Why else would he be getting himself worked up? Everything would become apparent in the fullness of time. Gabe pressed the end of the pen over and over. Click, click, click, click, click.

'Never mind, darlin',' said Oona, patting his hand. 'We all feelin' it, you know.'

'Shall we get on?' said Gabriel. 'There's a lot to get through.'

'Yes, yes, yes. I know.' She wiggled her bottom to try and get comfortable, a difficult task in the circumstances, of being wedged between desk and door. 'But, Yuri, love him. What he tinkin'? It ain't no hotel down there.'

That was it. If something smelt bad you followed the trail and the trail led back to Gleeson. Gleeson was pulling every scam in the book and a few on top besides.

'You arks me,' said Oona, 'they gonna sue the arse off this place.'

'Who? Who is going to sue? Anyway, he wasn't supposed to *be* down there.' For a moment he had been sure that Gleeson was renting the space to Yuri, charging extra for the mattress perhaps, but now the idea seemed ludicrous. Those empty bottles of Rémy Martin. You don't buy premium brandy on a night porter's salary, not at full price anyway. It wasn't Gabe's business, though. There was going to be an inquest. Let them find out what they needed to know. Let Mr Maddox find out the rest.

'M'mm,' said Oona, with some apparent satisfaction. 'Get their arses sued.'

'That's as may be,' said Gabriel. 'What we've got to worry about is getting this staff rota up to date.'

'Got Nikolai covering for Benny,' said Oona, 'he know his stuff all right.'

Nikolai, one of the commis chefs, was on a lower grade than Benny but Oona was right, he was more than capable.

'Rang the agency 'bout an hour ago,' Oona continued. 'Two porters on they way.'

'Two? Who else is missing?'

'The girl. What's the name? You know, washing the pots and all.' She rubbed her breast while she thought. 'Oh, she so skinny that girl she pass under doors, she so thin she hard to see. You want to sit her down with someting nice and hot and say, for Lord's sake, child, you eat now. Eat!'

'She call in sick?' Gabe checked the time. This coffee morning had to come to an end.

'Got it now – Lena,' said Oona, laughing. 'Hoo. She leaner than me, all right.'

'She call in sick?' Gabe repeated. He vaguely recalled this skinny Lena.

'No,' said Oona, 'but nobody saw her yesterday, so I hear, and she not in today for her shift. Probably she took a scare, with all the tings that happen, you know.'

'Have you called her house, then?' Gabe asked.

Oona looked at him and pursed her lips, clearly deciding if he was mad or simply joking. Giving him the benefit of the doubt, she began to laugh her deep and throaty laugh. 'Go on,' she said, 'go on.'

It seemed to Gabe that Oona did not laugh the same way other people did. Other people laughed politely or rudely, sarcastically or knowingly, helplessly, hopelessly, with sadness or with joy, depending on the situation at hand. But Oona had only one laugh, as if in reply to some never-ending cosmic joke. He said, 'She doesn't have a phone. Of course not.' It was pointless prising phone numbers from porters anyway. If you managed to get through, it would be to someone who spoke no English. Or to someone who, in broken English, vehemently denied that the person in question had ever entered the UK, let alone set foot in their house. 'Is she agency or permanent?'

Oona thought for a moment. Gabriel looked over the kitchen floor and saw Victor emptying a plastic bag of frozen chips into a deep-fat fryer. Frozen chips were banned; all frozen vegetables were banned since Gabriel took charge, five months ago. But there was Victor, the smartarse, carrying on as if he were a law unto himself.

'She come through the agency,' Oona was saying, 'yes, that's right, mmm.' The sentence finished but she continued, mmming and yesing, soft little soothing sounds uttered beneath her breath as if she had divined his mounting rage and would blanket it with her mumbles.

'She shows up, tell her to get lost again. I'm not having it.'

'I goin' to give her a warnin',' said Oona. 'Got to have two or three warnin's.'

'No,' said Gabe. 'She's only agency.' He shrugged to show he was taking no pleasure in this. 'I'm sorry, Oona, but she's fired.'

The kitchen, along with the rest of the Imperial Hotel, was a product of the Victorian age. But while the lobby and function rooms, the bedrooms and bathrooms, the stairways and corridors and vestibules had been transmuted into twenty-first-century spaces within a nineteenth-century shell, the kitchen – despite numerous refurbishments and refittings – retained its workhouse demeanour, the indelible stamp of generations of toil. It was a large, low-ceilinged room; roughly square with two dog-legs attached, the first containing the vegetable prep area, the other housing the industrial-size dishwashers, one each for plates, glasses and pans. Beyond the washers and sinks was a short corridor that led to the unloading bay, where trucks pulled up from the early hours of the morning until late in the afternoon and to which Ernie (a lifer even by Oona's standards) scuttled back and forth from the tiny prefab hut where he sighed over his poetry and the computer that scared him half to death. Going back into the hotel but out on a wing from the main kitchen, just before you reached the offices filled with toothy young marketing assistants, was the pastry kitchen. In contrast to the big kitchen the air in here was permanently cool, in theory because of the nature of the work, but whenever Gabe walked in or even past he could not help but feel it was because of Chef Albert, whose icy breath could chill the warmest of hearts.

From where Gabe was standing now, with his back to the pass and his hands on the edge of the hot shelf that ran two-thirds the length of the room, he could not see these far reaches of his domain. He could see the larder, sauce, and fish and meat sections. He could see the tiny work station where one of the commis dished up endless burgers and fries for room service, turning back and forth between stainless steel worktop and the fry baskets and grill, circling round and back, round and back, like a dog settling down for a nap. And he could see the way that decades of half-hearted refits, of misaligned edges and a mishmash of equipment, gave the place a desperate kind of look, as if it were only just managing to hold itself together.

Even the floor, he thought, gives up. The tiles, he judged, had been laid in the last few years, heavy duty red-brown stone. But they failed to make it up to the edges and into the corners where archaeological trails of slate, terracotta and lino could be found. When the kitchen was busy, when knives wheeled and pans slammed, when the burners hissed and flared, when the white plates marched, when the chefs shouted orders and insults and jokes, swerving and bending, performing the modern dance of cuisine, this place was transformed.

But today the lunch service was dead. One of the porters, a Filipino in a dark green boiler suit, pushed a mop over the tiles with such detachment that it was the mop that seemed animate, dragging the porter along. On the grease-spattered back wall, painted an institutional sage, a health and safety poster and a ripped-out Page 3 pin-up fluttered in the stale draught of the electric fan. In twos and threes, beneath the life-sapping fluorescent lights, the chefs gossiped and planned cigarette breaks. What a place, thought Gabe, looking away, at the grilled and bolted back door and the barred and lightless window. What a place: part prison, part lunatic asylum, part community hall.

The printer that stood on the pass and connected with the restaurant till began to whirr. Gabriel grabbed the docket. 'Battle stations,' he called. 'One consommé royale, two whitebait, one red mullet, one cacciatore, one osso buco. Let's go.'

'Chef,' said Suleiman, approaching with a Tupperware box, 'I have been playing around with the consommé garnish. A chiffonade of sorrel and chervil.' He displayed the contents of the box and then kissed his thumb and forefinger. 'Really, really tasty. You think it's OK?'

Suleiman was from India. He had spent less than three years in England but already his English was better than Oona's. He was the only person in the kitchen who showed any interest in food. A consommé royale did not have those herb garnishes. That would turn it into a consommé julienne. But Gabe did not want to discourage him. 'It's OK,' he said. 'Good work, Suleiman.'

Suleiman smiled. Though he brought to his smile the same thorough-going attitude with which he executed all tasks, stretching his lips wide and over his teeth, nodding his head and wrinkling his eyes, it did little to dent the seriousness of his face. Even in his white chef's hat and coat and apron, even with his short – slightly bow – legs in blue check trousers and with a skillet in his hand, Suleiman did not look like a chef. He looked like a loss adjuster wearing a disguise.

Gabriel decided to do a walk round and moved past Suleiman, dispensing a quick pat on the back.

In the larder section Victor was idling, kicking his heels against the under-the-worktop fridge. He was one of those young men who mistook their nervous energy and frustration for charisma, which made him impossible to like. The way he stood, jutting his chin and tilting his pelvis, he thought he was back in some alleyway in Moldova, waiting for a hustle to begin.

'Keeping busy?' said Gabriel.

'What team you support?' said Victor.

'What?'

'Team. *Team*. Football.'

Victor wore cologne and plucked between his eyebrows. The boy was clearly in love with himself. 'Rovers,' said Gabriel. 'Blackburn Rovers.'

Victor made a hand gesture which indicated that Rovers were, in his view, only a so-so team. 'My team – Arsenal. Back home – Agro.'

'Makes sense,' said Gabriel. 'Excuse me for saying this, but isn't there something you should be doing right now?'

'No,' said Victor. 'What?'

'Work,' said Gabriel. 'That's what we come here to do. Remember? That's what they pay us for.'

'Be cool, man,' said the Moldovan in a stupid American accent. 'Look,' he said, with a sweep of the hand, '*every*thing ready.'

Gabriel checked over the salad tubs and garnishes. He pulled open the fridge doors and did a quick count of the cold starters: aubergine and mozzarella towers and fanned melons with Parma ham. 'All right,' he said. 'Well.' On a whim he stuck a spoon in the gremolata and tasted it. 'No. I don't think so. Something's missing here.' He tasted again. 'What about the anchovy fillet?'

'Chef,' said Victor, folding his arms, 'there is no anchovy fillet. You want, I'll make the order.'

'Check the dry store downstairs.'

Victor looked at the floor.

'Haven't got all day,' said Gabe. 'The gremolata goes on the osso buco.'

'Chef,' said Victor. He held his palms in the air and grinned, labouring under the misconception that he could charm his way out of anything.

'Right now,' said Gabriel, keeping his voice low. He decided – it was a tactical decision – that if the bullshit continued he would 'put it on'. He never, hardly ever, lost his temper. But sometimes he put it on.

'No way I'm going down there,' said Victor. 'It spooks me, man. So he fell on some handle, right? Was it sticking in the back of his head?'

'Victor . . .'

But Victor couldn't stop talking. 'Shit,' he said. It sounded like *sheet*. 'You gotta have respect for the dead, see? Respect, see what I'm saying?' He spent a lot of time watching American movies. Pirated DVDs, no doubt.

'I'm giving you an order,' Gabriel barked. 'Do as you are told.' He set his mouth. His father used to fly off on one. Nought to sixty in three seconds flat. He'd come home from a bad day at Rileys and sit by the gas fire shuffling the local paper and his feet. '*Tea on the table at six. Is it too much to ask?*' Mum usually smoothed it over. Sometimes she yelled, 'Yes.' Then he'd go ballistic, shouting down the house and trembling, actually trembling, with rage. His ears turned crimson nearly up to the top where, it seemed, they went white hot. Gabriel waited out the storm with Jenny, sitting at the top of the stairs, and though his stomach felt funny, like he had a bout of diarrhoea coming on, he knew it was Dad who was pathetic because he couldn't control himself.

A cloud settled on Victor's face and he screwed up his features as though he'd been sprayed with disinfectant. 'Yes, Chef.' He spat.

'Never mind,' said Gabe, suddenly sick of everything. 'I'll go down there myself.'

The catacomb walls, white paint over brick, were studded with beads of water, as if pricked by tears here and there. Naked light bulbs hung in the corridor, casting Halloween shadows against doors. It was the kind of place you expected footsteps to clang and echo but Gabriel's polyurethane clogs made barely a sound on the concrete floor. He passed by the locker rooms, one for the boys and one for the girls. Someone had drilled a spyhole between the two and Gleeson fired the Italian waiter, despite a dearth of evidence, for possession, perhaps, of hot Latin blood. Gabe glanced into the old fish room, the paint on the door so flaky that it appeared to have grown scales of its own. Most of the fish came ready-prepped these days and only the frozen fillets (permitted in the fisherman's pie) made the journey underground. The air still smelt like low tide, of sand and browned-out seaweed. He walked and the air grew steadily clearer, and then began to smell of bleach. Overhead, somewhere, a trolley rumbled by. The pipes and ducts and fearsome screeds of wiring that coated the ceiling sounded a continuous muted distress. Turning the first corner, Gabe wondered how long the catacombs would be if you laid them end-to-end. They would be difficult to unravel; laid out in epileptic fits and starts, twists and dead ends.

The kitchen was hardly the ideal layout either. When he had his own place he would insist on starting from scratch. Refit from top to bottom, he would absolutely insist.

Charlie wanted to start a family. 'I'm not getting any younger,' she said. She was only thirty-eight. When she looked in the mirror her gaze was sceptical, as if the plump-skinned, green-eyed, red-headed siren in the glass wasn't fooling anybody, Charlie least of all. Working as a singer didn't help. There were plenty of younger girls around. 'You and your stupid plan,' she'd say, stirring her martini. 'Don't plan on me hanging around.' Gabe thought he would pop the question on the day the contract was signed. Do you want to move in together? He knew the answer, of course. They'd find a new flat, maybe on the river, where he could watch the silty banks and unmoving flow of the Thames. After a year, when they were sure, they could try for a child.

A child. He touched the bald spot at his crown and wondered if it was getting bigger. He was, he realized, standing by the yellow and black tape that marked off the place where Yuri had lived and died. He was puzzled, unable to remember what he had come here for. There had to be a reason. He supposed that he meant to spend a moment or two, simply to pay his respects.

'We could run away to Tobago,' Charlie had said, when she came off the stage. 'You dish up the surf'n'turf, I'll be pouring the drinks.'

Gabriel stared at the floor, the steel trapdoor that marked some long-forgotten coal hole, the treacherously bladed handle, flecked with Yuri's blood. The door to the old facilities office stood open, the light still burned inside. The police had left the mattress and sleeping bags. Everything else had been taken – two black bin liners containing Yuri's worldly goods. Gabe ducked under the tape and went into the office. He picked a sweet wrapper off the floor and put it in his pocket. The room was the size of a double bedroom with two shelved alcoves on facing walls. They had found a gas burner, a couple of pans, empty jars and spirit bottles, shaving foam and a razor, a change of clothes, a pill box with a lock of hair inside, and an old photograph – of a woman with a cleft chin and two little girls in big coats.

When she had sung her last set, Charlie's back always ached from standing so long in her heels. Her eyes ached from the smoke in the club. 'What about a cruise ship? I'll sing, you cook. Or the other way round if you like.'

A few more months and they'd move in together. She wanted to dock, not sail.

He looked around. He didn't know what to do. He had come to pay his respects to Yuri but had hardly given him a thought. He should have sent someone out for flowers. He would lay a bouquet on the spot. There was mould growing in the corner and one of the shelves looked charred, an accident with the gas burner perhaps. Thank God it was only himself that Yuri had managed to kill.

Yesterday morning Gabe had walked up to the body, stopped a couple of paces off and stood with his hands in his pockets, waiting a few blank moments before walking away again. Yuri was lying on his back, with thick, black blood like a hood cast up round his head. He had white hair on his chest, in short, singed-looking tufts. His stocky legs were skewed in different directions as though attempting to perform the splits or some kind of Cossack dance. The towel which he had been clutching had wrapped itself round a foot. He had a wise face, had Yuri: easy to miss when he was a man in a green boiler suit, shifting grease. But somehow, as he lay there splayed and naked, it wasn't hard to notice and his blue and kindly lips had parted, as if ready to dispense good advice.

'Don't know,' Ivan had said when the inspector asked what he knew about Yuri's family.

'No, no, nothing,' Victor said when asked what he knew about Yuri himself.

'I don't have any information concerning,' said Suleiman.

'Please,' said Benny, 'I don't know.'

Gabe didn't do much better. He handed over details of the agency through which Yuri had been employed.

Yuri was lying somewhere, unattended, on a mortuary slab. It was loneliness, certainly, that killed Yuri. For an instant Gabriel was desolate. He kicked at the mattress and tapped the wall, as though checking for damp or loose plaster, searching for an immediate job to be done. He swept his hand across a shelf and dislodged a soft roll of fabric that had caught between shelf and wall. A pair of sheer black tights, in a shrunken ball.

'So, he was naked, old Yuri. I think he was waiting for his girlfriend. You think so, Chef, eh, do you think?'

Gabriel sensed someone behind him, another beating heart. He stuffed the tights in his trouser pocket and turned and saw her. That girl, Lena, standing in the doorway in the jumble of shadow and light, let him look at her and she looked back at him. Her face was thin and rigid and her hands, which she held twisted together at her chest, were fleshless claws. This morning he had told Oona to fire her. It astonished him that he had never looked at her before. Gabriel breathed deeper, to breathe the air she had breathed.

He opened his mouth, without knowing what he would say.

Lena smiled, or he imagined it, and then she ran away, into the maze.

CHAPTER TWO

—◊—

THE IMPERIAL HOTEL, AS MR MADDOX WAS FOND OF POINTING OUT, had a history. Built in 1878 by industrialist and champion mutton-chop grower Sir Edward Beavis, on the site once occupied by Dr Culverwell's Bathing Establishment in Yew Street, Piccadilly, the hotel shouldered as many previous incarnations as it did flying buttresses and gargoyles on its Gothic Revival exterior. Following the respectability and 'discreet luxury' of the Victorian era when the smoking and billiards rooms kept the ladies out of harm's way, the Imperial enjoyed a roaring twenties reputation for dance, decadence and statutory rape. Charles Chaplin's 1921 visit (escorted through the fans by no fewer than forty policemen) had made the Imperial de rigueur with the stars and starlets of the British silent screen. In 1922, in a case widely reported, Tyrone Banks (best-known picture *Heave Ho!*) was caught with his pants down and three under-age flappers beneath the shot-silk sheets. The escapade remained curiously omitted from the hotel brochure but Mr Maddox had enjoyed relating it to Gabe when he interviewed him for the job.

After that he had appeared to lose interest and swivelled his chair round to look out of the window, so that Gabe was left staring at the column of iron filings that ran down the back of his neck. 'Noël Coward,' Mr Maddox had said, 'composed songs here. Big deal. The Aga Khan had a permanent suite. Theodore Roosevelt "gave his name" to the drawing room. Generous, would you say? Who else?

Haile Selassie. That's in the brochure. Bunch of marketing geniuses I got downstairs.

'I need five years from you,' he continued, coming round and sitting on the edge of the mahogany desk. A big man in an expensive suit. Careless with authority, as though he had much to spare. 'Be coming up to sixty then, Gabriel. Where *do* the years go? Been promised my last five somewhere more suitable. For a man my age, I mean. Bahamas, I fancy. British Virgin Islands. Take a gimp, I mean deputy manager, of my choosing. Ease off a bit, wind down.' He stretched his arms and clasped his hands behind his head.

Gabe noted the discoloured patch on his inside wrist where a tattoo had been removed.

'They're not expecting miracles. We're not talking Michelin and all that crap. Just some food you can eat without gagging. They spent a few bob on this place, you know.'

'They' were the PanContinental Hotel Co., which had purchased the Imperial from Halcyon Leisure Group a couple of years ago, marking, it was hoped, rebirth and renewal after the hotel's long half-century of decline.

In the war it had been requisitioned by the government, providing sickbays for convalescing officers and a transit point for soldiers on leave. Afterwards it went back into business but by the early fifties the doormen were fighting over the guests and the hotel was forced to close its doors. Somebody saw the potential for office space. A tobacco firm moved in, followed by an American pharmaceuticals outfit that put a cycle track in the roof space that was only for senior executives and a volleyball court in the ballroom for those from the lower floors and corporate rungs. In the seventies there was an attempt to restore the Imperial's former glory but by the mid-eighties it was hosting 'value breaks' and salesmen who packed samples and Alka-Seltzers and dutifully filled in the service questionnaires.

'Back when,' Mr Maddox had said, 'Monsieur Jacques . . . well, you know the story.' The restaurant still bore his name. 'Escoffier did a quick stint, not many people realize, before he buggered off to the Savoy. Think you measure up to Escoffier, eh?' He winked and laughed, with little pretence at mirth. His brow was low and heavy, a ridged escarpment above the potholes of his eyes.

'I give you five years, then what?' said Gabe. In his head he added £10K to the starting salary. Another friendly joke and he'd go up another five.

'Six exec chefs in two years.' Mr Maddox shook his head in a regal fashion, as though his crown might slip. 'Bunch of tossers. Tell you what, give me the five I'll give you my dick on a plate. Sit down, for God's sake. Relax. How about a cigar?'

'About the salary,' said Gabe through his teeth.

Mr Maddox stopped him with a flick of the hand. 'Sort it out with my deputy. I'll tell him not to disappoint you.' He banged the hand down and a stack of papers took flight. 'Loyalty,' he barked. 'That a word you understand? Where do you come from, Chef? . . . What? Where the fuck is that? Do they know about loyalty up there?'

Gabriel passed through the revolving doors and stood at the kerb looking up at the dark stone walls of the hotel. Midnight. Sixteen hours he'd worked today and the one time he'd tried to take a break he'd been dragged into a meeting with an environmental health officer who, despite finding no reason to close the kitchen, had found plenty of excuses to waste Gabe's time.

He spent a moment regarding the mullioned windows and the carved grotesques sulking beneath the parapets. The stone looked cold. The door released a guest and a blast of hot air that carried the vanilla scent of the lobby. Gabe looked in at the sleek black reception bar, the high perspex stools sprinkled among the distressed leather armchairs, the purple and chrome 'sculpture' suspended from the ceiling, the 'architectural' flowers that could take out an eye. Viewed like that, outside and in, the effect was somewhat schizophrenic. The Imperial would never be truly great again. Jacques would never live up to its name. Great restaurants, like great hotels, delivered coherent design and consistent standards. Gleeson's 'silk, please' flowers gave the game away. If the Imperial were a person, thought Gabe, you would say here is someone who does not know who she is.

★

By the time he'd walked up to Piccadilly Circus a soft rain had set in, caught in the headlights of the cars that edged fractiously around, crinkling the air and shining the pavement. The electronic billboards flashed the golden arches, Samsung, Sanyo, Nescafé. Above the fountain, the Eros statue looked glum, usurped by the monumental LED displays. Car horns sounded; a pair of young women tottered towards Haymarket screeching and cackling and holding each other up. On the fountain steps more drinkers, professionals who would dedicate their short lives to the cause. A hot-dog van let off steam and an oily onion smell. A businessman, officious overcoat and moustache, wanted to cross the road and struck the railings that blocked him with his sturdy umbrella. A middle-aged woman, a chihuahua tucked under her arm, hesitated beneath the foggy halo of a streetlamp, judging if it was better to ask directions or to remain a little lost. The rain, the smells, the billboards, the rumble of cars – Gabe walked and took it all in although his mind was engaged elsewhere.

He had seen Mr Maddox in action many times. With the hotel guests, the important ones, he was charming. He remembered their children's names. He was humble without being fawning. He knew what it was they wanted before they knew it themselves. With the staff he insisted that he was just one of the crew. He had come up the hard way, from the kitchen to the top floor. He walked the halls and corridors and spoke to everyone from PR chief to chambermaid, though he was more likely to be rude to the former than the latter, a fact which nudged Gabriel into grudging admiration. If someone was not work- ing properly he'd jump right in and tackle it. 'Never ask someone to do a job you wouldn't do yourself.' He would clamp a chambermaid's shoulders and move her gently aside. 'Now look how it's done. Bit of elbow grease, yes? You get me. I know you do.' He was cheerful and direct and always made sure to reiterate his point. He praised and punished openly like a good and honest man. In pursuit of managerial goals he deployed humour, incentives and a keen grasp of psycho- logical matters. In short, he was a first-class bully. And he induced in his underlings a fear that they often confused with respect.

Gabe knew it on that first meeting.

'Private client work,' Mr Maddox had said, 'it's the dog's bollocks. I know a lot of people. Month on a yacht round the Riviera, six weeks in a mansion in LA, couple of weeks in Aspen, London penthouse for a break, whatever the boss and the trophy wife are doing. You cook macrobiotic crud for her, steak for him, dinner party once a fortnight and you're done. How hard can it be? You're looking at filthy money. I mean a right filthy pile.'

'You could definitely do that?' said Gabe.

The general manager levelled him with his demolition stare. 'Are you in? Can I welcome you into the fold?'

For a moment Gabe was back in Blantwistle, ten years old, poking shepherd's pie round his plate while his mother started the washing-up and his father pushed back from the table and cracked his fingers as he always did before the sermon began. *Never pick on a lad smaller than yerself.* He would stroke the table firmly, as though to smooth out the cloth. He was built like a whippet but his hands were large and strong. Nimble too. At the mill the legend was that Ted Lightfoot could knot on faster than any machine. *Never pick on a lass neither.* There must have been a time, not that Gabe could remember it, when he was six or seven, maybe, when he had looked up to his dad. It was stupid the way he sat there after dinner like he was Moses, bringing down the law. *Never, ever, shake hands with a man and then go back on your word.*

Gabriel got up and shook hands with his new employer. It was an empty gesture and they both knew it. It was how the game was played.

At the Penguin Club Charlie was singing ''Taint Nobody's Bizness If I Do'. She wore her silver sequin dress and jade choker. Her heels were sharper than boning knives. The pianist kept his nose close to the key-board, collapsing under the weight of the blues.

Charlie put her hand on her hip and rolled her shoulder; her way of waving at Gabe.

Gabe bought a beer and sat at the bar, watching the punters watch-ing his girl. The room was dark with fake wood panelling and padded booths along one wall. The round tables in the middle had crushed velvet tablecloths and little art deco lamps that lit up the punters' chins. Some had their girlfriends or mistresses with them, fingering necklaces and earrings; some sat in twos or threes, clinking glasses and sometimes words; most just sat with their cigarettes, inhaling and exhaling and thickening the air.

Charlie and the pianist shared a small stage, elevated a mere six inches above the floor. The song did not suit Charlie's voice, which was too light for it, too teasing. She lowered her eyelids and pressed her lips to the microphone as though it were the object of her every desire. A bald man at a table close to the stage rose to his feet and saluted her with his tumbler. He swayed for a moment and then sat down.

'You like her, then, do you?' The punter at the bar had a heavy gold watch and heavy, hairy wrists.

'Yes,' said Gabe. 'She looks good to me.'

The stranger drained his glass. He slid closer to Gabe. He wore a good suit, silk tie. 'Listen,' he said, 'I can judge a character. In my business, if you can't do that, might as well cut your own throat. If you're interested . . .' He cocked two fingers in Charlie's direction and fired them like a gun. 'I could tell you the SP.'

Gabe laughed. 'Go on,' he said. 'Get me off the blocks. Give me the starting price on her.'

The man leaned against the bar. He squinted and burped and Gabe suddenly saw how drunk he was. 'Three Campari and sodas or one dry martini. Tha'sall you gotta do. She'll suck the tongue from your head, fuck like a rabbit and if you're lucky only steal the cash from your wallet, leave the bloody cards.'

If he had laughed Gabe would have punched him but the man was quiet now and looked sad. They both looked at Charlie. She was singing a love song, a Burt Bacharach number, loading every word with heavy irony; that was the way it sounded to Gabe.

For a moment he wondered if she had slept with this man.

'Well,' said the punter, 'best of British.' He tried to drain his glass but discovered he had already done that. 'I'd have a go myself but – got to be honest – she's out of my league, she is.'

Charlie's hair fell to her shoulders in thick waves. It was strong red, like an Irish setter, and her skin was creamy white. 'How was it today?' she said. 'How was work?' She laid her arm along the bar and took Gabe's hand in hers.

'Fine,' said Gabe. 'What do you want – red or white?'

She perched on the bar stool and crossed her legs. The dress was tight. It made her sit up straight. 'You're kidding me,' she said. 'Fine?'

He thought about the girl, Lena, darkness hollowing her cheeks. He raised his beer and drank slowly, as if to hide the picture in his mind.

Charlie twisted her hair over one shoulder. She sought him out with her cool green eyes and smiled in her lopsided way. 'Just another normal day. Nothing to report.'

'I don't know,' he said. 'Yesterday was . . . well, I told you. I'm half expecting the shit to hit the fan but nothing happened today, really. Maybe it's not going to.'

Charlie asked the barman for a large glass of Chablis. 'Accidents will happen, right?' She pressed a stiletto heel against Gabe's shin. 'I might break my neck in these.'

When Lena came in again he would talk to her, privately, about what she was doing there this afternoon. Her hair was blonde, almost colourless. He had never liked blondes much.

'Calling Planet Gabriel. No. No sign of intelligent life.'

'Sorry,' said Gabe. But Lena would not come again. She had been fired.

'My day was terrific, thanks for asking.'

'Was it?' He nodded. 'Good.' Though if she hadn't seen Oona, she wouldn't know that she had lost her job. So what made her run away?

Charlie swirled the wine round her glass. She wore a large amber ring that she had bought in a souk in Marrakech on a long weekend with Gabe. 'I spent the morning in a so-called studio – a tape deck in a bedroom, that's a studio – recording a song that may or may not be released as part of a compilation CD in Japan. And this afternoon I auditioned for a regular slot at some private members' club in Mayfair. The guy had sleaze coming out of every orifice and he thought I was too old, I could just tell, and I really feel like I'm getting somewhere now, you know, my life's just taking off.'

If she seemed to be inviting sympathy it was not a good time to offer it. Gabe had discovered this through a process of trial and error.

'Try out for one of those TV talent shows,' he said. 'It's the only thing left to do.' The police wanted to interview Lena. She would have to be found again.

'Thanks,' said Charlie. 'I'll do that when you have your own cooking show. How come you don't have your own cooking show? Nana Higson wants to know.'

Nana was Gabriel's maternal grandmother. She lived with his father now. Phyllis Henrietta Josephine Higson. Gabe called her Nana. Dad called her Phyllis or, in the old days, 'the shapeshifter', but only behind her back. The neighbours still called her Mrs Higson, even after twenty years. Only Charlie referred to her as Nana Higson, and she hadn't met her yet.

'I'm not telling you anything any more,' said Gabe. He put his hand on her collar bone, just below the choker. He thought, as he had thought so many times before, everyone here can see that I'm the one with her.

'Can't stay for the second set, sweetheart.' The man was a loser in a patterned jumper. He had a paunch and was going bald in the worst way, a forlorn ridge of hair between two receding tracks. He leaned between Gabe and Charlie to deposit some glasses on the bar. 'If I stay it'll be three more rounds at least and I get an acid stomach, you know. So I'm off now, sweetheart.' He winked. 'Don't take it personal. You're a cracker, you really are.'

Charlie kept a straight face. 'It's the fans that make it all worthwhile.'

Gabe looked round the club, at the smoked glass on the pillars, the slippery banquette seats, the penguin-shaped ashtrays and the waitress who was emptying them, old Maggie, who was reasonably penguin-shaped herself. Everything seemed unreal. This phoney life that he lived when normal people were in bed.

'Hey,' said Charlie, 'when are you going to take me Up North, anyway?'

He thought of Nana in her nightdress, the last time he visited, scuttling across the lounge with the drinks trolley that she used as support in preference to sticks or the walking frame. 'Now,' she said when she had kissed him and caught her breath. 'I was watching this chef on the telly, he was rubbish. Eee, I said to your father, our Gabe wants to look sharp. There's younger fellas now, not as good as him, who's jumping ahead and getting on the telly before he's had a go himself.' Her cheek against his felt powdery, as if she might crumble away to a heap of dust. 'Nana,' he said, 'you don't just get to "have a go". It's not about taking turns.' She settled into the wingback chair and put her furry bootees up on the footstool. 'I've got an irregular heartbeat, Gabriel. Did your father tell you? No. They suspect a touch of gout too. But I've got all my faculties, sunshine. I'll thank you to remember that next time you open your mouth.' She closed her eyes and grunted and it was a while before Gabe realized that she had nodded off.

'Nana'd like you,' Gabe told Charlie. 'She'd think you should be on the telly as well.'

'That doesn't actually sound like a plan. That sounds, in fact, like you think she would like me if only she met me but she's not going to so she won't.'

'What?'

Charlie sighed. 'What's wrong with me, Gabriel, huh?'

'Nothing,' said Gabe automatically. 'You're great.'

'I'm a cracker, I really am.' She slid off the stool and adjusted her dress. A sequin came away in her hand and she flicked it at his chest. He put a hand on her hip and she wriggled away. 'Can't keep the fans waiting.'

The pianist had taken up residence but was finishing his cigarette.

'My place or yours tonight?' said Gabe. He yawned and checked his watch.

'I'm tired as well, lover boy. I want my own bed tonight and I want to sleep alone.'

In the fridge there were three tomatoes, a slab of chocolate (80 per cent cocoa solids), an out-of-date bio yoghurt and a piece of Brie. Gabe ate a couple of the tomatoes and then took a piece of chocolate through to the sitting room.

The flat was at the top of a converted school building on Kennington Road, not far from the Imperial War Museum. It had long, casement windows and a view over the buses and chimneypots.

It was one of only ten flats and when Gabe first moved in he sometimes wondered how many schoolchildren had fitted into this space, which now was his alone.

The sitting room had new oak floorboards and recessed lighting. The estate agent who showed him round described it as being 'part-furnished' but it was furnished enough for Gabe and he rented it on the spot. There was a long, low sofa, ultra-modern and ultra-uncomfortable, upholstered in green with matching scatter cushions that were precisely as hard as they looked. The coffee table was an oversized sugar cube. A black leather and chrome Le Corbusier chaise longue stretched out next to the windows. Black shelving ran the length of one wall. Gabe had added books and a rug to the furnishings. The pictures that he had meant to hang were stacked against the shelves.

He sat on the sofa looking at the chaise longue, which was the only comfortable place to sit. The couple who lived across the hallway arrived home. They always stood outside their front door making a song and dance about keys. They were young and often stayed out late. She left early in the mornings, shouting goodbyes and last-minute instructions. He listened to Coldplay and Radiohead at top volume, and slammed the door when he went out and took the stairs at a run. They said 'hi' to Gabe whenever they saw him. They hadn't got as far as names.

Gabe ate some chocolate just to give himself the energy to get up and brush his teeth and go to bed.

It was all right that Charlie wanted to be alone. He wanted to be alone as well. That girl, the porter, Lena, kept inserting herself into his brain. Whatever he had felt, some kind of sickness, when she showed her ghoulish self in the catacombs had quickly passed but she had become a headache now. The police had questioned everyone else. She was a loose end to tidy up.

He wondered what colour her eyes were. He had spoken to her once, he thought, about polishing the wine glasses before they were racked up again. Her hair trailed out from beneath the green plastic porter's cap and caught in the side of her mouth. Yes, he remembered. He remembered now. How she looked. How she had looked at him.

She was nodding and staring down at a spill of soapy water and then she raised her eyes. They were dark, dark blue, wide and deep, and she parted her lips and he reached for her and kissed her. He kissed her hard and then harder still because that was what she wanted, he was sure of it, and the harder he kissed her the more she wanted, he knew it, and then she pulled away and he saw what he had done: there was blood all over her face.

The chocolate that was still in his mouth when he dozed off had melted and dribbled down his chin. Gabe went back to the kitchen for some paper towels and rinsed his mouth and spat. He noticed the answerphone blinking and pressed the button.

'Gabe, it's Jenny. I know you're busy – aren't we all – but I spoke to Dad today and I can't believe you haven't even called him back. Call him, Gabe, all right?' There was a pause and Gabe could hear her breathing. 'Right,' she said without much conviction. 'Cheerio.'

When had his little sister turned into the kind of woman who said 'cheerio'?

Dad had left a message a few days ago. 'Hello, Gabriel. This is your father calling you on Sunday afternoon, approximate time of three o'clock.' Messages from him were rare, invariably laborious and gloomy, as though the Angel of Death had called to make arrangements. 'I would like to speak to you. Would you call me please on the Blantwistle number. Thank you.' His telephone voice was both clearer and more strained than his normal speaking voice. If you were over a certain age, it seemed, it was impossible to speak normally into an answering machine. Call on the Blantwistle number – as if there were other numbers on which he might be reached.

Gabe had meant to call but it had been a bit of a week. It was too late to call anyone now.

He was about to switch off the light when the shrill of the phone sent a charge through his body.

'Gabe,' said Jenny. 'Is that you?'

'Jen, are you all right?'

'I'm fine, yes, fine, it's two o'clock in the blessed morning and I'm roaming around the house picking up socks and checking for dust on top of the picture frames and I've just unloaded the dishwasher but, you know, when you can't sleep the last thing you want to do is be in bed. I mean, that's not the last thing you *want* to do, it's the first thing you want to do but you shouldn't because it's not good sleep – oh, what's the word – *hygiene* is what my doctor says and we're trying to steer clear of the pills, though I wouldn't mind, sometimes I think, well, why don't I just give them a little try? Then I say to myself, Jenny, that's not a road you want to go down, not if there are other roads you can take, and there are. And, anyway, I wanted to call you and I know you're a night owl and so I picked up the phone and . . . I didn't wake you, did I? I mean, I called earlier and you weren't in so I guessed if I left it a while but not too much of a while—'

'Jenny,' Gabriel cut in. 'I was still up. I'm glad you called. How are the kids?'

He heard her sucking in and blowing out. She could have been lighting a cigarette or taking a puff on her inhaler.

'Harley's got a girlfriend, she's called Violet and she works over at Rileys on the Crazy Glazes stand and she's got her nose pierced and her belly and some other bits and pieces too that I wouldn't like to think about, and she doesn't look it but she is what I would call a good influence. Is on our Harley, anyway, because you know he's had his share of troubles and only the other day I was saying to him, Harley, I think Violet's got you under the thumb, I only mean in a good way because, well, when he was younger . . . and Violet is quite an old-fashioned name, don't you think? She's nineteen, year older than Harley, and . . .'

Gabe held the phone away from his ear. Two years ago – was it three? – he had been affronted when Jenny walked into the kitchen in Plodder Lane and he saw how old she had become, how middle age had enveloped her like the layers of fat on her arms, her legs, her neck. Jenny, who used to wear torn denim miniskirts and a fuck-off glare. Who used to drop one laconic word in the pub and send everyone scurrying to pick it up, frame it and hand it around. She used so many words now and all of them passed you by.

He pressed the phone to his ear again.

'. . . pleased about that but you can't help but worry. Worry about every little thing when you're a parent, you know, suppose you don't, not yet, but you know Bailey, always headstrong, and I said to her, Bailey, I know I'm your mum and you don't want to listen . . .'

'Jenny,' said Gabe. 'It's a bit late, even for me. I'll call you . . .'

'Tomorrow,' said Jenny. 'I'll call you tomorrow. You always say that.'

'Do I?'

'Yes,' said Jenny, lighting another fag or taking another puff on the inhaler. 'But you never do.'

'Don't I? I mean, I do. I'm sure I do, when I say it.'

'No,' said his sister firmly. 'You don't.'

There was a pause.

'Well,' said Gabriel.

'I need to talk to you, Gabe.'

Gabe went to stand by the sink under the kitchen window. The kebab shop opposite was closing. One man humped bags of rubbish to the kerb, another pulled down the metal shutter. Yellow light seeped from under it. A plastic bag flew across the road. 'I want to talk to you as well,' said Gabriel, finding, to his surprise, that he meant it.

'I'm sorry,' said Jenny, 'I haven't asked about you. How are you? Tell me how you really are.'

'Fine.' The word just popped out when he opened his mouth. He tried to think of something else to say.

There was only static down the line.

He tried again. 'Busy at work. Thinking about opening up . . .'

'. . . your own place . . .'

'. . . my own place . . . And me and Charlie are thinking . . .'

'. . . about moving in together . . .'

'. . . of moving in . . . but it's hard . . .'

'. . . to find the time . . .'

'Yes.' Did she end everybody's sentences for them? Why did she do it? Was everything he said really that predictable, that boring?

'I hope I'm going to meet her soon, Gabriel, time you made an honest woman . . . and I bet she thinks so too, even if she's not prepared to say. But I won't go on about that now, that's not what I'm ringing for, not at this time of night though I knew you'd be up most likely . . .'

Did they end each other's sentences, Jenny and her women friends in Blantwistle? Bev and Yvette and Gail and whoever else at the call centre.

'. . . and I wanted to talk about Dad . . .'

Perhaps they did. Perhaps having their sentences finished made them feel understood. Every completed sentence a small act of loyalty, of love. The thought of it was exhausting. Gabe wanted to go to bed.

'. . . those ships he used to build out of matchsticks, do you remember? Had all the drawings and photos of the *Titanic* and made her out of matchsticks, oh, so beautiful and the way he'd spend an hour just looking, deciding how to do the next bit . . .'

Gabe had taken one into the bath once without permission and broken it. He'd been terrified about telling Dad, but Dad only said, well, why don't we fix it together, as if it would give them something nice to do.

'. . . so I know you're very busy and honest to God believe me I'm not saying you're not but when I heard you hadn't rung him and this was three days ago now I thought . . .'

The light in the kebab shop was off. The moon was nearly full but so pale it made little impression, hanging sullen above the chimney-pots. The stars were weak too and few in number; they did not twinkle so much as flicker, as though at any moment they might go out. When Gabe was a boy there were more stars and they were brighter. That was the way it seemed. His sister's voice went on and on and it was a wonder she didn't run out of breath. He would finish her sentence if he could. If only he knew how, or when, or if it would ever end.

'. . . Dad wanted to tell you himself but, you know, by the time you get around to ringing him . . .'

If Jenny had got out of Blantwistle. If she hadn't saddled herself with a baby. What was the point, anyway, of thinking about that? She wore velour tracksuits now in purple or green. She had her hair done at Curl Up and Dye, drank in the Spotty Dog or the Turk's Head, and every Thursday was bingo night. It was strange how knowing every last thing about her made him feel as though he didn't know her at all.

'. . . so it looks like they didn't manage to catch every bit of it when they cut out part of his colon and it's spread to his liver now.'

Jenny had finally come to a halt.

'Oh,' said Gabe. 'I see.'

'Gabe,' said Jenny. She was crying.

'Jen?' He had heard the words but not listened. Spread to his liver. But Dad had not been ill. 'Jenny?'

He heard her blow her nose. 'He didn't tell me, either, about the colon cancer. He was only in hospital a couple of days and I didn't even know he'd been in 'til Nana told me and he said it was a "spot of bother with me bowels" and, well, I left it at that because Bailey was playing me up and Harley'd been in a fight and with one thing and another . . .' She tailed off.

'Nobody told me he'd been in hospital. When was this?'

Jenny sniffed. 'About eighteen months ago, maybe.'

'A year and a half ago? Nobody told me.'

'Nobody told me. Nobody told me. Is that all you can say? Honest to God, Gabriel. I never thought I'd say this but you've surprised me, you really have. I thought I'd never be surprised again by how selfish you are but I've got to hand it to you, you've managed it this time.'

Gabe turned on the tap. He twisted it until it would go no further. The water hit the steel sink hard and splashed out against the window, the wall, Gabe's shirt. He turned it off. 'So,' he said, keeping his voice even and low, 'he'll get over this too. There's got to be a decent chance.'

'Not with liver cancer,' said Jenny, sounding oddly prim. 'I've been reading up.'

CHAPTER THREE

—∾—

THE MORNING WAS BRITTLE-BRIGHT AND GABRIEL STOOD IN THE frost-starched loading bay watching the cheese van pull in through the gates. A single white cloud stood in the hard blue sky. Beyond the courtyard London hummed its morning song, endlessly reverberating, one crescendo piling into the next. A blackbird flew down from the wall and pecked the moss between the cobblestones. It returned to its perch and sang, its flute rising over the dying engine of the van. Gabe stepped forward, and the bird sang the warning call, flicking its wings and tail. Chook, chook, chook. A final rattle and it was gone.

Ernie sidled up with his hands in his pockets and a bobble hat on his head. He addressed Gabe in his usual manner, with his head ducked down, gazing up at a vacant spot approximately three inches to the right of Gabe's face. It made him look mentally deficient, which Gabe sometimes suspected he was.

> 'The blackbird is a canny wee fellow
> Wi' his coat of black and beak of yellow
> When the wind blows in fresh harm
> He is the first to raise the alarm . . .

'Ach, it goes on but Ah cannae quite remember how. Something, something every morn, watch something, something and warn . . .

No, Ah think Ah had morning and warning. One of ma early ones, that.'

'Hello, Ernie,' said Gabe. 'You got the order printout?'

'Oh, aye,' said Ernie, his chin practically on his chest.

Gabe held out his hand.

'On ma desk.' Ernie took a few sideways steps towards his wooden booth. 'Ah know their beaks are more, you would say, orange, but you cannae rhyme it. Purple,' he added. 'You cannae rhyme purple, neither.'

'Right,' said Gabe.

'Ah'm not so into the rhymes now. Ah'm more, you would say, *free flow.* Time was, Ah could list every word in the English language with no rhyme. Pint, nothing, silver, month, ninth, scalp, wolf . . .'

'Ernie,' said Gabe. 'The printout.'

The porter went off, a sideways scuttle. He walked back on his heels, flapping a handwritten list. 'Is it not on the system?' said Gabe.

'Och,' said Ernie. 'Oona's putting it in right now.'

Gabe turned and stooped to peer through the booth window. He watched his executive sous-chef tapping one-fingered at the keyboard while massaging her bosom thoughtfully.

'How long have you been on goods-in, Ernie? Wouldn't you like a change?'

'Change,' said Ernie. He drew his head into his anorak. 'No, no,' he said, somewhat muffled. 'Don't want some bugger messing things up. Just got it working nice. Och, Chef, no.'

'How long, Ernie? Since when?'

Ernie's head popped up. 'Nineteen seventy-three.' The head retracted. It was like speaking with a nervous tortoise. 'Year I come down from Fife.'

Gabe watched the cheese man roll the first boxes down on a fork-lift. 'They should give you a medal.'

'Been writing poems longer. Nobody's give me a medal for them.' Ernie sounded genuinely aggrieved.

'One day,' said Gabe.

'Oh, aye,' said Ernie, fixing an earnest gaze beyond Gabe's ear. 'Ah know. Or Ah wouldnae bother, would Ah?'

★

With the regular order out of the way Gabe climbed into the back of the van and began selecting the specials. First a Livarot, strong and herby, sassy as its green-striped paper casing. For subtle contrast he went for two dozen Crottin de Chavignol. The cheese man tried to push the Bleu du Vercors. Gabe tasted and rejected it. 'Your classic French mountain cheese,' said the cheese man. He named three celebrity chefs. 'Swear by it, they do, all three. Your classic creamy sauce cheese.' Gabe moved about the van, paring and tasting, getting high on the fumes. He had decided he would take a ten-kilo Cantalet that had just enough hazelnut edge without it overwhelming the fresh milk flavour. But he was reluctant to leave this sanctuary and plunge back into the daily round of meetings and spreadsheets. He sniffed rind after rind, trying to break down the smells into discrete and comprehensible units. After a while he gave up, gave in to the inevitable. The whole was more than the sum of the parts; the aromas knitted together were dense and intense and impossible to untangle. 'Something for you, Chef,' said the cheese man. 'Take one home.' He proffered a Bleu du Vercors. 'Thanks,' said Gabriel. 'I won't. But thanks anyway.'

Afterwards he went into the staff canteen to check on a problem with the deep-fat fryer. Another call to be made. This made him late for the management meeting in Mr James's fifth-floor office, with Gleeson, Pierre, the bar manager, and Branka, the housekeeping supervisor. Mr Maddox made an unscheduled appearance but then remained silent for the duration.

'Any further business?' said Mr James, addressing his superior. He offered an open palm, like a schoolboy about to be caned.

Mr Maddox affected to ruminate. 'Let's see, there was something . . . no, it's gone. Oh yes, table linen, let's talk about that.'

'Yes,' said Mr James smartly, 'I've been saying we should look into linen hire, the replacement cost is—'

'Christ alive,' said the general manager. He stood and pressed his knuckles on to the desk. 'I've got coppers still crawling up my arse. A whole week on, mind you. Don't they have anything better to do? I've got the PanCont lawyers wanking each other off, I've got sicko journos with a couple of column inches to fill . . . Jesus wept.'

'The porter?' said Mr James. 'I thought it was—'

'Yes it is. It better be.' Maddox leaned on his knuckles like some 300lb corporate gorilla. 'Parks called today. The post mortem's in. Exactly what he expected – injuries consistent with a fall. Awaiting the toxicology report, which will no doubt reveal he was bladdered, well it doesn't take a genius, does it? Parks says he's coming in today, tie up any loose ends. I don't like coppers in my hotel. Makes me itch.' He looked at Gleeson who narrowed his eyes at Gabe, trying to redirect the GM's gaze. 'What do you do if you have an itch, Stanley? That's right, you scratch.'

Gleeson sat straight-backed and righteous. 'Mr Maddox—' he began.

'Right, so I'll scratch around, shall I?'

Gabriel kept watching Gleeson and understood that he had made an enemy. The porter might have been on Gabe's patch, but now he was bringing unwelcome attention all round. Pierre looked uneasy too. Only Branka retained her usual demeanour, of ice-cold efficiency.

'Because,' continued Maddox, 'what we're after here is a clean result. It's a sad, sad accident, we are terribly, terribly sad, but we are not sorry – we're not sorry because it's not our fault and if you're sorry it'll cost you a mil – and they can stick that in the paper as well. Except they won't because they'll have forgotten all about it by then. And there isn't a problem. Unless . . . unless it's going to turn up something else. I don't know why, but this is what happens in hotels. A screw falls out of a door frame. Easy, you think, soon fix that, and just as you're giving it one last turn, that's when you notice the whole fucking door is full of rot and woodworm and it crumbles to dust in your hand. Am I making sense? Anyone read me out there?'

Everyone nodded. Gabriel looked at his watch. 'Bit pushed are you, Chef? Chef's a bit pushed, Mr James. Shall we let him go?'

Mr James, who clearly had no idea what the correct answer to this question might be, pursed his lips at Gabriel for putting him on the spot.

'You can go,' said Mr Maddox, 'thank you for your time, all of you. You can go. And if anyone's got anything they'd like to bring to my attention, please – as we say in the hospitality world – don't hesitate.'

★

Gabe split off from the others, who all had other meetings to attend. The vestibule by the lift contained the trademark arrangement of black lacquer occasional table, square-cut bowl with coloured pebbles submerged in water and a candle in a vase of sand. Above hung the portrait of Sir Edward Beavis, founder of the Imperial, flinty-eyed and wealthily whiskered, keeping watch over the management floor.

In the lift Gabe leaned on the handrail and thought about the pair of tights he had pulled from the washing machine that morning, tangled up inside a pocket. Dangling from his finger the tights were shrivelled and he had pulled at them with vague anxiety, attempting to give them shape. He had found a small hole and stretched it gently over his palm, watching the way it grew. The tights were on his kitchen counter and now he wished he had put them away. He told himself there was no reason to worry. Charlie had taken a week's job, singing in a hotel complex on the Red Sea, covering for a sick friend. There was no chance she would pop round and make the discovery. Even so, it left him uncomfortable, as if he had been told he had spoken in his sleep without knowing what it was he had said.

On the second floor the lift doors opened and three guests got in, two men with mobile phones held at their hips like guns, and a female hostage. They were mid-conversation about the 'Birmingham office', but something – he could not say what – made him think that two were lovers. The woman wore wedge heels and her hair scraped back in a bun. Lipstick smudged her front teeth. When she spoke she looked down and tapped her foot. *Rationalization long overdue*, tap tap, *more systems synergy to be had*, tap, tap, like a child reciting her two-times table.

When the police had called earlier in the week to ask if Lena had returned to work or if anyone had been in contact with her, Gabriel had told them no. 'No, nobody's seen her at all.' Why had he not told the truth? What need did he have to lie?

The lift halted on the ground floor with a shiver. The taller of the two men got out first, followed by the woman, and the other man followed her, his fingers playing up and down the curve of her behind.

★

Oona fanned herself with a folder of paperwork. 'Hotter than hell its own self, darlin'. One day I goin' find you all melt down. Just a lickle-ickle puddle on the chair, chef's hat on top. Hooo-hee.' She laughed her cosmic laugh.

Gabe looked down at his staff planner. There used to be a time, he could just about remember it still, when he actually cooked, rather than sat at a desk. He scanned down the document – all the commis where they belonged at the bottom of the food chain, Damian and Nikolai and the rest. Victor, he thought with a sigh, had been over-promoted by the previous head chef, who had made him a chef de partie – a decision no doubt taken in an alcoholic mist, why else put Victor in charge of a section? Unless, of course, it had been an honest mix-up, the wrong East European cook picked out of the line. At least Benny and Suleiman were up to the job.

Ivan's semi-autonomous republic as grill man was reflected in the way he'd been boxed off on the schedule. Gabe would have to do something about that. Albert too was out on a limb, but that was natural enough for a pastry cook. And then there was Oona at the top of the page. My right-hand woman, he thought, not without bitterness.

'Everything on target for tomorrow, Oona? You been checking things through with the boys?'

'Ho, yes,' said Oona, in a way that suggested she were responding to a double entendre. 'Don't you worry!'

'I'm not worrying, Oona, I'm . . .' He was about to say 'managing', but thought it might sound as if he were just getting by.

'No need to worry at all,' said Oona, laughing for no apparent reason.

The Sirovsky launch was tomorrow evening. All the chefs were in today, preparing everything that could be prepared in advance. 'Just take me through where we're up to,' said Gabe.

Oona pulled a sheet from her folder and studied it, mumbling to herself. 'Black bean cakes, salsa fresca, vitello tonnato . . . ho, was there a problem with the . . . no, it's all right . . . wild mushroom strudel . . . I think Victor said the chicken liver parfait was . . . ho, but he was . . . and then the devilled . . .'

'What's that?' said Gabe, looking round.

'What now, darlin'?'

'Scratching noise. If there's a mouse in here . . .'

'Ain't no mouse,' said Oona. 'A bitta dry skin on me heel. Just givin' it a little old scuffle on me shoe.'

Gabe looked at Oona's feet and quickly looked away. 'So. No questions, no problems, nothing else I need to order in.'

'Hopefully no,' said Oona. She showed her gold tooth and touched it like a lucky charm.

'Think, Oona. We don't have much time.'

'I hope it all OK.'

'Hope? Shouldn't come into it, Oona. Hope's irrelevant.'

Oona smiled at him with pity and forbearance, as if he were making an unwarranted fuss.

'Right,' he said, swallowing his irritation, 'let's decide what we're doing for service. Gleeson reckons he's only got three people to give us, so we need to call an agency, get five, maybe six more waiters.'

'Darlin', I know just who I goin' call and, you know, Suleiman was sayin' what he suppose do with the red pepper mousse? He suppose put it in the endive right away, or wait until the mornin'? And we clean out of the mushrooms, what's they called? Shanti-someting-or-other, fancy mushroom ting, you know.'

'Chanterelles. I'll go and see Suleiman about the mousse. Anything else, Oona, now you're in the mood to tell?'

The executive sous-chef pursed her lips and gazed up at the ceiling, waiting, perhaps, for divine inspiration. Her eyes had a sparkle, even in this dead, yellow light. Her cheeks were fat as ripe black figs. Despite everything she was a handsome woman. For a moment Gabe had a vision of Oona as a young girl in a white dress, kneeling in church, gazing up at the altar. She must have been a sight to behold.

Calling himself to order, he opened his notebook, thinking he would prioritize his workload for the rest of the day. In the kitchen the cooks bobbed and weaved. Suleiman slid on an oily patch but saved himself and earned a cheer. Gabe held his pen over the page. His mind became fogged. Impossible to pick out a single thought. His wrist locked and though he wanted to write any old thing, to begin the process, he could not make a mark.

He froze in the face of the endless tasks ahead. Would it make any difference if he remained at his desk, not moving, not speaking, not thinking? The world could go on without him, on its own relentless course. He stared at the page and admired its blankness; he wished that he too could be blank.

'Shoot me,' said Oona, 'if I forgettin' someting.' Her voice began to bring him round. It was like listening to a saucepan lid lifting on the boil, a little escape of steam. 'You lookin' a bit sleepy there, darlin'. I goin' make us a niii-ce cuppa tea.'

Gabriel threw down his pen, his energy abruptly restored. He looked at Oona and clenched his fists beneath the desk. Rage gripped him by the throat. He fought to draw enough breath. It occurred to him that he would, perhaps, drop down dead of anger. Gripping the sides of the desk as though he would turn it over he struggled to gain control. A nice cup of tea! Didn't she know there was work to be done? Were they to put their feet up with a nice cup of tea? Incredible. The woman was out of her mind.

'Chef?' said Oona.

There was a hell of a lot to get sorted. Gabe caught sight of a stack of suppliers' brochures on the floor. He had piled them there when he started the job, meaning to sift through and discard as many as possible. There had never been the time. No time like the present, he decided, jumping up. He was immediately diverted by a flyer pasted on the wall: *Kondiments King*, it read, *We've Got Sauce!* A grotesque tomato man with stick legs and arms grinned out, ketchup spouting from his head. The flyer was spattered and smeared and curling up at the edges. Why had he not taken it down immediately? He ripped it off the wall and tossed it on the floor. The patch of crumbling plaster which was revealed began to flake and fall. Gabriel looked round wildly, kicking over the brochures as he turned. There was fungus growing in a tiny damp patch over the skirting board. He began to rub it off. There was clutter on top of the filing cabinet. A tennis ball, one glove, a meat thermometer, a box of paperclips, a plastic box, a tin of lipsalve, two yellowing copies of the *Sun*. Who the hell kept making this mess? He cleared it all off, on to the floor. Too many things on the desk. He scraped everything into the drawers and closed them. He sat down again to an empty desk, feeling better. He could have a clear run at things now.

Barely had he noticed that Oona was gone when she returned with two mugs of tea. She looked at the littered floor but said nothing. She squeezed herself into the chair.

Gabe shoved the debris aside with his foot so it formed a kind of snowdrift against the back wall. 'Right,' he said. 'Bit of a tidy-up.' He took a sip of tea. There was a tremble in his hand as he raised the mug. What he needed was an early night. Tomorrow he'd be right as rain. 'How we fixed on the lunch service?'

'Chef,' said Oona, 'we fixed just fine. Suleiman, love him, havin' a few problems with the fresh custard. All this lumpy business. Have to pour it down the drain. The next lot look even lumpier and Suleiman, you know he so serious, he stirrin' and stirrin' and the lumps coming bigger and bigger, I say, "Suleiman, you got to let it alone. Sometimes a ting just ain't meant to be." '

'It's a question of temperature,' said Gabe, back, more or less, on an even keel. 'Of being precise.' His father was dying. He had to deal with a dead body. He had to deal with the police. His job was high-pressure, his girlfriend was away . . . He'd got a bit wound up. It was natural. But it had been brief, and it was over now.

Oona threw up her hands. 'You do every last little ting right, but sometimes it don' turn out like you plan.'

'Oona,' said Gabe, 'it's custard. If you do everything right, it turns out right.'

Oona blew sceptically through her teeth.

'Believe me, I know what I'm talking about. It's the protein in the egg that thickens the custard. At about forty degrees the proteins start to expand, they are what's called "denatured". As the temperature rises they begin to link up, network with each other and the sauce gets thicker. You need to get above seventy degrees. If you go higher than eighty, you start to get lumps. An ideal temperature is seventy-five degrees. It's chemistry, Oona, nothing else.'

'Don' know about that,' said Oona. She shook her head. 'Sometimes you have to say to yourself, this ain't meant to be.'

'Chemistry O-level. I did it as a project. Thought it up myself, actually.'

'And sometimes you have to say to yourself, this *is* meant to be.'

'I found a meat thermometer when I was clearing up,' said Gabe, hunting around in the snowdrift. 'That'll sort Suleiman out.'

'It's like my niece,' said Oona, rubbing at her bosom, knocking her diamanté hairclips on to her lap. 'Crying over this boy, boo-hoo, never let it alone. But what the point? I arks you. "Aleesha," I say, "you not *suppose* be with Errol. You *suppose* be with someone else."'

'He's a good lad,' said Gabe, strangely moved by Suleiman's dedication. He sniffed, and rubbed his nose.

'Nuttin but a ragamuffin, you arks me. She better off by her own self, that the truth.'

'Wouldn't mind making it myself,' said Gabe. 'Roll my sleeves up, you know.'

Oona fixed her hairclips back on to her coat. 'What? No, no, Mr Bird and his powder come to the rescue. You have a sit and relax. Chemistry,' she said, laughing. 'Don' know how it is with custard but when it come to boy and girl, chemistry the ting.'

For the next hour Gabe made calls to suppliers, marking pleasing ticks against his list. According to the list, the next call would be to his father. He punched two numbers and hung up. He scratched his head, burrowing around in the bald patch. Next time he got as far as five digits and again he cut the line. They had already spoken once and Gabe had promised he would call again today. 'Not so bad,' his father had said when Gabriel asked how he was. *Jenny told me*, said Gabe. *I'm sorry I didn't call you before.* 'Aye,' said his father, 'well. We've all got to go some time.'

Gabe wanted to say something significant. He couldn't manage a scrap. 'Love to Nana,' he said. 'I'll call you next week, Dad.' And this was the best he could do.

He would ring his father, but not without thinking what to say. *Get your brain in gear before you open your mouth.* Another sterling piece of advice from Dad. Never was short of advice, had to give him that. He'd be doling it out sometimes, sitting in his chair by the fire, big hands laced over knitted waistcoat, an inch or two of shiny leg showing between sock and trouser hem, and Mum would creep up behind him and start to act the fool. She'd do rabbit ears above his head, stick out her tongue, make kissy-kissy faces and cross her eyes. Gabe would poke Jenny to make her laugh and get in trouble. Jenny would pinch him, slyly, on the arm. 'I know what you're doing, Sally Anne,' Dad would say, without turning round. 'These children will grow up long before their mother ever does.'

Mum did grow up, thought Gabe, after Nana moved in. He never saw her acting silly after that. Maybe it was Nana's influence, maybe it was Mum getting old. Gabe preferred her before, when she did just as she pleased.

He was eight years old and hopped-up on life, running down Astley Street with the pincushion in his hand. He knocked on Mrs Eversley's door and old Mr Walmsley's, without even breaking his stride. If Bobby or Michael were playing out after tea they'd have a proper game of knock-a-door-run. He ran into the house and through the lounge. She wasn't in the kitchen. 'Mum,' he called. 'Where are yer?' The biscuit tin was on the table and he thought about raiding it but he wanted to show her first what he'd made. He'd worked on the pin-cushion nearly all term. It was in the shape of a daisy, with a yellow centre cross-stitched into the middle.

'Mum,' he shouted. He tackled the stairs like a rock wall, using his hands as well as his feet. 'Come on.'

He raced into her bedroom, thanking his lucky stars that Jen had gone round to Bev's after school. Now he would get Mum all to him-self. He slid right into the foot of the bed, banged his shin and dropped the pincushion. He bent down and when he straightened up again she said, 'Arise, Sir Gabriel,' and touched his shoulders with a curtain rod.

Gabe stood puffing and panting, chiefly out of surprise.

Mum laughed. 'Stop your gawping, Gabriel. And tell me what you think.'

She was twisting and turning in front of the mirror, wearing a pair of frilly bloomers, a skirt that seemed to be made of metal hoops joined by some sort of gauze, and a corset that pinched her breasts together. Her cheeks were pink as candy floss and she had ringlets, just like Jenny's porcelain doll. She twisted some hair around a finger and said, 'Rags. Nana used to do them for me, every Sunday for church. Know what?' she said, straining to see her back in the mirror, 'I used to hate them then.'

'Mum,' said Gabriel. 'You look . . .'

'Get away,' she said, 'wait 'til you see the whole thing.'

'Whole what thing?' said Gabriel, sitting down on the bed.

'The dress, you dummy. Haven't even got that yet.' She shrieked and jumped on top of him and tickled him under his arms.

'Well, I think you look right lovely,' said Gabriel, when she finally let him go.

Mum sat next to him and adjusted her corset. She held his face between her hands. He could see the bedroom window, the half-pulled curtains, reflected in both her eyes. Her long, slim nose was flecked with powder. The nostrils flared slightly as she breathed.

'I was born wrong time, wrong place. I've told you that before.' Her laugh was like a scatter of silver pieces. She jumped up and curtseyed, long and low, and held out her hand which he took. 'No wonder I'm never on time for anything,' she said, looking solemn. 'I'm a whole two centuries behind.'

They went downstairs and danced in the kitchen to whatever came on the radio, Val Doonican, Perry Como, the Beatles, The Who, moving in what they imagined to be the stately fashion of courtiers, breaking out occasionally into a frenzy of rock and roll. Dad came home, trailing Jenny and a cloud of poison gas. 'It's past six o'clock,' he said, his ears colouring.

Mum clamped her hands over her breasts as if she feared they would be confiscated. 'Don't,' she yelled at Dad. 'Don't tell me who to be.'

She burned some sausages and made chips that were oily on the outside and raw in the middle. Dad stood over Gabe and Jen until they'd eaten everything on their plates. 'It's good food, that. Yer mum's made it.'

Everyone had to suffer.

Mum had her dressing gown over her corset and crinoline; her ringlets looked greasy and damp. She stood at the sink, smoking, while the rest of them choked down the food. Jenny got up from the table, went out to the back yard to be sick and came back and ate the rest of her chips. Gabe heard her being sick in the night. The costume came out again a few times. Mum talked about what colour the dress would be, with how many ribbons and bows. Then Dad got a promotion and they moved away from Astley Street, up to Plodder Lane, and Mum cut up the crinoline and Jenny played hula with the hoops. Gabriel found the pincushion under the bed, when everything had been packed away. 'I made that,' he said, blushing. 'Did you, dear?' said Mum. He didn't remember seeing it again after that.

Plodder Lane sat at the north-east edge of Blantwistle looking down on the likes of Astley Street. Number 22 belonged to a newly built row of houses, with aluminium-framed windows, paved drives and carports. There was a garden at the back instead of a yard, and beyond the garden was farmland, great big runny-eyed Friesians staring into the wind. From the dining-room window, at the front of the house, Gabriel liked to watch the dark grey-greens of Rivington Moor, shifting shades beneath the hurrying clouds. Looking down into the basin between, he was gravely impressed by the sight of the mills, Rileys and Cardwells, Laycocks, Boorlands and the rest, the narrow streets flocking to them, the houses huddled in orderly queues. That he was surrounded by countryside surprised him. He had known, he supposed, that it was there. Sometimes Dad took them for walks on the moor. But when they were living in Astley Street, the world was made of red brick, yellow flagstone, grey cobble, and the coloured glass marbles that he liked to roll along the cracks.

The Howarths moved into number 17. 'You can breathe a bit up here,' said Mr Howarth. 'I've got nowt against 'em but who wants to smell curry, seven o'clock in the morning to eleven o'clock at night?'

Dad opened two tins of Watneys. 'Right you are, Tom.' He shook his head. 'Got nowt against no one, have we, but what I want to know is, have *they* thought it through? They bring 'em in now, all right, there's work to be done. But what happens, thirty, forty year from now, when it's them what's taken over the town?'

'Who?' said Jenny, looking up from dressing her doll.

'Breed like rabbits 'n' all,' said Mr Howarth, wiping ale from his chin.

'I want a rabbit,' said Jenny. 'Dad, can I have a rabbit? I won't let it poo in the house.'

She wasn't allowed a rabbit. Mum said she could but Dad said no, of course. Mum said let's *be* rabbits, then, if we can't get a real one. They spent an afternoon hopping round the house, rubbing noses and nibbling carrots, until Jen sat on Mum's feet and refused to let her hop any more.

Mum loved the new house, particularly the sliding doors from the sun lounge to the garden. She'd stand one foot in, one foot out, and say, 'This is the way to live.'

For a while there were no arguments about tea. Mum would wait by the front door for Dad, lead him into the kitchen and sit him down with a peck on the cheek. She bought some lacy white aprons and walked around in them, talking about baking chocolate cakes and waving a wooden spoon. Gabriel thought she looked beautiful, even more than when she wore the thing with metal hoops. She went to Lorenzo's and had a pixie cut, right over her ears, a wispy fringe that got in her big brown eyes. She wore the new style of trouser suits and shirts with collars that kept extending. She said her breasts were too small and she didn't like her nose but Gabriel thought everything was just right. 'I'm sorry, Jen,' she would say, 'you've got my nose. Just hope you get a bit more up top.'

After school they would rush in, hoping to find her in the mood for a game. They played knights and dragons and turned the whole house upside down. They sat at the kitchen table, 'reading' tea leaves and saying who or what they wanted to be when they were 'born again'. 'I'm coming back as an Arab stallion,' said Mum. 'Or maybe an astronaut, I fancy going into space.' Jenny wanted to know if you really could come back and have another life. 'Hindus think so,' said Mum. 'Is Mr Akbar a Hindu?' said Jenny, meaning the man who bought their old house. 'I expect so, love,' said Mum.

One afternoon, they got home and she'd turned the whole sitting room into a Bedouin tent, flowered sheets draping the walls, Mum sitting cross-legged smoking a hubble-bubble pipe. Another time she was stretched out on a plank between two ladders, painting the ceiling with clouds and butterflies, which Dad painted over, of course. The next week she had written a play, on the back of last year's calendar, a scene for every page or month, and wanted Gabriel and Jenny to star. Jenny threw her school bag across the room. 'I'll have your part, young lady,' said Mum, striking a theatrical pose. Jenny hurled herself at Mum's legs. She sat on Mum's feet and squeezed her knees. 'Just you wait,' shrieked Mum, trying to kick her off. 'What do you want me to do? Cooking and cleaning and shopping and cooking. I shouldn't do anything else! Just you wait, madam, it'll be your turn soon enough. See how *you* like it then.'

In the early days at Plodder Lane there would often be a new purchase to admire, displayed in the kitchen or lounge. A lamp like a fibreglass hedgehog, glowing purple at the end of every spine; a fondue set with twelve blue-handled forks; a clock in the shape of a cow, that went moo on every hour; Lladró porcelain figurines of elegant ladies, opening a parasol or sitting on a swing. After a while these purchases went underground. 'Come up,' she'd beckon, from the top of the stairs. 'Now, don't tell Dad, but isn't this divine? I'm putting it up the top of the wardrobe behind the blankets for now, but if you ever want to have a look at it . . .' wrapping up the pomander set, electric knife-sharpener, cigarette box with jet and onyx inlay, 'you just let me know and we'll come and take a peek.'

Sometimes she went out walking and forgot all about the time. Slipping through the sliding doors, mud streaking the backs of her trouser legs, pixie hair licked forward, tightening her face, she said, 'Well, that was lovely, I must say. A proper tonic. Don't tell your dad.'

The only thing that got her down, it seemed, was him. He drained the happiness out of her. Every cup of tea she put down in front of him was like a cup of her own blood. When she was sad she watched television, anything, she seemed to like the test card, or lay in bed chain-smoking Virginia Slims. Gabe crawled under the covers with her and stared at the ceiling. There was ash across the pillow. Mum sat up and stubbed out her cigarette. She left the ashtray balanced on her knee. Gabe looked at her and noticed for the first time that she was not much bigger than him. 'You know,' he said, 'how you wanted to be born two hundred year ago?'

She lit another cigarette and blew smoke across his face. 'Born too late. That's what I said.'

'But you wouldn't have had me then, see. Me and Jenny. Because we're only born, like, now.'

She didn't answer him.

'And we're, you know, like, glad that you're our mum.'

'I'm sick of this bedroom,' she said. 'Look at it. It's so *brown*.'

'Mum,' said Gabe. 'Do you think the Hindus are right?'

Mum lay down with her hair in the ash. She turned on her side, her face close to his, and adjusted her white lawn nightgown. 'Gabriel,' she said and clamped her hand across his cheek. 'Maybe I was born too *soon*. All the things Jenny will get to do. D'you see?' The Virginia Slim burned dangerously close to his ear. 'But you get this life, understand, you get this . . . and you must . . . because if you don't, all right, you see what happens, don't you, now, you've seen.' She moved her hand away and Gabriel caught sight of the white ash tower before it crumbled into the bed.

Gabe watched Chef Albert sigh over a tray of marzipan roses. There was a dusting of what looked like icing sugar on his moustache.

Hardly daring to say it, Gabe asked if everything was going well.

Chef Albert regarded him mournfully. 'Nothing,' he said, 'no.' His eyes, ringed by dark shadows, were wells of sorrow. Gabe did not like to look his pastry chef in the eye, lest he drown. 'How can it be,' Chef Albert went on, 'when I have zis muppet for assistance.' He gestured towards the apprentice, who giggled and lost control of his icing bag.

'But you'll have everything ready for tomorrow,' said Gabe. He forced a note of gaiety into his voice as if encouraging a small child.

Chef Albert planted his hands on his ample hips and executed a Gallic shrug. 'No, I do not think. I have to begin again with ze meringues and now I see how zees little flowers are . . .'

Gabriel shivered and moved away slightly, trying to make his movement invisible by coughing at the same time. He respected Chef Albert's perfectionism but, like all the self-sacrificing virtues, it was best appreciated at a safe remove. It was cold in here, anyway, particularly standing close to Albert.

Inclining his head to indicate that he was still listening, Gabe looked over the pastry kitchen. The Rondo machine still had a few scraps of fresh dough clinging between the rollers but everything else was sparkling clean.

Every pastry chef he had known was lugubrious. It went with the territory, he supposed. There had been one exception, Terry Sharples, down at the Brighton Grand. Terry was always laughing. Until he threw himself off Beachy Head, New Year's Eve, 1989.

Gabriel caught sight of himself in the refrigerator door. He had fancied he would look contemplative but his expression was somewhere between dismissive and harassed. He yawned in order to rearrange his face. In Blantwistle people would say, *doesn't he look like his dad*, but they said that no matter what. There was some resemblance but you had to search for it. Gabe didn't have his father's hard lines. Perhaps if you peeled the flesh back, you would see it: Ted as the prototype and Gabe the end result. He had the hair, though: thick, dark and curling on top, oddly foppish, like a playboy Italian count. Gabe worked his finger into the sparse patch at the crown. He wondered what age Dad had been when he started to go bald. Perhaps, when you lose your hair, that's when you really know that you're going to die, just like everyone else. Dad was going to die. An image exploded in his mind: the floor at Rileys, a hundred thundering looms, the battlefield noise, and Dad, striding around like a colossus, taming the machines with his big strong hands.

Dad would live to see Gabe open his own restaurant. That had to mean something, even if Dad would pretend that it didn't. Dad had to live long enough to see it. *Come on, Dad*, exhorted Gabe, as though everything would be fine as long as his father pulled up his socks.

Gabe glanced back at his reflection. He rubbed his hand across his face.

'Everything is not so good,' said Chef Albert. He spread his arms. 'You see for yourself how is all zis mess.'

Gabe administered a pep talk and fled. Gleeson and Ivan were holding a furtive conference in the passageway that led to the dining room. Why would a restaurant manager need to speak privately to a grill chef? Gleeson pranced on his toes, ready at any moment to cut and run. He had the wind up him all right. Every day, since Yuri's 'sad accident', he'd been a flutter of spite and nerves. Ivan stood fast but he was agitated, plucking at his red bandanna. Loitering at the corner, Gabriel wished he could read their lips. There was one thing he could tell from their body language: they did not wish to be overheard.

Gleeson saw Gabriel. 'Ah, Chef, you lost again? Kitchen's that way, I do believe. I've just directed your detective friend – Parks, is it? – to your lair. Try to keep him out of the dining room, would you? We don't want to frighten the horses.'

'I don't think I'll be able to stop him, Stanley,' said Gabriel, beginning to walk away. He smiled back over his shoulder. 'I think the police go wherever they want.'

When he reached his cubicle Parks was sitting at his desk. 'There you are,' said Parks. 'I've taken your seat.'

'Feel free,' said Gabe. 'How can I help?'

'Paperwork,' said Parks, pointing at the piles on the floor and the files poking out of the overstuffed drawers. 'Bane of all our lives.'

'Yes.'

'When I've got a file open that should never have been opened in the first place . . . and it's all about crossing the t's and dotting the i's, no real police work . . .' He trailed off. 'Not that I'm blaming the sergeant. Though someone else might have called it different, of course.'

'Was there something in particular?'

'Well, we've not managed to notify the family. Ran the usual immigration checks and naturally it's a false name. Usual story. You don't happen to know . . . of course not. Apart from that, I'm just checking back to make sure nothing's occurred to you, nothing out of the ordinary, before I start wrapping it up.' He referred to his note-book. 'One employee we haven't spoken to, another kitchen porter, I think.'

Gabriel nodded. 'She's not shown up again. If I can get to my files I can tell you which agency she came through.'

'I'm guessing your porters come and go all the time.'

'Pretty much.'

'So unless there's any particular reason . . . I think we'll leave it at that.'

'OK,' said Gabriel. 'Fine.'

Parks put his notebook in his pocket. 'Oh, there is one other thing.'

'Yes,' said Gabriel, tensing.

'My wife says she wants to go to a really good Italian for our anniversary, it's our twentieth. Had our honeymoon in Venice. Now, where would you recommend?'

Throughout the dinner service, Gabriel stood at the pass, checking plate by plate, adding garnish, wiping rims, admonishing waiters, sending back the overcooked, underdone or sloppily constructed with a pinch of encouraging zeal ground up with a measure of scorn. The tempo had been building from six o'clock and by half past eight the kitchen was in full swing. Gabe replated a chicken fricassée, and turned to look at his team.

Nikolai, the Russian commis, chopped salad onions with heartbreaking deftness and speed. Suleiman hovered by the Steam'N'Hold, waiting for his soufflé with evident anxiety, as though it were his firstborn son. Victor moved between the Bratt Pan, wilting off spinach, and the combi-oven, loading up potato röstis and cubes of butternut squash. A commis dropped a bowl of peelings and everybody clapped. Benny ran over to help him and ran back to his station, wiping his hands. A spit of fat from a wok hissed in the blue burner flame. In Ivan's empire the air pulsed with heat so that the grill chef appeared hazy, as though he were a mirage. He slapped a couple of steaks on the charcoal grill and took a hammer to a third, the sweat darkening the back of his white coat.

Victor sauntered over to the stockpots, threw a mock punch at one of the commis, moved him aside and lifted a lid. Steam rose in a column and dispersed, like an idea that can find no words. The extractor hoods roared momentarily and dropped back to their usual thrum.

'Hey,' said Victor, tossing his head at Damian who was standing, pigeon-toed, feeding noodles into a metal vat. 'Hey, come here, let me see.'

Damian pretended not to hear. He spilt noodles all around.

Victor took hold of the younger boy and pushed his chin up to inspect his neck. 'Wooo,' he screamed. 'What is this? Damian got a girlfriend. Everyone see this big, ugly thing? Love bite!'

The cooks beat on the work surfaces with whatever implement they had to hand. There were whistles and a couple of catcalls, all dissolving into laughs.

'I offer my congratulations,' said Suleiman.

'He's getting married?' said Victor, pantomiming shock. 'Man, he kept it quiet.'

'In my country,' said Benny enigmatically, 'the bride price may be no more than a case of Heineken and a slaughtered goat.'

'Well, that's way more than a commis can afford.' Victor banged Damian between the shoulder blades. 'Looks like you're choking, dude. Listen, I'm gonna give you a tip. Next time you wanna get dirty with this old bird of yours, ask her to take her teeth out first.'

The laughter was shrill but not hostile and even Damian giggled along.

Gabriel gave Benny a hand to make up more portions of bass and scallops en papillote. It was selling faster than Gabe had anticipated; perhaps because he had asked the waiters to snip the packages open at the table. It created a little drama which other diners were keen to reconstruct.

Benny worked quickly and neatly, wiping his station down almost every time he turned about. He was a small man who somehow gave the impression of being a larger man who had been condensed down to this size – something about the height of his buttocks or the spread of his shoulders or the way his head seemed a little too large. The whites of his eyes were yellow and his teeth were salty white. A jagged scar ran from the bridge of his nose almost across to his ear. Gabe thought about asking him which country he had left behind.

'Goal!' shouted Victor, chucking a romaine lettuce in the air and heading it on to a shelf.

'Give me strength,' muttered Gabriel. He picked up a scallop and sliced off the muscle tab.

'I know, Chef,' said Benny quietly, 'but that is the way he is made. Every one of us made differently.'

'Really?' said Gabe, flatly. 'Guess it's not his fault, then.' Oona was another one: *it ain't suppose to be.* A nice trick to have up your sleeve.

'If you don't mind, Chef,' said Benny, 'I'm going to sing a little now, keep going at the work and sing.' He sang, very low, in his own language, the words bubbling thickly like a rich and spicy stew.

Gabriel ran a mental checklist on the preparations for tomorrow's Sirovsky event. Some of the dips and sauces would be past their best by tomorrow night. They could be freshened up with a squeeze of lemon, a sprinkling of chopped herbs. He would have to go up to Blantwistle and see Dad. Dad and Nana. After tomorrow he'd be less busy. He'd think about it then, make a plan. He hoped Chef Albert wasn't going to ditch the marzipan roses. Not that they'd get eaten anyway, it was all about the show. Dad and Nana. Who'd have thought it? God, it made him laugh; to think they'd ended up together, those two.

It had begun, Gabriel supposed, by Nana visiting more often after they had moved to Plodder Lane. She couldn't say anything against the house, unlike the one in Astley Street, except it didn't have double-glazing. Her nemesis, Mrs Haddock, had double-glazing and since she, on a widow's pension, couldn't afford any for herself she felt that the least her son-in-law could do was to have it installed at number 22.

'You've to shop around, mind, for the best price. But there's a lot of cowboys out there, as'll part a fool from his money.' She sat primly at the edge of her seat, knees pressed together. 'Or her money,' she added, significantly.

Despite his promotion, Gabe and Jenny were given to understand, their father was somewhat lower down the social scale than Nana. This was on account of her husband having been a clerk at Rileys, who went to work in a shirt and tie rather than a pair of overalls. Dad was a tackler. They weren't called overlookers, not in Blantwistle, even the foreigners knew that. Dad was proud of his job. The people in the office, Dad said, didn't know warp from weft.

'*I* could never sit of an evening, not with shirts waiting to be ironed.' Nana was fond of mentioning shirts.

'A tackler,' said Dad to Gabriel, 'earns twice what a clerk gets. That's a fact.'

Gabriel believed him, but there was no withstanding the force of Nana's insinuations, insinuations being particularly hard to disprove.

'I've never seen such waste,' said Nana, arriving one bonfire night with a sticky black slab of parkin in an old Quality Street tin. 'Perfectly good clothes those Beesley children have put on their guy. Their mother should be ashamed.'

Mum was stirring vinegar into the black peas and staring into the kitchen window, from where she stared back at herself. 'Nobody's wearing straight-legs any more.'

'Sally Anne,' said Nana, touching the crisp curls of permanent wave around her head, 'I'm perfectly aware of that.'

Wasting money, in Nana's book, was vulgar. There was no higher sin. Those who had no money were also vulgar. Vulgarity took many forms and few in Blantwistle escaped its taint.

Gabe knew her for a snob while he was still a child. But for a long time it was impossible for him to see how anyone could be a snob unless they were also at least a bit posh.

When she moved in, it was Dad who encouraged it. Mum said, 'It'll be the death of me. Is that what you want?'

'This is what I mean,' said Dad. 'The way you get worked up. You've always been calmer when she's around.'

'But you hate her,' said Mum, wheedling.

'Aye,' said Dad, 'that's as may be.'

Nana moved into Gabe's room and Gabe had a camp bed in the sun porch at the back. He was at catering college by then, on day release to the Jarvis at Manchester Piccadilly. Nobody expected him to stay around for long.

Nana said she couldn't sleep in Gabe's old bed. She kept spraying it for bedbugs. Gabe came home at one, two, three in the morning and found her roaming in her nightie, support tights and Hush Puppies, making cups of tea that she left, half drunk, all over the house. She was partial, it transpired, to a glass of sherry, just a small one, now and then through the day. Exhausted by these and her night wanderings (on account of which Dad had slapped the 'shapeshifter' label on her) she was often back in bed by noon. When she needed something fetching – the newspaper, her bifocals, her medicine, two ounces of humbugs – she banged feebly but insistently on her bedroom floor and Mum growled and muttered before running up the stairs.

It was, supposedly, on 'account of her health' that Nana moved to Plodder Lane; yet it was only after she'd lived there for a while, as far as Gabriel could remember, that there seemed to be anything wrong. As was to be expected, her illnesses were refined in nature. Coughing she deemed to be vulgar, but breathlessness, from which she suffered, was not. When she had back pain it was sciatica, and most definitely not the lumbago of which any common labourer might complain. She had arthritis in her knees, which compared favourably to Mrs Haddock's varicose veins. Dr Leather was a frequent if somewhat reluctant visitor, though he seemed to spend less time in the bedroom with Nana than in the kitchen with Mum.

'She'll be the death of me,' said Mum, when Gabe got back, from time to time, from Glasgow, Scarborough, Lyon, wherever he happened to be. Perhaps, thought Gabe, she was. A heart attack at fifty-four. All that running around Mum did after Nana.

Nana was eighty-seven and still going strong.

From the corner of his eye Gabe caught sight of Damian holding his hand in the air and gurning while blood ran down to his sleeve.

'First-aid box, Damian. In my office, bottom drawer.'

Damian licked his finger and smudged his nose with blood.

'Doc,' called Benny. 'Take a look. Damian, let Doc see your hand.'

It was the crew's name for Nikolai.

Nikolai wielded his knife. 'The finger cannot be saved. I shall have to amputate.'

Damian laughed and waggled his finger but disappeared rapidly, nonetheless, into Gabriel's office.

Nikolai set down his knife. 'I propose a silence,' he said.

Everyone stopped working and turned to look. Gabriel wanted to object but he too was held in suspense. Nikolai was only a commis but he was older than the chefs de partie. He didn't say much, he worked hard, and when Gabriel wanted to put him in charge of a section Nikolai had turned him down. He had carroty hair and his face was bloodless as a veal chop, no colour in his lips or lashes. When he spoke it was with authority and sadness, like the gallows oration of a deposed king.

'Friends and colleagues,' said Nikolai, 'it has been a week since Yuri's death. I know how sad we all feel about this terrible accident. I would like everyone, with Chef's permission, to join in one minute of silence as a mark of respect to Yuri.'

Gabriel bowed his head. Why now, he thought, why in the middle of service, when every minute counts?

He counted off the seconds. 'All right,' he said, 'back to work.'

The silence hung about like a bad smell, until Victor broke wind.

'May I remind you,' said Suleiman, laughing, 'that this is a confined space.'

Victor went over to Suleiman and burped right into his ear.

'In Moldova, this is a sign of love. Am I correct?' Suleiman retreated a couple of paces on his little bow legs. Gabe smiled at the way he made his enquiry with apparent seriousness, as though he would inscribe the answer on to an official form.

'Too right, baby,' said Victor, attempting to grab Suleiman by the balls.

'Gentlemen,' Gabriel called, 'we're not in the fucking playground. Eyes down, go to work.'

'Yes, Chef,' said Suleiman. 'Chef? Extractor hood has a malfunction.'

'Report it to maintenance in the morning. Can't do anything now. Who's done this trout? Well, come and get it and do it again. Never mind "done", lad, put it in the sink and watch it swim.'

'In the morning, OK, I will make a report,' said Suleiman. 'When Yuri was here he used to fix always, very fast.'

'Right,' said Gabriel. 'There's your problem. You don't let the porter mess with things like that.'

'Oh, Yuri was an engineer also. Full qualifications. He understood very well the machines.'

Two plates were sent back to the kitchen, lamb noisettes and a chicken Florentine. The waitress said the customers had complained.

'Complained about what?' said Gabriel.

The waitress chewed her gum. 'The food.'

'The food. That's so much clearer now.' Gabe banged down the plates. 'And kindly take out that gum.'

He burned his finger on a jug of béchamel sauce and watched the blister rise. An order came in for a table of twelve. Gleeson had not warned him about the booking. Gabriel cursed the restaurant manager; once silently and then again aloud. 'Where's the red mullet?' he shouted. 'Come on! Two fries and one mixed salad. Don't make me ask again.'

Ivan slung a pork skewer and a fillet steak on to the pass, adding a little spin to the plates. He wiped his meaty forearms on his bandanna and went back to his station. His jaw was blue-black with stubble. He took a cleaver and with one clean slice chopped a chicken in two.

Victor stood in the grill section, attempting to burn Ivan with a stare.

Gabriel was about to tell him to move it, but wanted to see how Ivan would deal with the incursion into his domain.

'You smell like whore, Victor. You looking for pimp over here?'

Victor's face contorted. He had an in-growing hair between his eyebrows that was turning into a boil, visible even through the haze of heat. 'Fuck you,' he said, and turned.

Gabriel went to the sink for a glass of water. Gleeson slid up beside him, as usual standing a little too close.

'Here you are. Do I intrude on a break?'

'Can I help you?' Gabe folded his arms.

When Gabe had taken the job at the Imperial, he and Gleeson had gone out for a drink and weighed each other up.

The restaurant manager pretended to consider a moment. 'No,' he said, greasing the word. 'I don't think so.'

There were stories, of course, about Gleeson. He was screwing Christine, the head of PR, he was screwing a guest liaison officer, he was gay and he screwed all the waiters. Gabe paid no attention. Most likely everyone said he and Gleeson were screwing as well. Gleeson's sexuality, like his personality, was hard to determine, everything seeming to be put on for effect.

'And what did Inspector Morse have to say for himself?' said Gleeson, after Gabriel had declined to fill the pause. His manner was off-hand but Gabriel detected a pulse of anxiety. Whatever illegal stunts Gleeson was into meant he was uncomfortable with the police around. Gabe knew it would be unwise to wind him up. 'Asking about you, mainly. Said I didn't know a thing.'

'Quite the comedian, aren't we?' said Gleeson. 'There's a couple more people wanting entertainment in the dining room. They would like to see the chef.'

'I'm busy.' Gabe drew another glass of water. It was 'common knowledge' that Gleeson drove an Alfa Romeo Spider and went on holiday three times a year to places he shouldn't have been able to afford. In hotels, gossip was always known as common knowledge, even when palpably untrue. But, in Gleeson's case, it wasn't too hard to believe.

'Forgive me,' said Gleeson, 'but they are most insistent. Perhaps they are your friends.'

'I doubt it.'

'Don't you have any friends?' Gleeson smiled. He was a handsome man, slickly dressed and neatly trimmed. The light in his eye, though Gabriel mistrusted it, was both piercing and playful and it was likely that many had succumbed to his charms.

'I don't,' said Gabriel, sounding sullen when he had meant to joke.

'They are two gentlemen. One, you might describe as corpulent. Signet ring and paisley shirt. The other is pinstriped and blond, and I feel I've seen him somewhere before, can't say where. But I see it rings a bell with you. Well, if you don't go to them, they *insist* they're coming into the kitchen. Shall I lead them through?'

Gabe started at the description of Rolly and Fairweather. They had been in before, to sample the food, check they were backing the right horse, but he didn't want them coming into the kitchen. It was bad enough that they were asking him to go out there. 'I'll be out in a couple of minutes,' he said. He hoped Fairweather wouldn't switch into broadcast mode. If one of the waiters overheard, by tomorrow morning the whole hotel would know that Gabe was planning to leave.

'They'll be *so* pleased,' said Gleeson, with a smart little click of the heels. 'Want to convey their compliments, no doubt.'

Over drinks, Gleeson had told Gabriel that he grew up on a farm in East Anglia. It seemed a tall story, less likely than all the tales that were told behind his back. With his cufflinks and shoeshine, his soft-soap and sharp parting, with courtesy as his dagger and shield, it seemed that the only place Gleeson could have hatched was here, or some place like it, where you kept who you really were to yourself.

'Oh,' added Gleeson, over his shoulder. 'Mr Maddox is dining with us this evening. He's ordered the osso buco. I'm sure you'll see him. He's seated rather close to your friends.'

CHAPTER FOUR

—ᘑ—

JACQUES OCCUPIED THE GROUND FLOOR OF THE EAST-WING SEMI-circular turret that swept around from Yew Street to Eagle Place. The hotel's minimalist style had not been replicated in the restaurant; indeed, an attempt had been made to preserve or restore its old-world charm. The ceiling was high with quadrangular lacunae in the baroque fashion, the cavities hosting intricate flowers and unknown coats of arms. The walls were covered in fleur-de-lys wallpaper in a richly subtle colour somewhere between silver and beige. The colour was picked up in the carpet, and complemented by the table linen which leaned more towards pink. On the walls, at regular intervals, hung vast mirrors with rococo gilding and in the middle of the room stood a small stone fountain on which a pair of seahorses pranced. The French chandelier hid its ugliness in a blaze of light and this evening appeared to flirt charmingly with the scene below. Overall the effect was not displeasing though somewhat precariously contrived.

The restaurant was almost full. Gabriel paused at the edge of the dining room. To his side was the entrance to the cloakroom and the lectern where Gleeson or his head waiter greeted guests. Behind him the bar ran like a throat towards the belly of the hotel, the tables fanned out ahead. The diners leaned over their candlelit carousels, and the wine and the waiters flowed. The space was intimate and convivial, offering up both illusions at once.

As Gabriel stepped forward, a party of women – polished skin, bouclé and velvet, liver-spotted hands – set down their forks and exclaimed. The chef was in the dining room. They wanted a piece of him (why have a meal when you can have a dining experience?) but Gabe walked by with only a word. He spotted Mr Maddox, wiping gravy from his chin. He looked for his business partners. There were Rolly and Fairweather, damn them, a couple of tables away.

The noise of a hundred conversations hung overhead, pressing down gently but insistently, rounding Gabriel's shoulders and quickening his step.

'Must be a wonderful feeling,' said Fairweather, 'like coming out on stage to take a bow.'

'Can we make this quick?' said Gabriel, taking a seat. 'Aren't we due to meet next week?'

'He hasn't answered my question,' said Rolly. He waved a breadstick at Fairweather. 'That's what you get from a politician. They never answer the bloody question.'

Rawlins and Fairweather made an incongruous pair. The business-man, with his paisley shirt and fat pink hands, and the politician with his Savile Row suit.

'Gabriel was just saying' – Fairweather beamed at his companions – 'that he gets a terrific buzz when he walks through his restaurant.'

'My wife,' said Rolly, and shook his head. 'My wife thinks that if I leave my socks on the floor it's a personal insult to her.' His jowls vibrated. John Rawlins had none of the usual fat-man bonhomie. His eyes were small and hard, with few eyelashes, and he blinked a great deal, as though in disbelief at the entire idiotic world. 'It's genetic,' he said. 'Purely genetic. Women can multi-task. Men can't. There's scientific evidence. It's no use them trying to change us. Evolution takes thousands of years.'

'I *love* natural history programmes,' said Fairweather. 'David Attenborough and all that.' He twisted his wedding ring around.

Gabe kept watch on Mr Maddox, hoping to catch his gaze.

Rolly said, 'It's time the feminists admitted they've been barking up the wrong tree. Isn't it?' The question was appended with a slurp. There was always something moist about Rolly's speech: a touch of sibilance, a mulching of t's and d's, an abundance of saliva noisily drained.

'I think,' said Gabe, 'they're supposed to be post-feminist now.'

'Tits out for the lads,' said Rolly. 'Still bust your balls though, won't they?'

They had met several years ago on a salmon-fishing trip in the Highlands, a freebie organized by a supplier. The closest Rolly got to water was the soda siphon in the country house hotel. There was a fight. Take a fine array of single malts, one open-all-hours bar, a couple of chefs, add insults according to taste. Rolly sprayed them with the soda bottle, like a couple of scrapping dogs. Later, he sat in the billiards room with Gabriel. Above the fireplace was a stag's head. Its antlers were huge, powerful, majestic, and useless against the hunter's gun. I'm going to open up a restaurant in London, Rolly said, as soon as I've found myself a chef who can keep his cool. Gabe had looked up at the imperturbable glass eyes, the dignified head, and nodded his own.

'I agree very much with Gabe,' said Fairweather. 'On the one hand you can say we're subject to our nature, but what about raping and pillaging and all that? We can't just say we're designed for it. Infidelity too – well, we're supposed to be programmed to spread our seed widely, in an evolutionary sense, but I don't see that going down too well with my wife, or yours for that matter, Rolly. No, we have to rise above, sometimes, but I see what you mean about *difference*. Different but equal, isn't that the way?'

Rolly blinked his denuded eyes. 'See what I mean? You never get a straight yes or no.'

Fairweather laughed. He had a broad, pleasant face and his ruddy complexion lent him an endearingly bashful air. 'I rather fancy presenting a nature documentary. You've given me an idea.' He mused for a while, pushing back his blond fringe, as though preparing to face the camera. 'Power in the animal kingdom and power in politics – what does one world tell us about the other? Yes,' he said, 'yes . . . I should make a note.'

Gabe wondered if he should go over to Mr Maddox. But Mr Maddox was deep in conversation and Gabe could think of no reason to interrupt. Just then, the general manager's dining companion stood and excused himself. Gabe composed his face. When Mr Maddox glanced around, as he surely would, he would see that Gabriel was relaxed and had nothing to hide. Maddox surveyed the room. He looked straight through Gabe and then turned his head away. For God's sake, thought Gabriel, what game is he playing now?

'We're sorry to barge in on you like this,' Fairweather was saying. 'Aren't we, Rolly?'

The big man shrugged. 'Not really.'

'What he means is, we felt we had to. Speak to you immediately that is, and since you always seem to be working . . .' Fairweather gestured vaguely around the restaurant. 'The mountain must go to Mohammad, as it were. Jolly good, this food, by the way.'

Rolly leaned closer to Gabriel. His lips twitched. Gabriel could hear the saliva being squirted through Rolly's front teeth and sucked back into his mouth. 'Heard you mislaid one of your staff,' said Rolly. 'I think you forgot to tell us. Must have slipped your mind.'

'Read about it in the newspaper, actually.' Fairweather bowed his head and fiddled with his wedding band. 'Very sad,' he said. 'A tragedy.'

'What's the comeback?' said Rawlins. 'What sticks to you?'

'I'm clear,' said Gabriel. 'Maybe I should have mentioned it, but there's nothing that should affect our plans.'

'If there's anything I can do,' said Fairweather, as if Gabe had suffered a personal loss. 'Anything at all.'

A waitress came to top up the water glasses. She was pretty in an uninspired sort of way, a regularity of features, a sufficient spacing of eyes and nose and mouth. Fairweather fumbled with his hair. 'Now, I'll bet you're not really a waitress. Let me guess. You're between acting jobs.'

'No,' said the girl, rearranging the cruet. 'I am going to be a nurse.' She lingered a while and Fairweather flirted, teasing her about vampires when he discovered she was from Romania, asking her if she had a nurse's uniform yet. The girl affected an urbane tolerance, narrowing her eyes and smiling tightly, but by the time she left the table Gabriel could see something beautiful about her and credited Fairweather with the transformation. Fairweather was possessed of the kind of easy warmth that, from a distance, could seem suspicious and up close was impossible to resist.

They were an unlikely pair, Fairweather and Rawlins, but a pretty good team. Their egos didn't clash because they grew in different directions and Gabriel was grateful for that. Five years ago, when he'd tried to set up a business with a trio of experienced restaurateurs, it was like three chafing boils which finally erupted, leaving nothing but a big infected mess. After that, Gabe had decided he would only go it alone. No bank, it turned out, was prepared to advance the necessary amount of cash. He would have been looking at a greasy spoon north of Watford had he not found alternative private finance. The savings he'd built up, around sixty grand, would go in with Rolly's and Fairweather's contributions and his name would hang, finally, over the door of a fine central London restaurant. Looking at his backers now, Gabriel felt a constriction in his throat. Here, he thought, is my chance.

Forty-two years old and he needed a break. He'd expected his name above the door before now. But he made the plan when he was, what, fifteen, sixteen, and what did he know then? More than his father anyway, stuck as fast to Rileys as a shuttle caught in the loom. Fifteen he was when he planned his career and hadn't he pushed on through? My God, it made him shiver to think of some of the places he'd worked. That sadist in the brasserie in Lyon who pushed Gabe's face down to the pan of boiling mussels, so close the skin peeled back from his cheeks. The hotel in Scarborough where he'd spent nine months, the saddest place on earth; where the staff and even the guests were prone to sudden fits of weeping and where he shared a room with a deaf mute, a fellow trainee who had a passion for Pelmanism and hard-core porn. Of course he hadn't done the stint at a three-star. Hadn't needed to or wanted to, beyond the age of sixteen. As a kid he'd had a dalliance with patisserie, spinning sugar cages two feet high and entering competitions and, at the least, getting placed. He'd come to his senses, thank goodness, before condemning himself to life in the pastry kitchen, with the depressives and obsessive-compulsives, among the pink icing and chocolate mice.

'Are you all right?' said Fairweather.

'Wind, I should think,' said Rolly. 'Chefs have bloody terrible diets.'

'Do they really?' said Fairweather. 'It's a wonder no one's made a programme about that.'

'The Pimlico site is a goer,' said Rolly. He drained a water glass and poured some red wine which he pushed across the table to Gabe. 'Gentlemen, shall we toast?'

'Not here,' said Gabe, checking on Mr Maddox, who chose that moment to look straight back at him.

'Discretion is the better part of valour,' said Fairweather.

'My boss is over there,' said Gabe, shifting in his seat.

'Only one possible hitch with the Pimlico site,' said Rolly. He waved a pink paw at Fairweather. 'Fly-by-night here's thinking of getting out of Westminster. I mean, what's the point of setting up in Pimlico if he doesn't get all his MP buddies along?'

I'm going to get sacked, thought Gabriel. The restaurant won't happen either. Fairweather is going to pull out. Or Rawlins. They're both going to change their minds. Forty-two years old and going nowhere fast. He picked up the glass of red wine and knocked it back.

Fairweather laughed. His laugh seemed to trumpet down his nose. 'I'll still have *friends*. I may only be a very, very junior minister but I don't think I'll be forgotten all that quickly. And, you know, I might make some new friends. We fly-by-night types usually do.'

Gabe dragged himself back from the future, which seemed to have run away from him, to the present, over which, as far as he knew, he still exerted some control. 'Are you going to resign?' he said. 'You don't want to be an MP any more?'

'I won't stand again,' said Fairweather. 'I think the only respectable way out mid-term is in a wooden box.'

Gabriel looked round for a waiter. To his immense satisfaction, three started towards him at once. He ordered a 1962 Chateau Moulinet Pomerol and said it was on the house.

'Good man,' said Fairweather.

'Have you stopped enjoying it?' asked Gabe. 'Being an MP?'

Fairweather sighed. 'It's been such a privilege to serve. People complain about the caseloads from their constituencies but, you know, if I can help someone with their problems, however mundane they may be (I'm not denying they can be very, very mundane) it gives me profound satisfaction.' He gave a wistful smile and repeated the phrase. 'Profound satisfaction. Really and truly it does.'

Rolly snorted. 'Noisy neighbours, leaking roofs? I'll bet they give you a kick.'

'Why give it up?' said Gabriel. 'I can assure you the restaurant won't—'

'Of course,' cried Fairweather. 'It's not that. I'm sure you – you and Rolly – will keep all that running smoothly. But I've been getting so many media offers and most I'm not currently able to take up. I've done one or two, as you may know, and it seems I have this – this *knack*, shall I say, and it was sheer accident, you know, that brought it out. Who'd have thought it? Seems like something I ought to do.'

'Owes it to his talent,' said Rolly. 'Here comes that wine.'

'He loves to tease,' said Fairweather.

'Well, if you've got the talent.'

'A knack, perhaps it's more of a knack. Anyway, in the Department, we always say that workers need to think about multi-skilling these days. I'm not even sure if that's a word but that is what we say. I'm going to practise what I preach.'

Yuri, thought Gabriel suddenly. Yuri, it seemed, had been multi-skilled.

Fairweather's voice was running on. It was a perfect voice for broadcast, both gritty and smooth, like running your fingers through sand. 'And there'll be the restaurant. It's another way of serving, as I see it, because we'll be making people's lives that little bit richer. What could be better than making people happy? A restaurant *can* do that, I think.'

He's still in, thought Gabe, relaxing slightly. He poured the wine.

'Excuse me,' said a diner, coming up to the table. She bent down as she spoke to Gabe so her décolletage was level with his eyes. 'I just wanted to say that we've had a fantastic meal this evening. Thank you very much.'

Gabe lifted his gaze from the wrinkled valley between her breasts to the starched-and-ironed region of her eyes and brow. He asked what she had eaten, if the meal had marked an occasion and hoped that she and her husband would come again.

'*Splendido*,' said Fairweather, when the woman had blushingly retired. '*Bravissimo*. We must get you front of house as often as possible on charm offensives. They love all that, don't they, mingling with the chef.'

'Oh,' said Gabe, 'we've the television to thank for that. But I'll be needed in the kitchen, so if you don't mind—'

'Wouldn't be too clever,' said Rolly, 'to pour funds into a restaurant with a chef who's going to find himself on some type of corporate manslaughter charge. You sure nothing's going to stick to you?'

Gabriel gave a short laugh and rocked back in his chair. 'Forget about the porter. I already have. It was a sad accident but Yuri brought it on himself. He was drinking. It's not going to interfere with my life, though. I give you my word on that.'

'Good enough for me,' said Fairweather. 'Rolly? Good enough?'

Rawlins did his special tooth rinse. It was a wonder, given how much saliva he appeared to produce, that it didn't spray out when he spoke. 'How's business here, Gabriel? How's your bottom line?'

'Started out bumpy.' Gabe shrugged. Rolly looked like a bit of a clown. When he wasn't talking business he was usually talking rubbish, but in business, as he'd already proved, he was anything but a fool. With Rolly it would always be about the bottom line. 'Look, we're averaging seventy per cent capacity over the week now. The midweeks were killing the place before but you can see for yourselves . . . Let's crunch some numbers when we get together. I've got more projections to talk through but I need to get back in my kitchen, I like to keep things tight.'

'Off you go,' cried Fairweather. The alcohol had reddened his cheeks further, but they seemed to glow with health, as if he had taken a bracing walk rather than an immodest amount of wine. 'Mustn't keep him, must we, but do just tell me this: would you object very much to a *theme* week when we open up? MPs do like a theme. I think I can guarantee a full house.'

Gabriel put his forearms on the table. He set himself solidly in place. 'Traditional French cuisine – precisely executed classics with a clean, modern interpretation. Believe me, in London these days, that could be called a theme. If you want Pacific Rim with a Mexican molé on the side you can just pop round the corner. To get a decent steak béarnaise you've got to go to the ends of the earth.'

'Oh, I know,' said Fairweather, 'that's exactly what we discussed. That's why we're going to be full to the seams every night. There's no precision in anything nowadays. It's the same in politics, you know, a lot of flannel – flim-flam, my father used to call it – a lot of that about.'

'Look,' said Rolly, 'if you've got some secret lust for Michelin stars, I'm telling you now, forget it. Yeah, if you get them, there's payback. If you don't . . . It's a mug's game. It's one good way to go broke.'

'Not interested,' said Gabe. 'Never have been.' He looked across the restaurant at the treble-arched window. The open curtains, artfully swagged skeins of silver, framed the dark night beyond. People passed by indistinctly. Lights smudged colour into the street, but illuminated scarcely anything at all.

'Because if you are . . .' said Rolly.

Gabriel tuned in to the ticklish patter of the fountain, the clink of cutlery all around. Rolly needed handling, but it wasn't too hard to do. 'Who wants to end up like Loiseau?'

'Who?' said Fairweather. 'Oh, I do know. The chef who shot himself? He was worried about losing a star.'

'Besson,' said Gabe, 'had a heart attack when they took one away.'

'Jesus.'

'Senderens. He was smart. He handed them back himself. Wants to go back to cooking real food again.' Gabriel looked directly into Rolly's beady eyes. 'Why let other people be in charge of your cooking – your life – when you can be in charge of it yourself?'

Fairweather rubbed his hands together as the desserts arrived. '*Bravissimo.* By the way, you should upgrade to fresh flowers for the restaurant, plastic is a bit you-know-what.'

On his way back to the kitchen he stopped to speak to Mr Maddox, who was sitting alone now with an espresso and petits fours. 'How was your meal?'

The general manager took his time to reply, a small exercise of power. He stared with seeming deliberation towards Rolly and Fairweather, and then he glanced about the dining room. 'There's a man and a woman sat behind me, no, don't start looking now, they're staying in the hotel. I'd say he's her boss and what his wife doesn't know won't hurt her, if you catch my drift. Next table along, a brace of City types, and those squawkers right there are Essex girls come up to town for a shop.' Gabe studied Maddox's face, trying to read the signs. His brow was dark and heavy, as though authority resided there. His mouth, though in no way generous, had lips that were surprisingly full and red. His eyes appeared somewhat cavernous beneath the weight of the brow. These same features could assemble and reassemble to present one face to a guest and another to an employee who had failed to come up to scratch. But the process of transformation was mysterious and Gabe could divine nothing by scrutinizing the opening and closing of the mouth. 'The wax effigies at six o'clock,' Mr Maddox continued, 'fortieth anniversary, odds on. We're serving the pink pound over by the fountain, Soho's just waking up. What else? Ladies who lunch, doing dinner, ad execs on the mineral water, the lot of them on the twelve-step . . . I could go on. Point is, Chef – ' He paused and scratched the inside of his wrist where the tattoo had been removed. 'Point is, place like this, you got to cater for all of them and it looks like that's what you've done. Well, what you waiting for? I'm not about to fellate you, you have to get back in your kitchen for that.'

The new night porter was down in the catacombs operating the rubbish compactor. Everyone else had gone home. Gabe typed in his password to access his personal file, clicked to open the spreadsheet and drummed his fingers to fill the couple of seconds before the program got in gear. He looked away. Viewed from his cubicle the bare kitchen took on a desperate aspect, as though it had been abandoned for good. Even Ivan's grill station, his circle of fire, reduced to dull sheens and gaping holes, looked pathetic, as humbled as the rows of cookers and fridges that you see at any rubbish dump.

Gabriel began reading the numbers. He adjusted one of the assumptions, on staff costs, and watched it translate almost instantly to the bottom line. He took 10 per cent off dairy products, thinking that for the new business he'd be able to cut a deal. He ran through all the produce, making notional savings, and gaining the satisfaction of driving the gross profit up. If he raised the average spend per head, yes, he'd been too conservative there, he saw the possibility of moving into net profit before a year was out. Inching forward in his seat, he looked for new lines of attack. The computer purred and the numbers capitulated and Gabriel hunted deeper and deeper until he came to the costs that were fixed. Still he did not stop; he wanted very much to go on. He lowered the monthly lease and the price of gas and electricity, purely for the pleasure of seeing the numbers respond.

Rubbing his eyes he pushed back from his desk. He decided to go home. He hunched into the computer again and restored the fixed costs to their previous levels. Then he made another alteration to the projected volume of alcohol sales. If they pushed a mere twenty extra units per day – look at the effect it had. It was beautiful, setting up input and output like that. To make x happen you do y. Strange how easy it was to lose the connections in the course of an ordinary day.

There was nothing more he could usefully do tonight, except go home and get some sleep. He scratched, or rather caressed, the tiny bald patch. Was it visible yet, or was his hair sufficiently thick and way-ward to cover it up? Charlie had never mentioned it but that would be just like her – or rather it wouldn't, he thought she would have said something, to tease him, or to show that it was nothing, or just because . . . he couldn't think now, what it was that she might do. He really was extremely tired and he had to go to bed.

One thing he should do tomorrow was to think of a way of getting rid of Oona. It would hardly be fair to hand her on to the next executive chef. He had nothing against her personally, and it wasn't like she wasn't willing to do things his way. But even when she was doing exactly what he asked of her there was something so – what? – *static* about her. Even bustling about the kitchen, Oona had a way of seeming to stand stock-still.

A few times she'd covered for absences in the staff canteen and she'd always seemed happiest then, turning leftovers into curries and serving up huge portions of rice'n'peas. Her interest in food was basic and narrow, without imagination or zeal.

Gabriel looked down at his hands. They looked like chef's hands, callused and scarred, but gave no reassurance. Was he so different from Oona? Had he fallen out of love with food? It was all these numbers and forms, the meetings, the health and safety procedures, the staff problems, the countless emails. No wonder the passion waned now and again. A hard-on in a hailstorm would be easier to maintain. Classic French, a modern twist, cooked with precision. Just a set of worn-out words.

Well, he hated the alternative. A handful of this, a slug of that, depending on how you feel, lovely jubbly, tear a few leaves, do a dance, chuck in some chillies, there you go. He could still *feel* something about that. Yes, precision was something he could offer, a quality he would bring to bear. He had it all those years ago, even when he started at the Jarvis, and he had not lost it yet.

Bogie and Darren and the other commis used to go out and get shitfaced seven days a week while Gabe stayed late in the kitchen, test-grilling one-inch slices of steak and perfecting his soufflés. Their reading material began with *Penthouse* and ended with *Hustler* while he ground his way through *Le Guide Culinaire* and *Larousse*. They knew as much about food science as they knew about girls. For Gabe too, girls remained (literally) impenetrable, but he knew about polysaccharides, starches, gluten, protein, collagen, gelatin and gels.

No, Gabe knew about food all right, had forgotten more than most of them would ever learn. And if a dimming of passion was all he had to worry about, then, for God's sake, he was doing well. The business took over, that was reality. You couldn't go round tearing basil leaves and swooning with pleasure all day. He had no debts; he wasn't an alcoholic, he didn't take drugs, he didn't live on sugar sandwiches and Coke; and he had come this far without bankruptcy, coronaries, divorce or psychotic breaks. Looking sideways (for what man is strong enough to resist?) he could say that things were not too bad.

Gabriel turned off the computer, and at last got ready to leave.

He headed to the back exit through the loading bay. There'd be less competition for cabs; worth considering, even at this time of night. The cold cut his nostrils; it always shocked him after the day-long swaddling heat. He coughed and the back of his throat felt sharp. He wondered if he was coming down with a cold. As he walked past Ernie's prefab hut he saw a figure step away from the wall. He was not surprised. It seemed natural that he should have conjured her like this.

Lena had her hands in the pockets of her coat, a thin, navy trench. She shivered but looked at Gabriel with indifference as though ready to walk on by.

'It's you again.' Gabe hardly recognized his own voice. A streetlamp shrugged a sodium glow over the girl, and he had the sensation she was floating in the circle of orange light.

'Yes.' She carried a duffle bag over one shoulder. It slipped down and she hoisted it up.

'I'm going home,' said Gabe, his throat really hurting. 'What are you doing here?'

She raised her chin but did not speak. Shadow obliterated her eyes.

'It's very late,' he said, stupidly. 'Do you . . . do you have anywhere to go?' He knew that she had come for him, though he hardly dared believe it yet.

'I'll carry your bag,' said Gabriel. He took one step towards her. She didn't bolt so he took another. He approached her gradually, as he would a wild creature. 'There,' he said. 'It's OK. You can stay with me.'

CHAPTER FIVE

—ᴍᴍ—

LENA ROAMED THE SITTING ROOM AS THOUGH LOOKING FOR A WAY
out. She trailed her hand across a shelf, knocked a candlestick and set
it straight. She picked up a photograph of Charlie but barely glanced
at it. She put it down again. Standing by the long, naked window,
twisting her fingers, she regarded the door with infinite blankness.

'Tea,' said Gabe, 'coffee, cocoa, vodka . . .'

Lena switched her gaze to the window. Her hair, tied in a ponytail,
was limp and greasy. Her earlobes were stretched by thick gold hoops.
A row of studs ran up the cartilage of the left ear. The tendons of her
neck formed two thick cords.

She shook her head.

'Are you cold? I could put the heating on.' He felt shivery himself.
He bit his lip to stop his teeth from chattering.

Lena began to pace. She wore black patent shoes with a gold clasp
across the toes and low heels that tapped a nervy message across the
pale oak floor.

'We don't have to talk,' said Gabriel. 'You don't have to tell me anything.' If those were her tights he had found, if she had been living in
the basement with Yuri, if she was now homeless as well as jobless –
she probably didn't know where to begin.

'It's late, anyway. Time for bed.' His throat hurt when he swallowed.
He was coming down with something. Was he too cold or too hot?
For a few moments he closed his eyes.

He was back in the cab, coming over Vauxhall Bridge, looking out of the windows at the London Eye and St Paul's and all the other jewels scattered against the purple velvet sky, and his hand was not so far from hers and he breathed the thin damp scent of her and did not look at her once.

'If you want sex,' said Lena, 'I don't have problem.'

Gabriel opened his eyes. 'No,' he said. 'What? No.' He shook his head.

Lena shrugged. The deep slash of her top showed the sharpness of her collar bone and only the faintest suggestion of breasts. In front of the television she came to a standstill and faced him. 'I don't have problem. We do it, OK, now if you want.'

Again, he shook his head, staring at her cadaverous little frame. He scarcely believed those words had spilled from it, and he was appalled. He wanted very much to have sex. 'Christ, no. That's not why I . . .' He rubbed his face. 'Look. You don't know me, but if you think I . . . that's not how I am, I'm not like that at all.'

'OK,' said Lena.

'You don't believe me? I didn't bring you here for . . . you said you needed a place to stay.'

'OK.'

'Jesus.'

'OK.'

Gabriel got up. His throat was definitely inflamed and his head hurt. It was madness to try to help this girl. She could stay one night on the sofa and then she would have to leave. 'I'm going to take some aspirins and then get you a duvet. You can sleep in here. Right. You need anything else? Are you cold? I can get you a jumper, you know, if you're cold.'

He went straight to the kitchen, picked the tights off the worktop and threw them in the bin. He went to the bathroom and swallowed two aspirins, replaced the bottle, retrieved it and tapped out two more. In the bedroom he opened drawers and closed them until he realized he was searching for a jumper that would suit her and pulled out the first thing that came.

Lena was watching television in the dark. She had taken off her shoes and sat with her feet up, hugging her knees. Gabe held out the jumper. She took it without a word, pulled it on and stretched it over her legs.

Gabe wished it were already morning so he could put her out of his flat and out of his life. She wasn't in the least bit attractive. She was hostile. What was wrong with her? Offering sex like that but not a single word of thanks.

He would fetch a duvet and a pillow and leave her to it. He had tried to be charitable and she had thrown it back in his face.

He sat on the sofa next to her, but leaving the widest possible gap.

On the screen, some cable channel, a tedious 1940s movie played out. *Oh, how can you ask me that?* The woman wore a frothy nude-toned evening gown, although it appeared to be the middle of the day. The man was in a tuxedo. Through the open French windows was a swimming pool shaped like an internal organ; the way it glittered made everything look fake.

Gabriel turned to Lena. He would question her briefly but closely about Yuri. Wasn't that why he had brought her here? She wasn't his responsibility. If she had no job that was her own fault. Oona had never fired her because Oona hadn't seen her again.

Lena watched the television; his jumper formed a tent over her knees. The light from the screen played with her face, screwing the angles around. She had a feline nose, small and snub, high, skinny eyebrows and a pale scar of a mouth. It was difficult to tell, Gabe could not decide, whether she was pretty or not. She turned her face and now he could see her eyes, darker than he remembered, livid blue in the television's flame.

'Lena,' he said. It sounded like a sigh. He cleared his throat. 'Whereabouts are you from?'

'Whereabout,' said Lena flatly, as though that were the answer she gave. She looked at the screen.

'What country?'

The man laughed in an avuncular manner then kissed the girl on the neck. He was twice her age.

'Belarus,' said Lena.

Gabe reached for something to say. He looked at Lena. 'Oh,' he said. 'What's it like?'

Lena twisted her lips; scorn for the entire country or, perhaps, merely for Gabe.

Gabriel tried again. 'Which town?'

She ignored him. She plucked at the jumper, unravelling a thread or two.

'How long have you been in London?'

She rested her chin on her knees. Her earrings, though they were gold, spoke only of poverty. Curling her toes, she attempted to grip the slippery-hard edge of the sofa, and to maintain her slovenly position, Gabe knew, she had to hold herself rigid as hell.

'Were you living in the basement with Yuri?'

There's that whole darn mess with Mr Hammond! If only there was a way to clear that up. You see, I walked in on Celia that day when Bobby was supposed to . . . The girl was walking around now, swishing the folds of her dress. Get on with it, thought Gabe, wanting, in spite of himself, to know what it was that Bobby was supposed to have done.

Enough, thought Gabe. 'I said, were you . . .'

'Mazyr. My town. Mazyr.' Whatever quality it was that breathed life into words was missing from Lena's voice. The words that slid from her mouth were stillborn.

Gabriel let his head fall back against the sofa and stared at the ceiling, wishing she would speak again. How could he get her to speak?

The television girl prattled. She explained everything, the whole darn mess.

Gabriel sat up. The tux man strode masterfully across the room to the ottoman where the girl had flung herself.

Lena giggled, watching it all end happily.

'Yeah,' said Gabe, 'why do people watch these stupid shows?'

Lena rearranged herself, sitting properly and crossing her legs. She gave him a sideways glance that seemed playful but when she spoke it was in a petulant tone. 'I think is good show. I like.'

'How were—'

'You say you will not ask question,' said Lena, anger quickening her voice. 'But all you do is asking. Ask, ask, ask.' Gabriel saw how badly her fingernails were bitten, a ridge of crusted blood. 'Are you a police? Do I ask you question? No.'

She was hardly in a position to ask questions. She had asked him one. 'Go ahead,' said Gabe. 'Ask me. Anything you like.'

Lena drew up her shoulders. It was more a flinch than a shrug, as if the thought of finding out anything about him was disgusting. 'What is name?' she said.

'Gabriel.'

'Like angel.'

'Yes.' It was simple. He would talk to her and then she would talk to him. How could he have expected her to speak? She had not even known his name.

'Whereabout,' said Lena, shaping the word with care, 'you are from?'

'A small town in the north, Blantwistle.'

'Oh, what is it like?' she said without interest, turning his questions back at him.

I'll tell her then, thought Gabriel. I'll tell her what it's like.

Gabe picked up the remote control from the coffee table. 'My father says it's . . . never mind. It's small, it's a mill town, was, I mean—'

'What he is like?'

'Dad? I don't know. He's just a normal . . . ordinary, you know.' Gabe turned off the television. He had thought the room dark before, but it hadn't been. Now it really was. There was only the light in the hallway and the ghostly shimmer of the windowpanes. The white coffee table held a faint luminescence; the rest of the furniture thickened the blackness in places, and Lena, swathed in black, appeared disembodied, a little pale streak in the air.

'My father,' said Gabriel. He wanted to tell her. But what? Why did she come to him, anyway? *Had* she come to him? One look they had exchanged in the catacombs, what could one look mean? How much? Did she look at him, then, the way he thought she had? They had only seen each other for a second or two, the rest he had made up, invented now, tonight, because he was – what? – lonely? Was he lonely? Had he been lonely? Or was that something he had just now begun to feel? Was she making him lonely? It didn't make any sense. He was feverish. He couldn't think straight. He would take some more aspirins. 'My father,' he began again, 'is a bit set in his ways. Of course, he's of an age when. What I mean is he's always been like that. Knows what he likes and likes what he knows. Lot of men are like that, especially in Blantwistle, ha ha, maybe in your town too. Same place, same street, same friends, same job . . .' He ran on and on, scarcely knowing what he said. 'Doesn't have any idea what it's like for us, you and me, floating, I don't know, not that we're the same, I'm only trying to point out, when you have to make your own way . . . Sorry, I don't feel very well.' He tipped forwards, head in hands, and blew hard. Why was he talking like that?

Lena rose and switched on a lamp. She ran a finger over the shade. 'I stay here, two, three days, I clean for you. OK?'

'You don't have to clean,' said Gabriel. He was shuddery, as though at the end of a crying jag. She was only a pot-washer. An illegal one, most likely, she didn't want to talk to the police. 'I have to ask you about Yuri.'

She looked sullen.

'It's either me or the police.'

'I have do nothing. Is it my fault he drink?' The end of her nose went red.

Gabriel drew strength from her discomfort. 'So tell me what happened,' he said.

'Yuri have go for shower. He take long time but I don't think nothing. I go to sleep. I wake up—' She bit her lip. 'He is good man, Yuri. If I can help – but no way for helping him.' She bent her fingers so far back it was painful to watch.

'So you ran away? Why?'

Lena pulled a face.

'But you lived down there, with him?'

She made a sound that could have meant 'yes', could have meant 'no'.

'Why did you come back that day?'

She pulled her skinny shoulders up to her ears and let them slump again.

'Not good enough,' said Gabe. He stood up. 'That's not good enough.' She shrank as though she were afraid of him. He felt cruel, but he did not care. 'Come on,' he said, 'spit it out.'

'Money, I leave some money. Some little bit I save.'

'And? Did you get it?' said Gabriel, unsure where to take the interrogation next.

'How?' said Lena, her eyes blazing in her hard little face. 'How? I go and *you* are there!'

So that was the look she had given him. He was there. He was in the way. The shock of understanding made him laugh. Her eyes were bright and threatened to spill but he could only laugh and he was sorry, but he couldn't help it at all.

He made up a bed on the sofa. Lena perched on the edge of the chaise longue, her small flat body like a shadow that had slipped underneath the door. Gabe plumped the pillow. 'Right, then,' he said. 'All set.' His tone was brisk but the sight of her filled him with pity. She looked so dreadfully alone.

'Lena,' he said, 'tell me where you hid the money. I'll get it for you.'

She jumped up as though he had proposed to rob her and then she tried a smile. 'Back wall, count bricks from corner, four from right, seven up. That one is loose.' She stepped close and touched him, laying her hand on his chest. 'You are good man,' she said.

Finally, thought Gabriel, she was beginning to understand. 'I only brought you here to help you. I don't know what else you were thinking, but you should put it out of your mind.'

She patted his chest weakly and scanned his face and searched his eyes. Whatever it was she was looking for she seemed to have found. Abruptly, she withdrew.

Gabriel waited in the bedroom until he heard the toilet flush and the opening and closing of the bathroom door. When he passed the sitting-room door she was undressing in the lamplight with her back to him. For a few moments he watched her. He focused all his charity on the pathetic ridge of her spine.

In the bathroom he stood before the full-length mirror. His eyes were bloodshot, his hair a mess, stubble on his cheeks and chin. He tried to see what Lena had seen. He had changed into his jeans and fleece after service but still there was something of the kitchen about him and Gabe couldn't decide what it was. A tall man, big in the shoulders, strong in the jaw. He looked as if he were preparing to push something or someone out of the way. Perhaps he had been too rough on Lena; he should have let her take her time. It wasn't as if her answers would help Yuri – they were only a formality and he understood why she wished to avoid the formality of the police.

He would help her because he felt sorry for her, though – Yuri aside – hers was a familiar story and usually you had to steer clear. Not that he'd get sucked in. He'd find the money she mentioned, maybe make a few calls, get her a job within a day or two and then she'd be moving on. Though if it came out and the police, officially, were still looking for her, what would that mean for him? He laced his fingers together on top of his head and rested his forehead on the mirror, watching his breath steam steadily up.

Charlie would know what to do. He'd call her. She would want to help. He wished she were here now, he wanted to bury himself, let go of everything and lie down with her and see nothing but the hollow of her neck.

He splashed water on his face, picked up his toothbrush and wondered if Lena had used it. Lena, his charitable cause. He ran his fingers through his hair, pushing it back out of his eyes. Why did he think he looked like a chef? It was funny. If he'd spent his life in an office, would he look any different now?

He couldn't sleep and he was so hot that he was sweating. He stared at the cast-iron radiator that squatted fashionably low beneath the bedroom window, wondering if it was still on, though really he knew that it was not. At school, Gabe used to sit on one just like it at break time with Michael Harrison. 'Come 'ere, come 'ere,' Michael would squeak at any passing girl. 'No, get right close, I want fut tell you something.' He waited until she was close enough that she would jump away when he spoke again. 'Gabe'll give you ten pee if you let him cop a feel.' They did it over and over, sat there, warming their bums and cracking up. In those days if it was funny once, ten times was ten times as much fun.

He picked up a book from the bedside table. *The Universe in a Nutshell.* It was ridiculous how people bought all these science books, Stephen Hawking books, and never read them. Gabe seemed to have become one of those people but only because he didn't get time to read. He glanced at the cover and turned the book over and read the blurb, which he had looked at so many times he almost had it by heart.

He had to open the restaurant before Dad was too ill to travel. He would check with Jenny how long that would be. Get Dad to the opening. That was something he had to do. Get the restaurant on its feet, he'd be working all hours, Charlie would understand. They'd move in together. The restaurant would be going. They'd be living together. They'd have a kid. Good, he thought, good. Go to sleep.

He switched off the light.

He ran over it again. Get Dad to the opening. Get the restaurant on its feet. Move in with Charlie. Have a kid. Dad. Restaurant. Charlie. Kid. Tick them off, cross them out. Tick, cross, tick, cross.

He turned on his side and turned on his front. He flipped the pillow over.

It was Mum who should have been at the opening. Did he think Dad would even care?

Fuck it, he was awake. In a minute he'd get up and make a cup of tea.

In a minute he was asleep.

In his dream he descends to the catacombs and drifts in a phosphorescent light, a jellyfish glow on the walls, guiding him deeper and deeper still. He is afraid to touch anything and keeps his hands in his pockets, and lets the light pull him, lure him, pull him, until he comes to the place. The body is where he left it. He crouches to look at it carefully, beginning with the toes. Yellowing nails, a bunion, dry skin on the heel. Dense hair on the calves that peters out on chicken-skin thighs, and moving along to the genitals, don't miss anything out, a patch of eczema by the groin. The scrotum is hard and shrivelled, but the penis — he has to look at it — is soft and horribly long. Appendix scar on the stomach, leading to a chest that is, slightly but definitely, concave. He has to look at the face but he cannot. He closes his eyes and — gagging, retching — feels it with his hands.

CHAPTER SIX

—ᴍ—

IN THE KITCHENS WHERE GABE HAD SERVED HIS LONG AND VARIED apprenticeship, violence was not unknown, or, indeed, uncommon. He had been poked in the ribs, kicked in the shins, and – once – squarely up the arse. The chef at the Brighton Grand, an ex-trucker with a sweet little dog-fighting hobby, was a hair-puller, an ear-twister, a ball-grabber and was, Gabe sincerely hoped, locked behind bars by now. In his time he'd dodged a plate or two and taken one full force on the back of the head. There was that incident with the pan of boiling mussels and Gabe had witnessed still worse. These days, though, forget it. You had to mollycoddle them all.

Victor was at his station, filling and rolling trout paupiettes. His white coat was half unbuttoned, his right leg vibrated and his mouth puckered busily, as if limbering up for a quick knee-trembler against the wall.

'Take it off,' said Benny, pointing to his ears, but Victor was lost in the groove.

'Seafood frittata for the lunch special,' said Gabe, continuing his tour of the fridges. 'What else do we need to push?'

'Rabbit stew,' said Benny. 'Two portions. Three quail.'

Victor scraped out the last of the salmon mousseline, picked up the bowl and headed towards the sinks.

'Watch out,' said Gabriel as Victor tried to pass him. He stuck out his foot. The entire brigade was in today, on split shifts, in preparation for the Sirovsky launch. The catcalls went up as Victor went down, hitting the roof as he hit the floor. Gabe walked round to help Victor to his feet, and unfortunately trod on his hand. 'You see why it's dangerous to use iPods in the kitchen? Didn't hear me when I said to watch out.'

Victor acknowledged the cheers with a grin but when he looked at Gabe there was a new wariness written on his cocky little face. 'Sorry, Chef,' he said.

'Apology accepted. Now get your buttons done up.'

They had to dance on their toes today and that was the truth. He wasn't taking a bullet for anyone. The kitchen was on red alert, every last piece of artillery pressed into action, the munitions piling up all around. Sauces and stocks cooled on the windowsill, the fridge-tops, the floor; trays of rissoles, samosas, black bean cakes formed barricades; every flat surface was now in the front line, including the bin lids which formed staging posts between the commis and their chefs de partie.

He had all his best men on the party menu, including Nikolai and Suleiman. Gabriel watched Nikolai adding fines herbes to his spätzle mix, working the dough with his surgical white hand. Really, he thought, taking a moment, there was no better place to be.

Yesterday evening had passed in a dream, less real than the one in his sleep. It amused him now to think of it, the way the fever had messed with his perceptions, the way the cheap TV melodrama scripted his thoughts. Hadn't he been imagining Lena explaining 'the whole darn mess'?

In the morning he'd left Lena on the sofa watching television. Everything had snapped back together, the fever gone.

'It'll be late when I get back,' he said. 'There's stuff in the freezer. Use the microwave, you won't starve.' Looking out of the window, he regarded the carnival of traffic, three red buses, slow as floats. London, love it, was crazy. He could lock her up here for a month and no one would know.

Lena chewed what was left of her nails. 'You don't forget,' she said, meaning the money.

★

'Excuse me, Chef, could you taste for me?' Suleiman held up a slotted spoon with a dim sum. 'I steamed a test batch. Is it right?'

The embryonic pink of the pork mince seemed to pulse through the translucent skin. In his mouth, the soft explosion gave way to hot salty soy and a ginger tang. 'Yes,' said Gabe, 'it's good.'

Suleiman nodded anxiously. He had a way of peering, as though over the top of an invisible pair of spectacles, searching for the missing detail. 'The gorgonzola custards – did you try?'

'I'll do it now.' The flavour palette was not enough to describe it. He dug another spoonful from Suleiman's little ramekin. It wasn't baked cheese; it was peat, moss and pinecones, a roaring hearth on a frost-cracked day. 'Awful,' said Gabe. 'Terrible.' He laughed.

'I surmise that you are joking,' said Suleiman, gearing up his most industrious smile.

'You'll go far,' said Gabriel. At least as far as the new restaurant. He'd definitely take Suleiman with him, maybe a few of the others as well.

Continuing his troop inspection, he came to Damian, dicing carrots for mirepoix. The boy chewed his tongue as usual; he'd choke on it one of these days. There was something scurfy about him, though he kept his chef's whites clean enough. Ten to one he was a bedwetter. He needed to toughen up.

'What do you call these carrots?'

'Who?' said Damian. 'Me?'

'Yes, you, what do you call them?'

Damian put his knife down. 'Carrots, Chef, just call them carrots.' He jerked as if Gabe had hoisted him on a gibbet, which, in a sense, he had.

'Carrots, Chef.' Gabe let him writhe a short while. 'Fine dice, standard or large cut? What are these?'

'Standard?' said Damian, beginning to puff.

The boy was useless, even at breathing. 'They're not standard,' said Gabe, slowly. He wrapped an arm round Damian's shoulders. 'I'll tell you what they are. They're shit is what they are. Get the bin, throw them away and start again.'

★

'Was I too hard on him?' he said to Benny, on the way back to his desk.

'To be honest with you,' said Benny, 'no.' Benny was a natural-born peacekeeper. They could probably use him in Rwanda, or wherever the hell he was from. 'In my country we have a saying: the empty sack doesn't stand up.' He wiped his board and replenished his towel stack. 'I never saw you give harsh words with no reason. You're fair. If you're asking me, I'll say that you stand up.'

Gabe made a detour through the pastry kitchen. The light, operating-room bright, made the space look like some sort of clinic. He could almost hear the sigh of rising dough, neatly tucked beneath hospital-white cloths. Chef Albert moved a toothpick through pink icing with laser precision and speed. He was working his way across a tray of biscuits, writing 'Sirovsky' on them all.

'Look,' he said, pausing a moment and holding up his hand. 'No – how do you call? – tremor. Absolutely none.' He patted his breast pocket and Gabe heard the rattling of pills. 'Beta blockers. What miracle! *Magnifique*. I have stress, I am stressed, my muppet – he muppets around – but all the time I remain calm, absolutely calm.'

'These are terrific,' said Gabe. He wanted to get away from the yeast smell, and Chef Albert's shiny, sugar-glazed face.

'Yes,' said Chef Albert. 'Beautiful. But you know what will happen to my little work of art? It goes into the mouth and – a few hours later – it comes out of the arse.'

'Such is life,' said Gabriel. 'If you need me I'll be at my desk.' He almost ran back to his office and found a fresh pile of paperwork on his in-tray, peppered with Post-it notes from Human Resources.

'It *all* witchcraft and wizardry,' said Oona, blowing into the cubicle and cackling over his shoulder. 'It all about the codes.'

'I thought F17 *was* the sick-pay code,' said Gabe. 'God, it's the second time I've filled in these forms.'

'Want me to do it for you, darlin'?' said Oona, squeezing into a seat.

It was why he had kept her on in the first place, he supposed; why the chefs before him had too. Oona's knowledge of the Imperial's by-laws and footnotes was encyclopedic. He used her to fend off red tape.

'A ting I need to arks you, sweetheart . . . it OK with you I take tomorrow afternoon off? I can swap a half-day holiday with Benny, he suppose be home tomorrow but he can come. Oh, no, not Benny, I mean it was Suleiman and then he gonna trade half a day with . . . wait . . . now I'm getting muddled but it work itself out in the end.'

'No,' said Gabe. He handed her the sheaf of paperwork.

'I wouldn't arks but . . .' said Oona, one hand sinking into her breast.

'No.'

Oona's eyes twinkled, because she knew he was pulling her leg.

'I'm serious,' said Gabriel. 'The holiday rota is fixed. It doesn't *work itself out*. I work it out and that's that.'

'Ho,' said Oona, sagging. 'Well.' She slipped off her shoes and rubbed her feet together like a praying mantis. 'What about Mr Maddox's little meeting, in the Roosevelt? Want me to rustle up some nice tasty plates?'

Shit. He'd forgotten all about it. He'd have to divert Suleiman for a couple of hours. 'Thanks for reminding me. Consider your part of the job done.'

'*Harn't* you lovely?' cried Oona, leaning forward and, for one alarming moment, seeming to prepare for a hug. 'I'll whip up some nibbles quick enough.'

'Oona,' he said, 'no offence, but that's not a risk I'm prepared to take.'

Ernie nearly ran him over with a fork-lift piled to invisibility level with cartons of milk and cream.

'Driving blind today?'

Ernie parked the trolley. He scratched his head. 'There's no motor on it. Ah'm just pushing it along, you know.' For a poet he could be somewhat literal-minded.

'How's the world of goods-in?'

Ernie thought. 'Not bad. Not bad at all. The goods come in and Ah put 'em away. That's how it works, you know. Ah cannae complain.'

'I see.'

'Chef,' said Ernie, sliding a plastic folder out from between cartons of organic full-fat. 'Chef, would you be interested in buying a valentine poem? It's a new business. Three pound for two verses, six pound for four.' He extended and retracted his scrawny neck.

'Valentines? It's only November, Ernie.'

Ernie blinked proudly. 'Aye. Ah'm ahead o' the game.'

Ernie's trousers were too short for him. His socks showed and the elastics were gone. His haircut was an institutional scalp job and there was something defective about the way the Adam's apple bobbed in his throat. Gabe flicked quickly through Ernie's folder, time running through his hands. In this job, sometimes, you had to play social worker, whether you liked it or not.

'This one you'll like,' said Ernie. 'See what Ah've done? That's what you call an acrostic – see – it spells VALENTINE down the side of the page. Ah reckon to sell ten a day, say for the next month, and Ah'll be adding more, you know. Mothers' Day, Fathers' Day . . . You've got a Day in every month, at least.'

'Good plan, Ernie,' said Gabriel. 'I'm afraid I've got to run.'

The phone was ringing in his cubicle. Gabe snatched it up.

He was just hanging up again as Mr Maddox filled the doorframe. 'Good news,' said Gabe. 'That was the inspector.'

Mr Maddox was still blocking the door, so that his deputy was forced to stand meekly behind.

'We can just about squeeze the three of us in here,' said Gabe, offering his own chair.

Mr Maddox took up his offer and Mr James scurried in. 'Ah, there you are, Gareth,' said Maddox. 'Thought I'd given you the slip. Keeps following me around like a doggie. Can't imagine why.' He gave his humourless laugh.

The general manager, Gabe decided, liked to pretend to be a bully, to disguise the fact that he really was.

'Actually,' said Gabe, 'Parks said he was wrapping things up.'

'Actually,' said Mr Maddox, 'I know. He called me first.'

There was a silence, which Gabe resisted the urge to fill.

'Gareth,' said Mr Maddox, 'our executive chef is wondering why we're here. Does either of us know? Do you have it written on your clipboard, or is that your shopping list on there?'

Mr James fingered his tie anxiously. 'Meetings at the Imperial are generally insufficiently minuted. We've agreed to tighten up.' If it weren't for his officiousness, Gabriel would have felt sorry for him. 'The directors' meeting lunch—' he continued, before his boss cut him off.

'Taken care of?' said Mr Maddox. 'I'm assuming yes.'

'Yes,' said Gabriel. 'Yes.'

'Not just a pretty face, is he? Now, I'll tell you what.' He picked a stapler from the desk and punched a few staples on to the floor. 'This business with the porter, it's been cleared up – all well and good. Pretty much a formality now, is what I understand. Which is good, because if it had played any different – do I even need to tell you?' He tossed the stapler aside. He pulled out the top drawer and closed it, pulled out the bottom one and kicked it shut. 'Don't mind me, I'm just thinking.' He smoothed an eyebrow. 'What I'm thinking is this. You've been here – what? – five, six months now, Chef, long enough, I'd say, to start noticing anything that smells wrong. If there was no funny business with that porter, then marvellous, pleased as fucking punch, me and Gareth, you can tell he's pleased by the way he's clenching his buttocks, that's a sign of happiness.'

Mr James was, indeed, smiling. Though he had made no marks on his pad, Gabe imagined he was taking mental note of the torsion technique Maddox applied to his staff, twisting in two directions, to get the best out of them. It was a technique that was bound to come in useful when Gareth became a GM himself.

'But there's only two things certain in hotel life,' Mr Maddox continued. 'Number one: to make your margins you screw every last drop of blood from your workers. Number two: they screw you right back.' He paused and locked his missile gaze on Gabriel. 'So we know there's something going on, always is. What I need from you, Chef, is the who, when and how. You with me? Good, well, you know what they say.' He rose. The meeting was over. 'Gareth,' he roared. 'For fuck's sake, don't tell me you're taking a minute. Jesus wept!'

★

The who, when and how, thought Gabriel. I could give him the who. Maddox wanted dirt. If you're not with us, you're against us; that was what he said, or didn't say.

He was more than half an hour late for his regular sit-down with Stanley Gleeson.

'Nice of you to come,' said Gleeson. 'Better get straight to business – shall we run through the specials, or shall we talk about tonight first?' Gleeson's new frostiness at least served as a reminder – if reminder were needed – that Stanley was not a man to trust. Gabriel ran through the specials, and in his mind ran over the scams which were stocked like basic ingredients in any London hotel. Gleeson would have something going with Pierre, the bar manager, topping up vodka bottles with water, pouring singles instead of doubles and splitting the dividend. Pierre, who clearly took his own medicine, dealt marching powder to his regulars and Gleeson would take a cut. Sometimes he 'rushed' a handwritten dinner order to the kitchen, which doubtless bypassed the till and ended up in his pocket. There'd be kickbacks from the alcohol suppliers, of which Pierre and Gleeson retained charge. And if Gleeson didn't 'comp' his friends in the restaurant then Gabe didn't know his elbow from his arse.

'Ah,' sighed Gleeson, as the waitress cleared the coffee cups, 'if it weren't for the sexual harassment laws this place would be heaven on earth.'

In other words, nothing. There was nothing going on, as far as Gabriel knew. No more than Maddox would guess as a matter of course. Yet Gleeson had whined like a lobster on the grill over Yuri. There had to be something else.

It could be anything, any number of reasons why Gleeson didn't want the police around, not necessarily connected to the porter, but something he didn't want them stumbling on, something more than a pilfered bottle of vodka or brandy, which Gleeson would be only too happy to brazen out. Gabriel tried to imagine, tried to make up a story with Gleeson at its dark heart, but he couldn't make anything stick. Anyway, it was futile, there were things that went on that you could never imagine; he'd never have believed that mess at the Dartington, unless he'd been there and seen it with his own eyes when the police and the environmental health scooped up the Ghanaian sous-chef. They'd traced the bush meat from Hackney market back to the Knightsbridge hotel, and Gabriel had stood behind them when they broke the lock on the spare chest freezer, peering in at the gorilla steaks, smokies and grasscutter rats.

'I'll let you skidaddle,' said Gleeson. 'I can see your mind is racing to pastures fresh.'

'You know what it's like,' said Gabe, in spite of himself slipping into a faux-Gleeson drawl. Gleeson was a fake and a phoney. He affected an upper-class manner, like a butler who believed himself part of the world which was his only to serve.

For lunch service Gabriel folded Nikolai back into the crew, dunking fresh pasta and working the skillets of frittata for those docile enough to take the special, the same punters who ate all the breadsticks and asked for water out of the tap.

'Yuri loved my omelettes,' said Nikolai. He ceased his labour for a moment, letting the egg whisk rest in the bowl.

Gabe picked up the whisk and watched the viscous slide of yolk.

'Very simple,' said Nikolai, 'tomato, parsley, salt and pepper, and of course the eggs.'

Gabe stirred briefly and stopped.

'Really, it was his favourite,' said Nikolai, modestly, patiently, as if he would hate to influence anyone's opinion but was honour-bound to state the facts.

Gabe wondered if Nikolai had gone down to the catacombs and cooked on the gas burner, had raided the kitchen stores, or brought the food from home. Not that it mattered anyway, not that he wanted to think about it at all.

'A little caviar and sour cream to go with it, that's what we needed, but Yuri was too much of a gentleman to say a word about that.'

Gabriel started beating. The whisk against the metal bowl sounded good. It occurred to him that Benny too had known about Yuri's bunk hole, had been paying a quick visit when he'd found him on the floor.

Nikolai didn't say much in the kitchen. He had the ability to keep his mouth closed, a quality which Gabriel liked, though now that he came to think of it, sometimes it made him uneasy, as if Nikolai were watching and judging and waiting for the opportunity to report back.

Report back on what, to whom? Gabe beat the eggs harder, too hard, getting too much air. He'd just got rid of the Yuri problem, he didn't want to be thinking about him now.

'His daughters,' said Nikolai, 'they were—'

Gabriel forced himself to stop beating. He wiped his hands. He folded his arms across his chest and waited for Nikolai to go on.

Nikolai shook his head.

Come on then, thought Gabe, come on. There was something odd about Nikolai, the way he refused to move up from a lowly grade. The man was clearly intelligent. He was like some overgrown student, no, some underground revolutionary leader, watching and waiting, biding his time.

'His daughters,' said Gabriel. 'What?' He issued it like a challenge, because he'd had enough of Nikolai.

'Nothing, Chef.'

Gabriel smiled at Nikolai, to show there was nothing difficult between them, and then went back to the pass, dismissing Oona with another smile.

Lunch was brisk but not catastrophic, they easily held their own. Tonight – let's face it – might be a bloodbath, but they weren't on the run just yet. In a lull he leaned with his hands behind him pressed to the hot shelf, secretly revelling in their toughness. Breathing a little deeper, he was forged afresh, benign. He knew it would not last. He was like a general on a brief tour of the front line who, receiving a valiant and superficial wound, feels at one with his men. Still, he looked at his kitchen and brimmed with something that he wouldn't say was love. It wasn't love but it was something, when he took in his brigade, a United Nations task force all bent to their work.

Every corner of the earth was represented here. Hispanic, Asian, African, Baltic and most places in between. Oona had taken on a new dishwasher, from Somalia or somewhere pretty much like that. The other one was Mongolian and the third was from – where? – the Philippines? Gabe had worked in places where porters came as a job lot, the first getting along a cousin who recommended a brother-in-law who also brought his friend. Before you knew it there was a gang of them, and that only spelled trouble ahead. The room-service guy was fresh from Chile and Gabriel doubted that his English extended beyond *fries* and *burgers* and whatever else was on the menu. He'd fitted in all right. It was touching, really, to watch them all, every race, every colour, every creed.

In Blantwistle there were only the Asians, or the Pakis as they were called then, maybe still were. They did only the night shifts at the mill, were just coming out as the morning shift went in. That was the way it was at first. Gabriel remembered the journey on the number 72, going down from the heights of Plodder Lane to the market square and across the coccyx of the narrow streets that lay like old men's backbones, decaying, grinding down. Michael Harrison's family lived there, 'marooned', said his father, among the Asians, and when the bus pulled in at the bus stop the conductor shouted 'Khyber Pass' and rang the bell. People said things about the Asians. They never scrubbed their doorsteps, the children pissed on the flagstones, they made curry with Pal dog meat. Gabriel played a game with Michael, walking behind them making monkey noises, he didn't know any better then.

When the kitchen had dispersed for the afternoon break – to the betting shop, the pub, or any warm quiet cubby hole for a sleep – Gabriel went down to the catacombs to fetch the money for Lena. He passed the dry-goods store and the old fish room, turned to the right and passed the rubbish chutes and breathed through his mouth to combat the smell. He had a girlfriend once who was a mouthbreather. That was nearly all he remembered about her, blocked sinuses and musty breath, and the mouthbreathing which he couldn't tolerate in the end.

After her there'd been Catherine. He'd given it a good try, moved into her Putney cottage, with all the retro floral prints and lime-washed pine. What had happened? They wanted so much from each other that every day was like being eaten alive. His parents, their generation, their friends, he'd seen them, they never expected that: to drink lifeblood from a spouse. It was enough to rub along after the honeymoon period, to knit together slowly like a broken bone, and to do it over the chores and children or in the allotment pulling weeds. And if they found that they hated each other, well, that was something they had in common, stuck in a life they did not want.

With Catherine, they'd suffocated each other, too many needs, too imprecisely defined. Charlie was different, anyway, independent, light on her feet. It was a bonus of marrying late when they both knew their own minds.

Of course he was going to marry her. He'd known it for a long time, without putting it into words.

He'd taken a wrong turning. He would have to double back. The corridor here was so narrow his wrists scraped on the walls. A more fertile imagination would place skeletons behind these rusty-bolted doors.

On an early date with Charlie she took him to meet a potential manager, an unexceptional man in coach-driver slacks and sleeveless jumper who spoke quietly and respectfully and stood all their rounds in the bar.

'What did you make of him?' said Charlie. She was undressing in that languorous stripper's way of hers.

'Not much,' said Gabe.

'Not much?'

'It's up to you,' said Gabriel. 'But if you ask me, I think he's slime.' He had no reason to think so. In fact, he didn't really think it at all. But at that moment he was looking at her with such unspeakable and piercing desire that he had no option but to banish him instantly, this unknown other man.

It turned out the guy was a sleazeball, he'd ripped off a friend of a friend. 'You're acute,' said Charlie. 'I've got to say I thought he was totally straight.'

'Not as cute as you,' said Gabe, losing his hand in her hair.

She still said he was a good judge of character. You *see* people. Well, there'd been nothing to prove her wrong. He'd go along with that. And she liked that he held back a little, wasn't a prattler like her previous boyfriend, on and on, she said. When they lived together she'd probably grow to hate it, this thing about him that she loved. Why do you never talk to me? And he'd tease her and she'd toss her head but she would laugh, and they would be fine together, the two of them – the three of them – they would be just fine.

He came to the old facilities office. The light was still on, the naked bulb dangling like a suicide, casting fear and gloom. Gabriel went to the back wall and knelt. He counted, four from the right and seven up. The brick was loose. Prising it away he caught his fingernail and sucked on his finger until the throbbing died. Gingerly, he poked at the cavity.

Nothing there. Maybe he had got it back to front. Seven from the right and four up from the ground. He scratched at the mortar, using his other hand. Perhaps she said left, not right. He checked the positions and then stood up and watched the purple bruise spreading under his nail.

Who could have taken the money? Presuming there was any. Why should he believe a word that she said? Perhaps Yuri himself had stolen it, she rushed to confront him, pushed him, felled him, manslaughter they called that. What if there was someone else, someone else who came down here? And was Lena having sex with Yuri? It was none of his business. She might have offered it, like she offered it to him. Sex for a bed for the night, was that it? Well, it was her body, she could do with it what she liked.

He grabbed leftovers from a bread basket and ate two energy bars he found in his desk drawer. He wasn't really hungry, felt like he'd been grazing on this and that all day. When the new place opened he'd institute a 'family meal', the floor staff and kitchen staff sitting down for something decent and home-made, not the slops and defrosted burgers they dished up on a pound-per-head budget here in the staff canteen. They'd have chicken stew, or meatballs; Charlie would be there, he could see her, checking her make-up in a compact mirror, wanting to look good for the front-of-house. She had a kid on her lap; that was him, their son, their first. Gabe would take him into the kitchen, he'd have to be a little older, how old would he have to be and what would he tell him, what would the first lesson be?

He'd been no more than eight or nine when Dad first took him to

102

Rileys, in through the wrought-iron gates, across the smooth-rubbed flagstones in the yard, past the twist and cloth warehouses, pointing out the pale stone quoins and copings over the dull red of the brick, taking a detour to the engine house to see the original coal-fired boiler inscribed with Yates & Thom, ushering – no, pushing – him into one of the weaving sheds, a firm hand pressed to his back to steady him against the unholy din.

Gabriel had looked up with fear and reverence at the cast-iron columns, the rolled steel beams, which seemed to him more beautiful than the pillars of any church. Dad squeezed his shoulder and steered him between the thundering machines into the tacklers' room.

'Happen you'll get used to it. First day in the mill, you come out, you can't hear a thing. After a bit you don't even notice – unless there's a machine what's making a worrying sound.'

Mr Howarth was there, reading the racing pages. 'I fancy a flutter today.'

One of the weavers came in, picking lint out of her hair. 'Tom,' she said, 'there's a mash on number nine. Some silly so-and-so's gone and left her scissors in the back.'

Gabriel did an impression of her later, stretching his mouth to the corners of his face. Mum doubled over with laughter, she was in one of those times. Had you not noticed before, she said, my little poppet, that's what all those women do. If you want to carry on gossiping while you're standing across on different looms, there's only one way it's possible, you've got to read each other's lips.

'Rita, Rita, Rita,' said Mr Howarth, looking her up and down. 'What silly so-and-so would that be? It wouldn't be you, my love?'

'It wouldn't,' said Rita, primping her curls. 'Anyhow, it wants tackling. I've wrote it on the board.'

They watched her go and Dad said, 'Gabe, did I ever tell you, back in the old days, a weaver would kiss her shuttle in the morning. Kiss it for good luck. That's an old Lancashire tradition, something what was traditionally done.'

Mr Howarth sighed and made a show of rattling his paper. 'Ay,' he said, 'that Rita, she can kiss my shuttle any time.'

★

The first lesson was yarn. Ted left Gabe on the bench for a bit, picking his scabs and kicking his heels. When he came back from his rounds he had a bobbin in his hand.

'Now this – is what we call a pirn. Can you tell me what's on the pirn?'

'Thread, Dad.'

'You'd call it thread if it was in your mum's sewing basket. Here we say—'

Gabe shot his hand up and yelled out at the same time. 'Cotton!'

Ted laughed. 'We call it yarn. Can you say that, Gabe – yarn.' He had a fresh oil-spot on the leg of his boilersuit, screwdrivers in his top pocket, an infinite manliness to the steely cut of his nose that made Gabe faintly ashamed of the way that he had said 'thread'.

'To produce the yarn, there's a process, to get it from cotton balls to this. First you've got to untangle it, that's called carding. You straighten the fibres down into long strings and you've got roving, that's right, roving, and that's about an inch or so thick, light and fluffy and you couldn't be weaving, not even for string vests, with that. So then it's got to be spun. I'll take you to a spinning mill one day, so you can see for yerself, but it's basically drawing and twisting it and turning it into the yarn.'

Gabriel looked at Ted's hands, which kept moving, as if moulding his words into shape. They were scarred along the knuckles, hairy, and missing the left little fingertip. It was brilliant, this, thought Gabe, wagging a day off school.

Ted pulled some yarn off the bobbin, the pirn, and gave it to Gabriel who pretended to study it hard. 'The sizing's a kind of coating that goes on next . . .'

Gabe became aware of his mouth hanging open; it happened sometimes when he tried to concentrate. He felt the saliva pooling, smelt the changing-room smells of the bench, watched the dust motes spiral in a shaft of sunlight like a fairyland tornado, shifted his weight a little closer to Dad.

'I'm trying to give you the big picture here. You're not too young, are you – no – good lad. You're wanting to get on to the weaving, but there's a lot of stuff comes before. Now, look at you. Put them tonsils away.' He put his thumb briefly to Gabe's chin. 'Blimmin 'eck, that reminds me – is that the time – your mother'll be stood at the gates b' now, calling for my head.'

'Dad,' said Gabe, 'can you tell me that bit again?'

'What bit?'

Gabriel shrugged. 'Well, sort of . . . like . . . all of it, I suppose.'

'Aye,' said Ted. 'There's a lot to teck in.' He stood up and stretched his arms. His arms were that long, thought Gabe, he could reach right to the tops of the looms.

'Look sharp,' said Ted, 'you've a dentist appointment. That's why your mum said you could stop off school.'

He hadn't thought of it in a long time. It wasn't like remembering another time and place, but another world. Can you tell me again, Dad? He needn't have worried. Dad kept dragging him along there until he hated the sight of the mill.

Gabriel logged on to email, it was the first chance he'd had. Thirty-six since last night, mostly junk. He opened the one from Gareth James because it was marked with a red flag. There was going to be a meeting for 'team leaders' about 'human capital' and 'leading from the middle'. Gabe had been to that kind of meeting plenty of times before, and his aim – like everyone else's – was to get out of there having agreed to nothing, while seeming to be 'on board' and 'part of the team'.

He looked up and checked the kitchen floor. Victor was over with Ivan, the two of them with their arms folded, facing each other, as if they both had something they were unwilling to say. Ivan adjusted his bandanna, put his hand to his crotch and shifted his balls as though they were lead weights. Despite his cauliflower ear and powerful build, you didn't look at Ivan and think boxer, rugby player. Somehow there was nothing sporting about him, but his physical presence would be ideal in a prison, either as a con or a screw, and maybe it was the way he held himself that made him seem built for the giving or taking of grief. He was a worker, though, Ivan, a proper Trojan, no messing. Gabriel had seen him sustain – it made him wince to think of it – a severe burn on the arm, the kind that writes a sick note for a week.

Three hours later he was back from Accident & Emergency, working one-handed at the grill.

Gabe filleted out the emails that he'd need to attend to and dragged the others into the bin. If a kitchen were as wasteful as emails, he'd be permanently surrounded by stinking mounds of crud.

Victor and Ivan were talking now, Victor circling, moving nervously, a yipping terrier to Ivan's unmoving pug. Victor was a troublemaker, Gabriel could see clearly the way he was trying to wind Ivan up.

Let them sort it out. There had to be a pecking order, cooks like wild dogs raised their hackles now and then, testing out their position in the pack. Gabe looked back at the screen.

Now they were yelling at each other and could probably be heard in the penthouse. He was going to have to break it up. He kicked back his chair, left his cubicle and rounded the corner in time to see Ivan pick up the bottle. For one long, hovering moment it looked as if he would smash it into Victor's face. Instead he flung the contents on the stove-top behind Victor's back, sending a wall of flame, red, gold and blue, to the ceiling with a force that sucked the oxygen from the room and sent Victor leaping with a scream.

CHAPTER SEVEN

—◆—

SHE WAS SIX FOOT TWO IN HER HEELS AND APPEARED TO BE SPRAY-painted in gold. Several versions of her circulated around the ballroom like some complicated mirror trick, balancing trays of Chef Albert's beloved confectionery on upturned palms. The models had been provided by the Sirovsky PR people and seemingly selected for the load-bearing strength of their earlobes, on which a tonne of Sirovsky silver crystal swung, and for the length of their femurs, guaranteed to excite any palaeontologist if suddenly exhumed on a dig.

Gabriel declined a miniature meringue and reappraised the spray paint as catsuit as he watched the sway of her back and traced the line of the zip. The ballroom, 'dressed' for the occasion, was a scandal of fur throws, floor-standing candelabras and a ceiling of billowing silk. In the alcoves, little crystal deities lolled on dark velvet beds. These, Gabe had been informed, were the launch products, 16cm sculptures of reindeer, puppies, lions, a bird at a bath, priced at 'upwards of two thousand pounds'. At the centre of the room was a life-size Sirovsky cherry tree complete with glass blossom and a carpet of turf. And from behind a bowling-lane-sized perspex table, lit from within, agency waiters served flavoured vodka shots while front and centre an ice swan glowed magnificently and began, at this late hour, to drip.

He'd catered for three hundred and it looked like they'd all turned up. Gabriel assessed the crowd. Among the women there was a predominance of jutting hip bones and big, expensive hair. The younger ones worked a pout or smile and looked pleased with their handbag brand, while the more mature generation had no doubt discovered tennis, joined a book group and raised funds for a cause, which gave them plenty to talk about without needing to pause for thought. The men, to Gabe's eye, were no more varied than the women. There was a sprinkling of pretty young things, at whom it was impossible to look without the vague accompanying sensation that you might have seen them somewhere before, who were or had been celebrities or who were confidently waiting for their birthright of fifteen minutes of fame. The older men, greying, balding, spreading, were glossed by success and the confidence with which they took up more space than was strictly necessary. As an ensemble the guests had one uniting feature, discerned by Gabe in the way that gazes slid over shoulders, feet pointed and tapped, a general air of mobility that made him think of quivering antennae, tuning in and tuning out.

He exchanged a glance with a woman who wore a diamond the size of an artichoke and her hair in a French pleat. He looked around. Champagne, inevitably, came his way and he drank it down. The woman still looked when he looked and he touched the tiny bald patch at the back of his head.

This place wasn't so bad. For an instant he thought about staying on at the Imperial, blowing Rolly and Fairweather out, but he knew that it was madness to allow a momentary gratification to deflect him from his path. In truth, he liked this party, liked this vibe. He could look at it and not be fooled by it, but he liked the flow and buzz. Sometimes he had to get out of the kitchen to appreciate what it was that he did.

He lifted another glass and made a silent toast of welcome to one and all, because he needed this sometimes, to be some small part of this and get out of the cauldron below. Victor and Ivan had said nothing about the blow-up, sticking to some Slavic criminal code.

'Nothing dangerous, Chef,' said Ivan. 'All big show.'

'All show, man,' said Victor. 'Yeah, all show is right.'

Victor, Gabriel suspected, had been cut out of some deal and was hustling for his share. Ivan and Gleeson, was that it? Doing what, though? What?

Victor had squawked like a hen but he was still strutting, nothing injured apart from his pride.

'Seen what the buggers are charging for those glorified paperweights?' said Mr Maddox, over his shoulder. The GM had sent for Gabe to come up.

'Community outreach programme,' said Gabriel, turning, 'providing relief to those unfortunates burdened with excess cash.'

Mr Maddox snorted. He held up a hand to block a waiter who made the mistake of trying to slip through between Maddox and Gabe. 'See that girl – there – the one stroking the swan. Look at the tart factor on that. Is she a hooker or a filthy rich Russian? Even I can't tell them apart.'

'I've no experience of either,' said Gabe.

'Is that right, my friend? Is that right? Then you've clearly no hotel experience. I should fire you on the spot.' Maddox gave his malfunctioning laugh. 'Never too busy to enjoy a joke. Now, I wanted to get you up here before this lot buggers off. We want this crowd, Chef, we want to please them, we want them to come back and bring their friends. What did they think of the food, eh? Asked them? No, me neither, didn't need to, because know what they did, they ate it, there's more food gone in their bellies than the bin and that's what you call a minor miracle, some of these girls wetting themselves over the calories, be a few fingers down throats tonight.'

Mr Maddox, being as affectionate as his nature allowed, punched Gabe on the arm as he departed. Gabriel imagined him with Mrs Maddox, lovingly exchanging blows.

Left alone once more, Gabe insinuated himself deeper into the room, gathering fragments of conversation, bright useless things, which were all that he needed right now. When he saw Rolly and Fairweather for a moment he wished he could disappear, but Fairweather smiled at him with such boundless enthusiasm that Gabriel said good to see you and found that he meant it; they were partners and surely friends.

'My wife collects this stuff,' said Fairweather, pushing his fringe out of his eyes. 'We're not checking up on you.'

'I am,' said Rolly, 'speak for yourself. There's a function room at the Pimlico site, we need to make it pay.' He was wearing a suit tonight, of a rather violent blue. His tie, which bore a daisy motif, had been loosened, the knot pulled down to the point on his chest from which his belly swelled.

'Fabulous,' said Fairweather, making an inclusive gesture. 'Wonderful. And the wives are over there, getting to know each other. They'll get along famously. Lucinda gets along with anyone, all part of the job, like being a vicar's wife.'

'Tell you what Geraldine's good at – spending,' said Rolly. 'Used to be amateur, when I met her, now she's turned into a pro. *I have to have it.* What does that mean? I say to her, Geraldine, if you can't buy it are you going to go up in a puff of smoke?'

'Women.' Fairweather ruffled the top of his head, petting himself to mark his own incorrigibility which nobody, least of all Fairweather, could resist.

'I sent the revised business plan,' said Gabriel. 'Think it's looking good.'

Rolly blinked rapidly. 'It's getting serious. Getting down to the serious stuff.'

'What pretty girls,' said Fairweather, accepting a crystallized fruit from a golden Sirovsky specimen. 'Where in the world do you get them from?'

'Keep them in my desk drawer,' said Gabriel, 'one or two in my locker as spares.'

'What do you say?' began Fairweather. 'Let's take a little boys' trip, just a couple of days. We could go to France, look at some hand–built ovens I've been told about, do a bit of the old male bonding as well.'

'Hand-built ovens?' said Rolly.

'Weren't you just saying, Gabriel, that you could do with a bit of a rest, a bit of a boost?'

Gabriel found himself nodding, though he was sure he hadn't said anything of the kind. But it was true enough, he supposed, and sensitive of Fairweather to pick it up.

'Mancini's called in the receivers,' said Rolly. 'The fish place in

Tooley Street is about to close. Chez Nous won't be far behind from what I hear.'

'Dreadful,' said Fairweather, 'the poor things.'

'Right. It breaks my heart. But restaurants are a cruel, hard world. And when I've finished crying for them I'll be over there, to see what bargains I can pick up.'

'Oh, he's the greatest, isn't he,' said Fairweather, 'he's the best. Ding-a-ding. Round two.'

'Anyway,' said Rolly. He wiped a little sweat from his brow with his tie. He looked, Gabriel thought, like a children's entertainer, down on his luck after a false accusation. Was he trying to be flamboyant? Was it Geraldine who dressed him like that? 'Anyway, you know something, if Gabriel's depressed then it's a cross he has to bear. It's the 5-HTT gene, read it in the papers today.'

'I'm not depressed,' said Gabe.

'Aha,' said Fairweather, 'we always have this conversation. We could say it's a *predisposition*, rather than, you know, written in the stars, as it were.'

'It's not in his horoscope,' said Rolly. 'I don't believe in that.'

'Of course not. I think you're absolutely right.' Fairweather beamed. He had a remarkable ability to agree and disagree at the same time. 'And we all take responsibility, don't we, for looking after ourselves. Quick tune-up needed sometimes. Nothing wrong with that.'

'What you want is the short gene, the short version, transports serotonin. Hang on, no, that's what you don't want. You want the long 5-HTT.'

'I'm actually not depressed.'

'Well, I need my beauty sleep. Giving a speech in the House tomorrow. Shall we rendezvous next week?'

A woman touched Fairweather's forearm. 'Excuse me – hope you don't mind me asking, but – are you somebody?' she said.

Gabriel thought about it as he stepped on to a Juliet balcony to get a breath of air. The guests were dispersing now, collecting goodie bags and brushing cheeks to signify a kiss. Are you somebody? Fairweather had managed to blush and bumble about being a mere *junior* minister of state. He was delighted, of course. He was somebody. What was the alternative? A nobody. If you were more than your own self you were somebody, and if you weren't 'somebody' perhaps being yourself amounted to nothing at all.

'Hello, Romeo, isn't this where I'm supposed to be?' She was a little older than he'd realized, a few grey hairs in that slick French pleat. Good-looking, though, handsome, with a broad, compelling mouth.

'Why's that?'

'Oh, you know, the girl stands on the balcony and looks down . . .'

'And I clamber up with a rose between my teeth.'

She laughed. 'Listen, shall we cut to the chase?'

'Do you want me to chase you?'

'You are funny. That's exactly what you don't have to do.'

'If I were a free man,' said Gabe.

She shivered. She waited a moment, considering perhaps her exit or giving him time to change his mind. 'Well, Romeo, we're only as free as we want to be. It's your funeral. You enjoy it,' she said. 'Goodnight.'

Gabe looked down at the street and then looked up at the sky. It was his funeral, was it? Charming. If a man said that! He shook his head and laughed.

He was hardly burying himself with Charlie. They'd had that trip to Marrakech, a present that he'd organized, a little surprise. Maybe they needed something else like that, something spontaneous. He'd have to plan it in.

It was well past midnight and Gabe was at his desk. When he went home Lena would be there. Or maybe she had gone. It didn't matter either way. But she'd be there, of course she would, waiting for the money that he didn't find. Then what? He'd had it all worked out. It wasn't complicated, it was simple, he would just . . .

Damn it, he wasn't wasting any more time on this.

Benny was the last in the kitchen. Gabe went out to see what he was doing.

'One gallon of court bouillon,' said Benny, lifting a lid. 'Two litres of demi-glace, nearly done.'

'Good man,' said Gabe. He watched as Benny skimmed the

demi–glace. 'We've got to get twenty-four-hour room service started,' he said. 'It's to do with star ratings, now they've finished the refurb. We need to cover between midnight and six.'

'Yes, Chef,' said Benny. 'It's a long time to go without food.'

Benny stirred the bouillon. The scar across his cheek was faintly silvery. It was a big ugly scar but it didn't make him look ugly. In an odd way it suited him, if it was possible to suit such a wound.

'Problem is, it's the thought of having it rather than actually having it and that's why the numbers don't add up. It's why I haven't sorted it out before now. Mr Maddox wants every new initiative to show a profit. Insists on it, in fact.' Gabriel hitched himself up to sit on the worktop. 'But with the extra staff costs, waiters as well, remember, we're not coming out ahead.'

'So, Chef, what will you do?'

'You a bit of a night owl, Benny? Fancy the graveyard shift? It'll be soups and salads, fries and burgers, no real chance to cook, but I need a reliable man.'

'What about the profits? What will Mr Maddox say?'

Gabe shrugged. 'I'll punch in some different numbers. It'll look OK.'

'Yes, Chef.'

'Look,' said Gabe. 'This is the way it'll work. I put in some numbers to give the right projection, so Maddox can sign it off. His nose is clean. Then the orders don't come in at the projected rate, it's nobody's fault, we've got the extra star which is what we want. We fold the night-service profit and loss in with the rest of room service, which is what is going to happen anyway. We've made the problem disappear.'

Benny was quiet. He seemed to be loaded with questions, which he would now refuse to ask.

'What?' said Gabriel. 'What?'

'Nothing, Chef. I was just wondering, would it be easier to tell the truth?'

Remember, Gabriel, a lie is as worthless as the feller what's told it.

It was all very well. But at work, these days, truth and lies didn't come into it. What you had to think about was what 'they' did or didn't need to hear and how to make yourself heard.

'Truth is, Benny, it's going to work fine. All I'm doing is de-risking it for Mr Maddox so the worry is mine alone.'

Benny smiled again, showing his salt-white teeth. 'Let me work some doubles, Chef. I can sleep until the afternoon, come in and work until six.'

Gabe nodded. 'I'll pour this bouillon for you. Let's stick it straight in the fridge. There's one that's empty. No, I'm OK, you strain the demi-glace. Then we can both get home.'

They worked and cleared in silence. The night porter came in and made a start on the grease traps. They exchanged nods, one apiece.

'Right,' said Gabe. 'We're done.' He wiped his hands with an unnecessary flourish and smacked them together a few times. 'Home,' he said, and then, more weakly, 'home.'

'I have to go down and get my things from the locker,' said Benny.

'Right. Of course. Right.' Gabriel folded his towel. He picked it up again and scrunched it, then lobbed it at the laundry bin. 'OK.'

Benny started to move.

'Wait,' called Gabriel. 'Wait. Do you want to go for a drink? Do you need to get home? I'm not in a hurry myself, I mean, it's not that late really and – come on, let's do it – I know a nice little bar.'

Dusty's was a cook-infested basement dive in Heddon Street. The eponymous Dusty was a Geordie with a legendary CV including working the rigs in Saudi, bootlegging whisky, also in Saudi, gun-running in unspecified southern African states, managing a fairground attraction in Mexico City as a front for some hinted-at nefarious activity, and 'bodyguarding', as he put it, for celebrities. 'Yeah, they were cunts,' he liked to say, 'but no more than the other cunts. No more than you cunts in here. Come down to it, I've travelled the world and it's the same all over, it's what you get everywhere, and everyone, basically – I'm talking brass tacks, behind the scenes, boil it down – is more or less of a cunt.'

The cooks didn't give him any grief. They took their fights outside. The bar was like a warm, dark mouth which held them while they wet their troubles or joys, or rinsed off the boredom with Jack Daniel's and Bruce Springsteen.

Tonight there was no sign of Dusty. A girl in a ripped black T-shirt, sporting a ring through her lip and a cold sore besides, guarded the bar with a belligerence that must have taken months of training to perfect. She raised her chin a millimetre, an economical way of saying, *yes, what can I get for you?*

'Kronenbourg,' said Gabriel. 'Benny, what do you want?'

'Good evening,' said Benny to the girl, who had merely to slacken her jaw muscles to tell him what she thought of that. 'Do you have Blue Curaçao?'

The girl touched the tip of her tongue to her lip ring but disappeared down behind the bar and then rose again as if from the grave holding a bottle of the glowing blue spirit.

Gabe and Benny took their drinks and sat close to Spunker's Corner where Dave Hill, at that time Garde Manger at the Connaught, was said to have come in his pants while recounting the contents of a pornographic film. If you drank at Dusty's for long enough you learned a legend about everyone in the game.

'Where the fuck have you been?' Nathan Tyler came out of the gents, zipping, and spoke as if Gabriel had stood him up. In a sense, Gabriel supposed, he had. Since he'd got together with Charlie, he either went to the Penguin or went home.

'I've got to split, mate,' said Nathan, in a tone that suggested Gabe had begged him to stay. 'Listen, give us a call, yeah, you little fucker, give us a call.'

'We were at the Dorchester together,' Gabe told Benny. He smiled to himself. Ten hours a day 'turning' potatoes, carving them into a roundness that nature did not see fit to provide. Doing that shit forged a bond between you, somehow, like living in a trench. Yeah, he'd give Nathan a call.

'Cheers,' said Benny. He lifted his glass. The contents looked radioactive. Benny cocked his little finger daintily as he drank.

'It's good to . . . you know, wind down after work,' said Gabe. 'Have a couple of drinks.'

'Yes, Chef,' said Benny. He had changed into stone-washed jeans with neatly pressed creases, a black leather jacket with a tiger embroidered on the back, and traded his work clogs for a pair of grey slip-ons so shiny they could easily be employed to look up a skirt.

'So,' said Gabe, glancing around. 'I used to come here sometimes.'

'Yes, Chef.'

Neither one of them, it seemed, was winding down. 'You don't have to call me Chef now. Gabe will be fine.'

'OK, Gabe.'

'Did you come that night we went to the Penguin? Place with the jazz singer, my girlfriend? Night Damian got legless and puked down his shirt.' The detail was extraneous; there hadn't been any other nights.

'No, Chef. I was not in that day.'

Soon after he'd started at the Imperial, Gabriel had taken the crew out, his first and so far only initiative in the building of team spirit.

'We'll do it again some time soon,' said Gabe, without meaning it. He wanted to ask Benny where he was from. Benny's English was excellent but deeply accented, each syllable a heavy mouthful, formed – so it seemed – with a degree of physical effort at the back of the throat, and released with an audible exhale. Gabe had been working with Benny for nearly six months now. It seemed a little awkward to be asking him where he was from. He decided to come at it from the side. 'Salim,' he said, naming one of the night porters. 'He's Somali, isn't he? Do you know much about it? Somalia, I mean?'

'I know a little,' said Benny with an enigmatic smile. He lifted his drink. 'You know this is made with oranges. How does it end up blue?'

Gabe had only ever seen one person drink Blue Curaçao before and that was Nana. She liked the green stuff too, crème de menthe, which tasted like medicine as far as Gabe was concerned. 'Search me. He looks quite sad, Salim. I wonder what his story is.'

Benny shrugged. 'He is from Somalia. That is a story, for true.'

'What about you, Benny?'

'Chef?'

'Well,' said Gabe. 'I don't know. I guess we're just having a bit of a chat here. What about your family? Have you got someone waiting for you at home?'

'It depends,' said Benny, slowly, 'on what you mean by home. You have your lady friend waiting for you?'

Lena was waiting for him. Gabe shivered. The thought of her drew and repelled him, like an image of an atrocity at which he could not look and from which he could not turn away. 'Not tonight,' he said, 'she's working abroad for a while. What do you call home, then? You tell me.'

'Ah,' said Benny. He shook his large head and gazed at Gabriel with his yellowy eyes. Head aside, Benny was compact, undersized even, but there was nothing stunted about his physique. He made Gabriel feel his extra inches as something superfluous, extra blood and bone and tissue which could be removed without taking anything essential away.

'Only making conversation,' said Gabriel. 'Let's talk about something else.'

'A friend of mine,' said Benny, 'is Somali, like Salim. He lived in Mogadishu and he was a driver. If you heard his story . . . eh, heh, heh.' Benny's laugh was deep-throated, laden with a meaning that was not clear to Gabe.

'Go on,' said Gabe, 'what happened to your friend?'

'Too many things,' said Benny. 'Chef, is there anything about work you are wanting to discuss with me?'

Gabe had considered asking Benny about Victor and Ivan, what lay behind the flare-up today, but Benny had a diplomat's gift for deflection, was a master at smoothing things over. They could talk but nothing, he knew, would be said. 'We're off duty, Benny, let's give ourselves a break. I'd rather listen to a story about your friend.'

'Do you know,' said Benny, 'you can buy a national insurance number, you can buy a passport, an identity, and also you can buy a story. If you think your own story is not strong enough, if you worry that your own suffering is not sufficient to gain permission to stay in this country, you can buy a story and take it with you to this government office in Croydon. Somali stories can get a high price.'

'I suppose,' said Gabe, 'that everything is for sale.'

'And if you tell your own story, you may not be believed. "Lack of credibility." That is the stamp they use. I know somebody that this happened to.'

Gabe yawned comfortably. He knew the type of thing that was coming, but he didn't mind. 'Where was he from?'

'The Democratic Republic of the Congo. He was a professor of economics at the University of Kinshasa, a very clever man.' Benny chuckled, as if to say, well, there is the problem, right there.

'And? He got put in prison?' Benny, he could see, was hesitating, not knowing how much to say. After-work drinks meant bitching, ribbing, gossiping, not telling tales of woe.

'He was involved in opposition politics. The first time he was arrested, they extracted most of his teeth.' Benny looked at Gabriel, checking, it seemed, whether he had gone too far. Gabe nodded, as if this detail was only to be expected. 'The next time,' said Benny, speaking quickly, 'that they locked him up they did not torture him, but when he was released he went home and discovered that they had killed his wife and children. With the help of a colleague he fled to Zambia and from there he came to the UK. A happy end, you think?'

'I'm guessing no,' said Gabe. Benny, who had antique good manners, had got the story over with as fast as possible, not wanting to be a bore.

Benny lifted his glass with his peculiar one-finger salute. 'No,' he said, and took a gulp. 'Lack of credibility. They asked him all sorts of questions. They asked how many children he had and how many had been killed. Eleven, he told them. And how many, they asked again, have died? Eleven, he said again. He should have said two or three. That was his mistake. We do not believe your story, they told him. It lacks cred-i-bil-ity.' He made the word go on for ever, a long indictment, a litany of crime.

'After all that, they turned him away?'

'They were right. But also wrong. It is not credible but it is true. What is a man to do?'

Gabriel bought more drinks. He went to the jukebox and scanned it. Nothing had changed. Dylan, the Stones, Springsteen, Neil Young, Deep Purple, Meat Loaf and the Pogues. Dusty had been known to ban people who had the temerity to ask for new tunes. 'What's the point of having my own place,' he'd say, 'some cunt comes along, tells me what to do?' The jukebox was vintage, a '73 Wurlitzer that played 45s, with a design aesthetic that hovered somewhere between spaceship and Tiffany lamp. Gabriel punched in the number for 'Southern Man' and gave the old beast a slap on the flank as if it were a pit pony on its way to the knacker's yard.

'I have talked too much,' said Benny, when Gabe sat down again. He rearranged the table, straightening the napkins, the bowl of peanuts, the cardboard coasters, the drinks, his fingers working deftly, flying over the objects and moving them as if by magnetic force or magic, displaying the dextrous touch of an able chef.

'No,' said Gabe, 'not at all.'

'If I had a woman,' said Benny, 'I would not bring her here.' A couple at the bar had locked mouths. 'This is killing romance. Romance is better than sex.'

'Ideally you get both,' said Gabe, thinking about Lena's offer. He'd have to go and face her soon. 'Did you say you were from Congo as well?'

'Liberia,' said Benny. 'Small country, big troubles.' He shook his head.

'Right,' said Gabriel, vaguely. 'Good idea to get out.'

'There was fighting. I ran away.' Benny shrugged.

'You came straight to London?' Gabriel was grateful for this abbreviated history. On the one hand he was idly curious to hear Benny's background, on the other he did not wish to be burdened with it. If he had to yell at Benny about something, or even give him the sack, he preferred not to know about any terrible things he might have been through. He was only keeping him talking to put off the inevitable: going home.

'I went with some others to Cairo because I heard that they help Liberians there. After two years of waiting I was interviewed by the United Nations officials and after another year of waiting I was offered resettlement here. I used these years of waiting to improve my English.'

'Your English is excellent,' said Gabriel.

'Thank you. English is our official language in Liberia. But if I talk Liberian English,' he said, his accent thickening, 'it g'wan vex you plenty-plenty.'

How did I get myself into this thing with Lena, thought Gabriel.

But it wasn't even something he had got himself into. It was something that had happened to him. He didn't, after all, ask for her to appear like that in the yard. 'So,' he said to Benny, 'Liberia is not a good place to be.'

'I can tell you another story,' said Benny. 'Perhaps it is more interesting than my own.'

'Please,' said Gabriel, 'go on.'

'This friend, Kono, is also Liberian. He is around my age, and we are very close. He is from Nimba county, one of the Gio people.' Benny stopped. He appeared to have a change of heart. 'Well, it is getting late.'

'We haven't finished our drinks,' said Gabriel. *Lena*, he thought. *Oh, God*.

'All right,' said Benny. 'When Charles Taylor's men first came through this area, in 1989, Kono's village was untouched because the Gios supported Taylor. But the following year the trouble began. Taylor's men – he was the rebel leader and later he was the president – had some disagreement with the headman of the village. This man was Kono's father. Two days later, these rebel soldiers, they returned.

'They dragged Kono's mother and father and his four brothers and sisters out of the house. The parents they shot. The children they beat to death with rifle butts. It saves on bullets, you see. Kono lived because he was the eldest and a boy and the rebels recruited him in this way. He was twelve then.'

'Christ,' said Gabe. He knew what was going to happen with Lena. That was what he was trying to avoid, sitting here listening to this stuff that nobody, to be honest, wanted to hear.

'I know,' said Benny, laughing, 'I know. The rebels took Kono and they put him to work. At first he fetched water and dug latrines. After a while, he was taken on a raid and ordered to shoot one of the prisoners – a pregnant woman. The rebels beat him, but still he refused. Are you sure I should go on? A short time later, on another raid, he was told, "It is time for your initiation now." Kono was reluctant but the unit leader took a knife and started to cut Kono. This gave him the encouragement he needed.'

'So now he was a rebel soldier himself?' *He knew what was going to happen with Lena*. But where was the knife at Gabriel's throat? He was free to choose, was he not?

'A child soldier,' said Benny. 'This is what my country is famous for. They put him on a checkpoint, another Liberian speciality. This one was decorated with human skulls and it was called No Way Back because . . . well, I think you can guess, eh, heh, heh. For nearly three years Kono went on raids and guarded the checkpoint. This was his life.' Benny, it turned out, was quite a raconteur, once he got going. 'All the child soldiers had nicknames. Death Squad, Lethal Weapon, Killer Dog . . . Kono was not very tall for his age and his nickname was General Shoot-On-Tiptoes, for obvious reasons I think.'

'I get it,' said Gabe. He had to admit there were places, there were times, when your life was taken out of your hands.

'He did what child soldiers do and had cornrows and cowries in his hair, and every day he got high.'

Gabriel had no such excuse. If he wanted to sleep with Lena, how could he kid himself that it was 'just going to happen'? As if he were the victim of history, of war, of fate.

'Then one day Kono went on a raid and they did the usual stuff, raping, looting, killing. When they had finished this work they relaxed for a while in this village. Some of the boy soldiers began playing football and Kono went to join in. He saw that they were using a woman's head for a ball. Kono joined in the game.'

Gabriel looked sharply at Benny.

'I can see what you are thinking,' said Benny, 'heh, heh, you are thinking how can a human being do this? Even myself, I am thinking the same. What is it that makes us human? Are we just animals, after all?'

'This is your friend?' said Gabe. Lena, he thought, with a sudden, low ache, would be pacing, waiting for him to get home. How could he be thinking of Lena, right now, this second? What was wrong with him?

'We are very close. After this day, he knew he had to get out. He decided he would rather die than stay. So when he was sent to the market one day to get food – take it, not buy it, you understand – he ran away. For a while he lived on the street in Monrovia, expecting every day to be his last. Then he met a friend of his father's, a Libyan businessman, who helped him get to Cairo. That is when I met him, ex-General Shoot-On-Tiptoes, Kono, my good friend.' Benny laughed. He clapped his hands, wrung them together briefly and then put his jacket on. Gabe caught a flicker of understanding. For an instant he saw it clearly, knew why Benny laughed. He knew it deeply, instinctively, momentarily before he lost the perception again.

'Now,' said Benny, getting up, 'all he has left of that time are the nightmares. But nightmares won't kill you, he says.'

They left the bar and Benny walked towards Oxford Street to wait for the night bus. Gabriel watched him for a few moments, the tiger dancing on his back, stepping in and out of the shadows, his stories packed and stowed; a small black man on his way to or from a shift, hurrying, looking down and walking away, until the city claimed him and Gabriel turned and hailed a cab.

CHAPTER EIGHT

—〜〜—

HE WATCHED HER SLEEPING NOW, HIS HAND HELD AS IF IN A FORCE field directly above her throat, as though to absorb or else heal her through the pulse that throbbed at the base of his thumb. Lena, in the marbled moonlight, was a carved beauty, a dying swan. Her lips were sheened to perfection, her flawless cheeks were pearled, and the unfathomable beauty of her eyelids would make a convert of any man. There she lay, his irritant, his ache, his skinny girl, colourless hair spread across the pillow, his salvation, his ruin, or neither, but simply his release.

Lena stirred and opened her eyes. Gabe, on his knees at her side, pulled back with guilty speed, as if he had been stealing. Her mouth stretched to form an 'O' and closed again. For a long, frozen moment they looked at each other and Gabe's ears filled with the pounding of blood. She raised an arm and put her hand against his chest. She slid it inside his shirt. When he moved on top of her it was with a grace and ease he had not known he possessed. Her hard little fingers moved through his hair. Am I the kind of person who does this? he thought. Is this me, am I this type? And then there was only the movement, the heat, the wet, the rub, the glide, the ripples across his back, and he dissolved, no *I*, no *me*, no *who*, but only this, their bodies, and nothing more.

They unwound from each other and parted, Gabriel sitting on the sofa and Lena tugging down her skirt but still reclining, head against the sofa's arm. Gabriel came back to himself. Oh shit, he said silently, but it was mere experiment, the regret that he expected had not reported for duty yet. He ran his fingers around her kneecap and stroked her thigh, waiting for his breath to settle down. Lena was looking at the ceiling, her lips pressed together, arms crossed on her chest, laid out like a graveyard statue.

'Lena,' said Gabe, tenderly pinching the thin, soft flesh. 'I looked for the money.'

Lena let out a slow exhale. 'I know what you will say.'

'I went down there,' said Gabe. 'I counted the bricks, four from the right and . . .'

'I know what you will *say*.'

Gabe removed his hand from her leg. He was accused, but of what? He reached for the lamp and switched it on. 'What am I going to say?'

Lena snapped upright as if jolted by her own internal current. 'You say you did not find. I am right or not?'

Was she saying that he had not bothered to look, or that he had taken her money for himself? He looked into her eyes, trying to gauge the level of her anger, but he could not see inside her, could as soon see her liver or intestines as the state of her heart. 'You're right,' he said. 'I didn't.'

'No,' said Lena, drawing up her knees to form a barrier. 'No.' She plucked at the rings in her ears, stretching the lobes.

There was another possibility. The money never existed. She was working some plan to twist cash out of him. 'I'm sorry,' he said.

'Why sorry? For what?' She pulled harder at the earrings. 'How I was so stupid, leave money like that?'

Gabe took hold of her wrists. 'Don't,' he said, 'you'll make them bleed.' Gently, he lowered her arms and held her hands, or rather her fists. 'I've got some money saved,' he said. So what if it was her plan? He didn't care. 'I can let you have some, we'll call it a loan but you can pay me back whenever that's going to be possible for you. OK? Lena, OK?'

She turned her sharp face up to look at him. Her beauty had a fragile quality; it could break at any moment. 'If you think . . .' she said, trailing off. She released her fists and they held hands.

'I think that would be fine. How much do you need? How much did you have?'

Lena hesitated. He imagined the calculations running through her head. How much to ask for? How much was too much? How much not enough? 'Two thousand,' she said, finally. 'But . . . is up to you.'

'Two thousand?' Gabe whistled. 'OK.'

'I accept this offer,' said Lena, and Gabriel understood the attempt to make it real, binding, a done deal.

He pulled her into his chest and they sat for a while in silence, Gabriel smelling the anxious, unwashed smell of her hair, so different from Charlie's, which was safely fresh and citrus, as full as Lena's was thin.

'When?' said Lena. She said it softly. 'When you will make this loan for me?'

'I have to . . . you know, make the withdrawal. I have to actually go into the bank. Can't get that kind of cash out of the machine.'

Lena pulled away. 'Yes. I understand, yes.' She smiled. He could see the tension in her neck, the way the tendons stood out. 'When you will go?'

'Soon as I can,' said Gabriel. They were walking the high wire, both of them, facing each other over the canyon of their conflicting desires. 'Might be tricky the next couple of days, lot on at work.' He wanted her to go, of course he did, as much as she wanted to leave, but he didn't want it now, not yet.

'Two days,' said Lena, 'is nothing. I wait.'

In bed, while Lena finished up in the bathroom, Gabriel looked at the furniture: the pine chest, the melamine stacking chair, the home-assembly chest of drawers, and thought about putting them into storage. He should get some furniture of his own, choose stuff that was more 'him', though he was not sure of his taste in furniture, and it would be better to get Charlie to help. This room was so anonymous. But maybe he liked it that way. In Plodder Lane every chair, every object had a history so that nothing was just what it was.

Lena came in wearing her blouse and pants. She hadn't brushed her hair. She sat down beneath the pastel-framed print of the water lilies, half in, half out of the circle of lamplight, back bent, hands on thighs.

He looked at her serious little face. He said, 'Have you heard the one about the chef and the kitchen porter? The chef says, see these pans here . . .'

'You want to make fun for me. I am not care,' said Lena, her accent thickening. 'I am not give shit.'

Gabriel patted the empty pillow at his side. 'Come here. I'm not making fun, I was trying to, you know, keep it light.'

Lena stared at her knees.

'You can't sit there all night. Come on, hop in.' He lifted the duvet. She sat still, resisting, wretched, and he decided to be firm with her to put her out of this self-inflicted pain. 'Get in bed, Lena, now. Stop pissing around.'

She got in bed and he covered her with the duvet. Lying propped on one elbow, he traced the lines of her thin high eyebrows.

'When you were growing up,' he said, 'when you were a little girl, what did you want to be?'

'I don't know,' said Lena. She looked directly at him. Her eyes were a clear, dark blue but he saw nothing in them, as if they were clouded by cataracts.

'Ballerina,' said Gabriel, 'princess, acrobat, Eskimo.'

She made a dismissive sound. 'Tchh.'

If he could make her laugh, he decided, there was nothing to be sorry about. Though she had started it, touched him, she was behaving as if he had taken something from her.

'Astronaut, actress, lion tamer, mystic. Bank manager, accountant, florist, mortician. Am I close? Damn.' He rolled on to his back. 'Got it,' he said, punching the headboard. 'Kitchen porter at the world-famous Imperial Hotel. Your dream came true.'

'You are bad man,' said Lena, but she gave a short, dry laugh, and it was she who came to him, sliding across the bed and fitting under his arm.

There were footsteps in the courtyard. People went out there some-times in the night to smoke. The traffic maintained a steady rumble, a soft underblanket of noise on which to float off to sleep. When she spoke again he realized he had been drifting.

126

'Italy,' she said. 'I want for long time, go to Italy.'

'Oh, Italy. Why not? Italy is beautiful.'

'For work in care home, be carer for old people. Is not dream. Little girl dream . . . I don't know, not this. But now, seem like dream, even this.'

'London's not so bad,' said Gabe. 'We'll get you back on your feet. You'll see.' The police weren't looking for her. Even if they interviewed her they wouldn't care if she was illegal or not. There was no need for her to hide. He thought about telling her but it was almost the middle of the night and he didn't want to think about all of that. Something else to keep in the bank, sterling currency in his gift. 'What do you think of this room? Bit characterless, would you say?'

Lena sat up. She looked into the middle distance but whatever she was seeing it was not the pine chest, the stacking chair, but something in her head that made her pinch her arms. 'In my home, in Mazyr, there is gypsy woman. She have big gypsy nose and one eye green and one eye blue. This gypsy woman she tell for me fortune. You know what is fortune? Yes, future. She use tea leaves for this. She tell me, you will meet man, beautiful man, tall and dark hair, yes, like fairy tale, and beautiful man he have mark on neck, back here, is mark from birth, yes, birthmark, and he will take you to your life.' She rocked gently, back and forth. 'He will take you to your life.'

Gabriel ran his hand up and down her spine. She grew still.

'There's time,' said Gabriel, 'your life's only starting. What are you, twenty-five? Twenty-four?'

'My father say, in old days, Soviet days, is easy to tell what is lie. Everything is lie. Now, he says, is more hard. What is truth and what is lie? How we can know?' She pulled her shoulders up by her ears and let them drop. 'But he is wrong. There is no truth. Is only a new kind of lie.'

'My father,' said Gabriel, not realizing what he would say until the words left his mouth, 'is dying.'

She wormed down and lay on her side, their bodies not quite touching. 'He is old?'

'Seventy-five.'

'He is old,' said Lena.

Gabe looked into her cold blue eyes.

'But is sad,' she said, without a flicker of emotion.

Gabriel took her hand and pressed her fingers to his mouth. He kissed the bitten nails. He kissed the palm. She was hard and cold, and he was grateful for it. Their exchange, after all, was equal. They wanted something from each other, and what was theirs was theirs to trade freely, they didn't need to deceive themselves.

He descends again into the aquarium glow of the catacombs. He is drifting on the light, and the light is not light, it is dark like the sea, the night sea but lit from within, a current of dark-light that sucks him down, sucks him in, and he is nearly at the place though he would turn from it if he could. He crouches over the body and begins with the feet, yellowing nails, a bunion, dry skin on the heel. He tries to move to the legs but is held, and must consider the feet again. Hair on the big toes, left little toe is bent, insteps white and purple with an eggshell texture, a wedge of tissue under the right big toenail to stop it growing in. Why must he look? They are only feet. He has seen feet before. And he is hungry. Oh, he is hungry. He calls for food. Who will feed me? I, who have fed so many, am hungry. Bring me food. Let there be food. Oysters on a silver salver. He drinks them from their shells. Sweet skewers of pork with a peanut glaze. He tears them with his teeth. Filo parcels of feta and spinach. He breaks them with his hands. His prayer is answered. The feast surrounds him. He is loved. He is loved. In gratitude, he weeps.

'Caught you,' said Charlie. 'Admit it.'

The phone was at his ear. He must have answered it in his sleep. He tipped out of bed and went to the kitchen, leaned a forearm on the cool black granite. 'No,' he said. 'What?'

'Sleeping and what time do you call this?'

'I missed you, sweetheart. What time is it?'

'Ten thirty. I called you at work.' Charlie laughed. 'Oona covered your arse, said you'd probably gone straight into a meeting, but that's after she'd said you hadn't turned up.'

'Oona,' said Gabriel, putting his hand in his boxers, weighing, arranging, freeing, making his habitual adjustments to start the day.

'Never mind Oona. How was it? Tell me everything. I missed you, sweetheart.'

'I know,' said Charlie, 'you just told me. Tell me again.'

'I did. I do. I want to see you. Why aren't you here with me?' He meant it, every word. Except the part about Charlie being here right now, because that would be difficult with Lena still in his bed.

'Cheap flight,' said Charlie, 'bloody Luton in the middle of the night. Listen, baby, if you're not working, I'll . . .'

'I wish. Oh God, do I wish.' He still had his hand inside his pants. His penis, he noted, concurred with his expressed desire. He gave it a consolatory stroke. 'I overslept, that's all, late one, and it's going to be a fuck of a day.'

'Be like that, then,' said Charlie. 'Know when I'm not wanted.'

'Oh, you're wanted, believe me.' He had a full erection now and turned to face the cupboards so that Lena, if she walked in, would not catch him. He knew Lena would not affect his desire, his anything, for Charlie. That was why he could let it happen. No one could touch his relationship with Charlie, not Lena anyway. 'So tell me about Sharm el-Sheikh.'

'I spoke to you practically every day.' She stifled a yawn. 'Maybe I got up too early. Might go back to bed. Did I tell you about the golf buggies? The hotel's all spread out, you know, bungalows, and you ride round the marble paths on these little carts. I drank pomegranate juice and detoxed, think I lost about a stone.'

'You'd better not.'

'One of the security guards was Mossad, Israeli secret service, apparently the Egyptian resorts are crawling with them. Everyone said it, but no one really knew. You know how it is in hotels.'

'Aah,' said Gabriel, 'mmm.'

'You with me, Gabe?' said Charlie. 'Oh, and how's your dad?'

His hand stopped what it was doing. He removed it from his shorts. 'Well, you know, no change.'

'You've spoken to him, though?'

'Yes, spoken, of course.'

'The phone is useless, though, isn't it? We'll talk . . . I'm not working tonight.'

'Shit,' he said, 'tonight. Tonight's not good, there's a launch party, big bash, goes on really late. And tomorrow there's . . . a . . . um . . . PanCont. Directors' conference, banquet and stuff, got to show my face.'

'If I didn't know better,' said Charlie.

'Sweetheart,' he said, '*sweetheart.*' They laughed, she blew him a kiss, they made an arrangement, he hung up the phone. When he turned he saw a ghost in the doorway, Lena in his white shirt. 'What is name?' she said, twisting her skinny fingers. 'Your girlfriend, what she is called?'

When he walked into his office, Oona was sitting in his chair. 'Praise be,' she said, 'the wild rice and buckwheat finally on they way.'

Gabriel sighed. 'Praise be?'

Oona extricated herself from the chair and spread a buttock over the desk. 'Giving tanks to the Lord. Go on, darlin', settle yourself down.'

'You're not thanking JD Organics?'

'The good Lord,' said Oona, 'provides.' She shifted her weight and released it, getting comfortable, making herself at home.

'Is there anything else, Oona?'

'We muddlin' through,' said Oona happily. She was roosting like a pigeon, all swelling chest and sleepy eyes, bedding down amid the paperwork for a little bill and coo.

Gabriel thought he should thank her for this morning, for holding the fort while he slept. What he said was, 'Have you thought about retiring? You know you could after all these years.'

She looked at him as if he had suggested they start planning her funeral. Then she smiled and her gold tooth caught the light, a little sunburst, sparkly as false hope, and she said, 'Retirement? Hoo! Not me, darlin', I goin' stay here 'til I drop.'

Gabe grabbed a notepad and took the back stairs on his way to the communications meeting. The meeting would be a farce, as usual, dressed up as a worthy ensemble play about Working Life. Word was that the menus had to be rewritten in the PanCont house style, with a maximum of five ingredients listed and a minimum of three. It was another Initiative. Initiatives were generally designed to remind you that you shouldn't show any of your own. He'd give Lena a call afterwards, she must be bored out of her skull. She owned a mobile, it had turned out, when he told her not to answer his phone. She had been sullen this morning and they'd rowed about the phone business. 'I have phone,' she said. 'I am not give shit. I am not need nothing from you.' He'd only told her not to answer it in case Charlie called, or Jenny, or Dad. He let her be angry. It was kinder to let her be angry. She needed her anger right then.

On the way into work he'd thought about it. Was it rare for a porter to have a mobile phone? Or did the others just not own up to it, preferring to remain untraceable?

The bus hummed its way up Bridge Street, the sky watery blue over the Houses of Parliament, Big Ben sounding noontime, baleful as a knell. In the seat in front of Gabriel, teenagers ate chips for a mid-morning snack. Tourists in cagoules and sunglasses littered the pavement. The window creaked as Gabe rested his head against the pane. And then he saw it, a rag-and-bone cart, and he twisted his neck and looked and looked until he lost it as the bus turned into Parliament Square. Did you see it? he wanted to say. Did you see the man, the horse, the blinkers, the way the fetlocks shook? Did you see the pile of old clothes, the television, the toaster, the vegetable rack? The man had a hole in the knee of his trousers, he wore a brown cloth cap, and did you notice how lightly he touched the whip to the horse's neck? The top deck was almost full. Gabriel looked at the faces around him, each locked in its own private space.

Thirty-five years, must be, since he'd seen the rag-and-bone man, heard the call that sounded nothing like any old iron, a wordless, timeless, animal cry and he could hear it now, from down the decades, and the clop of hooves on the cobbles, and he could see the cartwheels turning pretty circles and feel the heat of the horse as it stopped right by him, smell its dark, packed smell. One thing he couldn't fathom. Another picture, another memory, this one without root or reason. What tricks the mind can play. But how clearly he could see, though the angle was oblique, over the steaming haunches, up to the seat behind, a woman, madly staring, tangles in her hair, his mother, his mother, and the old rag-and-bone man, dark as a gypsy, with the devil in his eye, winking and grinning, holding her elbow as she raised and turned and lowered herself, stiff as a candle, to the ground.

Checking his watch, he saw he was running later than he'd realized. He turned out of the stairwell to go to the lifts and there, coming towards him from the other end of the corridor, were Ivan and Gleeson, walking fast, tied at the hip, heads inclined, rough with smooth, a gross mating, an unnatural sight. Gabriel stepped into an alcove and flattened against the wall. At once he regretted it. They would see him. Was he a child, imagining himself invisible if only he closed his eyes? He pressed his back and arms to the walls and breathed in. It was ridiculous. The alcove was shallow, not deep enough to conceal his chest, and anyway when they walked past there would be nothing to hide behind. They were close now, very close. Should he step out and continue walking, as if this were nothing unusual, to be standing in an alcove like this, or should he jump out and yell, pretend to some sort of prank? His heart became drunk and disorderly, lurching around in his chest. It was ridiculous. He was ridiculous. He held his breath.

Ivan and Gleeson muttered past him and stopped at the next door, Gleeson fumbling with the key card while Ivan looked around, up and down the corridor, seeing nothing but his own cleverness, filing a thumbnail on the stubble on his chin.

The smug clunk of the door freed Gabriel's lungs. He put a hand on his chest as it heaved. What were they doing in a guest room? How did they get the key? It stank. But it wasn't a smell he recognized. Gabe peeled himself from the wall. He thought for a moment. These rooms were directly over the kitchen. There'd been complaints. The kitchen started up too early in the morning, the guests were woken by noises from the underworld. It had come up in the management meeting, the rooms were being left empty until they could be re-configured into an office, a sauna, a meeting room. Gabriel crept to the door and listened. He heard nothing but the shush of a carpeted corridor, the faint tick and purr of the building, white noise that thickened the air in this as in every hotel.

Nikolai stood in the delivery yard in the narrow shaft of sunlight that had punched a hole in the clouds. The sun striped the brick wall behind him, brown, red, brown. It lit his ginger hair. It caressed the smoke from his cigarette, curling and lifting it in a high, voluptuous trail. Gabriel watched him, the way he was smoking. These days, smokers took hurried and furtive puffs. But not Nikolai. He made space for the cigarette. The cigarette made space for him. It was an elegant punctuation, a pause in the sentence, indispensable to the rhythm, the sense.

Gabriel crossed the yard. Nikolai accepted his presence with a nod.

'Taking a breather.'

'Yes,' said Nikolai, 'good.'

He offered Gabriel a cigarette. Gabe hadn't smoked in eight, nine years. He took one and Nikolai flicked his lighter, lit another for himself.

Dizzy with the first hit, Gabriel drew less deeply the second time and everything was fine. They smoked together. Gabe remembered how good it was to stand with a colleague and share something, man to man, a smoke.

Nikolai squinted into the sun. He was so pale he could be albino, but for the sand-red hair. A Russian, like Lena. Belarussian, she'd said.

'A man,' said Nikolai, 'feels he is essential. He knows he is only a cog. Not even that – a drop of oil in the machine. But his life is so real to him he cannot imagine a world without him. How incomplete the world would be.' He took a long, slow drag of the cigarette. He took his time. 'And then he is gone. The waves close over his head. Is there anything to mark him? Is there a ripple? No.'

He was speaking about Yuri. Gabriel lowered his cigarette and tapped the ash.

'Two daughters,' said Nikolai. 'One studying economics, the other in the second year of a medical degree.'

'Things happen,' said Gabe, 'all the time.'

'How small we are.'

They stubbed out their butts against the wall. 'Listen,' said Gabriel. 'There's something.' He pulled a weed from between the bricks and pulped it between finger and thumb. 'Ivan and Stanley. Stanley Gleeson. Is there something? Because if there is I need to know.'

'Something,' said Nikolai, 'something,' as if pondering a philosophical conundrum, the answer to which lay in deep contemplation, without reference to external events.

'Something they shouldn't be doing,' said Gabe, as if it needed explaining. 'I know they are, but I don't know what it is.'

Nikolai nodded, acknowledging this state of affairs.

'Chef, I didn't know you were a smoker.'

'I'm not.'

'Smoking is bad,' said Nikolai, 'but it's like life. Bad, but the alternative is worse.'

You never entered a walk-in and closed the door. Someone passing might pull up the lever to complete the seal and then you'd be locked in a more or less soundproof fridge. Victor was handling a thirty-pound beef rib when Gabriel stepped inside and pulled the door shut.

'Hey,' said Victor, dumping the meat and wheeling round.

'Cosy in here,' said Gabriel. 'Quiet. Good place for a chat.'

'Hey, the door.'

'Can't be overheard. No one listening in.'

Victor sniggered. 'You gonna put me on a meat hook, Chef?'

'I can do that. If you like.'

Victor's snigger grew higher and wilder; it struggled to find purchase on Gabriel's stony gaze. Gabriel let it peter out.

'I don't squeal,' said Victor. He shoved a saddle of lamb that hung at shoulder height. He caught it as it swung and pushed a thumb into the yellowy fat.

'Victor, you can speak to me. I am not your enemy.'

'I do my job, Chef,' said Victor, 'my nose is clean.'

'What about Ivan? What is it?'

'Why you asking *me* about Ivan?' He tossed his head and stirred his foot, as if he were a bull about to enter the ring. Gabe was meant to smell testosterone, not the adrenalin surge of fear. 'Ask Ivan about Ivan. Not me.'

They faced each other. Without noticing, Gabe had mirrored

Victor's stance, squared up to him as though he were a serious adversary rather than an employee who needed a kick up the arse.

'Let me look at those ribs,' said Gabriel, so that Victor was forced to stand down, step aside. 'Did the rib-eyes arrive as well?'

With the door closed, the smell in the meat locker was beginning to become a third presence. They were squeezed uncomfortably close. Gabriel ran his hand along the bones. 'Nice piece.'

'It's good meat,' said Victor. He shivered. 'Man,' he said. 'Check this. In Moldova, yeah, few years back, there was this woman. A cleaner at the hospital and she took body parts from the hospital. Get me? Body parts that were supposed to go to be burned. She sliced them up, yeah, and sold them in the town centre. Two dollars a kilo, half the market price. She made a killing, man, a killing. People bought it, they ate it, they loved it. They came back for more.'

'She get caught?'

'Somebody got suspicious.'

'Eating human flesh.'

'Dog eat dog,' said Victor. 'You Brits, you think . . .' He shook his head.

'It's your country we were talking about.'

Victor snorted. He pawed the ground. 'We're talking about flesh for sale.'

'Don't get in too deep with Ivan. I'm offering you a way out. I'm holding out a hand.'

'I told you, my nose is clean.'

'But what you know . . . nothing comes back to you.'

'Two dollars a kilo,' said Victor. 'For that price you don't want to know what you're eating. You don't want to think about it.'

'Dog eat dog.'

'Man,' said Victor. 'Seriously.' He tried the door and it opened. He held it with a hip. 'Point is, you're better off not knowing. It's better not to ask.'

CHAPTER NINE

—〰—

THEY HATCHED FROM THE CINEMA AT MARBLE ARCH, RUBBING THEIR arms and stretching their necks, shaking off the shell of wakeful slumber that had encased them during the film. They drifted north, arm in arm, along the Edgware Road. The light was dying. Neon signs flickered into life, Beirut, Al-Ahram, Al-Dar, Café du Liban. Office workers began the route march home. The matinee was over and the evening show yet to begin.

'Intelligent thriller,' said Charlie, 'appears to be a contradiction in terms.'

'Weren't you thrilled? Clever plot. Give it that.'

'Yes, but that's a bad thing. All plot, no story. Nothing unfolds, everything is forced.'

'You were on the edge of your seat.'

'I was slumped right down.'

'Peeping through your fingers.'

'What happened to make him a star? It's like, *watch me acting now*. We're supposed to forget he's acting, and he's waving a big bloody flag.'

'Got something. Six million a movie.'

'What's he got? A lucky break. Six million a movie or flipping burgers in Kansas. A toss-up, I'm telling you.'

Gabriel put his arm around her shoulder. 'You fancy him. That's what it is.'

'Eyes left, that means *thinking*. I mean, come on.'

Gabe laughed. 'His entire life is a fluke. If you say so. Anyway, you chose the film, let's not forget. The story wasn't bad.'

They kept going, towards Charlie's place, past shops that sold reproduction French furniture, Louis XIV plus twenty-first-century bling, past slot-machine arcades, jewellers, pawnbrokers, estate agents, restaurants, the signs in English and Arabic. In a café window, an old man lifted a newspaper, concealing his white beard, underlining the red and white turban wrapped around his head. Two women in burkhas trailed a toddler by the arms and were overtaken by a girl in a pink tracksuit with SEXY stitched across the bum.

'See that,' said Charlie, 'seems strange, don't you think? Having a Union Jack flying here.'

'It's the Victory Services Club. For old army buffers. Fought for king and country. Surely they can have a flag.'

'I know,' said Charlie. 'But . . .'

'We need to buy food, I'm cooking, remember.' He removed his arm from her shoulder and they broke apart as they entered the shop.

They carried a bag apiece and wove in and out of the human rush hour. When the pavement grew freer they walked side by side. Shazia Food Hall, Al Mustafa, Bureau de Change, Meshwar, Al Arez. On the other side of the road was a pub.

'What about that, then?' said Gabriel, tipping his head.

'What?'

'Burn the flag, close the pub.'

'Don't be silly.'

'Old English Gentleman. Seems strange. Maybe they should change the name at least.'

Charlie swung her bag at him. 'All right, you've made your point.'

They stopped for coffee at their usual place. Fazal was busy stoking a hubble-bubble but waved them to a table. The chairs were an odd assortment, stacked deep in velvet cushions, but the tables were identical – octagonal wooden fretwork inset with a copper tray. On the far wall a silent television screen showed Arabia TV and from somewhere Middle Eastern music played its endless lament. All the customers except Charlie were men, hookahs squatting faithfully at their feet. The artwork added a touch of the exotic: a pastel of an English country cottage, a collage of postcards depicting the Tower of London, Prince William and the Queen.

Fazal flapped his way across the café, cawing in anticipation, heralding his arrival with arms thrown wide. 'My friends,' he said, on landing, 'what can I get for you?'

'How are you?' said Charlie. 'Busy?'

Gabriel took an exaggerated breath. 'What's smoking today? I can smell cinnamon, what else?'

'Gentleman over there has apple, the one opposite asked for mint. We have strawberry behind you . . .'

'I think I'll try one. I'll have a pipe.'

'Excellent,' cried Fazal, hopping from foot to foot as though his wings had been clipped. 'I'll bring it right away.' He stayed where he was. His face darkened suddenly. 'But you cannot enjoy for long. Westminster Council – these people are killing us. Soon they will kill us with their smoke-free environment. Twenty thousand a year rates, sixty to seventy thousand rent. How can I survive?'

'Don't you get special exemption?' said Charlie. 'It's your culture. You could argue that.'

'Letters, meetings, protests,' said Fazal. He shook his head. His hair, which he wore long, was like glossy black feathers. A small patch of bristle grew on either side of his nose. 'Let those who don't like it go to their places,' he said. 'Nobody has to come here unless they want.'

'True,' said Gabriel. He'd spent two more nights with Lena. Last night she'd had an orgasm. He thought so, anyway.

'They say if you get ill by smoking it costs money for the state,' Fazal said, stretching his wings again. 'But what about junk food? What about alcohol? Those things are worse. Why not ban them as well?'

Gabriel sucked on the mouthpiece and watched the bubbles chase through the water, the smoke puffs gathering like a miniature storm above the silver bowl. Charlie sipped her coffee.

'Taken up smoking,' she said. 'What else is new? What else have I missed?' She unbuttoned her coat. Gabriel pressed his knee against hers. He told her about work, about Ivan and Gleeson, and she wrinkled her nose, confirming something wasn't right. She asked about Yuri, but there was nothing much more to tell. The workplace Health and Safety people had been. There was a notice in the basement, past the dry-goods section, saying NO UNAUTHORIZED PERSONNEL. Yuri hadn't been authorized, of course. Such a shame, said Charlie, such a waste of a life. He had to lie to her after that about the launch party, pretending it had been on the day after she got back. He almost came unstuck when she asked about last night's banquet, forgetting the lie he had told, but managed to recover and surprised himself by how easily he could speak about something that had never happened, as though recalling rather than imagining the event. By the time he had finished the memory seemed lodged in his mind.

Charlie was a good listener. The way she listened, the intelligent light in her clear green eyes, invested his words with meaning, with depth. He was lucky to have her. Of this he was sure.

This thing with Lena. He drew on the pipe and coughed.

'Are you really enjoying that?' said Charlie.

He'd given himself a couple of days to get things sorted out, thinking Lena would be gone by then. But the kitchen had nearly been outflanked by a number of large bookings, had only just held the line, and he hadn't managed to get to the bank.

Charlie told him about snorkelling in the Red Sea, the astonishing electric colours of the fish.

This thing with Lena. One point of clarity – it reinforced what he had with Charlie, a perfect fit.

Fazal swooped down with a coffee pot and topped up their cups. 'Let the smokers smoke together,' he said. 'What is wrong with that? If they have to smoke at home, where the wives and children are, how does it make things better? Better leave things be.'

Gabriel nodded, without knowing whether he agreed. Maybe he had needed that: to test his relationship with Charlie, to see how solid it was.

'People can choose,' Fazal continued. 'In this country, you're supposed to choose for yourself. Is this a free country or not?'

Or – wasn't this more like it? – he had been tightly wound and she offered him a release. If someone passes you a plate you take it automatically, before you realize your hand has moved.

There had to be a better explanation. Lena, after all, was no femme fatale. She was too skinny. She was rude and petulant. Last night they'd sat on the sofa for three hours in front of the television and she'd hardly said a word. They were only using each other. But what, really, was he using her for?

'Is the Pimlico site settled?' said Charlie.

'Wrangling over the rent,' said Gabe. He wasn't a monster. He felt something for Lena. More than she felt for him.

When he'd got back from work yesterday, Lena was in the bedroom. She hadn't heard him come in. In a cast of amber lamplight she knelt on the floor beside the contents of a ransacked drawer. Mouth drying, he shrank back in the doorway and watched. Lena bent to her task. She lifted a pair of his boxer shorts, shook and folded them in one neat movement and placed them in the drawer. Then she was rummaging, obviously looking for something, money, jewels, documents, anything she could sell. She held up two socks, discarded one and held up another, measuring them against each other, toe to toe. They matched. The search began again. When everything was back in the drawer, she reached up and pulled out another and tipped the contents out – vests, T-shirts, sweatshirts, all crammed in anyhow. She worked quickly, smoothing and folding and putting away. If she didn't want him to know she'd raided his drawers, why not leave them as they were?

Lena held up a blue sweatshirt. She pressed it against her chest, flicked the sleeves around to the front and, gathering them in one hand, began to stretch them out, pulling harder and harder as though she would like to tear them off. After a few moments she sagged again. Her head drooped to one side. She sat back on her heels and looked across the room at the mirror. Gabriel drew back further though the mirror was angled away from him. Wraith-like she rose from the floor and drifted, not walking but disintegrating, her slender black figure reassembling in front of the looking glass. She was held there, hypnotized, staring, dissolving into the reflection, and then she snapped her shoulders back, filled her tiny chest with air and spat at the mirror. A string of saliva hung from her lip.

He'd crept back to the kitchen then, waited a few minutes and started rattling about. When she came through she was stretching and yawning as if she'd just taken a nap.

'We should make a move,' said Charlie.

'I want you to think about something. I'll need someone for front of house.'

'Me? Is that what you're asking? And give up my promising career?'

Gabe went to the counter to pay the bill and Fazal clucked and fussed about how he should be relaxing in his seat. The other customers sat talking quietly or simply sat as if they might never move again. There was never much time for relaxing, not in Gabe's life, not yet. On a website Gabriel had heard about you could choose an avatar and live a virtual other life. You could pretend to be whatever you wanted to be, get what you wanted, good looks, wealth, women, a fast car. Might as well sit here and puff these magic dragons, dreaming dreams. If you wanted another life you had to stop the dreaming and make a proper plan.

The mansion block, off the Edgware Road, was four storeys of Victorian pomposity painted an inexplicable house-of-horrors red. Charlie's attic flat had sloping ceilings and porthole windows and was decorated with the kind of casual chic that described Charlie so well. Fifties film posters hung above Moroccan leather floor cushions, a Murano glass light fitting over a salvage-yard chair, effortlessly gathered in a pick'n'mix assembly that mysteriously became a unified whole.

Charlie waltzed out of her shoes and into the living room and put some music on. After a couple of bars she changed the CD. Turning to Gabriel, she pulled a face and shook her head. 'No,' she said, 'not this.' She changed the track and then the CD again.

She turned the stereo off.

'I'm not really a musician, am I? Not really a singer. Don't even know what I want to listen to.'

'Know what you really are?' He pulled her to him. 'Bloody gorgeous, that's what you are.'

She kissed him on the lips and then broke free. 'Gorgeous and gagging for a glass of Sauvignon Blanc.'

They settled in the kitchen. He rubbed her instep through her sock and she wiggled her toes.

'I saw a rag-and-bone man. A couple of days ago, Parliament Square.'

'In some sort of parade?'

'No.' The question annoyed him.

'OK,' she said, giving him time.

'That's it. The bus went past.'

'And it made you think of . . . ?'

'I don't know. Nothing. I saw it, that's all. Didn't know they existed any more.'

She switched feet, offering him the other one to massage.

'Sometimes,' she said, 'I just want silence. I want the music to stop. Then I think, but there's something wrong here, music is supposed to be my life.'

'I don't want to eat all the time. I don't always want to cook.'

'You said your mum hated cooking. Is that why you started? You wanted to help her out?'

'Didn't cook at home, hardly ever. I wasn't allowed.'

'Some amazing meal, then, in a restaurant, on holiday?'

'When I turned up at catering college, I'd never tasted a fresh herb. I thought gammon with a pineapple ring was haute cuisine.'

'Oh,' she said, 'it isn't?' She pressed her foot into his groin.

'Hope you're going to finish what you've started here.' He leaned back with his hands behind his head.

'Right,' she said, laughing, 'you hope away.' She got up and went to the fridge and returned with a dish of olives. 'Something turned you on to it, to being a chef.'

'Lured by the glamour, the easy money, easy waitresses . . .'

'No, seriously.'

'Seriously,' said Gabe, 'I'm not sure. In those days you didn't have all the celebrity chefs. It wasn't the thing to do, not really, not at all. But something always appealed to me – you take a piece of dead animal, some plant leaves, some other vegetation and extracts and you change them. You transform them into something else. It's the process. I like the process, the science of it. And then there's seduction, of course. If you can cook you can always get laid.'

'Very funny,' said Charlie. 'You're a funny guy.'

'Oh, you think I'm joking?' said Gabriel.

'Hadn't really started, had it, back then? Chefs on the gossip pages, all the shows, the *channels*, the competitions, the photospreads.'

'But more people cooked back then. Now it's the microwave and ready meals and takeaways. People don't actually cook.'

'They like to watch the shows and buy the books and the magazines. People like to look, they get off on it, there's more and more of that stuff.'

'Food porn,' said Gabriel. 'Right. And they wouldn't last a day in a kitchen, a real kitchen. They wouldn't last a minute, you know.'

'What's it all about then? Why? And who is cooking – the immigrants? Or are they just washing up?'

'Look at the other stuff in magazines, all the beautiful clothes – but then look at people walking around.'

'Who ends up in the kitchen, Gabe?'

'Have we finished that bottle already?' He poured out the dregs. 'Misfits,' he said, 'psychos, migrants, culinary artists, and people who just need a job.'

'Ah. Which one are you?'

'Dad thought I was mad, of course. Or stupid, anyway.'

'Bet he's proud of you now.'

'Charlie,' he said, 'my father . . . When I was a little boy, do you know what he used to test me on?'

She shuffled her chair a little closer and searched his face. Maybe it was the sweater she was wearing, but her eyes seemed greener than ever.

'He'd bring a sample home from the mill and lay it on the kitchen table.'

'Yes,' she said. 'Go on.'

He'd bring a faulty sample home, knock the crumbs off the oilskin cloth with the back of his hand, and lay it on the kitchen table. Gabriel would hazard a guess. 'Weaving over,' he'd say, kneeling up on the chair. 'Double end?'

After work, before he'd been for his bath, you could smell the mill on Dad, a hot metal smell, like he'd just been pressed out of a machine. 'With a double end you'd get a thicker line. This un's got an end drawn wrong. See?' He would trace the fault with an oil-blacked finger, and Gabe would say yes, Dad, thanks, and run upstairs with the cloth and stow it carefully in the box file under his bed.

It must have been his second or third visit to Rileys when Dad led him through the trembling air of the Sulzer sheds to Maureen's domain.

'Maureen's a cloth looker,' said Ted, pulling Gabe up on a stool so he could see what she had on the dressing frame.

'Used to be a proper looker in my time,' said Maureen, winking at Gabriel.

'Showing the lad around,' said Ted.

'Oh aye,' said Maureen, 'why not?' She pointed to a felt board to which a dozen or more pieces of cloth had been nailed. 'These is what I look for. This one here with the loose thread that's weaving over, that's a double end, there's a mis-lift, and that one's where the 'ook's gone down. See that – easy to spot, in't it – weaving without weft where you've just got the thread goin' one way. 'Ave yer had enough? No? Short broken pick, contaminated end, tailing and tufting and give yer three guesses what's up wi' this.'

Gabriel looked up at the overhead pulley that lifted the rolls of fabric, the rubber belts and big metal hooks. He thought he knew the answer but it seemed too easy. Dad never told him there'd be a test. Screwing up his courage he said, 'It's dirty.'

They both laughed but Dad put a hand on the back of his neck and said, 'That's right. There's oil in the warp.'

'You've to put in for the outin' now, Ted, don't forget,' said Maureen. When she wasn't speaking, Maureen's bottom lip covered her top one, like a bulldog. She had to stand at the dressing frame all day, keeping watch, that was probably what made her like that.

'I've put in for the Illuminations,' said Ted. 'How many's goin' this year?'

'No,' said Maureen, 'it's fer the panto, fer t' kiddies. Yer comin' in't yer, Gabe? You and your little Jen?'

★

Charlie, standing with her back to the kitchen counter, dug her hands into her jeans pockets. Her sweater, samphire green, showcased her curves. Once he had said to her she should be on a tailfin, a mascot for our brave boys as they went to 'liberate' whichever godforsaken country they were sent to next. You mean I've got World War Two hips, she said. He knew, by then, that she said these things as a parody of female insecurity and also because she was insecure. He said nothing because, confirm or deny, either way it would be taken as an attempt to patronize.

'Did he want you to follow in the Lightfoot tradition? Did he expect you to go into the mill?'

'No future in it. He said that even then. Thought I should train as some sort of engineer.'

'He knew you liked sciences. At school.'

'My grades were pretty good.'

'Gabe,' she said, curling a piece of hair around a finger, 'I've been thinking. You know, I'm not really getting anywhere. I'm thirty-eight. I might have to do something else.'

'I told you — I need someone. You could manage the place after a while.'

'The family firm?' As she said it she looked self-conscious, as if she had mentioned something inappropriate, something that might make him head for the door.

He should ask her to marry him. Have done with it. It was on his list to do. But how could he ask her now, this instant, with Lena infesting his couch, his bed? 'Charlie,' he said, 'look . . .'

'I was thinking of teacher training,' said Charlie, a little too quickly, too brightly. 'Thought I might look into being a classroom assistant, see if it's going to be my thing.'

'Can't see it myself . . . but if you want.'

'I'm good with kids,' she said, and then hurried on, fearing, it seemed, that she had compounded her mistake. 'And, you know, sometimes you have these moments — that make you think about stuff. So yesterday, I was sitting on the tube, I was only going three stops up to the dentist. One minute I was fine, I was watching this woman eating a bag of crisps. She was reading a book and eating and the crumbs kept gathering on her chest and I was thinking she's going to brush them off now, now, now, but she never did. And the next minute I was, like, what if there's a bomb? It's a thought that pops up and you expect it to pop itself right back down, but this time it didn't. I'm sitting there thinking, what if there's a bomb?

'And I'm only going three stops. So I'm thinking, why didn't I just walk, it would have been so easy. Getting really annoyed with myself. Then it gets worse, I start looking around to see if anyone in the carriage could be the one with the bomb. Looking for dark skin, beards, big coats, and I'm pretty disgusted but I'm doing it, can't kid myself about that.

'Thing is, it's ridiculous. What are the chances? What kind of statistic are we talking about? But it invades us. We've been invaded, not by anyone, just by a nightmare.'

'This is when you thought you'd like to try teaching?' said Gabe. 'Must have had quite a fright.'

She pretended to laugh, a skittish, airhead giggle. 'Yeah. I'll say that in my interview. No, that was a bit later. Actually, right then I had the weirdest mix of big and tiny thoughts. It was like, if I'm going to die right now have I been doing the right things – have I been *living* enough? And then if I live I have to start doing all the right things straight away, choose better, be smarter, know what I really want. Do you know what I decided? Sitting there, terrified by this non-existent bomb? I decided I was going to upgrade my fish oil tablets – go for the more expensive kind, the Omega 3 mix. If I got off the train in one piece I'd go straight to the chemist. Because I always think about it and never do, so it became like this huge, important thing, something worth staying alive for' – she was really laughing now, hair swinging over her face – 'so that was my moment, my epiphany, my blinding light. Some people see God in their moments of crisis, but not me, not people like me – we get consumer insight, that's what we get.'

Gabe stretched his legs and twirled his empty glass. 'Hey, don't knock it. We don't want you ending up as a nun. Did you say there's another bottle somewhere?'

'It's here. I'm opening it.' But she kept her hands in her pockets.

'There's always this stuff hanging over us, isn't there? The way the media is today. We get it all the time. And it's really huge – all the terrible poverty, terrorism, climate change.'

'I suppose. But it's been the same for every generation, there's always something, a big threat. At least we didn't have to live through the war, and then there was the Cold War after that.'

'I don't know. In a funny way I think I'd have preferred it. It was more *collective*, but our things just make us turn in on ourselves.'

'The enemy within,' said Gabe. He'd get a ring, that's what he'd do, though with the money for the restaurant and the money for Lena he'd have to work out how much he could spend.

'Yes,' said Charlie. 'No, not Islamist cells in Birmingham, that's not it. I mean, we don't know who the enemy is, not with any clarity – and we can't be sure it's not us.'

'It's not me. I promise.' All this anxiety. This wasn't the Charlie he knew. And she'd got things back to front. It wasn't bomb fear that gave her single-woman-going-nowhere fear. It was the other way round. Once he'd proposed she'd stop dwelling on this stuff.

'Somewhere in the backs of our minds,' said Charlie, 'there's this nagging doubt – that we're our own worst enemies. What a horrible thought.'

'The war on terror making more terrorists?'

Charlie sighed. 'I suppose. We can always try blaming everyone but ourselves for global warming and third world sweatshops but, you know . . .' She trailed off. She picked up the bottle and the corkscrew. 'It's all bitty and blurry and muddly. You know, in a proper war, or even in the Cold War, there's a really clear enemy and it all makes sense, like a story with a beginning, a middle and an end and you know what you want the end to be, but now we don't have a good story, the plot's all over the place.'

'That's not so bad, is it? You said that film was rubbish because it had too much plot.'

'I did. But I was probably wrong. Anyway,' she said, approaching with the bottle and an exaggerated sashay, 'I had a little moment and it passed. Normal service has resumed.'

'But you're serious about the teaching idea?'

'Me, honey?' She put on her breathy, jazz-set voice. 'Who, me? Can you picture it? Chained to a classroom every day? I like my freedom too much. I like saying yes or no to a gig.'

He ran a bath for her, adding a block of bath salts that he'd carried in his coat pocket all day. When they dissolved they released dried rose buds that floated to the surface, and he said he would come and scrub her back when things in the kitchen were under control. I'll have to go away more often, she said, if this is what I get.

Emptying the shopping bags, Gabriel lined up his ingredients – couscous, garlic, root ginger, coriander, a jar of harissa sauce, a tin of chickpeas, and lamb chops. Dad, he thought, would hate this meal. He'd have the lamb chops, grilled, some boiled potatoes on the side. Gabriel sighed and broke the garlic bulb. It would be a lot less fuss.

Mag's café every Friday lunchtime, dinner as they called it; that was Ted's weekly treat. He took Gabriel once and they had chicken pie with chips and baked beans and steamed jam pudding with custard. It tasted like heaven. They'd been at Rileys and Gabriel must have been sick of going there by then. Maybe not, maybe that came later. There came a time when he refused to go.

Wide-eyed still that day, yes . . . now it was coming back, they had been in the warp room and it blew his little mind. The room was long and low and two, three times the size of the school hall, with three vaults across the ceiling, northern lights, the same as the weaving sheds. He walked slowly up and down the length of the creel, drinking in the rainbow colours of the multitude of spinning cones as though he were visiting the crown jewels. An enormous, elongated spider's web vibrated across the machinery, as the yarn wound on to the drum.

'Lovely when there's a coloured job on.'

'Dad,' said Gabe. 'It's cool!'

'Come up here, by the cylinder. This is Hattersley's latest. Best make in't world is that.'

'How's it work, Dad? What's it do?'

'First things first,' said Ted. 'This beauty's what you call a warp machine. Rileys've took the section warping road, but there's many in this town won't know what a section warper is.'

'Is Rileys' way the best way, Dad?'

'There's some as says so, aye.'

'So the yarn comes through here,' said Gabriel, putting his hand up, 'and then . . .'

Ted pulled him back. 'Watch out. There's fingers been lost before now. Man's been scalped on this machine.'

'Is it dangerous, Dad?'

'Can be,' said Ted. 'In me father's time, yer granddad, the warpers wore ties and this one time he heard a scream and came running.' He bent down, his face level with Gabriel's, and rolled his eyes. 'And there's the warper, got his tie caught, there he is goin' round and round on t' beam.'

They went for a brew in the tacklers' room and Mr Howarth was there, checking the form. 'Pick a number,' he said, 'any number, one to thirty, go on, lad.'

'Twelve?' said Gabriel. He hoped he'd got it right, though there wasn't much to go on and really it didn't seem fair.

Mr Howarth ran his finger down the page in his newspaper. 'Piper Marie, hundred to one, you've picked a blimmin' donkey there.' He raised his voice and called, 'Bill, Bill, give me a number, quick, make it a good 'un.'

In the corner, a pile of clothes stirred and Gabe saw that they contained an old man, his chin resting on his chest. 'What? What? Come again.'

'Number, Bill, for the gee-gees. Be my lucky charm.'

The man's head lifted and Gabriel stared at the geological wonders it revealed, the ridges and crevasses and potholes. 'Bugger off,' said the ancient, 'I'm on a break.'

'Dad,' whispered Gabriel, nudging Ted, 'when's he going to retire?'

'Retired about a century ago,' said Mr Howarth, 'did Belthorne Bill.'

'Why's he still here then?' Gabriel whispered.

'Deaf as a post,' said Mr Howarth. 'Bill, you deaf or what?'

'Aye,' said Belthorne Bill, 'I'll have a cup.'

'Fifty-odd year he worked here,' continued Mr Howarth, folding his paper. 'Can't grudge him a place in the corner and, aye, I'll mek 'im a brew. Take a good look at 'im, son, that's a living legend you got sat there.'

Bill, it turned out, came from over the hill, in Belthorne, a distinguishing mark in Blantwistle when migrants from such distant lands were practically unknown. He walked the seven miles to work and back every day and was famed for his stringent timekeeping and for never having a day off sick. One winter, when the snow had fallen marvellous deep overnight and all the roads were closed and half the mills were sleeping in a hypothermic daze, Belthorne Bill had taken a shovel and cleared a path over the hillside, yard by freezing yard, clocked in with a touch of frostbite and said he was sorry for being late.

'Tell you what,' said Mr Howarth. 'Yer dad and Bill, much alike, very much a pair.'

Gabe looked at Ted. He looked at the crumbling man.

'Don't you know what I'm talking about? Best of British, that's what they are.'

Charlie pressed her body up behind him and wrapped her arms around his waist. The head of garlic was still in his hand.

'Hey, I thought you were going to join me. The water was getting cold.'

He turned round and kissed the top of her head. 'Sorry. Look at me. Useless. I haven't done a thing.'

'Should we get a takeaway?'

'Would you mind?'

'I've got five places on speed dial, how could I mind?'

'I keep thinking about the mill, about Rileys. It's a shopping centre now. Hadn't thought about it in years.'

'Thinking about your father, you're bound to, now that he's . . . you know.'

'God, you smell good,' he said.

She pulled her head away. 'Are you all right, Gabriel? It's so awful about your dad.'

She was wearing a red kimono. The silk felt like a balm. 'I'm all right,' he said, automatically, but as he said it he decided it was true. 'Worried about Dad, of course, but I'm fine.'

'You know I'd like to meet him. If you're not ashamed of me, that is.'

'I know, I know,' said Gabriel, 'but I thought I should see him first on my own. You said it yourself – can't say much on the phone. And I've planned it in already. I'm going up tomorrow on the train.'

CHAPTER TEN

—〰—

BETWEEN EUSTON AND WATFORD, THOUGH THE TRAIN WAS CROWDED, he managed to change seats three times. The first time he was getting away from a malevolent child with swinging feet and an oblivious mother, then there were the mobile phone abusers, and just when Gabe thought he was safe in the 'quiet carriage', the stink of catering food packages unwrapped at his table forced him to beat yet another retreat. He'd found, so he thought, a haven at the end of the train when a woman boarded at Watford and quickly set about colonizing his space. She wore a tweed suit and good strong shoes and had an equally sturdy face. As she talked at him, the clink of fine china in her voice, Gabriel thought you don't see many like her any more. She was empire-building stock, no doubt about it; she was Jam and Jerusalem, God and Golf, Gin Rummy and Croquet Lawn. And she talked and she talked until Gabriel staged an uprising, reaching overhead for his bag and explaining he was getting off at the next stop. 'But that's not for another hour,' said the woman. Gabe nodded and staggered away, the train rolling side-to-side beneath his feet.

He squatted at the end of the next carriage, his back against the luggage rack, and closed his eyes. There was only the thunder of the track. There was only the dark space behind his brow.

When he'd gone back to Kennington in the morning Lena was standing by the long living-room window, leaning against it, as though she wanted to push herself through the glass.

'I've got to go home,' he said, 'just for a couple of days. My father – I told you. I'm sorry, but it's something I've got to do.'

She didn't turn round. The only sign of life was her breath steaming up the pane.

'There's a set of spare keys. Look, I'm leaving them here. But maybe it's best if you stay in.' He didn't know why he said that. Why should she not go out?

Still she made no response.

'Sorry,' said Gabe. 'We'll sort out everything when I'm back. You'll be here, won't you, when I come home. Won't you? You'll be here.'

Lena rolled round so that her back was to the glass. Gabriel felt a touch of vertigo. He wished she would step away.

'Two, three months I hide,' said Lena. 'In cellar, in flat – what is difference to me?'

'Hiding? In the basement with Yuri? What were you hiding from?'

Lena gave a slovenly, lopsided shrug. 'What is difference?'

'You had to hide the fact that you were down there? Or you went down to hide from someone? From what? From who?'

She melted against the glass, her eyelids drawn insolently low.

He reached her in a couple of strides and grabbed her arm, his fingers digging into her flesh. 'Can't you answer me? Answer me. Or get the fuck out of here.'

She rose at him in a rigid fury, veins standing proud on her neck. 'Pimp,' she spat. 'I hide from *pimp*.'

He was still squeezing her arm but he was frozen, and his fingers wouldn't release.

'OK,' said Lena. 'You are happy now?'

His fingers opened and she walked away from him.

'I think . . .' Lena began. She rubbed her arm and looked around. On her pale pinched face a bloom of red flowered across her nose. 'I think . . . I know this man. I think . . . but he is not . . .'

He wanted to go to her but his legs betrayed him. 'What did he do to you?'

Lena rubbed her nose with the back of her hand. She sniffed. 'Took my passport. Beat me.' She punished Gabe with a smile. 'This is all.'

He'd grabbed her arm. He'd hurt her. For pity's sake.

'I run away,' said Lena. 'I hide from him.'

'I'm sorry,' whispered Gabriel.

'Yuri,' said Lena with a defiant jut of the chin, 'help me. Only from goodness of heart.'

'Yes,' said Gabe, 'when you ran away he helped you.' He was edging slowly towards her, ready at any moment to stop.

'Later, few months later.' She settled like a small black cloud on the arm of the sofa.

'How did you meet him?'

'Now you know everything,' said Lena, ignoring the question. 'I am disgusting, yes, you think. I get fuck out of here like you say.'

'No,' said Gabriel. 'No.' He touched his fingers to her shoulder. He waited, to see if she would cast him off. He dropped to his knees and caught hold of her feet and traced the line of each toe inside the black tights. He felt her ankles, her calves and up to her knees, pressing and moulding as if she were clay. When his hands were on her thighs he laid his head on her lap and she began to stroke his hair. He reached up and took her hands and massaged from the tips of her fingernails to the palm and on to the wrist. Tracing small circles, he worked his way up her arms and then rose to tip her gently back on to the sofa where he pressed his lips to hers.

He worked at her with an urgency he had not known before. And yet he felt little desire. In this coupling they would be made new; from this they would draw their strength. He needed this, to wipe the slate, and to brand his indelible mark. Sweat rolled off his brow and into his eyes. It made them sting. He buried himself. He needed this. To engrave himself so deeply that the others would be erased.

He'd had to catch a later train because for a couple of hours he'd tried to keep her talking, gathering up her broken sentences, her scattered words and thoughts, piecing them together, making sense out of the senselessness, creating a coherence that wasn't there in the telling.

The flat in which she had been kept was in Kilburn, the eleventh floor of a tower block that reminded her of her home town. There were bars on the windows, she told him. You can't jump out of an eleventh-floor window, he said. 'Tchh,' she said, 'you can.' After a couple of weeks Boris brought another girl who had an iron mark on her arm. He put them to work first in a Golders Green sauna and then in a walk-up brothel in Soho. The men, she said, were mostly OK. They didn't beat her. That was Boris's job. No, said Gabe, these men (he wanted another word, one that did not include him) are not OK. Husbands, fathers, sons, she said. Men. There was one who was different, a very bad person, but she did not want to talk about him. She had been with him on the day she ran away from the Soho walk-up, Boris hadn't locked the door, he was getting lazy because he thought she was completely broken by then, thought she would never run.

For a few days she slept out. She didn't know exactly where, except it was close to the river. She met a girl, a Ukrainian, who took her home and got her a job at a café. It was hard, she said, standing up all day when you're used to working on your back.

One day she saw Boris walk past the café and she didn't even get her coat, straight out of the back door and never went there again. The Ukrainian girl knew Yuri and Yuri knew the perfect place. Living underground was OK once you got used to it though one time she had woken with a rat curled on the pillow and she had screamed and screamed.

You've got to go to the police, said Gabriel. They'll lock this Boris up and throw away the key. Maybe, said Lena. But I will be dead by then. Boris will kill me first.

Gabriel mined the depths of his coat pocket for his mobile phone. If he called Jenny she'd pick him up at the station. He needed to talk to someone, even if it was only Jen. She wouldn't judge him. He didn't think so, but then he didn't really know her now.

That panto trip, Dad put in for it and Gabe went with Jenny and Mum came as well to help shepherd the kids around. *Aladdin*, it was, at the Manchester Apollo but he couldn't remember a thing about it except the coach journey. They'd had their photo taken before they boarded and then all the children were pushing and shoving because everyone wanted to sit at the back. Gabe got a back seat next to Michael Harrison and he saved a seat for Jenny, she was wearing her white fur hat with the pompom ties that she twisted on top of her head like bunny ears and she kept it on all the way. They had a Wagon Wheel each and a drink of Vimto. Mum had packed extra for Michael because she knew his mum would forget. The other mothers crammed the front seats while Mum, on brilliant form, walked up and down the aisle, giving out sweets and getting the kids to sing. She had brown platform boots on, and a white coat that swung open and closed over her skirt. Gabe could tell by the way some of the other mums looked at her they were jealous, and Mum must have known as well because after a while she went and sat by the driver and talked to him, keeping herself out of the way.

There was one Pakistani kid on the coach. They didn't come to the socials, the football, the Christmas parties, though they'd come to the cricket and bring their own food. He was a bit of a runt, this kid, hair in all directions like a turnip top, shorts sliding off his arse, but he was tolerated because he'd do anything for a dare. Word spread round the back half of the coach faster than you could say 'impetigo' – the Paki kid was going to do something and everyone wanted to see. Gabe pushed his way through and pulled Jenny with him, the two of them pressed against prickly upholstery, peering over as the kid knelt on his chair and dropped his pants and, without a moment's hesitation, inserted a pencil up his prick. 'Fuckin' ace,' said Michael. Swearing was a religion with him. 'Fuck panto. Bet Aladdin can't do that.'

It was always the best bit, the coach journey. The windows never opened, they sweated in their coats, flicked snotballs at each other and ate their snacks. Their hands had a wet-dog smell after they'd wiped them on the seats. But they were the Rileys kids, going somewhere, on a treat. The air was thin on oxygen but thick with excitement that began to dilute as soon as they went down the steps. Michael's dad had got the sack from Rileys, worked a few days at the foundry when he was sober enough to stand, but the other parents must've chipped in for Michael, the little poppet, still one of us then, still one of the tribe.

Yes, they could never live up to their billing, those days out, always went downhill because they started out as perfection and that could never be matched. There was a row at home that night, a big one, and Gabe and Jenny sat hand in hand on the stairs. 'What they yellin' about?' said Jenny. 'You're too little to know,' said Gabriel, who had no idea. 'You're too little to understand.' Jenny pushed the tip of her nose up, splaying her nostrils. 'Pig,' she said, 'pig, pig, pig.' They thought they heard someone coming and scrambled up and back to their beds. Gabe decided he would creep down without Jenny who always made too much noise and gave them away. He'd have to wait for a while until she was asleep but then he must have drifted off. When he woke, there was Mum sitting by him, saying, 'I didn't wake you, did I?'

'No,' said Gabe, 'what's time?'

'I want to show you something. Here's your dressing gown.'

They went through the back garden, the frosted grass crunching beneath their feet, and climbed over the fence into the field. They were on a different planet. A few dim lights glowed in the valley and dark life forms stirred up ahead.

'Not scared are you?' said Mum. 'It's only the cows.'

'I know,' said Gabriel, shivering. Mum was in her skirt and blouse, but didn't seem to feel the cold.

'I was out here,' said Mum, standing behind him and holding his shoulders, 'and I saw a shooting star. There's going to be another one, I just know there is, any second now. Thought Gabe would love to see that. He's never seen one before.'

The cold had his feet in pincers. His slippers weren't up to much. 'Where we looking, Mum? Which side will it be?'

'Up. Just look up, you'll see it. It was lovely, the one I saw. You can wish on them, know that? Make a wish on a shooting star.' She let him go and moved off, walking deeper into the field. He could hear her singing softly. Catch a falling star.

'Mum,' he said. 'Mum.'

'Imagine putting a star in your pocket!' she called back to him.

He could barely see her now. 'Mum.'

'Isn't that wonderful? Isn't that beautiful? Oh, Gabe, look! Look up. Up, up, right over your head.'

Gabriel tilted his head as far back as it would go. 'What? Where? Where?'

'Quick, quick, you'll miss it.'

Gabe pushed back until he thought his neck would snap. His jaw hung open and steam poured from his mouth. He twisted left and right.

'There. Up there,' called Mum.

All the stars seemed to go off like flashbulbs, making his eyes water at the corners, but none was actually moving. Which was the one? How bright the sky was now, when a moment ago the stars were only pinpricks in the black. He swung round, he stepped back, he swung round again and the ground was treacherous; he slid right off his feet and landed on his bum.

Mum stamped her platform boots and hooted. 'Oh, Gabe,' she said, shaking with laughter, 'look at you, sat in a cowpat. What *are* you like?'

She made two cups of cocoa when he'd washed and got fresh pyjamas on. 'After all that,' she said, 'I think it was only a plane.'

'What about you?' he said. She'd set their cups in the sink and told him to get himself up them stairs. The kitchen clock said half past four.

She lit a cigarette and stood with her ankles crossed, like a picture in a magazine. 'I'm not sleepy. I've got loads to do and it's easier when I've got you all out from under my feet.'

He changed trains at Manchester without calling his sister and sat numbly looking at the floor. As he stepped on to the station platform, beneath the canopy of glass and green iron girders, it began to rain. At once the weight was on him, slumping his shoulders. In Blantwistle, it seemed, he lived in a state of suspended animation, in constant oscillation between unbearable tension and annihilating lethargy. It was the agony of familiarity, the awful inevitability of home.

His phone began to ring inside his pocket. He snatched it up as if he had been offered a lifeline.

It was Lena. 'Hear that,' he said. 'That's how it rains up here.'

'I want to ask —' said Lena. 'You can do something for me?'

'I have to see my father. It may be the last time.'

'If you can do this thing. Please.'

He wanted to tell her, don't worry. He wanted to say, I'll take care of you. Could he say those things, did he mean them? What would they mean to her? The connection was poor, her voice flickered, he pressed the phone to his ear. It wasn't raining. That was sleet pounding on the roof above. An announcement on the loudspeaker, Lena's broken voice, a boy running past, sorry, mate. He was at the station entrance and in a moment he'd have to go out and get wet. He told her that he would help her. She couldn't hear him. He told her again. The signal was weak. Repeat for me, she said.

'Yes,' Gabriel shouted. 'I'll do it. Of course I'll do that for you.'

CHAPTER ELEVEN

—◊—

NANA, IN THE FRONT PORCH, CLUNG TO THE FROSTED-GLASS DOOR like a shipwreck, sleetwater bogging her slippers.

'You'll never guess,' she called up the garden path. 'Go on,' she urged, tottering off the step and clutching the window ledge. 'Have a guess. You'll never guess what's happened.'

Gabriel kissed her and took her arm. 'Hello, Nana. Let's get out of the wet.'

'Gladys died,' trilled Nana, unable to contain herself any longer. 'It's Gladys. Fit as a fiddle, me, she'd say. Well, that's how she was. Loved to blow her own trumpet, that one.'

'I'll just take my shoes off and leave them in the porch. Can you manage? Grab on to that door handle there.'

'Last week it was,' said Nana. 'Or do I mean last month? Poor Gladys.' She sagged. Her top lip, her honest-to-God moustache, began to twitch.

'Gladys. I'm not sure I know—'

'Gladys,' cried Nana. 'You know. You *do*. *Gladys*.'

'Ah,' said Gabe, to calm her. 'Oh. If you hold on to me now and I get the door . . .' He manoeuvred them into the hall.

Ted, planted firm in the kitchen doorway, nodded at Gabe. 'Kettle's on,' he said.

They sat in the lounge in the strange, brief afterglow of the storm, the UFO light in the sky. Nana, deeply entrenched in the wingback chair with her feet up on a stool, sucked on a tea-soaked Hobnob with both eyes firmly closed. Ted cracked his knuckles and laced his fingers together on his lap. The teapot, the good blue one, stood on the coffee table with the milk jug and biscuit tin. The carriage clock ticked on the mantelpiece, the Victorian lady in the framed print peeped from under her parasol. The leaves of the rubber plant were covered in dust.

'Nice send-off,' said Ted. 'Gladys – Mrs Haddock – you remember her, Gabe.'

Mrs Haddock, of course he remembered her. Nana's old sparring partner, her best friend and enemy rolled into one.

'Never the same after they stuck her in that home,' Ted continued, 'but they saw her right in the end. Lovely bash, eh, Nana? Fine spread for Gladys, eh?'

Nana swallowed her biscuit and dabbed her eye with a piece of kitchen roll. 'Cradle to grave, me and Gladys. There's not many friends as can say that. Come over closer, Gabriel, my eyes are not what they were. Gone and left me, she has. Mind you, I'll not be long behind.'

Gabe patted Nana's hand. Ted rolled his eyes and said, 'Have another biscuit. Go on.'

'Well,' said Nana, seized by a sudden coquettishness, 'there's nobody watching my figure now.' She had, over the last decade, grown a barrel chest on which her chin could comfortably rest for a snooze. Gabriel handed her the biscuit tin.

The clock said quarter past four. Maybe it had stopped. Had it really been only twenty minutes since he'd arrived?

'Mahogany,' said Nana. 'With brass handles. *What* do you make of that?'

'Nana,' said Ted. 'Come on, now.'

'Fancy,' said Nana. 'What a waste.'

Gabriel looked at Ted, who shrugged. 'Coffin,' he explained. He stood up and switched on the lamps. Gabe looked at the way his trousers hung from the waist, nothing filling the seat.

'Your programme's on soon, Nana. I'll pull the curtains to.'

They had the gas fire on and the television with the sound turned low while they waited for the programme to begin. Nana closed her eyes. Gabriel struggled to keep his open. The hiss of the fire, the babble of voices, the blanketing heat. This house was never the way he remembered it. The ceilings were too low. Everything had a cardboard feel. When they'd moved in it felt like a palace; it felt like an overgrown Wendy house now. All the colours were faded, the sofa covers had slipped from maroon to dusty brown, the walls from cheery yellow to a life-sapping shade of cream. The whole place was heartbreakingly tidy, as if nothing much ever happened, which probably it never did.

Gabriel tried to formulate a question for Ted. He wanted to ask in a way that would get Ted to open up. 'How are you?' was all he could think of.

'Can't complain.' He was thinner, definitely thinner, but he was strong and straight. His face perhaps was pulled a little tighter across the steely cut of his nose, and at the edges of his no-nonsense mouth, but you could still read his character there.

Shaking off his irritation, Gabriel tried again. 'You've lost some weight.'

'Aye,' said Ted. 'Part of the process.' His shirt, Gabe noticed, was frayed at the collar and there was a stain on his sweater sleeve.

'Dad,' said Gabe.

Ted shuffled his feet. 'I'm not doing so bad. Bit tired. It don't take you too bad 'til the end.'

'What did the doctor . . .'

'Nana's took it hard. When she remembers, that is.'

'Her memory's going?' Gabriel looked at Nana, a strand of drool on her lip, the sheet of kitchen roll tucked into the neck of her blouse. Her hair, short grey wisps, stood up on either side of her head, making her look vaguely shocked or lightly electrocuted, sprawled across stool and chair.

'Comes and goes,' said Ted. 'Still finding new ways to drive me mad. How's work?'

'I'll be leaving soon,' said Gabe. He leaned forward. 'Dad, I'm setting up my own place.'

Ted snorted. 'Leaving? You've only been there five minutes.'

'Five months. Six. But it was never meant to be for long.' Gabriel sighed. There was no point arguing now.

'Your own place,' said Ted. 'Good for you. That's grand, it really is.'

'Have I missed it?' said Nana, waking. 'Turn it up. Ted, are you having a sherry? Because I'll have a small one myself.' She slid her feet off the stool and levered herself a little more upright.

'That's right, Phyllis,' said Ted, winking at Gabriel, 'I've been at your sherry again.'

Gabe got up and loaded the tea tray. 'I'll get it, Nana. Dad, any beers in the fridge?'

When he returned they were watching the television, one of those chat-cum-freak shows, where the host talked about 'healing' and hoped one of the guests would throw a punch.

'Can't cope,' said Ted, 'that's all you hear on this show. He can't cope. She can't cope.'

'Shush,' said Nana. 'Six kids, this one's got by, what is it, seven different fathers? In't it shocking, Gabe?'

Gabriel laughed as he poured her sherry. 'I demand a recount,' he said.

Ted smoothed the arms of his chair, that old familiar gesture. 'In my day,' he said, 'that's what we did. We coped. That's what we had to do.'

Nana, on her third sherry, grew sufficiently animated to sit up straight in her chair. The loose, soft skin of her face trembled with words that sought to escape while her mouth prepared itself slowly for action, warming up with a few mouldings and partings of the lips. Gabe studied her closely, trying to remember how she used to look when he was a boy. The years, it seemed, had robbed her of the singular, all her features melting into a generality of old age. No matter how hard he looked, he couldn't really see her, just the lines and folds and wrinkles, a second caul at the other end of life.

'Listen to this, Gabriel,' she said finally. 'It's Edith who told me and you can't say truer than that. Happened to a neighbour of hers. Well, she lives down the beaches, doesn't she, been there since . . . well, you're going back a long time now.' Nana hesitated, floundering for a moment. She plunged on. 'Anyway, this chap's sat there of an evening, in bed, minding his own, when he hears a noise. From up there,' said Nana, pointing to the ceiling with a finger turned querulous by arthritis and an incipient sense of outrage. 'That's queer, he thinks. Sounds like there's a rat got into the attic. A big one.'

'Nana,' said Gabriel, beginning to suspect where this might be going.

'Prince Street, it was,' said Nana, dabbing her left eye, which appeared to suffer some continual low-grade seepage. 'Down the beaches, you remember, Gabe.'

'The beaches, course I do, Nana. Where I learned to ride my bike, remember. Only the other side of the main road from Astley Street. But we're talking about thirty-odd years ago now, aren't we, Nana? We're not talking about today.' 'The beaches' was a stretch of concrete with a mouldering fountain and a bench that lay between the terraces of the old town, where a German bomb had cracked the rows apart. Gabe, in the days when the earth's circumference could be described in the swing of a conker, had spent many an hour there, perfecting the art of mooching about.

Nana leaned so far forward Gabe feared she would topple out of the chair. 'That's queer, he thinks, this chap.' Nana's features might have blurred with time, but her voice was distinct enough. It moved up a register and she began to enunciate more carefully, the better to articulate her disgust. 'So he goes to fetch a stepladder and he climbs up to the loft. He gets the trapdoor open and he's got a torch with him, of course . . .'

Gabriel knew what she was going to say and fervently wished that she wouldn't. He looked at Ted, sitting with his hands on the sides of the chair, the snub of the left little finger, its final joint missing, pressing into the fabric.

'Well, you'll never guess what he saw,' said Nana. She clamped her lips together.

'Oh,' said Gabe, 'I think I will.'

'The whole attic,' said Nana, in an ecstasy of indignation, 'was full of Pakistans.'

'No, Nana, not this . . .'

'Yes, oh, yes. Got their mattresses and whatnot, and there they all are in a line, sleeping between their shifts, and there's others what come and take their places when this lot go off t' the mill. The chap got right to the bottom of it, you see, and you know the way all the attics in them terraces are joined, well there's Pakistans all down the row, right to the end of the street. Bartlett Street, it was. June told me all about it because this chap's a neighbour and she said to me, Phyllis, what is the world coming to, and I said, June, I just don't know any more, I really don't.'

Nana sat back and dabbed at her eye.

'Nana,' said Gabriel, 'have you heard the phrase "urban myth"?' He must have been nine or ten years old when he first heard that story.

'Best leave it, Gabe,' said Ted. 'Clock's broken, if you know what I mean. A bit confused, now and then.'

'Who's confused?' snapped Nana. 'And I'm not deaf, neither.'

Ted smiled. 'Still the full shilling, that's right. What was it Albert used to say? If our Phyllis was any sharper she'd cut herself. Isn't that the truth?'

Nana's mouth puckered and twitched. 'Eee,' she said in a long, whistling sigh. 'It's been a good life. That much I can say. When I married Bert, seventeen years old, that's all, and he was twenty-one, and we'd never a cross word,' said Nana, her voice and face aflutter with emotion. 'Not in all those years.'

'Never a cross word,' said Ted. 'That's right, Phyllis, that's right.'

Gabriel stood in the kitchen peeling potatoes. Nana wanted egg and chips for her tea. The kitchen, at the back of the house, used to look out to the field but now looked over a housing estate, in which all the houses were 'individual' (to increase the price at which they could be marketed) but basically identical, sharing an architectural style – a Tudorbethan mishmash of stone cladding and fake timbering – that found favour with the upwardly mobile.

Gabriel drew the curtains. The peeler was blunt. He put it down and took a kitchen knife from the drawer. It was blunt as well. He ran his hand along the spice rack that was fixed to the wall, a rickety affair that trapped tall narrow bottles of ancient cumin, paprika and chilli. Mum had bought it long ago. Gabe doubted it had ever been used. The tiles by the sink needed regrouting, all the cupboard handles seemed to be loose, and only two of the spotlights were working, two stabs of unforgiving light over the general shabbiness of it all. But the kitchen was spick and span. The surfaces wiped clean.

Why did the walls close in so quickly? How had the place shrunk so?

He set the chip pan on the stove and lit the ring. He sliced the potatoes, dried them on kitchen towel and loaded them into the basket. If Charlie were here she'd stave it off, this sense of decay, just with a flick of her hair. Her perfume would mask the smell of death. He needed her; he'd thought it before and he knew it now. The test chip sizzled and somersaulted in the hot fat. Gabriel lowered the basket in. What he had to do was tell Charlie about Lena. Not that he'd slept with her, of course, but the rest of it. The sex had to stop. Now that he knew. He had to protect her now.

It would be a little awkward to tell Charlie. *I've got this girl staying at my flat.* But he could fudge it, blur the timeline and once Charlie knew what Lena had been through that would be all she was interested in.

'My brother is in London,' Lena had said. 'Please. Help me find.'

'Of course I'll do that for you.' Why did he promise that? Where would he begin?

This morning she had put on his shirt to cover herself and left him on the sofa while she curled up on a corner of the chaise longue. She told him all that had happened without looking at him, her unseeing gaze directed to the centre of the room. The gypsy woman in Mazyr, she said, that bitch. Probably she was still doing it, may she burn in hell. Boris was the man, yes, the tall and dark and handsome man, with the mark here, on his neck. He came for her, just like the tea leaves said, and he was the one. She was supposed to go to Italy, to look after old people, that's where he said he was taking her, but he took her to a different place. It was a new life, OK, the gypsy bitch did not lie about that.

He watched her knot her fingers together. Her knees were gathered to her chest. When he only imagined her she seemed so real. But when he was with her she seemed to fade. She was so pale it compromised her existence, as if you could put out a hand and sweep it clean through her body, as if she were merely a trick of the light.

Lena, thought Gabriel, the word running through him like a shiver.

'Getting on all right?' Ted was at his shoulder.

'Just taking these out for a bit, then I'll put them back in to crisp up.'

'I'll set the table,' said Ted, opening the cutlery drawer. His clothes, dark brown trousers, beige V-neck and checked shirt, were the same off-duty uniform that he'd worn for as long as Gabe could remember, a kind of standing protest against change that had continued down the decades.

Gabe found a frying pan. He took the eggs from the fridge. He wished he could be himself with his father, talk to him naturally, the two of them shooting the breeze. Whatever had gone before, though they had never been close, though the common ground on which they could stand was small and parched, he wanted to speak to his father before the time was gone. He wanted to set aside the irritation that arose so easily in Ted's presence, but it seemed to exist in a part of him that was impossible to reach, like an itch in a phantom limb.

'Nana and Granddad never had a cross word,' said Gabe. 'Is that right?'

'That's right,' said Ted. 'And I'm the Queen of Sheba. No, they got on all right but they'd their share of troubles, just like the next couple.'

'Dad, do you think Nana's going a bit, you know . . .'

'Oh aye, she is a bit. Tells anyone who'll listen her Albert was an accountant. Well, you know, he did a bit of bookkeeping, and he wore a tie to work.' Ted laughed and then started coughing. He stood breathless for a while and Gabriel saw that he was leaning on the chairback for support. 'Mind you,' he went on, 'she said that before. And she believes it now, of course.'

'I used to think Nana was posh,' said Gabe. 'She had me fooled.'

'Had herself fooled n'all,' said Ted. He went to the sink and filled the water jug. He set it down. 'Used to bug me. But now I think . . . I don't know. What's the truth of anything, anyway? Nana says she'd never a cross word with Albert. Seems like that to her and it makes her happy. Makes sense to her. You follow? What really happened, it don't make a whole lot of difference, not to Nana. The way she remembers it – now, that makes all t'difference in the world. You know? You know what I mean?'

'Yeah,' said Gabriel. 'Sort of.' His father looked him in the eye. This was, Gabe sensed, an opportunity. This speech, with its hesitations and uncertainties, its vague and – frankly – shaky idea, its appeal, finally, for understanding, was an opening. It was not the kind of speech his father usually made. The spotlight shone on Ted's bald head, the scalp tight and red. A small band of hair, fully white, remained above the ears. When he was a boy – Gabe had seen the photos – he wore it long enough on top to let it curl, but by the time Gabe was born he had it short and under the strictest control.

'Them chips going back in?' said Ted.

'I was trying to remember,' said Gabriel, 'how you lost the top of your finger. I know it was at the mill.'

'Before you come along,' said Ted. 'Little mishap in the weaving shed.'

Gabriel looked down at his own hands, the old burn marks and scars, the calluses, the blackened nail, the lump on the index finger of his knife hand, the duck's-foot webbing between the first and second finger of his left where a third-degree burn had fissured the skin and healed all wrong. When he was a kid he used to look at his father's hands. Ted's hands held an entire world, of work, of manliness, and now Gabe wanted to hold his own aloft for inspection because Dad had never realized that his son had worker's hands.

'How many eggs?' said Gabriel. 'Two each?'

'I've not much of an appetite, truth be known.'

'You have to eat.' He'd missed the opening, he knew, and now they would struggle on in the usual way.

'I'll just sit down a minute before I fetch Nana.'

'Dad,' said Gabriel, 'how will you manage?'

'I'm all right. Just having a moment here, son.'

'But, I mean, you and Nana, how do you . . . how will you . . .'

'A right pair. I know.' Ted swept some imaginary crumbs from the table. 'We've a home help comes in the mornings. Jenny does what she can. Nana's on medication now she's been diagnosed. And the nurse comes to see to me from the . . . what's-it-called.'

'Hospital.'

'Hospice.'

'Right,' said Gabe. He wanted to put on his coat and walk out of the door. This business of dying was not his business. It could continue just as well without him. 'What's Nana been diagnosed with?'

'Dementia,' said Ted. 'They used to say so-and-so's gone senile, but they say so-and-so's got dementia now.'

'Can they treat it? What can they do?'

Ted shook his head. 'Not much really. She's on some tablets, might slow it down a bit. There's good days and bad. Got her on a good day today.'

'That story she told,' said Gabriel, 'about the Pakistanis in the loft. Funny how you can lose your memory but not your prejudices.'

'She misses the old days, is all.'

Gabe emptied the chips into a bowl he had lined with paper towel. He wasn't going to argue with Ted, but he couldn't let this simply go by. 'The old days when you could start a joke with "an Englishman, an Irishman and a Paki walked into a pub". That what you mean?'

'Don't,' said Ted, 'be so bloody daft.'

'The days when we had the good old National Front and swastikas sprayed on every railway bridge and underpass?'

'That's not what we're talking about,' said Ted. 'We're talking about how it was, when people round here cared about each other. When you knew everyone in the street and they knew you. Not that that means anything to you.'

'You're changing the subject.'

'This *is* the subject, but you don't want to know. You dismiss all that. But there was a community – aye, turn yer nose up, that's right – a community here and that's been lost.'

'It's not even the subject.' Gabe slammed the frying pan on to the flame.

'It is the subject,' said Ted, 'because this town is dying, Gabriel. There's no cure for it now.'

'What's the disease, Dad? Foreigners? Progress? What?' Gabriel was close to shouting. He ripped back the curtains. 'And, anyway, look – look out there, the new estate,' he looked himself but saw only his own image peering menacingly from the dark, 'doesn't look like death to me.'

'You understand nothing, son.' Ted lifted his hand, as though to knock Gabriel's words away. 'Houses are only houses. Them houses could be anywhere, they could be on bloody Mars.

But this town's had the heart ripped out of it, I tell you that for free.'

'For God's sake.' Gabriel began cracking eggs into the pan. 'A lot of old people are racist, I wasn't blaming Nana . . .'

He was interrupted by the unmistakable squeal and rattle of the drinks trolley that heralded Nana's arrival. It had long served as her Zimmer frame and long ago been cleared of booze but Nana had brought her precious bottle of Harvey's amontillado with her to the kitchen and when she came to a stop by the table the bottle slid forward and Gabriel dived to catch it, landing badly on his shoulder as the green glass shattered and the amber liquid rolled down the linoleum to form a puddle at his ear.

The eggs were burnt underneath. Gabriel put down his knife and fork and picked up a chip with his fingers. He dipped it in the ketchup.

Nana said, 'Honest British food. Nothing to beat it, is there?'

'Careful,' said Ted, 'you'll have our Gabe accusing you of racism in a minute.'

Gabriel felt his face contort even as Nana smiled up at him. He was furious with his father and he was furious with himself for being so angry, and he was furious most of all that his father was not the raging giant of Gabriel's childhood but this gaunt and sick old man at whom it was implausible to direct all this rage.

'I have never,' said Nana, waving her fork perilously close to Gabriel's cheek, 'been a racialist.'

Gabe kept quiet.

'What I don't understand is,' said Nana, 'why do they make such a fuss? The Pakistans, the Asians, or what have you – always on about something, aren't they, complaining about this and that. There was this lass in the paper, Gabriel, only t'other day, she wants to wear the veil to school. Well, I mean. This is England. If they want things exactly like home they can bloomin' well go there, can't they? There's no use try-ing to make it like home, is there, because they didn't like it at home and that's why they've left and come here.'

'They came for the work, Nana,' said Ted.

'That's right,' said Nana, 'I tell you what disgusts me. When people say it's all about colour, well that's just nonsense, because I've nothing against any colour, black, white or brown. It's what you do that's important. You do right by me and I do right by you, isn't that the way?'

Gabriel scraped and stacked the plates. Ted and Nana were what they were. What did he expect from them? 'Glad we've got that straight, Nana,' he said.

Nana beamed at him. 'It's lovely to see you, Gabriel,' she said. 'It's such a treat.'

After tea they continued to sit at the table and Mr Howarth came round and sat with them.

'Gabe's opening a new restaurant,' said Ted.

'Are yer, Gabe?' said Mr Howarth, blowing on his mug of Ovaltine. 'Something fancy is it, down south?'

'Now,' said Nana, 'I've to go and get changed else I'll be late. And I'm expected at . . . oh, where is it again?'

'That's tomorrow night, Nana,' said Ted. 'You sit yourself back down.'

'He says that every night,' said Nana. 'Don't know what kind of fool he takes me for.'

'What kind of restaurant is it, Gabe?' said Ted. 'Has it got a name?'

'I might just call it Lightfoot's. What do you think of that?'

'I think,' said Ted slowly, 'that's not such a bad idea.'

'What I don't understand,' said Nana, 'is why they always make such a fuss.'

'Who?' said Mr Howarth. 'These chefs?'

'The Pakistans, the whatyercallums, Muslims, is it now?'

'I don't bother with the horses any more,' said Mr Howarth. 'I take bets on your nana now, Gabe. Never know which way she's going to go.'

'There's this girl in the paper, only t'other day, she wants to wear the veil to school. Well, I mean. She's forgot what country she's in.'

'Ah,' said Mr Howarth. 'But it's not their fault, the way I see it. Can't blame them for asking. Human nature to ask for what you want. It's the council, that's what it is. Bunch of right rollickin' idiots, and I only put it that way due to the lady present. So far up their own backsides with this – what's that word? – "multiculturalism", they've got no common sense.

'I give you an example. I was down Tesco's yesterday, and you know Sally Whittaker, she was on the till and she's a right lovely girl, and I says to her, how's your mum? And she says to me, me mum's all right, Mr Howarth, but she's a bit upset at the moment because they're stopping the library van and she can't get out, you know, the way she is. Spending cuts is it, Sally, I says. She says, do you know what they spend their money on, Mr Howarth, I went in there meself and talked to the librarian and she wasn't happy about it at all. Every leaflet they do they've got to translate it into fourteen different languages. That's a hell of a lot of money is that. And they buy these books by Muslim preachers what are in prison some of them, what say you should take up arms against the infidel, that's meaning you and me, and they make a nice little display with them. It's a multicultural society, says Sally, I don't disagree with that. But what about me mum, she says, who's paid her taxes all her life and she can't get her historical romances what don't do no one any harm. Who's going to stand up for her?'

The great thing about London, thought Gabe, was that everyone was just a Londoner. The city bound everyone together or kept them all equally apart. Or maybe it didn't but at least everyone was too busy to give much thought to it. 'That does sound unfair,' he said.

Nana was nodding like a puppet with a broken spring. 'Yes, oh yes,' she said, 'I've had a wonderful life. Wonderful, wonderful, it's been a wonderful life.' Both her eyes were leaking and her chest began to heave.

Ted scraped his chair back. He went to stand behind Nana and patted her shoulder. 'You're all right, Phyllis. You're all right. Good night's sleep and you'll be right as rain.'

He helped her to her feet and guided her to the trolley, a tender shuffling dance across the kitchen floor.

The moment seemed to Gabriel unbearably intimate and he had to look away. He stared at the table. The pale pine looked soft as sawdust but it had proved itself tough enough over the years to bear the weight of this family, absorb all that activity, history, into the grain. The kitchen was where they ate, the dining room being a mausoleum of china, glass and candlesticks. They used to mix scones at this table, Mum laid out her dress patterns here, they cleared a corner for home-work, spilled glue and glitter and Tizer and argued about who should clear up. He used to kick Jenny's shins under this table and she couldn't quite reach across to pinch his arm. This table had heard all the arguments, seen all the fights, given loyal service, and would one day, not too far from now, end up being tossed in a skip.

The back door opened and a fat, beaming blonde woman stepped inside and threw up her arms as if she were at the top of a roller-coaster ride. 'You're here,' she shrieked.

'Jenny?' said Gabriel.

'All right, Jen,' said Mr Howarth. 'Good job you've arrived. Think your brother's had enough of us old folk by now.'

Jenny sat down. 'Well,' she said, 'what do you think?' She touched her hair.

'Very . . . um, nice,' said Gabe. He had thought it was a wig, a platinum bob that licked up the sides of her face.

'And I've lost a few pounds. Not that you'd ever notice, right.'

'I was just thinking you had,' said Gabe.

'Get away,' said Jenny happily. 'I'll go and pop my head round the door to Nana. And then I'm taking you out for a drink.'

The night sky above the moors was the colour of an old bruise. The land trailed from light-refracted milkiness away to folds of black. Jenny dipped the headlights as they passed another car. They used to walk this way sometimes, the best part of an hour, up to the Last Drop Inn when they were sufficiently hungover to want the fresh air and not so hungover they couldn't face a pint at the other end.

'I'm sorry about Harley and Bailey,' said Jenny. 'If I've told them once, I've told them a thousand times it was today but do they listen . . .'

Jenny had overhauled her entire look and ditched the velour track-suits. Gabe glanced at the way her boots cut into the top of her calves, the broad, round knees that emerged from the hem of her skirt. 'Sorry,' he said, 'what's that?'

'They'll come round and see you tomorrow,' said Jenny. 'They've only the one uncle after all and mind you you've only the one niece and nephew and oh, but Bailey's a one, she is . . . But I need a drink in front of me first and then I'll tell you, a drink and a fag

173

and a good natter, that's me, well that's all of us really I suppose.'

The car smelt of cigarettes and the Magic Tree air freshener that dangled from the rear-view mirror. Gabe cracked the window a little.

'Well, if we're having the windows down I'll have a quick one now,' said Jenny, reaching for the Silk Cuts on the dash. When she pulled on the cigarette it was with such measured intensity that she was transformed, as if the nervous chatter would never return.

Every time he saw her he knew her less. The years didn't add up, they only took away. He watched as she blew streams of smoke out of the window that sailed back, sure enough, as clouds. Her hair was truly extraordinary. There was something violent in it, though whether turned in or outwards was difficult to say.

She saw him looking and said, 'I've wanted to try it this way for ages but Den always said he hated bottle blondes. So now I've got my freedom . . .' She touched her hair. 'Again!'

Gabriel wondered if he'd ever met this Den. Jenny always seemed to have someone new.

'I know you liked Den and he was quite a fan of yours too but what will be will be. To tell the truth we weren't suited and he could be a bugger he really could but he was all right, I mean we had our moments and it's company isn't it at the end of the day . . .'

Jenny talked on as she parked the car. Gabriel had no clear idea of what it was that she was trying to say about this Den and neither, he suspected, did Jen.

The pub had remained unchanged, pretty much, over the years and so lacked the 'traditional' feel of the pubs that had been revamped with old church chairs and agricultural tat. At the Last Drop Inn the seats were upholstered in fake leather that had long ago cracked and split and laddered many a pair of tights and even sliced a finger or two. There was carpet on the floor. There was a slot machine covering the fireplace.

'Getting done up next year,' said Jenny. 'About time. Needs it, don't you think?'

On their way through to the snug (a small and draughty room with a tiled floor but it was where they had always sat), they said hello to a few people. Remember Gabe, course you do, trilled Jenny at every stop. All right, they said, all right, Gabe, which encompassed everything – enquiry, acceptance, a general statement that all was as it should be. Bev was there with her husband. She moved her coat and bag to let them sit but Jenny said no, I'm having him all to myself and steered Gabriel by the arm.

'I wouldn't have minded,' said Gabriel, 'if you wanted to sit with Bev.'

Jenny stirred her vodka tonic. 'See her every day, don't I? In the chicken shed.'

'The what?'

'The call centre. Big old shed full of squawking birds.' She laughed. 'Seen her near enough every day of my life since I was about six. Think that's when we became official Best Friends.'

'I remember you crying one time because you said Bev had gone off with—'

'Gone off with Mandy Palmer. I know! But she came crawling back.'

'Boys don't really have best friends,' said Gabe. It must be nice to have someone know you so well. But Charlie knew him as well as any human could know another; he was sure of that.

'That's right,' said Jenny. She looked at him carefully.

'I suppose Dad's got Tom Howarth.'

'Yes.'

'And it's not as if I don't . . .'

'Have friends.'

'. . . have friends. What happened to Michael Harrison?'

'Michael Harrison? Oh, I don't know. That poor little lad with the dirty jumpers and scabby head. You really took him under your wing.'

Gabriel sipped his pint. He felt unaccountably sorry for himself. Jen had Bev and Ted had Tom. Bev wasn't just a friend, she was a witness to a life. There were parts of Gabe's life that Charlie could never know about, however much he told her. There were parts of Gabe's life – stretches in half-forgotten hotels, rooms he could no longer summon with people he could no longer recall – which it seemed he himself did not really know. They did not exist, except in his mind, and then not even there.

'I don't know about that,' he said. 'I don't know why we stopped being friends.'

Jenny took a puff on her inhaler and then lit a cigarette. She tucked her hair behind her ears. 'He started getting in trouble, police and stuff.' Gabriel held out two fingers and she passed the cigarette. 'I don't see him around. Must have moved away. Keep that one, I like lighting them anyway, first drag's always the best.'

She narrowed her eyes as the lighter flared. They were pretty eyes. She had Mum's long, fine nose and her top lip curved up in a sculpted arch. The oval that contained her features sat on her face like a mask, untouched by the fat of her jowls and chin. She didn't suit being fat. It didn't seem right. It seemed unnatural, a joke, as if she were about to burst out of there.

'Tell me about the kids,' he said. They talked about Harley and Bailey and Jen asked about Charlie and they talked about her as well. Gabriel wanted to tell her about Lena but the words stuck in his throat. They moved on to Dad and Nana and Jenny explained the rotation of visits to the GP, specialist and nurse; she itemized the medications, their dosage and timings and purposes, though all would be futile in the end; she explained how the shopping got done and the cooking (she made an extra shepherd's pie on a Monday, Mary Mahoney at number 82 popped a hotpot round on Thursdays); and she listed the home visits, both official and unofficial, which had been carefully structured so that someone looked in at least twice a day. Gabe began to appreciate the enormous industry that went into it. What had looked to him like two old people muddling through was in fact a carefully orchestrated plan. He'd had no more idea of it than a diner presented with a beautiful plate, who knows nothing of what goes on below stairs.

Jenny finally stopped speaking. She seemed exhausted, as if she too had been surprised by all the labours involved. Slowly shaking her head she said, 'I hate to do it, but it's got to be done, Gabe. She'll have to go in a home.'

'Nana? But you've set everything up so well.'

'For now. Just about. Oh, think about it, will you, it doesn't get any easier from here. Dad's going to get worse, Nana's going to get worse and I can't give up work and I don't suppose you will.' Her eyes flashed in the old way.

'I'm sorry. You know what's best, I'm sure.'

Jenny sucked on the inhaler. 'Allergies,' she said. 'Listen, let's talk about you. I want to hear about this new restaurant of yours.'

'It's not going to be anything fancy. Old-school French, but done to perfection, that's the idea. Not a steak-frites bistro with red check tablecloths and candles stuck in bottles. More upmarket than that. And really classic food – blanquette de veau, trout meunière . . . that sort of thing.'

Jenny laughed. 'Not fancy? Well, I suppose if you want to get them stars, Michelin stars, you've got to have all the posh food on the menu or you won't even get a look-in.'

'Trust me, Jenny, all I'm talking here is old-school French . . . beef and carrots, peach melba, it's certainly not Michelin star stuff.'

Jenny looked sceptical. 'It all sounds posher when you say it in French. And don't do yourself down like that. You'll get your stars in the end. It's what you've always wanted and you deserve it after all these years.'

'I've never wanted them, actually. I mean, it's not something I've ever aimed for and I certainly wouldn't be trying to get in that race now. It's a whole other world, I promise you.'

'If you say so,' said Jen. 'But you did want them *something rotten*. It's all you could talk about for a while. I remember when you came back from that place in France where you worked in a two-star and you were only starting out really back then and you were so full of it, excitement, about the things you'd seen and what you'd tasted and the way they did things and you'd sleep on the laundry pile because you were on your feet sixteen hours a day. My goodness, you were keen. I've never seen anyone so keen on anything before or since. And it was lovely. It was lovely to see.'

'But it wasn't something I wanted for myself,' said Gabe. 'I just wanted to learn as much as I could.'

Jenny touched his arm. 'We all had our dreams, didn't we, but here we are.' Her fingers tightened conspiratorially on his forearm. 'Here we are,' she said.

While Jenny was getting the next round in, Gabriel's mobile rang.

'Where the fuck were you?'

'Rolly,' said Gabriel, 'wonderful to hear your voice.'

'Two o'clock today, on-site, kitchen fitters – ring any bells?'

'Shit, sorry.'

'You need to get your act together, I'm telling you.'

'I'm sorry. I had to come up north to see my dad.'

'Well, that's all right then isn't it? There I was thinking you'd let your partners down for no good reason at all.'

'Rolly,' said Gabriel. 'Fuck off.' He hung up.

'Everything OK?' said Jenny, dangling a packet of peanuts from the corner of her mouth.

'Yes,' said Gabriel. 'No.' He rubbed his bald patch and a few more hairs came away in his hand. 'Everything's fine. I'm going for a slash.'

He called Rolly from the toilets and got no reply. He left an apologetic message saying that his father was dying. As soon as he'd hung up he wished he could take it back.

The packet of dry roasted was torn open and empty when he returned to the table, and Jenny was dabbing at the crumbs.

'I could eat these 'til the cows come home. What's your favourite food then, Gabe? Your favourite meal?'

'I like all sorts. French, Italian, Japanese.'

'Toad in the hole,' said Jenny. 'That's me. With onion gravy. What about you?'

'I don't know. Look,' he said, 'that stars business, it's a mug's game. It's never been part of the plan.'

'Do you remember Mum's meatballs?' said Jenny. 'I made a paper-weight out of one of them.'

'Dad standing over us until we'd eaten up,' said Gabe. Where did his sister go? He wished he could reach inside this fat woman and find her again. But if he got beneath the fat there'd still be this unknown woman in the polyester cap-sleeved blouse. He'd have to chisel through the breathless chat. And another casing which was made of cares, of Harley and Bailey and Nana and Dad. And then scrape away the small-town thoughts and habits and go in and really in, like open-ing up a Russian doll, until he got to the real Jenny, the one who lay on her stomach on the bed in a torn denim miniskirt and said, 'If I'm not out of this place by the time I'm eighteen, just shoot me. Shoot me, please.'

'I felt so sorry for him,' said Jenny. 'Poor old Dad.'

'Poor old Dad? Poor me, poor you, poor Mum. She was never allowed, anyway . . . I don't know. What about you? Don't you want to, sometimes, just get back to being yourself?'

She looked at him through slitted eyes. 'I am myself. What you see is what you get, Gabriel. And if you don't like it you know what you can do.'

'I didn't mean . . .'

'You didn't mean? What? Forget it, Gabe, no, just forget it, I don't even care. And about Mum, you shouldn't sound so superior because Dad did his best and you've never had family to cope with, not like that, not when there's someone ill for years and years and it's not even understood properly and you're just struggling on your own. Put yourself in his shoes, why don't you, and then you'll see how things really stand.' She smoked a cigarette the way Mum used to, always held close to the face, always smoked down to the butt.

'Nana wasn't ill, not really, she was a hypochondriac and it was Mum looking after her anyway, not Dad.'

'Not Nana,' wheezed Jenny. 'Mum.' She could hardly catch her breath.

'Where's your inhaler, Jen?'

'You were always,' Jenny gasped, 'so wrapped up in yourself.'

Gabriel opened Jenny's handbag. 'My God, how do you find any-thing in here?'

Jenny snatched the bag and shook it gently to sift and separate the contents, as if she were panning for gold. 'She frightened me some-times. Especially when she'd run off. I thought she'd never come back.'

'Run off? Are we still talking about Mum?'

'Her *little holidays*. That's what we called them. When she'd run off with another bloke, some random person she'd met at a bus stop or in the launderette, though one time it was Daniel Parsons and he brought her back after one day and said, I'm sorry but I've bitten off more here than I can chew, and it was awful because Dad had to work with him and it was worse even than when she took up with the milkman and rode around with him on that bloody float and of course he denied there was anything going on but she could ride with him if she wanted to, he wasn't going to stop her if her husband didn't, and everyone set their bloody alarm clocks, didn't they, to make sure they'd be at their curtains when the bloody milkman came by.'

Gabriel stared at Jenny. He saw the rag-and-bone man leering, his mother descending as plumes of steam rose from the horse. 'You're talking about Mum. Our mum.'

'She was ill,' said Jenny. 'Four or five times that happened and then there was all the shopping, endless stuff from catalogues that Dad and me would wrap up and send back. That was the mania, the manic episodes, and then she'd be depressed. Bipolar they call it now.'

Gabe shook his head. He opened his mouth and closed it again. He went back to shaking his head.

'I didn't know she was so ill,' said Jenny. 'Not until later. She was sectioned one time, Dad never told me for years. It was the stigma. Carted off to the loony bin, children mustn't know. The children did know, of course, the ones at school, God, kids can be so mean.'

'You can't tell me about Mum like that, as if . . . as if . . . Do you even realize what you've said? What you've accused her of?'

'Oh, grow up,' said Jenny. 'When are you ever going to grow up?'

One of the pub staff worked his way round the tables, emptying ashtrays into a bucket and flicking a cloth about. There was a nasty taste in Gabriel's mouth – the cigarettes, the beer – and he swallowed and swallowed and the bile rose in his throat.

'I'm not accusing anyone of anything,' said Jenny, when Gabriel didn't reply. 'She couldn't help it. She was ill. And she probably wasn't even having an affair with the milkman, she just didn't see anything wrong with riding out with him. She was like that when she was on a high.'

'But the others . . .'

'I don't know exactly and it doesn't matter now but yes, I'm sure that some of the others . . . one or two at least.'

Gabe shook his head. 'No. I'd have known. If you knew, I'd have known as well. I'm older than you.'

'You didn't *want* to know, Gabriel. I tried saying something to you once or twice when we were kids.'

'Mum was on Valium,' said Gabriel. The pint glass was clammy in his hands. 'Around the time Nana moved in with us. But lots of housewives were. It kept them quiet, kept them in their place, I suppose.'

Jenny sighed so long and hard that Gabe nearly expected her to deflate. 'That's not the half of it. She was on serious stuff, more like a chemical cosh. And Nana moved in to keep an eye on her and you'd started your training and you were hardly ever around and Mum said we've not to trouble Gabe, he's going places, that boy, and it's not for us to drag him down with cares. And she'd sit and watch the phone because you'd said you'd ring on such and such a night and so she'd sit and stare at the phone, take a chair into the hall and set it by the little table, I don't know why everyone kept their phone out by the stairs, and of course you wouldn't ring and in the end she'd go up to bed and she made the staircase look like a mountain, it was such a heavy climb.'

'I was a little shit, right?'

'You were her golden boy. And she was your fairy queen, until you left home, anyway. I sometimes used to think it wasn't the medication that made her go all flat . . .'

'Just say it.'

'It was like she had a broken heart.'

'You've waited all these years, and you've never once said anything, and now you're trying to tell me these things . . . that are not . . . they are *not* . . . and I'm supposed to take all this from you?'

'Listen to you. Does it always have to be about *you*? And it's not like I've never tried before. But you've always been the protected one, and you've never had to hear. You've never been around. What am *I* supposed to do? Sing hosanna when you ride into town?'

'She embarrassed you,' said Gabe, his eyes beginning to smart in the smoke from Jenny's cigarette. 'It was you as well as Dad. You could never just let her be herself.'

'I wouldn't bother telling you now,' said Jenny. 'Not for your sake, I wouldn't bother, not in a million years. It's only for Dad, that's all, because he's dying and you need to understand.' She started to cry.

'Jenny,' said Gabriel. 'Jen.'

'I'm OK,' she said and continued to weep.

'Remember,' said Gabe, 'when she turned the sitting room into a Bedouin tent?'

'And she had a tea towel on her head.' Jenny laughed and then groaned. 'But we always do this. Turn her into a fairy tale.'

'I know she wasn't perfect. But she could be fun, couldn't she?'

Jenny looked at him solemnly. 'What happened between you and Dad? I've always wondered. It's like he was your hero and then overnight, you must have been eleven or twelve, and it was like, wham, woke up one morning and hated his guts. I've always wanted to know what it was.'

'I think you might be rewriting history here,' said Gabriel. He squeezed her hand. 'Me and Dad, we always rubbed each other up the wrong way, and I'm not blaming him for anything, before you have a go at me again. Though he did keep dragging me off to the mill.'

'You loved going,' said Jenny. 'And then you suddenly refused to go any more. Something must have happened and from then on it was like everything he did was wrong.'

Gabriel, all in a rush, was seized by a sense of things left undone. He'd forgotten an important meeting. He should have told Oona to finish the stock-take. Maddox was still on his case. He hadn't found out what Gleeson was up to. Charlie needed – she deserved – something better from him. And Lena, for God's sake, Lena. What a mess he had made of that. A vertiginous feeling came over him and he held on to the edge of his seat. 'We never got on,' he mumbled. 'I thought, you know . . . I was taking Mum's side, but then everything you've been saying, if it's true, I don't know, maybe I didn't understand.'

'Let's get you home,' said Jenny. 'You look fit to drop. But isn't it about time you sorted things out with Dad? Whatever happened, Gabriel, it's time to let it go.'

CHAPTER TWELVE

—◊◊◊—

IN HIS SLEEP THE VERTIGO RETURNS AND PINS HIM ON A HIGH LEDGE.
Then he is falling, this ancient, bottomless dream. He plummets into
the darkness, gives himself up, lets go. The dead black weightless fall.
The light begins to creep in and now he is underground in the endless passageways. He squats on his heels by the corpse and begins the
examination, closing his hands around the feet, feeling each toe
between his fingertips, tracing the lines of each instep. Kneeling, he
presses the ankles as he scrutinizes the calves, and now he lifts the leg
a little and cradles the slack flesh in his palm.

Gradually, he becomes aware of the food. It is piled high around
him, around the body, and in every direction, glorious and glistening,
and at last he will enjoy it, for this is his favourite meal. He tears the
leg of a roast chicken, and bites into the crisp and bubbled skin. It
makes him want to sob. He breaks off a piece of meat between his
fingers, crawls along and pushes it gently between Yuri's black lips.

He woke with a crushing weight bearing down on his chest. Gabriel
tried to sit up but he couldn't move. He pushed the covers down and
then lay motionless until the pain had eased. He sat up, switched on
the lamp and checked the time. Five thirty, which meant that he'd
never get back to sleep. He wished he had a cigarette. There was no
way he'd go back to being a smoker, but right now he would like
nothing more than a fag.

No sooner had he thought it than the idea of it made him retch. He was nauseous, definitely, perhaps he wasn't well. He lay down again and the dream came back to him. He curled up, trying to stave off the sickness, the sense of disgust. He wasn't responsible for a dream.

It was impossible to sleep properly in this single bed. His knees were pushed up against the wall. He turned over. In the corner, under the window, was the wicker-bottomed cottage chair that he used to jam beneath the door handle when he needed privacy, when he'd lie on the bed with a box of tissues and an underwear catalogue. Whenever he was ill, laid up with flu or tonsillitis or tummy ache, Mum would pull up that chair and sit by him and the cool touch of her hand on his forehead made him safe.

She was never ill, not in those days. Not that he'd known. She was either brilliant or sad, but that was just her, so he'd thought. When he lost her it was a gradual fading, a merging, a blending of grey upon grey, and she seeped away so slowly that he failed to pay attention. When she died he realized she had been gone for years and he scarcely mourned her because there'd been little left, by then, to mourn.

She had become a shuffler. Her feet never left the ground. Whenever he came home she said, 'You've got it all ahead of you,' as if it was all over for her, and she'd whisper in his ear, 'Don't feel you have to stay,' the moment he'd stepped in the door.

If he'd known. If Jenny had told him. Jenny and Dad and Nana, they hadn't told him a thing. He was twenty-eight when she'd had the heart attack. An adult. He should have been told long before. Gabriel pushed his face into the pillow to wipe away the tears. He lay for a while on his stomach and allowed himself to cry. He moaned into the pillow. His breath was hot on his face. He pushed his hips against the sheet. When he groaned the sound travelled down his body and flexed his feet back and forth. His hips rocked softly. He hadn't cried for years. His lips brushed the pillowcase as the blood thumped in his head. His tongue moved between his teeth. With his eyes tightly closed he saw her, she came back to him, his waif, his stray, Lena, stretched out on the sofa, all skin and bone.

He raised his head and let out a horrible noise, half-yelp, half-groan. What kind of man was he? In his grief, even in his grief, he was penetrated by desire, and for a girl he did not want. Gabriel rolled over and sat up. He tugged down his boxer shorts and surveyed the treacherous region. His penis stared up at him, a one-eyed implacable foe. It bore no sign of remorse. Gabriel closed a fist around it and slumped back again, his hand working up and down in a fury, as if to say, right, you asked for it and you're not getting out of it now.

After breakfast he called Charlie. 'I'm looking at my thigh,' she said. 'I'm in bed, watching the news, another car bomb in Baghdad, seventeen dead, but I'm more concerned about the way my thigh is starting to get these little dimples.'

'It's only the one thigh? Perhaps you could have that leg removed. It's the second most common cosmetic surgery procedure in LA, after the full-body lift.'

'It's both thighs. These utterly trivial thoughts. Could I have them surgically removed as well?'

'You're so hard on yourself.'

'But I'm not. I only said that because it's a way to absolve myself – and have you absolve me – and that doesn't make it better, it makes it worse.'

He decided not to stumble further into this minefield. He said, 'I wish I'd brought you with me. I can't talk to Dad. Nana's pretty much senile. Jenny's bleached her hair white and she screeches, it's like she's always about to fall off the edge of a cliff.'

'It all sounds very enticing. I'm sad you never invited me.'

'I don't know what to say to him. My own father.'

'You twit,' said Charlie. 'It doesn't matter what you say. Talk to him. About work, about anything.'

'Charlie,' said Gabriel. It wasn't how he'd planned to do it, but he was suddenly gripped by the thought that this was one thing he could sort out right now. If he felt a little light-headed it was only because of the giddy ease of it, the plunge he was about to take. 'Charlie, will you marry me?'

For a few moments there was silence.

'I hope you're down on one knee,' said Charlie. 'Just how I dreamed it all those times.'

'Sweetheart,' he said. He got off the chair and knelt on the bedroom floor. 'I'm down on two.'

Ted was in the dining room, bending over the *Mary Rose* which he had set on newspaper on the table, next to a tube of glue, a box of matches, a bowl of water and some cotton buds. She'd stood on the mantelpiece once, but the heat from the fire began to melt the glue and bits of the gunwale fell off. 'She's seen better days,' said Ted.

'Still beautiful,' said Gabe. 'I kind of like her like that. She was a wreck, wasn't she, anyway?'

Ted dipped a cotton bud in water and began to clean the dust from the stern. 'I've fixed up two already – HMS *Endeavour* and the *Titanic*. There's a couple more I'd like to see right, if I've the time. You've six months to live, what'd you do? It's a pub conversation. Well, you say, I'd go on a cruise around the world. Or you say, I'd go and find that little redhead from Fleetwood, see what she's made of. Summat like that.'

'Restoring matchstick ships doesn't make it to the top ten,' said Gabriel, smiling. He took a cotton bud and started to help his father, working his way up the mizzenmast.

'Neither does spending it with a nurse with a needle in yer arm and a sick bucket by the bed. Don't occur to anyone, that.' Ted laughed.

'I'll come up in the next few weeks,' said Gabriel. 'I won't leave it so long. Another visit before Christmas, at least one.' He did love his father, but his love had a fugitive quality; it was always up to him to hunt it down.

Ted tried to unfurl a paper sail that had rolled in on itself. It crumbled between his fingertips. 'Take Nana out for a walk,' he said. 'While it's fine. Give her an airing. I can't push the wheelchair any more.'

'You could come to London when the restaurant opens. And Jenny and Nana. We'll sort it out somehow.' He watched Ted carefully but discerned no response. When he was a boy he used to scour his father's face for warning signs. Like some amateur meteorologist he tried to see the clouds forming, attempted to predict the storm ahead. But the anger, if it came, even when – especially when – Gabriel had predicted it, stunned him every time.

Ted continued his tender labours, one hand cradling the prow of the *Mary Rose* while the other attended to the stern. 'What I said last night – don't pay any mind. About leavin' yer job. Wouldn't blame you if you left the country, never mind a bloomin' job. Way things are goin', them as can, they up and leave.'

'We've found a brilliant site.'

'Great Britain,' said Ted, without looking up, 'no one says that any more. United Kingdom. Well, we're hardly that. It's going to the dogs, Gabe. Going to the dogs.'

'This kind of opportunity . . . I've waited a long time for it.'

'We've lost the "Great". Know what else we've lost? Britishness. People keep talking about it. That's how you know it's gone.'

Gabriel looked round the dining room, at the spare chairs waiting against the wall for visitors who would never come, the best china trapped, as ever, in a glass cabinet, doomed to a lifespan of uselessness by constantly being 'saved'. 'Dad,' he said, 'things change. There's no point trying to keep everything the same. And just because things are different doesn't mean they're worse.'

Ted put down his cotton bud. He cracked his knuckles. 'Britishness tests,' he said. 'What daft bugger dreamed that up? Eh?'

Talk to him, Charlie had said. She didn't know how difficult that was. And this was not even his father; this was an impostor, one too weak for the role. It was galling. Now that Gabe was big enough to stand up to him, his father had conveniently disappeared. 'It's a citizenship test, that's all.'

'We used to know,' said Ted, 'what it meant to be British. We didn't have to discuss it, because we knew. We used to know what it meant to be English. It's a dirty word now, that is.'

'Oh, I don't know,' said Gabriel, determined to dispel the doom and gloom. 'Tolerance. Fairness. Fair play. There are definitely British qualities. I think we'd both agree on that.'

'Just words,' said Ted. 'Don't mean owt now.'

'Come on,' said Gabriel, laughing. 'It's not as bad as that. That's part of the British character – always doing ourselves down.'

'These sails,' said Ted, 'they turn to dust in yer hand.' He shook his head. 'British character,' he said. 'There's no such thing. Not now. You see them, these politicians, talking about it, and it's like a Punch and Judy show. No, there's no substance. Time was, you could talk about decency. And it meant something. In this country, it did.'

'You should see my kitchen, Dad. I've got every nationality in there and everyone gets along.'

'Pleasure without responsibility,' said Ted. 'That's how it is, you see. Character don't mean anything, don't count for anything any more. To lose yer good character, that were a terrible thing in my day. But now – you take a pill, you talk about it on TV, you blame everyone but yerself.'

'I've got Somalis, Poles, Serbs, Russians . . .'

'British character,' said Ted, snorting the words. 'It's gone the way of maypole dancing, has that.'

Gabriel was only mildly irritated, and he viewed this as a sort of victory, if not over Ted then over himself. 'A bit of an exaggeration, maybe,' he said. 'And I think you're mixing up two things. When I said "British character" I meant, you know, national identity, as the politicians say. But what you were just saying about character was about individuals, about personality. That's a different thing.'

'Aye,' said Ted, 'maybe. I don't know. You always were a clever lad.' The low winter sun broke the clouds and pierced the folds of the net curtain, lighting dust motes that stood in layers across the room as if the air itself were pleated. 'But I'm saying the same thing, either way.'

'Which is what?' said Gabriel indulgently. 'Let's have some coffee and then I'll take Nana out.'

'There's nothing there, that's what I mean. Nowt to get hold of at all.'

'But "having character", that was just a way of saying you did what was expected of you. It's almost the opposite of having a character, a personality, of your own. Now you've got to know yourself, what you really are.'

Ted nodded. 'That what it is, eh? I wouldn't want to be starting out today.' He picked up the *Mary Rose* and inspected the hull. 'We used to build ships in this country, Gabe. That was part of who we were. We built merchant shipping for the world over. I reckon when you built a ship you knew you'd done a job. There's no ships built on Teesside these days. It's a breaker's yard now. They send ships there from all sorts of places, full of asbestos and oil and God-only-knows, and they break 'em up.'

'That kind of manufacturing . . .' It was hardly worth finishing the sentence. Gabe got up and patted his father on the shoulder. 'I'll get us that coffee now.'

Nana wore a mustard-and-brown fur coat which, though Gabe did not remember them, must have seen better days. It was somewhat chewed and balding, and resembled a number of mangy tabbies sewn together. The thing smelt like a dead cat too. 'Lovely coat, Nana,' said Gabriel, wheeling her along Plodder Lane. 'Is it real?'

'Real?' shouted Nana. 'Real? Of course it's real. Real fur coat, is this.' She looked about her, this being information worth disseminating more widely, but there was no one else to tell.

'Lovely day,' said Gabe. He was beginning to sound like Nana. 'Turned out nice.' There was an icy sort of sunlight in the air but the day was hardly lovely. Across the valley there was mist on the moors; the wind was cold and damp.

'Lovely,' said Nana, chin in her coat, hands in her pockets, boots splayed indecently on the wheelchair footplates. 'Lovely, lovely, lovely.'

Gabriel stopped for a moment and looked down across the town, the houses and mill chimneys and spires huddled for warmth in the basin, the streets that marched crookedly up the hill, the long sheds of the industrial park where Jenny clucked down the phone, the bright cars scattered across the grey and brown canvas like spatters of metallic paint.

'She's a lassie from Lancashire,' sang Nana, vibrato. 'A flounce on her petticoat, a comb in her hair . . .'

Gabriel started wheeling. He picked up the pace.

'Oooh,' sang Nana, turning a streaming eye to Gabe. 'If those lips . . .' Her mouth continued to work, but it was a few seconds before the sound was restored. 'If those lips could only speak. Ta-da de-dum da-dum.'

'We'll cut down this way, shall we, Nana? Down the side of the park?'

'Gabriel! Gabriel!' shrieked Nana. 'I've forgot me hat. I can't go to church without a hat.'

Gabriel leaned over her but carried on pushing. 'It's all right, we're not going to church. You wanted to go to the market, have a look around.'

Nana sniffed loudly. 'I am perfectly aware of that.'

The houses on Park Street were Victorian mansions with porticos and sweeping bay windows, which had been turned into care homes, social security offices and temporary employment agencies or given over to charities. Only a few remained as family homes, and they belonged not to wealthy mill owners but to wealthy Pakistanis who owned the local bingo parlour, a string of convenience stores, a pickle factory and curry houses either side of the East Lancashire Pennines. As they came closer to the centre of Blantwistle the streets began to narrow and steepen. Gabriel slowed his pace, fearing a skid that would send Nana flying off down the hill. They were nearing Astley Street now, passing through the old back-to-backs with the front doors that gave straight to the street, front windows that displayed overstuffed lounges crammed with fake leather suites and gargantuan TVs. Some of the houses, in an advanced state of disrepair, stood empty. Others, equally dilapidated, had steamed-up windows and slamming doors.

'We used to sit in front of the fire a Sunday night,' said Nana, 'after me mother had been baking, and we'd bread and barm cakes all round the skirting boards. Ooh, the smell, it was lovely. But we hadn't to eat them, because warm they weren't good for your tummy. But we did sometimes, when Mother weren't looking, we'd smuggle a barm cake up our jumpers and take it up to bed.'

At the corner a group of young Asian men, some in skullcaps, some in hoodies, were engaged in kicking a portable television to pieces. They appeared to take little pleasure in the task, which they performed with an air of weariness as if, were it up to them, it would be the last thing they would choose to do.

They were on Astley Street now, the row of two-up, two-downs where he'd begun his life. Here they were, passing the house. HAPPY EID was spelled out in tinsel across the ground-floor window and an old man sat on a chair in the doorway, a tiny child on his knee.

Gabriel was expecting Nana to comment – on how the Asians had depressed the house prices, how they never scrubbed their doorsteps, how they butchered goats in the backyard. But Nana was lost in her childhood, not seeming to notice where they were.

'I had it across here from me mother, many a time, for answering her back. She were a good woman, right enough, and she knocked the goodness into me. I've her to thank for that. And we'd respect our elders then. Fetching and carrying, with no excuses. I'd try one, now and then, and she'd never let one slip by. "That's a tackler's tale," she'd say.' Nana popped an Extra Strong Mint in her mouth; it clacked between her dentures.

'In and out each other's houses, we were. Well, that's how we lived. Never locked the door. And we helped each other out, clubbed together, you know. Funerals were the best. There'd be a whip-round and there'd be a wake, and the body'd be in the parlour, that's the way we did it then. Oh, there were some right good funerals, and all the adults would sing, especially when they'd had a few.'

Gabriel looked down on the delicate eggshell of Nana's skull, visible through the nest of hair. 'You'll have to show me some photos, Nana, of the old days. Let's get the albums out when we get back.'

'Are we meeting Sally Anne?' said Nana. 'Are we meeting her here?'

They had just wheeled into the covered market. The place had a distinct smell of vegetation and decay, like wet and rotting leaves. Gabe, startled by the mention of Mum, failed to make a reply.

Nana turned to him in agitation. She seemed to sense something amiss, half fearful, half embarrassed, and at a total loss. 'Sally Anne,' she said, 'Sally Anne.'

'We'll see her later,' said Gabriel. 'After we've got the shopping done.'

They trundled slowly over the flagstones, between the stalls selling halal meat, pork pies, discount electronics and undergarments in stupendously large sizes. Christmas lights dangled between the girders. They were unlit, which suited the atmosphere of scrimp and save. The shoppers were elderly and white or young Asian families pushing prams, the more mobile having fled long since. Gabe and Nana were overtaken by a motorized wheelchair, its occupant mountainous and old. 'Mind where you're going,' shouted Nana. 'The *size* of her,' she grumbled. 'Stop a minute,' she said as they came to the next stall. 'We'll get some cold meats for lunch.'

Gabe surveyed the slabs and rolls slapped down on the metal trays. There was black pudding, lunch tongue, jellied veal, corned beef, luncheon meat, pressed beef, boiled ham, potted meat and ox heart; all slightly grey at the edges. Nana wanted ox tongue and jellied brisket and Gabe said 'lovely' and hoped she'd forget about them by the time lunch came around.

They sat at Granny Bun's for a cup of tea. 'It's grand to be out,' said Nana, lifting her shoulders the way she did when performing her most dazzling smile.

'What would you like for Christmas, Nana?'

'We used to hang our stockings up,' said Nana, 'and in the morning there'd be a tangerine and some nuts inside, maybe a toffee as well, and maybe a ball and maybe a peg doll and hair ribbons and, oh, we were overjoyed. All the things they get given these days.'

'I think I could stretch to a peg doll,' said Gabe. He'd call Lena when they got home, just to check everything was OK.

'We'd not get new clothes for Christmas, though. We'd new clothes for Whitsun, you see, and then they'd be Sunday best. D'you know, those Whitsun Walks . . .' Nana trailed away, her eyes closed and her chin drifted down to her chest. Gabe was wondering whether to wake her or push her home still asleep when she lifted her head. 'Maytime, they were, and everyone turned out just so, whole town dressed to the nines, and we'd more processions in June. I've walked in many a procession, girl and woman, we'd walk with our churches, well, you'd a chapel on every corner, I'm going back of course. The Catholics had theirs too, you see, they'd march for Our Lady, first Sunday in May. The Sacred Heart's been pulled down. But they were lovely days for families, all these marches. You know, many's the time I walked in my wedding dress under a banner, Mothers' Union, and I was proud to do it. Yes, oh yes, we took pride.'

Gabe said, 'Did you march with your mother? Did she wear her wedding dress too?' The distant past, it seemed, grew brighter as the recent past began to dim. It was a place of safety now.

'She were a weaver,' said Nana, 'on a shoddy loom, making plain cloth, it's all it'd make – you just threw the shuttle across. But she stopped work when she had her children, because Father said that's the most important job a woman could do.'

Gabriel thought, soon I will have a wife. He could scarcely believe it so he said, 'I'm getting married. You're the first to know.'

But Nana didn't hear him. She cocked her head to one side and seemed to be listening to something far away or long ago. 'We'd go to New Brighton for our holidays. Sometimes Blackpool, but Mother preferred New Brighton because Blackpool could be a bit coarse. Wakes Week, you see . . .' The very words seemed to put her into a trance. 'The whole town shut down, all the mills, and we'd that week for enjoyment and we knew how to enjoy ourselves.' She smiled and looked at Gabriel and then all around, seeming increasingly doubtful and concerned. 'Gabe,' she hissed. 'Gabe! What time's the appointment? Here we are chatting on in the canteen.'

'What appointment?' he said, stupidly. He should have got the hang of her by now.

'We're at the hospital, aren't we?' said Nana in her best voice, all proper and strangled. 'For my check-up with Dr Patel.'

At twilight a red sun sank behind Rileys and a paper moon floated over the shell of Harwoods, that once-mighty rival, the few remaining shards of window glass glittering like tears. A flock of starlings fretted and swooped in the distance, a black kaleidoscope constantly shaken against the blood-tinged sky. It was just past four and Gabe and Ted were going to Rileys because there was nothing else to do.

Coming towards them up the hill an old man in an army surplus coat, left over perhaps from the Crimean War, bent his back to the incline at a remarkable angle, snailing forwards with the top of his head on show. To keep moving seemed like something of an achievement, given the shopping he was carrying, the deep stoop that he suffered, and his broke-back shoes which were only loosely appended to his feet.

When they reached each other Ted stopped and the man, to Gabe's surprise, instantly straightened up. Greetings were exchanged. 'You remember my son,' said Ted. 'Gabriel, you remember Mr Nazir?'

'Ah,' said Gabe, who didn't, 'good to see you.'

'Fine boy,' said Mr Nazir. 'Strong like an ox.' He giggled and set down his bags.

'Rileys,' said Ted to Gabriel, seeing he hadn't a clue, 'twenty year or more.'

Mr Nazir giggled again and if Gabe had closed his eyes he would have heard a young girl rather than this old and bearded man. 'Yes, yes,' he said, 'twenty-two.'

'Wind's picking up,' said Ted, folding his arms behind his back.

'Chilly,' said Mr Nazir. 'How is your grandson? And your grand-daughter too?'

'Bailey's all right, she's a Saturday job at Rileys, settling down, you know. Harley, well, Harley's out o' work . . . he's a good kid, but some-times I think . . .'

'Right in the heart,' said Mr Nazir, grooming his beard, 'but wrong in the head, isn't it?'

'Aye,' said Ted, gravely. 'Aye.'

'They don't want to listen to us old ones,' continued Mr Nazir. 'They think they will never be old.'

'How're your grandsons? All right?'

'Asif is difficult. *Very* difficult. Always telling me what is written in the Qur'an. The Qur'an says this, the Qur'an says that. I say, Asif, you are not the keeper of the light. This is my religion too.' He shook his head. 'These young people. Thinking they know it all. No humility and no respect, this is the problem. It's the western values they pick up, wanting everything their way.'

'This is it,' said Ted. 'Yer not wrong there.'

'What is the point in blaming?' said Mr Nazir. 'I was the one to come here. For everything there is a price.'

'What about Amir?'

'Amir was in the newspaper. His case has gone to court. Charge is vandalism – spray painting, breaking window, damaging a car. Even in crime he lacks ambition. His mother cries for him.'

'The devil makes work,' said Ted. 'The lad needs a job.'

Mr Nazir involved his fingers in his beard. 'He *needs* a job,' said Mr Nazir, 'but where is the job for him? I myself am taking him for job at that distribution place, at the warehouse, everywhere, but nowhere has job for him. Always they are taking the Poles.'

'I've heard it often enough,' said Ted.

'They say these Polish are good workers, and they don't care what they do, undercut the wages, sleeping fifteen, twenty, to one house.'

'This is it.'

'This is it.'

'Well, you'll freeze stood 'ere.'

'Catch our deaths,' said Mr Nazir, giggling. He grabbed Gabriel's hand and shook it with startling vigour. 'But tomorrow will be fine, isn't it? Red sky at night, shepherd's delight.' He released Gabe's hand and picked up his bags. Gabe watched him tackle the hill, his back angled against the slope.

'Decent,' said Ted, turning up his coat collar. 'A decent sort.'

Gabriel pretended he wanted to look in a shop window to give Ted a chance to catch his breath. They dawdled along the parade. Outside a jeweller's Gabe blurted out, 'Dad, I'm engaged.'

Ted laughed. 'Don't sound so terrified, son.'

Gabe said, 'God, I think I am.'

'It's wonderful news,' said Ted. 'Perhaps we'll meet her now. Set a date?'

'Haven't even got a ring yet,' said Gabe. 'But it'll be soon, definitely.'

'Got you tearing yer hair out already, has it?'

'What?'

Ted gestured vaguely towards him.

Gabriel lowered his arm. He hadn't realized he was doing it. He hadn't felt it. 'The thing is . . .'

'Let's keep walking,' said Ted.

'There's this other girl. I slept with her. More than once.'

Ted lengthened his stride, hoping perhaps to leave this news behind.

'It's over, anyway. With this Lena. I won't even see her again.'

Ted remained silent.

'I don't know why I told you that.' He could think of no reason, other than the thrill of speaking her name out loud.

'I remember,' said Ted, 'when I decided to marry yer mother. Blackpool it were. She's there with her folks and I'm there with mine. I'd seen her before, course I had, seen her around, but I didn't know her then. Anyhow, I'm walking down the pier and there she is, having her portrait done, penny portrait on the end of the pier. I says, "Hello, Sally Anne," but she ignores me. Aye, that's right. Bit later, reckon around tea time, I'm on the beach and summat hits me on the head. So I look up and she's there, up on the promenade, throwin' chips. I says, "Sally Anne," call out to her, you know, and she smiles at me and then she's off and running. And I know. She's the girl I'll marry. I see it – clear as the back of my hand.'

Gabe said, 'She was really something, I bet.'

Ted blew his nose. 'I'd to hang on to her, Gabe. From that day on. I'd to hang on for dear life, sometimes.'

'I didn't really know,' said Gabe. 'I knew she had her ups and downs . . . but . . . I was talking to Jen last night and she said . . .'

'We've a hard time remembering now, the way we didn't talk about things then. And she didn't want it. Didn't want you bothered with all that.'

'There were a few dramas, weren't there?' said Gabe. It was easier to talk like this, not facing each other, but walking side by side.

'We'd a temper on us, both of us. Can't have been easy for you and Jen.'

'Oh, we were all right.'

'Always the one for me,' said Ted, speaking quietly, as if to himself. 'And she knew it, because I always brought her home again. That's how I knew it meself, truth be told.'

'Your feelings didn't change, not in all those years?' His parents' marriage, which had seemed – at best – like mutually indentured labour, began to seem like something of an achievement.

'Feelings?' said Ted, chewing it like a foreign word, the way he said 'vol-au-vents'. 'I felt angry, a lot of the time. People are always on about how they feel. I tell you one thing I've learned in old age. You don't always know how you feel, not at the time, anyway. And it's easy to mix up feelings, muddle up anger with fear. Maybe what's important – it's not what you feel, it's what you do.'

Rileys Shopping Village was, according to the sign that hung over the entrance, A LEGENDARY EXPERIENCE. It had begun, after the last of the jacquards and looms had been shipped to Egypt, as a small retail outlet selling remnants and seconds that had been discovered when the warehouse was cleared out. Over the years it had grown into a sizeable emporium with a coffee shop and restaurant, landscaped gardens, an indoor children's play area and free parking for the coaches that brought the visitors to experience shopping the Rileys Way.

Ted and Gabe followed the signs to the Hungry Tackler Café. It was hot inside the old shed but the customers, mostly middle-aged and old, wore their coats and anoraks as they worked diligently through the concession stands. The 'Victorian Arcade' was filled with 'ladies' fashions', ceramics, bakeware, handbags and accessories, crystal vases and 'personalized' coffee mugs. Gabe saw signs to Candleland, Gnomeland and Bubbleland, and more pointing the way to FlowerWorld, Cat'n'dogWorld and GadgetWorld. In the 'Weaver's Court', they brushed by the fake bow window (complete with bubbled glass) of Thow'd Calico Shop and witnessed an exhibition of toffee being pulled by hand.

At a stand selling tea towels three old ladies, their hair freshly 'set' for their day out, picked through the offerings with great deliberation as if selecting for their trousseaux.

'Look at this,' said Gabe. He picked up a towel from the 'novelty' shelf and read aloud to Ted. ' "Rules to be Observed by the Hands Employed in this Mill". It's got the date on, 1878.'

'Oh aye,' said Ted. 'I've seen that one before.'

' "For single drawing, slubbing, or roving, 2d for each single end. For any bobbins found on the floor, 1d for each bobbin. For every oath or insolent language, 3d for the first time, and if repeated they shall be dismissed. The Grinders, Drovers, Slubbers and Rovers shall sweep at least eight times a day." '

'Hard times,' said Ted. He chuckled. 'But at least they got paid for being here. Now look, it's t'other way around.'

They installed themselves at the café where, despite it not yet being five o'clock or even quite December, a coach-party Christmas dinner was in full swing. They were, the piped music informed them, simply having a wonderful Christmas time. Plastic holly and fir branches, studded with glittery red ribbons and baubles, decorated the walls.

Ted and Gabe sipped their tea in congenial silence. Gabe stared at the pillar to his right. It bore the scratches and knocks of a hundred years and more and the letters that he thought he'd made out were small and barely visible: he'd struggled with his penknife to leave any mark at all. But, no, there they were, a G and an L, underscored with a wobbly line. He'd worked at it, quickly, feverishly, when Ted had been called away to deal with a mash on one of the machines.

It was in the summer holidays and Dad had brought him to Rileys for the day but they were shorthanded and he kept leaving Gabe on his own. When Dad came back Gabe had slipped the penknife up his sleeve.

'Right,' Ted had said, 'I'll start from the beginning. This here's a knotting machine. Everyone calls it the Topmatic, that's how it's known.'

'Can I have a go with that blower thing, Dad? Can I? Can I have a go?'

' 'Old yer 'orses,' said Ted. 'OK. The Topmatic goes on top right here, on the warp-tying frame. Remember what we're about? What's the job we've to get done?'

'Easy,' said Gabriel. 'I know. The loom's run out of warp. It needs a new beam on. Dad, can I have a new bike?'

Ted started up the machine. It looked like something Gabe could build with his Meccano set. Ted operated it with loving precision, breathing hard down his nose. He checked the first few knots individually then speeded everything up. The Topmatic trundled along.

Ted was speaking and Gabe stared at him closely to tune out the background noise. 'Go on, you can use it.' Dad handed him the blower, a simple nozzle and rubber pump. 'That's it, you get rid of the fluff so the knots don't get stuck in the healds and break. Know what a heald is?' Gabe pointed to the flat steel strips with eyes in the centre through which the yarn had to run. 'Champion,' said Dad.

After Gabe had finished, Dad worked along the knots with a little brush to make sure they all lay down nice and smooth.

'Dad,' said Gabe, 'when did you decide you wanted to work at Rileys? How old were you?'

Ted snorted. 'Decide? That's just what you did. Them days, they said, "Put a mirror under their nose. If they're breathing, get 'em in."'

Gabe put his hands in his pockets and wiggled his penknife into his hand. He worked it open and managed to cut his finger on the blade. It didn't seem right, what Dad said, as though any idiot could do his job. 'But you could have been, like, a train driver? If you wanted, Dad?'

'Aye,' said Ted. 'I suppose.' He wound the handle again and showed Gabe how the threads went through the pins to the reed. 'Right, the knotter has to call the tackler at this stage. But,' said Ted, 'guess what?'

'I know,' said Gabe, bursting with the answer, 'you *are* the tackler, Dad.'

'The tackler tightens what's known, in this town, any road, as the temples, have a look, these spiky rings what hold the cloth in place. It's an important job, is tackler. Not anyone can do that.

'Then I tighten up the warp, come with me round the back. And now we're ready to weave a few inches, then I put a docket on the board says the loom's been gaited. The weaver's help checks the cloth over for faults and – if it's all OK – the weaver starts the loom.'

'Dad,' said Gabe. He could feel the blood draining rapidly out of his finger. He was surprised there wasn't a pool of it on the floor. If he took his hand out of his pocket and showed Dad what had happened he'd get a bollocking. If he didn't he would bleed to death. He couldn't decide which of these options he preferred.

As he dithered he noticed a crazy woman running towards them, flapping her arms.

'Take a breath, now, Rita,' said Ted. 'You'll set yerself on fire.'

'It's Jimmy,' said Rita. 'Jimmy. A beam's fell on him.'

'Go and find Maureen, stop with her,' Ted told Gabe. 'You know where she is. Go on.'

'But, Dad,' said Gabriel. Ted was already striding away. 'Dad.'

Gabe ran through the sheds with one bloody finger aloft. Dad didn't even care. He didn't even look round when Gabe was shouting out. Gabe ran smack into Maureen, straight into her pillowy bosom, and she said, 'Oh, there you are,' as if she had been expecting him.

On the drive home Ted had been quiet. 'Dad,' said Gabe, eventually, 'is Jimmy all right?'

'I'd a pint with him after work,' said Dad, 'only yesterday.'

'Did he go to the hospital? Did an ambulance take him? Did you go with him, Dad?'

Ted indicated to turn right. The tick–tick filled the car like a time bomb, nobody speaking, and Gabe felt his stomach contract, wishing now he'd not said a word.

When the car was stopped at some traffic lights Ted said, 'Course in the old days you'd to do knotting on by hand. There's a few as can do it still. I can do it. Jimmy could do it. Aye, there's only one or two. I remember when I was learning, this old feller he tried to show me what to do. But he was that fast I couldn't see what he were doing wi' his fingers. And he couldn't do it slow. It were ingrained in him, ingrained.'

It was Mum who had told Gabe about Jimmy, the morning of the funeral.

A waitress brought a Christmas pudding to the long table, the weight of it forcing her tongue out between her teeth. She set it alight. The coach party said 'ooh' and 'ah'.

Ted said, 'Have you handed in yer notice yet? They know you'll be moving on?'

'I'm waiting for the right time,' said Gabe.

'Mr Riley had a way of knowing who were about to leave. It were uncanny. Like he had a sixth sense. Well, he seemed to know everything, even who'd clocked on late, and he'd a lot of things to see to, but he always knew. What about your boss now? Good sort, is he, good man?'

Gabriel shrugged. 'I don't know. But, you know, the hotel doesn't belong to him. He's only an employee like me.'

'Oh,' said Ted. 'I see. Who's it belong to, then?'

'Shareholders,' said Gabe. PanCont had hotels all over the world and was listed on the US stock market. 'American shareholders, I guess.'

'What about your colleagues. You told 'em yet?'

'Not yet, Dad. They won't care. The catering business, it's got a very high turnover. People move around.'

Ted said, 'Not done too much of that meself.' He smiled to acknowledge the understatement. 'No, not done so much moving around. Maybe I should of, but it's a bit late to be thinking of that. Loyalty,' he said, 'that don't mean anything any more. It means points on your Tesco clubcard. It means buy five teas and get one free.'

'We're a nation of shopkeepers, Dad.'

Ted blew his nose. The effort of it made him pause a while. 'But I don't look back and wish I'd done it different. Only the small things, maybe. D'you know, I was stood by the window waiting for Jen, t'other week, is this, and there were a blackbird on the lawn and I was stood there watching, the way he's trying to pull up this worm, and there's a fascination to it, if you've a mind to notice. Well, we never really look. You see the colours in the feathers, like a slick of oil on water, you see the beauty in it when you take the time.'

'You know what,' said Gabe. 'You know we were talking about "British" – what does it mean? There's your answer, that's what we've always done as a country: trade. We're a trading nation. If anything's our national identity, that's it, that's what it is.'

Ted set his hands on the table and ran them along the paper tablecloth. 'Once upon a time,' he said, 'yes. But not any more. D'you know what the balance of payments is? Aye, expect you do. When we were the workshop of the world we sold to everywhere and we'd a healthy surplus, you see. But we've a huge deficit now because all as we can do is shop. We're not a trading nation, we're a nation of consumers, that's all.'

'Where does the money come from, then? You've got to be making money to spend it. If people want to spend it on shopping that's up to them.'

'Of course it's up to them. I'm not telling anyone what to do.' Ted folded his arms, as though – even if begged – he would refuse to direct the nation now. 'But this country wants waking up. It's in a dream world. How long can it go on?'

'How long can what go on?' Gabe tried to keep the irritation from his voice.

'There's no industry any more,' said Ted. 'We don't produce anything. You can't build a pyramid upside down, it'll fall over, you've to get the foundation right.'

'You mean, we don't make ships any more? Cars? Cloth? So what, Dad? So what? There's more people employed in curry houses now than in all those old industries combined. But so what? What's bad about that?'

'You can't buy a box of matches what's made in this country, never mind a ship. You can't buy a television, a washing machine or any electrical product made here – all the components are foreign, and all as we've got is a few assembly plants, most of them foreign-owned.'

Gabe had his elbows on the table, his knuckles pressed together. As he listened he gnawed his fist. 'We've moved on,' he said. 'We've moved up. People have got money to spend. At the top restaurants in London you can't even get a table and these are places charging a hundred quid a head. It's invisibles, Dad, you know, banking and finance and advertising. All that stuff.'

'Invisibles,' said Ted, making it a clumsy word. 'The emperor's got no clothes on. The whole country's living on tick.'

'The economy is booming. What's so wrong with that?'

Ted sighed. 'You understand these things better than me. To an old man like me it's a house of cards. There's nothing solid, that's all I'm saying, but you don't have to listen to me.'

Gabe disliked this new ploy of Ted's, saying 'you're clever' or 'you understand' and then contradicting everything Gabriel said. 'You don't have to understand the entire economy to make a good living. You can just get on with it and not worry about it. I've got enough to worry about.'

'Aye, there's the wedding,' said Ted.

Gabriel bit his tongue. He wasn't worried about getting married, he'd meant the restaurant. Typical of Dad to read absolutely everything wrong.

★

In the evening he rang Lena on her mobile. It went to voicemail and he left a message. He tried again later and then once again before he went to bed. He sat in bed with his mobile phone and dialled her number, counted the seven rings before the message service cut in and then hung up. He switched off the lamp and lay down with his phone on the pillow. Why hadn't she called him back? Where could she be and why didn't she take her phone? He picked up his mobile and scrolled through his contacts list. There was her name, Lena, this little scrap of lettering on a tiny glowing screen. This was all he had of her and it was better than nothing so he lay there in the dark, imagining he would never see her again and looking at her name.

CHAPTER THIRTEEN

—〰—

OONA SUCKED THE END OF HER PENCIL AS SHE TOTTED UP THE numbers from the previous night. She jotted down a couple of figures, licked her finger and turned the page in the reservations book. 'Now,' she said, 'I clean forgot where I counted to.' She flicked the page back again.

Gabe pushed his foot against the wastebasket. He balanced his shoe on the rim and rocked the basket back and forth.

'Nineteen tables of four, that makes . . . seventy-six.' Oona crooned a little as she bent over the book, as if the numbers could be lulled into submission. 'And seventeen twos – thirty-two, no, thirty-four.'

'Oona,' said Gabe, 'there's a calculator here.' A ball of paper rolled on to the floor. Gabe righted the basket again but his foot still fretted around the rim.

'Hoh,' said Oona, 'calculator.' She laughed her cosmic laugh.

'Give me the book,' said Gabe. He stabbed at the calculator with a pen.

'Hexercise,' said Oona, 'got to hexercise the brain.'

He'd picked up a message from Rolly this morning about some problem with insurance at the venue. Rolly didn't sound in the best of moods. Gabe said, 'Let's just crack on. Give it to me.'

'Nearly done,' said Oona, 'just have the walk-ins to do. Now what did I have? Sixty-seven and thirty-two?'

'Seventy-six and thirty-four,' said Gabe. To be a successful restaurateur you had to know about more than just food. There was health and safety, tax law, fire regulations, employment law, building regulations, licensing, environmental protection and sanitation. There was insurance to deal with. There was marketing and promotion and publicity. And more, always more.

'Sixty-seven and thirty-four,' said Oona, dragging the words from here to eternity.

'Seventy-six,' said Gabe. 'SEVENTY-SIX.' The bin rolled and clattered as he leaped from his chair. He snatched the book from her hands. 'Christ,' he said, as he sat down again. 'Look, I'm sorry, but we haven't got all day.'

Oona took her hair slides off the front of her chef's whites. She cradled them in the palm of her hand, contemplating, perhaps, whether to turn in her badge.

'Don't worry about it,' said Gabe. He needed an extra shot of coffee, after yet another night's broken sleep. 'Tell Damian to bring me a double espresso and get everyone together in ten minutes. I need to run through some stuff. OK?'

'M'mmm,' said Oona, her almond eyes drowsy with indifference. 'OK.' She clipped the diamanté slides back on the front of her coat. When she paused a few moments Gabriel had to restrain himself from jumping up and tipping her out of her chair.

The kitchen brigade seemed less like a United Nations assembly this morning and more like a pirate crew. Ivan wore his red bandanna, Benny had his trousers rolled and Damian stank of booze. Chef Albert stood at the front parrying and thrusting with a dough hook at some invisible foe, and an unlit cigarette dangled from Victor's lips. Gabriel stared at Victor until he removed the cigarette and tucked it behind his ear. Gabe ran through the specials. Damian leaned on the worktop and burped. Someone needed to take him in hand before his drinking got out of control.

'Pastry section,' said Gabe. Oona had fucked up again. And now Gabe was going to have to listen while Chef Albert bitched and moaned. 'The function tonight – they didn't want a big cake, they want individual cakes and a candle on each one.'

Chef Albert hung the dough hook on his belt. 'Ninety-five guests, no? Ninety-five birthday cakes for tonight?'

'Yes,' said Gabe. Oona hadn't read the sheet properly. It was all down on there. It wasn't only the extra work for the pastry section, it was the hike in the food cost as well.

Chef Albert pouted and shrugged with his hands on his hips. 'I am a pâtissier,' he said.

'Well,' said Gabe, 'there's no point moaning about it. Better forward planning next time.' He nodded at Oona, hoping she would get his point, but she returned a smiling, contented nod that made him realize once and for all that it was completely futile expecting anything from her.

'Moaning?' said Chef Albert, looking round. 'You hear moaning? Does a pâtissier not love to make ze cakes?'

'You feeling all right?' said Gabriel. It was inconceivable that Albert should miss an opportunity to complain. To quit complaining, where Chef Albert was concerned, was pretty much giving up on life. He would not be the first pastry man Gabriel had known who had decided to abandon all hope.

Chef Albert widened his sorrowful eyes. 'Ye-es,' he said, elongating the vowel with astonishment. '*Je suis en pleine forme.* I am – how you say? – tip top.' He reached in his top pocket and extracted a pill bottle. 'My docteur – he gives me more zan ze 'ealth. He gives me *me!*'

'Jolly good,' said Gabriel, anxious to move on down his list before Albert launched into some full-blown Gallic lament. 'Right . . .'

'Ow I wish,' said Chef Albert, 'zis man was in my life ten, twenty years ago. All zis sadness and suffering – I thought it was simply my temperament, my sensitivity, the artist in me. But, no!' Albert was certainly quite animated today. And he seemed to have lost his aura of crackling frost, though maybe he had less starch than usual in his whites. 'No! There is no meaning in zis suffering. Only a chemical imbalance! *Alors,* another miracle! My first birth is from ze mother – God rest her soul – and my second is from ze pills.'

'Good for you,' said Gabriel. 'Holidays. Not long until Christmas, it's busy as hell from here until the New Year. Anyone wants time off over Christmas, get your request in by the end of the day and I'll think about it. If you don't get your request in until tomorrow you're too late. Clear?' He looked over his bunch of ill-assorted brigands. Damian looked back at him glassy-eyed, the involuntary twitch of his eyelid the solitary sign of life. What was wrong with the lad? Where was his ambition? The kitchen drove plenty of men to drink but Damian – what was he? seventeen, eighteen? – had scarcely had time to work up a thirst.

'I thought my first boss was a bastard,' said Gabriel, attempting to hold Damian's unsteady gaze. 'Ranting off orders, do this, do that, and when he gave you a bollocking he'd push you up against the wall with his arm across your neck. We didn't put in requests for holidays. He stuck a list on the noticeboard and you took whatever you got. The bad old days. But, you know what?' Gabe placed his hands on the worktop and ran them along to the edge. 'I realized after a while I wasted a lot of energy on hating that man and I took that energy and I turned it into something useful. I spent it on making a plan – to learn as much as I could, to get out of there, to move on to somewhere better and then to somewhere better and then I'd get to be the boss. And that's what I did. Put some energy into it. Followed through.'

Nikolai, who was standing next to Damian, shook his head. 'A nice story,' he said. 'This is what stories are for, to make order from the chaos of our lives.'

'Oh, really?' said Gabriel. 'And what is a commis chef for? Chopping vegetables, that's what.' He hated the way Nikolai made out he was a philosopher king in rags, an intellectual in the gulag. It was a free country. Nobody was keeping him here. He rejected even a minor promotion, the better to feel oppressed, rather than working his way up like an honest man.

Victor, grinning, shuffling an imaginary deck of cards, said, 'Man, you get to be the bastard now.'

'Victor, my friend,' said Gabriel, beginning calmly enough, 'I'm sticking close to you today. I'm staying closer to you than those pimples between your eyes. I'm on you like the boils on your backside. Understood? IS THAT UNDERSTOOD?' Gabe yanked down his hand – it had strayed up to his head – and stood clenching and unclenching his fists. He controlled his breathing, slow and deep. 'Now,' he said, 'does anyone have any more business?'

Ivan pushed past a porter and a couple of commis. 'I have a business,' he said. 'What bastard have stolen my knife?' The way he glared at Victor suggested the question was purely rhetorical.

Victor quivered. 'I never touched your filthy knife, bro.'

The grill man put his hand on his crotch and adjusted his balls in a manner that was oddly menacing, as if they rather than his brain would dictate any course of action he might take. His cauliflower ear was as red as his bandanna now. 'Henckels knife,' he growled. 'German knife. My knife, you give back to me.'

'Listen, homey,' said Victor, 'I ain't got your knife.'

'Homey?' said Ivan. 'Homey? You bend over and spread the buttocks and I show you . . .' He performed an obscene gesture with his fist. 'I show you who is homosexual.'

Though the scene wearied him, Gabe wanted to laugh. Everyone was straining to see what would happen next. Even Damian was standing more or less straight.

'I saw a knife,' said Benny, 'near the dishwashers. Maybe that one is yours.' He hurried across. 'It is this?' he said, returning.

Ivan muttered something that didn't convey much in the way of gratitude. He rolled one sleeve and tested the blade by shaving the hair on his forearm.

'You are most welcome,' said Benny. His manners never deserted him. If he got mugged, Gabriel imagined, he would say *you are most welcome* as the thugs went on their way.

'Show's over,' said Gabe, clapping his hands. 'Get on with your prep. Shift it, people. Go.'

A few of the cooks mumbled yes, Chef, as they turned.

'Can't hear you,' called Gabriel. 'What did you say?'

'Yes, Chef,' they chanted, loud and clear this time.

Gabe pulled Oona aside as she attempted to shuffle off on her flat square feet. 'Can I have a word?'

'I'll make us a nice cuppa tea.'

'No, Oona, no tea. This won't take long. It's this cake business. Well, it's not really that, it's everything, that's just the icing on . . .' Gabe started over. 'Oona, I'm giving you a formal warning. I'm going to write it up. You've cost us time and you've cost us money, again.'

'But, darlin',' said Oona. 'That wasn't . . .'

'No, Oona, enough chances. I'm doing things by the book from now on.'

Gabriel sat in his office and scanned through his list. He crossed off one item and added three more. Looking in his drawer for a new biro he found another list. There was yet another in the notebook in his bag, and another at home and one that he had started typing on his computer. In all probability there were more, lurking beneath the piles of paperwork, languishing in jacket pockets, trapped in files somewhere. If he got himself organized now he could put together a master list, with absolutely everything on it. Or maybe what he needed was one set of clearly separated lists, filtered into categories of . . . well, the place to start would be to make a list of the lists that were needed. That was what he would do right now. After he'd checked emails again. Perhaps he would call Lena first.

She had been curled in a foetal position on the sofa when he'd returned to the flat the previous night. All the lights were off and the television was on. She was watching a reality show.

'Hey,' said Gabe, lowering himself on to the couch. 'I missed you.' It was a ridiculous thing to say.

Lena slid one leg over his lap. He rubbed the arch of her foot.

'Why do you like watching this?'

'Is live television,' said Lena, 'anything can happen.'

'And what does happen?' They were watching someone wipe down a kitchen surface. The camera cut to two young women, one combing the other's hair.

'Tchh,' said Lena. 'Nothing.'

'So why do you like it?'

'Is not for reason. Only for – ' She sighed at his stupidity. 'Only I like.'

He looked at her face in profile in the darting light of the screen. One moment her hair was greasy and she was hollow-cheeked and gaunt, and in the next flicker her hair was slickly groomed and her features finely drawn. She was like one of those Escher drawings; what you saw depended on how you looked or what you were looking for.

'I called you and left messages,' he said. 'Two or three. Didn't you pick them up?'

'Yes, I think,' said Lena. She sounded as if the subject was of no conceivable interest.

'You didn't call back. Were you here?'

'Tchh.'

She was like some moody teenager. She had no grace. She couldn't think of anyone but herself. 'Lena,' he said, 'this thing about your brother.'

Lena sat up. 'I have photo.' She scavenged through her bag, which was on the floor. 'Pasha,' she said, poking the photograph at Gabe. She got up and switched on a light. 'Very handsome, yes.'

The brother didn't look anything like Lena. He was dark, he sneered with his eyes and there was a purple hue to his lips. 'Tell me again,' said Gabe, 'what happened. How did you lose touch?'

'When I live with girl from Bulgaria, I speak to Pasha and he say he comes soon to London. Then . . . I tell you before, Boris comes to my work and I run.'

'Bulgaria?' said Gabe. 'I thought the girl was from the Ukraine.'

Lena twisted her earrings. She turned it into a gesture of contempt. 'Ukrainian girl first, Bulgarian girl later. Why, what is difference to you?'

'Nothing. Your parents must know where Pasha is. Can't you ring them and find out?'

'Their phone is not work.' She spoke as if he had subjected her to hours of interrogation.

'Maybe it's fixed now,' he said.

'Is not work. Maybe they gone to other place.'

'Doesn't your brother have your mobile number?'

'Why you are asking this?'

'I'm trying to help you, Lena.'

'Why you ask if Pasha have this number? Yuri buy this phone for me. After I run Pasha have no way to find. You think my brother will not lift telephone for me?'

There was something about Lena's story that did not add up. But if he could help her he would, the poor kid. 'OK,' he said gently, 'OK. What do you want me to do?'

Lena attempted to soften her face and succeeded only in looking sly. She looked up from half-lowered lids as she spoke. 'Maybe Pasha is in language school. You find him there. Some places you can look, where Russians are going for talking and drinking. Coach station also – you know where is? Victoria. Is place for job. Many people are going there for job.'

It was a ludicrous request. How many language schools were there in London alone? And even if Pasha had registered at one of them, to gain a student visa, there'd be no guarantee he'd actually turn up there. More likely he had disappeared into the black economy and would not want to be found. 'I'll try,' said Gabe. 'I can't promise anything, but I'll try.'

She rewarded him with a pat on the chest. 'You are good man,' she said, and settled back to look at the screen again.

It would never occur to her, Gabriel thought, to ask about his father. Unless it might bring her some benefit, encourage Gabe to do more for her. At least she hadn't asked about the money again. Though that would probably be coming soon. And that was fine. It was straightforward. The more he thought about it, the clearer the situation became. It was fortunate, really, if he was going to have an affair – an indiscretion, rather, because 'affair' was too grand a word – that it had been with Lena. Things could have got complicated if he'd chosen someone else, that woman on the balcony, for instance, whose emotions and expectations would lack any clarity. With Lena, at least, the exchange was simple enough.

There was nothing between them. They were poles apart with nothing in common. When he'd met Charlie he'd known pretty soon that it was likely to work. They had the same sense of humour, she was the right age, they both liked food and music, and they kept similar hours. It was a bit like cooking, he supposed. If you had the right ingredients you could cook up something pretty good.

But Lena . . . just look at her there, in a state of suspended animation in front of the screen. He could keep watching her, because she was barely aware of him. She was so devoid of charm it was funny. It was quite charming, in its own way.

After he'd been to the bathroom he found her stretched out naked on his bed. The way she lay, so stiffly, she seemed to be waiting not for him but for a winding sheet. He wanted to cover her and tell her no, that this was not right. He sat on the edge of the bed. He put his hands on her feet. He kissed one big toe and then the other. Slowly, he examined each toe. He massaged along her insteps. He held her ankles in his hands. He tested the sharpness of her shin blades with his fingertips. If he could have her one more time, it would be done and spent. It was nothing but a bloodletting, to cleanse her out of his system, purge her once and for all.

When he'd finished he held her against his chest and she slept. He could not sleep but was content to be lying there. The next moment he was falling. He jerked awake. Better not to sleep than to have that dream again.

Lena rolled away to the other side of the bed. Gabriel got up and went to the kitchen. He drank a glass of water. It was only a nightmare and nightmares will not kill you. Someone, only recently, had said just that to him.

Gabe had picked up the phone to call Lena when Ernie trundled through the door, an art folder hugged to his chest, his trousers flapping at the shin.

'Chef,' he said, 'Ah've a special offer on Christmas cards. Would you care to have a wee look?'

'I'll take a pack,' said Gabriel quickly. 'How much do I owe?'

'Ach,' said Ernie, retracting his head. 'Ah dinnae think o' that.'

'Got to have a price list, Ernie. Come on now, I thought it would all be in your business plan.'

'Oh aye,' said Ernie, gazing wistfully to the left of Gabriel's ear, 'Ah dinnae think o' packs.'

'I'll take ten, OK?' Christ, he thought, as if there weren't enough to do. The other thing Rolly had said in the message, *there's a new bistro deluxe opening every time I turn around*. He'd never said anything about a bistro deluxe to Rolly. That was not what Lightfoot's would be. 'Just give me ten or a dozen. Give me twelve.'

Ernie laid the art folder on the desk and unzipped it. 'See, what Ah've done – they're all the same on the outside, just with the Christmas tree stamp. And then you choose the verse you want. Different prices for different lengths.'

'Terrific,' said Gabriel. Classic French food executed with the kind of rigour he would bring to bear – it wouldn't surprise him if the kitchen ended up with a star. The inspectors went incognito, and if they liked the place . . . well, they liked it, and that meant you could put your prices up.

'This is the price list,' said Ernie, 'and here's a list of first lines, all alphabetical, and Ah've kept a list of the ones Ah've sold. That way I know which ones are most popular and Ah can plan for next year.'

Gabe opened a card and read. *Ding dong, hear the angel's bell, Ding dong, hoping you are well* . . . He took a twenty from his wallet. 'Give me whatever I can get for this.' It irked him that he was forced to play social worker, but there was something about Ernie's lists that was touching, heroic in the way of all hopeless endeavours.

'Our very own Poet of the Polywrap, our Bard of the Unloading Bay.' Mr Maddox's massive frame filled the doorway and darkened the office. In his black suit, dark shirt and toning tie, his hands clasped at his groin, he looked like a professional pallbearer waiting for the next coffin of the day.

'Ernie's made some cards,' said Gabe, tucking the twenty into the porter's top pocket.

Mr Maddox loomed in. 'How's it going, Ernie? How's the old poetic inspiration, eh?'

If Ernie had had a cap he would have doffed it. 'Very good, Mr Maddox, thank you, very good.' He stood to a kind of dog-eared attention, scrunching his shoulders and clicking his heels.

When the general manager inspected the rank and file it was like watching members of the public in a line-up to meet the Queen. They became afflicted by self-consciousness, deference and embarrassment, even the bolshiest among them, the below-stairs republicans.

'Well done,' boomed Mr Maddox. 'Off you go.'

The GM sat on the desk. 'Get in here, Gareth, sit yourself down. What you waiting for, a bloody telegram?'

Mr James, who had been whipping about like a rat's tail in the doorway, trying to see round his boss, slunk on to the spare chair.

'I've been in your kitchen, giving out a few pats on the back,' said Mr Maddox. 'You've got to give exactly the right amount. Too few and the natives get restless, too many and they expect a bloody pay rise. Got to get rid of Ernie, by the way. You need to let him know.' He scratched the inside of his wrist, along the ghost of the tattoo.

'Oh, Ernie,' said Gabe, 'he doesn't do any harm. Been here for ever and a day.'

'Then give him a bloody carriage clock, but get him out of here.' The GM picked up a hole-punch and took it apart, spilling little disks of white paper all over the floor.

'Now, we've got the date for the inquest,' Mr Maddox went on, 'you know, for that night porter – his name, Gareth, his *name* – are you clearing your throat or is that what he's called? Yes, all right, I've got it. Yuri. Stick it in your diary, Chef. You'll be wanted, I suppose.'

'Will his family come over?' said Gabriel.

Mr Maddox laid a mocking finger across his lips. 'Oh dear, I didn't think to ask.'

'He had two daughters,' said Gabe, 'one studying economics, the other in the second year of a medical degree.'

'Toxicology report came in. Completely legless, of course. Give him the date, Gareth. It'll probably change. Go on, write it down.'

'Actually,' said Gabe, 'Yuri was an engineer, fully qualified.'

'It's an inquest, Chef, not *Mr and Mrs*. You'll be telling me the colour of his toothbrush next,' said Maddox. 'Well, we lost a good man. That's what I'll say when I'm called to give evidence. A good man went down.' He paused to savour this line, which he clearly felt would resonate well in the coroner's court. 'That's the news we bring for you today, Chef. And what do you have for us?'

'Yes,' said Mr James, 'what do you have for us?'

Mr Maddox put a hand to his ear. 'Anyone else hear an echo? Is there an echo in here?'

Gabriel watched the deputy manager clenching and unclenching his buttocks, a glaze of pious suffering over his face. 'What were you expecting from me, Gareth?'

Mr James consulted with the clipboard. 'The numbers for last night and the night previous to that. The coffee shop three-month forecast. Final budgets on the night-shift room service.'

'We're not in the bloody F&B,' said Maddox, shifting his haunches, knocking a mug and spilling coffee dregs over Gabriel's list.

'Chef missed the food and beverage meeting this week,' said Mr James, as though citing a capital offence.

'Gareth . . .'

'Yes, Mr Maddox?'

'Shut up.'

Gabe turned to Mr James. 'I'll come up to your office, go over the figures with you.'

Tipping back and toppling a pile of suppliers' brochures, Mr Maddox sniffed the air long and hard. 'Smell anything?'

'I smell lunch service,' said Gabe.

'In this business,' said Mr Maddox, speaking loudly over Gabriel, 'you develop a nose. A nose for trouble. A nose for anything rotten. The fishy stuff. You don't know what or where it is, but you find it in the end because you follow your nose.'

'I'm not sure I—'

'All I'm saying – the conversation we had the other day – have you got anything for me? I've put my trust in you.'

'No, not really. I'm on the lookout, of course.'

'Of course, of course,' said Maddox, 'you're one of us, aren't you? Isn't he, Gareth? One of the team. You happy here with us, Chef? You settled? Not planning to cut and run?'

'Me?' said Gabe. 'No.' The words rang out so alarmingly clear and false that he panicked. He needed to divert attention. 'Stanley Gleeson,' he said, 'I'm sure he's up to something.'

'Yes,' said Mr Maddox, 'go on.'

'I don't know yet, but I'm keeping an eye on him. And then there's Pierre,' he babbled on, naming the bar manager. Gabe stood up and fiddled with the air-conditioning. There was sweat running down his back. But what was the worst that could happen if Maddox found out he was planning to leave? He'd get ejected six months ahead of schedule but so what? So what! He couldn't afford for that to happen.

He'd put his money into the pool, there were already costs – the architect had put his invoice in – and Gabe couldn't go six months without pay. Even worse, Rolly and Fairweather might use it as an excuse to back out of the venture. Do a year at the Imperial, they'd said; prove yourself. A year, they'd said. Not six months. Maddox, what a bastard. *I've put my trust in you.* What a bastard thing to say.

Gabe adjusted the thermostat. 'Yes, I was going to mention it . . . Pierre, sometimes puts handwritten orders through from the bar and never rings them up on the till, so either he's pocketing the money or giving meals away.'

'No shit, Sherlock,' said Maddox, 'giving meals away? The barman? You'll be telling me he's poured doubles and charged for singles next.' He laughed. His laughter, which contained no mirth, was like a series of heavy objects falling to the floor, lead balls perhaps, something that made you want to skip out of the way.

'I'm just being straight with you,' said Gabriel.

For a moment Maddox leaned in towards him, sweeping his gaze like a wrecking ball across Gabriel's face. He seemed satisfied. 'It's appreciated. And, as you say, keep an eye on Stanley. There's something about that man. I don't know what it is, but I can smell it. He's up to something, as sure as I've got a hole in my arse.' He got up and looked round at the desk. 'Maybe you should tidy up a bit. Don't know how you find anything in all that mess.'

Front of house turned lunch service into an unexpected bloodbath by fucking up at every turn. Plates were sent back cold which Gabe knew for a fact had gone out hot. The Swedish waitress was mixing up the orders, taking them to the wrong tables and wandering back in leisurely fashion to the kitchen to announce that the 'wrong dish' had been sent.

'Sort her out,' said Gabe to Gleeson, 'before I do it myself.'

'Little stressed in the kitchen today, are we?' Gleeson looked like a waxwork dummy, all stiff and unreal, not a single hair out of place.

'What is she – on drugs or something?'

'Come, come,' sang Gleeson, 'that's a serious allegation to make.'

'What *is* she on then? The end of your dick? Stanley, the girl's a fucking space cadet. Oh, hello, here she fucking comes. Ready on nine? Who's ready on nine? Stanley, get her out of my frigging kitchen, put her on coffees because if you don't, I'm telling you, I'm going to chuck her in a chest freezer and lock her the fuck in there until the end of service tonight.'

'Coming from you,' said Gleeson, a dishonest sparkle in his eye, 'I'll take that seriously. After all, there's been one death below stairs.' He prowled over to the Swedish girl and curved his arm solicitously behind her back as he steered her away.

'You piece of shit,' shouted Gabriel, only managing to find his voice as Gleeson reached the swing doors. 'You fucker! You fucking fuck!'

Gleeson turned with his hands over his ears and rolled his eyes. 'Temper, temper,' he mouthed. 'It'll get you into trouble one of these fine days.'

Oona joined Gabriel at the pass mumbling incantations. ' "Come unto me, all ye that labour and are heavy laden, and I will give you rest." Matthew eleven, verse twenty-eight.'

'He's a fucking wind-up merchant,' said Gabriel, 'he's . . .'

' "For what will it profit them if they gain the whole world but lose their soul?" '

'Jesus Christ,' said Gabe, wiping his brow.

'M'mm,' said Oona.

'Look, can you take over? I need a break.'

Oona made little clucking noises. 'Didn't I just say so, darlin'? You go and get some rest.'

His cubicle was as hot as the kitchen. Gabe knocked the thermostat down another five degrees. He called Charlie on her mobile and the only word he'd spoken was her name but she said, 'You sound a little frazzled, fiancé, can you get away for a while?'

'No,' he said, checking his emails. 'Not really, but I will. Where are you?'

'On my way to the British Museum. Come and meet me. I'll bring you some smelling salts.'

At the newsagent where Gabriel stopped to get cigarettes there was a cardboard tray of adjustable 'sweetheart' rings on the counter for little girls to buy when they came in for a Curly Wurly or a copy of *Sugar* magazine. Gabe bought one and slipped it in his pocket. He walked north up Charing Cross Road. The walk was clearing his head. They'd try for a baby straight away when they got married. It wasn't as if Charlie had time to lose. The first few years would be hard, with him working all hours at the restaurant, but he guessed she'd bring the child in most days. He'd grow up in the kitchen. It would be like a second home to him. Would he mind being dragged along? I used to go into Rileys, thought Gabe. Never did me any harm. He smiled at the cliché. Well, it didn't. And the boy would learn at his side.

What would he teach the kid? What would the kid have learned today, if he'd been with Gabe? It wasn't a good day to witness. Was it so different from all the rest? Gabe sighed because it was all very well a generation ago, to take your son to work as Ted had done, and show him how to be a man. The values Ted preached at home he practised at work. But the world wasn't like that any more. Gabe wasn't proud of the way things were. And he wasn't ashamed either. If he wasn't straight with Mr Maddox today, it was because that was how it had to be. The GM asked for loyalty. In the same breath he wanted Ernie to get the sack after thirty years. Trust, loyalty, commitment – they were only bits of management-speak. You had to have tactics, get into the meeting mindset, be seen to cooperate. It said nothing about a man's character, the way he behaved at work.

Family, thought Gabe, *that's where you show what you're made of.* He'd have his own family soon. He ran up the museum steps to where Charlie was waiting and wrapped her in his arms.

She kissed him three times on the lips. 'You must have been a boa constrictor in a previous life. This is a new coat you're crushing, you know.'

'Sorry,' he said, setting her free. 'I got you this.'

'Tiffany's,' she said, 'you shouldn't have. So now we're officially engaged.'

'We'll go and choose one together, but I couldn't resist the thought of putting a ring on your finger this afternoon.'

Charlie laughed and held out her hand. 'The silly thing is, I quite like this one.'

'Right. Orange is good, matches your eyes. Charlie, I've been thinking

– let's not hang about too long, there's Dad to think of . . . and, anyway, we could book a register office, nothing too fancy, just get it done.'

They were walking into the Great Court now, the glass dome stretching above, encasing the people, the buildings, like one of those snowstorms you shake and put on your desk.

Charlie took Gabe's arm and steered him towards the stairs. 'An incurable romantic,' she said. 'Don't I get to arrive in a coach with white horses? Don't I get to wear a meringue?'

'We'll do it however you want,' said Gabe, wondering how quickly he could get her out of here. It was so airless. There were too many school parties. They always ended up looking at bits of broken old pots.

'So, tell me about Nana Higson,' said Charlie, 'and tell me about your dad.' They trailed along the beautifully lit aisles speaking in the hushed voices of worshippers and stopping now and again to lean against a cabinet of ancient coins.

'I thought we'd go to Bronze Age,' said Charlie. 'There's a bit about feasting you'd like.'

They looked at numerous bronze ladles and buckets, and 'flesh-hooks' made of pieces of bronze linked with crumbling shafts of oak. *Feasts were important social and political occasions for the people of the Bronze Age*, Gabriel read. *Hosting a feast could reinforce loyalty and bind guests in obligation. It provided an opportunity for hosts to display their status and valuable possessions.*

'Don't you find it a bit . . . you know,' said Gabe.

'What?'

'Boring.'

'Gabriel Lightfoot,' said Charlie, crossing her arms and tossing her flaming hair. 'Now that we're to be wed you're not going to come out of the closet as a secret philistine?'

'No way,' said Gabriel, 'I'm as cultured as they come. But I think I need some coffee. Let's go to the café.'

They got the coffees to take away because Gabe said he needed fresh air too, and sat on the wall that bounded the front lawn watching the coaches disgorge, the genteel bustle of Great Russell Street, the lazy lamp lights yawning on in the dimming afternoon. Gabriel sparked a

219

Marlboro Light. 'I see,' said Charlie. 'That's why you wanted to come out. Since when have you *smoked*?'

'Gave up years ago,' said Gabe, 'before I met you. But . . . I've not taken it up again.'

Charlie shivered and put her hands in her coat pockets. Her coat was cream with a dark fur trim and collar, just right for hailing a cab to the Savoy, not jumping on a bus back to the Edgware Road. 'I'm hallucinating,' she said.

'I've always had one or two, at work,' said Gabe. Why was he lying to her? What was the point? 'Nip out to the loading bay, have a breather – no harm in that, is there?'

She looked at him. 'No,' she said, 'I suppose not.' Laying her head on his shoulder she said, 'Am I coming to yours tonight or are you coming to mine?'

Gabriel sucked courage and nicotine into his lungs. This was it. He had to tell her now. 'Charlie, this is going to sound . . . Let me start at the beginning. Remember I told you about the porter – he was living in the basement.'

She pulled away. Already there was suspicion in the angle of her shoulders, in the tilt of her head, and he hadn't told her anything yet. 'Yuri,' she said, 'the one who died.'

He had to get it out quickly, not sound as if he was beating about the bush. 'There was a girl living down there with him, one of the dishwashers, we didn't know about her at first. Then I saw her, she came back to look for some money she'd hidden in the wall, and it had been stolen, and she'd come back to look for it and she didn't have anywhere to go. She had no money and nowhere to go and she was terrified – if you'd seen her – really terrified, that she'd be blamed for something, get in trouble, so I decided to help her. Didn't think about it, just offered her a place to stay.' He finished the cigarette and tossed the stub. It had sounded all right, he thought.

'You mean,' said Charlie slowly, 'that this girl is staying at your flat?'

'Yep,' said Gabriel, 'you'll meet her, skinny little thing, scrawny, terrible hair.'

'What's her name?'

'Lena. God, it's really freezing now. You know I go from a boiling kitchen into the cold like this – hot, cold, hot, cold, it's a wonder I don't get sick. Lena. The thing is, I found out, she told me about all these horrendous things – stuff that's happened to her, you wouldn't believe, she's only a kid.'

'Try me,' said Charlie, giving him a lopsided smile.

'The reason she was hiding out in the basement with Yuri is that she was running away from her pimp.'

'Oh God,' said Charlie. 'East European?'

'The pimp? I don't know. I guess so, he's called Boris. Lena's Russian, Belarussian. From Mazyr,' he added, embellishing unnecessarily, a liar's habit which he seemed to have acquired.

'She was trafficked,' Charlie said, as if explaining things to him.

'That's right.' He checked his watch. He'd have to get back to the Imperial soon.

'We have to help her,' said Charlie, taking charge as he had known she would, 'get her to the police and file charges, find her some counselling.'

'No, she won't go to the police. She's too scared of Boris. She thinks he'll get her somehow.'

Charlie put her hand on his arm. 'Gabe, those men, her clients, they raped her. There's no other word for it.'

'I knew you'd want to help,' said Gabriel. He hugged her, looking over her shoulder at the museum entrance, the learned Greek colonnade suffusing him somehow with the confidence that everything would be dealt with calmly now.

'So when did you find her?' said Charlie. 'Today?'

'No,' said Gabe, 'a couple of days ago. Will you come round later? I'm finishing at ten.'

'You mean before you went to Blantwistle? She's been staying at your flat since then?'

'I guess,' said Gabriel. 'Yes. You're shivering. Your poor little hands have turned to ice. We'd better get moving, don't you think?'

'You guess,' said Charlie. 'You guess? You came and stayed the night at mine before you left, do you *guess* she was at your place then? I see. Or maybe I don't. We spent the evening, the night, together but she slipped your mind, this Lena, because you didn't mention her.'

'Of course she didn't "slip my mind". Charlie . . . don't be like that. This girl – if you saw her you'd understand. She's such a wretch. And she made me promise not to tell anyone about her. Maybe I should have told you, but I promised her, and now that I've won her trust a little, she's agreed . . . she's agreed to let us help her.'

Charlie slipped down off the wall and stood in front of him, breathing frosty columns in the air. She turned her head, watching the people come and go, stepping crisply along the path. 'I have to ask you. I'm only going to ask this one time and then it's done.' She still didn't look at him. 'Did you sleep with her?'

He could tell her and they would get through it. She was big enough for that. But he wouldn't do it to her. He cupped her chin and drew her face round. 'No.'

She smiled gingerly, as someone smiles after difficult dental work, risking pain. 'I had to ask.'

'It's OK.' He kissed her forehead.

'So, you ran into her in the basement and then she came home with you. You offered her a place to stay, just like that. Not many people . . . they're usually scared to get involved. I'm sorry I asked you that question. You're a kind man, Gabe. You really are.'

Gabriel lit up a cigarette. 'Well,' he said, exhaling, 'you know me.'

Charlie watched him smoking. She didn't say anything. She looked down as he tapped ash, looked up as he blew smoke, tracked the progress of his cigarette, the arc that it travelled as he raised and lowered it again. 'Do I?' she said, finally. 'Do I know you? I didn't know you smoked.'

'I told you. I just have one or two. What difference does it make?' She looked angry; he'd have to tread carefully. Was she shivering or shaking with rage?

She shook her head and turned as if to leave and then turned again and flew at him, knocking the cigarette from his hand. 'You fucked her, didn't you? You coward. Sitting there smoking, you coward. Did you think I wouldn't know?'

Gabriel turned up his palms. He looked around to appeal to the judge and jury. 'What? Because I'm smoking, that means I fucked someone?'

'Yes,' hissed Charlie. 'Yes.'

He was calm. All he had to do was deny it. In a minute she'd be apologizing again. 'Look at me, Charlie.' He paused a moment. 'OK, yes. I did it. You're right.'

Charlie hugged herself. A wind started up and blew her hair across her face. When she pushed it back he saw, but did not quite believe, the damage that he'd done. She said, 'How many times?'

'Charlie . . .'

'How many times? Well, was it once? Was it twice?'

'I don't know. It's not what you think. She needed—'

'—you to fuck her? Are you out of your mind?' Charlie was yelling and he could not make himself heard. 'This girl – this poor girl – who you say has been abused.'

'Please,' said Gabe, 'stop shouting. I know it was wrong. But I could have lied about it. At least I told you the truth.'

'You *lied*. My God, you lied, and I believed you.' Her eyes glittered darkly with tears.

'Not for long,' said Gabe softly. He reached for her. 'Sweetheart, I'm so sorry. Honestly, I don't know how I got us into this mess. But we can get out of it, can't we? And we can help her too.'

She rested her brow on his shoulder and snuffled about for a bit. Then she lifted her head and looked him straight in the eye. 'You think you know someone,' she began, before her voice cracked. 'You think you know someone . . .' She took his hand and placed something in it and pressed his fingers closed. 'I hope you do help her. She sounds like she needs it. Don't make things worse for her.'

She backed away from him, her hands in her pockets, and she looked magnificent, backlit by the streetlights, her coat cinched tight at the waist, the deep burnish in her hair. Gabriel gripped the ring. It seemed important not to lose it, not to give up like that. 'Wait,' he called. 'We need to talk about it. There are things you don't understand.'

'I understand enough, Gabriel. The question is, do you?' She turned then and left him and before she was out of sight he lit up a cigarette and started planning what he needed to do to get her back.

CHAPTER FOURTEEN

—∾—

GABE WATCHED ERNIE AND OONA SCUTTLE AND SHUFFLE TOWARDS THE prefab from opposite ends of the loading bay. Oona had a low centre of gravity; any lower and she'd be rooted permanently to the ground. Ernie looked distressed and distracted, which was how he always looked on the move. He needed a pillar to lurk beside, a rock to duck behind, a shadow in which to rest. It was a perpetual hazard of his porter's job that no sooner had he reached a place of relative safety than he was forced to break cover again. Perhaps it would be kinder to put him out of his misery, effect the 'restructure and redundancy initiative' outlined in Mr James's sickly little memo yesterday.

In swift light strides Gabe passed his executive sous-chef.

'Good Lord,' said Oona, as if Gabe had spread his wings and flown.

'Morning,' said Gabe, hurdling a packing crate. He jumped into the back of the cheese van.

'Hernie need a little bitta help,' called Oona, sing-song.

Gabe watched the pair converge at Ernie's hut. He owed Oona an apology. He'd filled out the wrong details for that birthday party and then given Oona a formal warning about it. Ernie and Oona both stepped into the doorway at once and became, momentarily, wedged in the frame.

Gabe turned away laughing and groaning. 'Crack troops,' he said under his breath. 'Top team.'

He picked up a Vacherin du Terroir and lifted the lid. He put it to one side. He examined the Roqueforts next and they failed to inspire. It had been a week since he'd seen Charlie and he hadn't called her yet. The plan was to call her today. Give her a week to cool off and then ring her when she'd given up expecting him to call. Maybe she'd still be furious. Maybe he should have run after her straight away.

He used his penknife to slice a piece of Demi Pont l'Évêque. He held it under his nose. Why had he told her? This was the question he could not answer. He'd decided (hadn't he?) not to tell her. And then he told her. Just like that. He did it without thinking. But that was only an expression (wasn't it?), a manner of speaking. *I did it without thinking.* You dodge a fist without thinking. You step around a pothole without thinking. You *breathe* without thinking. You don't tell your girlfriend you fucked someone else without thinking. Anyway, he'd considered it, played the angles, rejected it as an option. Then he spoke and somehow it all came out.

It must have been in his mind to do it, to tell her. You can't speak the words without the thought. The thought comes first and the words give it shape. They follow along, however infinitesimally small the delay. So he'd decided to tell her. Why? He'd had that thought. Tell her, he'd thought. *It was my thought. But where did it come from? It wasn't my idea to think something stupid like that.*

He was going round and round in circles. What did it matter? Whatever way it had happened it was done. But he could not let the subject rest. What he wanted to know was this: did he produce the thought or was the thought something that happened to him? *It just popped into my mind.* People said that, didn't they? But if he wasn't responsible for his thoughts, then what was 'he'? Was there a 'he' that was separate from the bit of him that thought? He didn't think so. How could he know? And what was the point of all these questions? They just turned in and in on themselves in one big tangled mess.

I said it without thinking. Maybe it made more sense that way. The thought followed the words. Subconscious, that was it. Deep down he wanted to break it off with Charlie, wanted to destroy the relationship. He groaned at this marvellous insight. It made no sense, that he'd want to fuck everything up. It all went round and round. He could scarcely pick out one thought from the next.

He jumped out of the van and the cheese man was waiting. 'Sorry,' said Gabe, 'but I don't really want anything today.'

A giant bullfrog in a tuxedo had been positioned strategically across the entrance to Dusty's. It moved aside to allow a couple of girls dressed in two or three sequins to trip fawn-like down the stairs. Gabe looked at Nikolai. 'There's never been a bouncer before.'

A gaggle of girls brushed past them and the bouncer unclipped the red velvet rope. Gabe glanced at the girls' legs. They looked like they might snap. The knees were the widest part. It certainly wasn't the usual Dusty's crowd.

'Members?' said the bouncer, his hooded eyes swivelling between Nikolai and Gabe. He didn't wait for a reply. Pointing up at the sign he said, 'Members only now.'

'Ruby in the Dust,' said Gabriel. 'Where's Dusty? What's he done to this place?'

'Who? Never 'eard of him. You're not getting in.'

Nikolai put a hand on Gabriel's arm. 'Plenty more places. Come on.'

'Look,' said Gabe, 'I've been drinking here for . . .'

'Not any more, mate.'

'Fuck's sake,' said Gabe. 'Do you think I *want* to go in there?'

'I don't know what you want, mate. All I know is you're still hanging around. And you ain't getting in.'

Gabriel flew up to the red velvet rope. He was eye to eye with the bouncer. He could almost feel the fat throb of his neck. 'You,' he said, spitting the words, 'are not very civilized. I asked you about Dusty. This used to be Dusty's place.'

'Chef,' said Nikolai, 'this gentleman is not in the mood for conversation. Let's find another establishment.'

Gabe allowed Nikolai to steer him away.

'I can't believe it,' said Gabe, though he believed it only too well, property prices being what they were. 'Dusty's has always been there.'

They tried a couple of pubs but there was nowhere to sit, a bar at which they were (politely) refused at the door, and another in which the music was intolerable and the clientele unbearably loud and young.

'I have a bottle of vodka,' said Nikolai. 'In my locker.'

Gabriel did not want to drink vodka at work with Nikolai. He did not want to sit in this bar. He did not want to traipse any longer around these streets. He did not want to go home to Lena. The only thing he did want was to call Charlie, and that he could not manage yet. 'Let's go, then,' he said.

Though it was strictly against regulations they smoked in the locker room. They drank Nikolai's cheap vodka from plastic water-cooler cups. Little spots of colour appeared in Nikolai's dead-white cheeks. He could almost be albino, Nikolai, with his white eyelashes and brows. He had the eyes of a mouse. But his hair was ginger and nutmeg, to keep you guessing, as Nikolai always did.

'What shall we drink to?' said Gabriel, topping up the cups.

Nikolai smiled but did not speak.

'To Yuri?' said Gabe.

'If you like,' said Nikolai.

'There's a dream I keep having,' said Gabe.

Nikolai nodded.

Gabriel sat on his right hand to keep it from flinging up again to his head. He clutched the plastic cup in his left and tossed the vodka down.

'Why do they call you Doc?' Nikolai's English was barely accented. He was clearly educated. What was he doing, chopping onions all day?

'Ah,' said Nikolai.

'You don't say much.'

'I got out of the habit,' said Nikolai.

'Don't let me force you,' said Gabe.

Nikolai smiled. Gabe looked around the locker room. It seemed the right place to be drinking with Nikolai. It matched his austerity. There was something Soviet in the strip lighting, the metal lockers, the two that gaped open utterly bare. Though Russia, of course, was totally different now. Moscow was all glitz and glam, what he'd seen in the supplements, gangsters and molls, the Wild West gone east. But that wasn't Nikolai. Nikolai was cheap vodka, bread queues, empty shelves.

Nikolai liked to make himself an enigma. Well, Gabe wasn't playing the game. He wouldn't ask him anything. They'd sit here in the bowels of the Imperial and listen to the rumble and whine in the walls. Might as well drink vodka in silence with Nikolai as do anything else he did not want to do.

'Drink to the year ahead,' said Nikolai. 'May it be full of joy.' He saluted with his cup.

'My girlfriend left me,' said Gabe. 'We were engaged.'

'A beauty,' said Nikolai, as if that explained it all.

'Oh,' said Gabe, 'you saw her. That time at the club.'

Nikolai lit a cigarette and offered it to Gabe, who slid his hand out from under his bum. When he was smoking his arm behaved itself.

'She's a cracker,' said Gabe, like some no-hope punter. 'I fucked up.'

'You were together long?'

'Three years. Three years and a bit.'

'And before? You were married before?'

Gabe shook his head. 'Waiting for, you know . . . the right time.'

Nikolai crossed his legs. He drank off another shot. His eyes were pretty much pink.

Gabe matched him with another drink. He needed a few drinks tonight. All this stress. He needed to relax. 'The thing about Charlie is, she's very independent. She likes her freedom. Likes to do her own thing.'

Nikolai poured again.

'But she can be very needy. Biological clock, all of that. You know how women are.'

Nikolai assented with a slow blink.

'She'll look in the mirror, see all kinds of faults with herself. She knows it's daft.'

'Ah,' said Nikolai.

They drank.

'She's not stupid, though. She sees through all that magazine stuff. Botox, implants – she'd never go there. I don't think so, anyway.'

Gabe ground a cigarette butt beneath his heel. 'She's pretty serious, interested in politics, culture . . . and music, she's serious about that. Although sometimes she says she's not.' She sounded pretty unstable the way he was describing her, but he hadn't said anything about her that wasn't true. She was changeable, that was the thing. Be one way and then another. Contradict herself. Hadn't she said to him, *I'm only going to ask this one time* – and then she asked him again. Forced him to say yes, I slept with her, like it was exactly what she wanted to hear.

'When I was growing up—' said Nikolai. He broke off to deal with the bottle again.

Gabe spilled a little vodka down his chin. *God, I'm drunk. But not so drunk I don't realize how drunk I am.* He determined to rectify this situation and emptied the rest of the cup down his throat. What he wanted to be was drunk and oblivious. He did not want to think about degrees of drunkenness.

'When I was growing up, in the Soviet Union,' said Nikolai, 'femininity was a simple thing. A woman was a worker. A woman was a mother. A woman was a wife. My mother, she worked in a factory. In the factory she wore blue overalls, like a worker. When she came home, she wore an apron, like a mother. And once a month she went out with my father to listen to music and drink a little vodka, and she wore lipstick. It was bright red.' When Nikolai did talk, the talk turned into a speech. He spoke in his usual modest, precise tones but the cadence drew you in. His authority was like an undertow sucking you gently away from shore.

Gabriel closed his eyes. There was a pleasant kind of swimming in his head.

'On those nights they made a lot of noise when they came home. There was only a curtain across the room. We slept on one side and my parents on the other. Even with my head beneath the pillow I heard everything.'

Gabe opened his eyes again. There were things about Charlie that irritated him. The way she got into bed. She folded one leg under her and swung the other one in. There was nothing wrong with it. But it was always exactly the same. If they got married he'd have thirty, forty, years of it, watching her get into bed, and always precisely, exactly the same.

Nikolai passed him another cigarette. His hand was as white as a surgical glove.

'But now,' said Nikolai, 'what does femininity mean?'

'Search me,' said Gabriel, leaning back rather faster than he'd intended and cracking his head against a locker door. The thing about Charlie was . . . no, it was gone.

'My mother had one lipstick,' said Nikolai. 'We all knew what it meant. How many lipsticks does your girlfriend have?'

'Charlie? Oh, dozens. I don't know. Every shade.' She never closed the door when she went for a pee. Now that was annoying. And he'd never mentioned it.

'This is like a metaphor for women today,' said Nikolai. He seemed remarkably sober, or Gabriel was, at last, remarkably drunk.

'Women,' said Gabe. 'Lipshtick.'

'My mother had only one lipstick. It was bright red. We all knew what it meant.' Nikolai had said all this before. Perhaps he was pissed as a fart. 'But now a woman has many shades. She might wear them all in one day. It depends on her moods. It is very confusing for men.'

Gabe reached for the bottle. It was empty. 'Let's borrow one from the bar.'

'And we'll drink to Yuri,' said Nikolai.

'To Yuri,' said Gabe with a wild laugh.

'A good man.' Nikolai burped loudly as though in tribute. 'He saved his money for his girls. Every couple of months he sent it home. Lucky I knew his hiding place. There was money waiting there and I sent it to his family. The coroner's office gave me the address. Very lucky for them, or this money would be rotting still inside the wall.'

In the couple of weeks since he'd returned from Blantwistle, he had fallen into a routine of sorts with Lena. When he returned from work they'd get a takeaway or a pizza delivery or have a bit of bread and cheese in front of the TV. Sometimes they didn't bother to eat. Lena's monumental capacity for indifference extended, of course, to food. And sometimes Gabe could not bear to think of food again after a day in the kitchen, or he was simply not hungry, or he was hungry but too tired to care. Today, though, Lena had broken the routine and cooked a meal.

They sat in the kitchen. Lena had used a white sheet as a tablecloth. She'd folded two pieces of kitchen towel into triangles for napkins and found two candle stubs and set them on jam-jar lids. The table was burdened with dumplings, fritters, pancakes and rolls, pickles and salads and breads.

'Eat,' said Lena. She'd washed her hair and spread it out over her shoulders. She began with the varenyky and explained every dish to him. The Ukrainian girl had shown her how to make the cottage cheese fritters with raisins. The cabbage rolls stuffed with rice and mincemeat they used to have at home.

'Beautiful,' lied Gabe, tasting the potato pancakes. 'You're quite a chef.'

'Tchh.'

She picked at some mushrooms and beetroot, but mainly she watched him eat.

'So, Lena?' he said. 'Why the feast?'

'You like?'

'Yes.'

'OK.'

'Because you thought I'd like it?'

'Why not?'

'OK.' He couldn't stop looking at her. He had to force the food down. 'You found the dress.'

He'd bought it a fortnight before because he wanted to see her in something other than her black skirt and top, but he'd left it at the back of the wardrobe in a plastic bag. This evening she had been waiting by the door when he came in and she was wearing it, a poppy-print dress with short sleeves, a girlish summer dress, all wrong and completely right. 'How old are you, Lena?' he'd blurted and she had only shrugged.

'Yes,' said Lena now. 'I find.' She had a marvellous ability to kill conversation. When Gabe thought he'd found an opening, she managed to close it down.

He tried again, 'Must have taken you ages.'

'Yes.'

What was it with all this food? He hadn't told her about his little chat with Nikolai. That money wasn't hers. If it had been hers she would never have left without it. It only occurred to her later and she must have thought nobody else knew. She hadn't mentioned the money since he'd got back from Blantwistle, which was suspicious. Maybe she'd sensed, somehow, that he had found out. She'd still want money from him. Maybe this was a new strategy of hers.

'So Valentina taught you to cook this, when you were in the flat in Edmonton?'

Lena said, 'Maybe. Maybe Edmonton. Maybe Golders Green.' She lifted her wine glass in two hands. She really did look like a child.

He tried to catch her out sometimes and it wasn't difficult. Her story always changed.

Gabe choked down the last of the dumplings. He looked at her, tried to hold her gaze. 'Beautiful,' he said. 'Lovely. Gorgeous.'

She rolled her eyes.

'Do you remember Victor?' said Gabe. Ivan and Victor had been at it again. Lena might know what had gone on between those two – East European gossip below stairs. Maybe Nikolai had told Yuri and Yuri had told Lena, and maybe Lena would tell Gabriel now.

Lena twisted an earring. 'No.'

'What about Ivan?' said Gabe. He still hadn't made time to go and check on that guest room, the one Ivan had gone into with Gleeson. Not that he'd find anything – they were bound to cover their tracks.

'I don't remember,' she said.

'Yuri must have known them.'

'Maybe,' she said, or half said, the word aborting on her tongue.

He gave up. He didn't feel like talking anyway. All he felt like doing was looking at her and in a second he would get up and clear the table and then they'd sit in the half-dark in front of the television and he would be able to scan her over and over while she pretended not to notice, until finally when he judged her sufficiently hypnotized, he would slip to the floor and take hold of her feet.

She spent, so she said, most of the day in front of the screen. He gave her a little money before he left in the mornings. Not enough that she could run away. She spent it at the shop on the corner. One time he'd waited out of sight to see what she did. He'd stood in a doorway for a couple of hours, craning his neck to see, and when she came out of his building she went into the grocer's and then back home again straight away.

The neighbours hadn't said anything. He'd had his answers prepared, about both Charlie and Lena, but now he knew he wouldn't be needing them. That was the great thing about London. Nobody interfered.

One day she had started weeping in the morning as he was about to leave. He tried to hold her but she disintegrated beneath his fingers, collapsing to the floor. She howled until he thought that surely the neighbours would come and bring the police. This can't go on, he decided. But the next morning she rose early, and when he walked into the kitchen she was humming tunelessly and doing the washing-up.

Sometimes, as now, he had the sensation that if he reached out his hand it would pass straight through her.

'Thanks for dinner,' he said.

She stared into the middle distance, as though it were Gabe who didn't exist.

If they moved through to the sitting room, they could float together in the half-light, neither one truly present, neither one truly getting away.

Gabe pushed his chair back. He fingered his bald patch. That was real enough. It had grown. With Lena the situation was getting to be absurd. It was time to look at it clearly and get it sorted out. He wasn't going to let it run on and on. Why did he hold his breath around her? As though if he said the wrong thing she might go up in a puff of smoke.

'I've been thinking – we should go to the police. This Boris has to be stopped. There's other girls out there.'

Lena said, 'You want that I leave.'

'Listen to me,' said Gabriel. 'He has to be punished.'

'Your girlfriend have something to do with it,' said Lena, the tendons in her neck standing proud.

'You'll be safe, I promise you.' He would set the process in motion and one thing would follow on from another. He would look back on this episode with Lena and marvel at how quickly it had unfolded and packed up again, once everything was back on track.

'Your girlfriend have—'

'Forget about her.' He cut Lena off. 'She's got nothing to do with this.'

Lena started scraping plates. She knocked a serving spoon to the floor. 'I know girl,' she said, 'she come from Chişinău. You know where is? Moldova, OK, you know, maybe. She is whore like me.'

'Lena . . .'

'Whore like me,' repeated Lena, scraping hard, as though attempting to remove the pattern from the crockery. 'She run away and she go to police and she tell them what have happen to her. They say to her, where are your papers? They say to her, you are illegal immigrant. They say to her, you go home now and they put her on aeroplane. These men, they meet her at airport and they bring her back again.'

'I hardly think . . .' said Gabriel.

Lena let the plate drop on to the table. 'They bring her back to pimp.' She spoke quickly and there was heat in it, though the words as usual lacked inflection, as though she were racing through a list. 'The police have come and arrest him and asking many, many question and then they let him go. He say to her, see, you cannot touch me, bitch. And then he beat her like never before. After that he sell her to Boris. You see what good it do for her, Irina, when she go to police?'

He didn't know what to believe. She would lie, certainly, if it suited her, but did she have the capacity to concoct a tale so fast? It was hard to tell. He said, 'They don't do that any more. They changed the law. Girls don't get deported now. They let them settle in this country.' He didn't know if that was a lie or the truth. He had no idea about the law, but there was such a thing as justice and you got it by going to court.

Lena twisted her skinny fingers together. The dress, now he looked at it properly, was too big for her. It hung off her shoulders, the waist-band sat on her hips. She looked like a little girl in a hand-me-down. He would never, ever touch her – not in that way – again.

'You have papers?' said Lena. 'You can get for me?'

'No,' he said. 'I can't do that. We have to go to the police.'

Lena lifted a fork. She extended her arm, then opened her fingers and let the fork clatter to the floor. She picked up a knife and repeated the operation. She did the same with a blue and white dish that smashed and sent a splash of beetroot juice up her leg.

'Enough,' said Gabe.

She continued with a plate and a spoon.

'All right,' said Gabe. 'Stop.'

She went on smashing the crockery until Gabe rose from his chair and held her arms.

'He know,' she said, 'where my grandmother live. My parents have move somewhere but my grandmother is in village very close. He will send someone.'

Gabriel bent down slowly. He knelt among the beetroot and cabbage rolls, still holding her by the arms. 'It's OK,' he said. How stupid he was being. He knew that this Boris was terrifying to her. 'No police.'

'My grandmother, she look after me very good.'

He released her arms tentatively. 'Lena, why don't you go home? Forget about everything. Start again.'

She drew her bare feet up on to the chair and hugged her knees. She looked at the ceiling. 'Home,' she said. 'People like me, no, we don't have.'

'Of course you do,' said Gabe, still kneeling. 'Trust me. It'll be fine.'

She lowered her chin and her eyes were level with his. It was awkward looking at her, because she seemed not to see him. It was like staring into a blind person's face.

'Fine?' said Lena. 'No, I don't think. I have hear so many stories. You like to hear one story too?'

'I'll buy you a ticket,' he said.

'This girl, sixteen years, Romanian girl, this is story I have hear.'

Gabe put a finger to his lips. 'Shhh!'

'Her pimp he is from Albania, and he take her first to Italy and then Holland and then . . . I don't know. Some time they spend in England and then I think they go to Italy again. And one day she is rescue by police, they go for raiding, kick door, take her to shelter with charity ladies and hot soup.'

'Sweetheart,' said Gabe. 'Don't.'

'For six months she have not speak.' Lena lapsed for a few moments into her usual silence. Gabe inched closer to her on his knees. 'Only slowly words are coming. And she have no teeth here at front, the pimp have take out to make easy for give blow jobs.'

'Hush,' whispered Gabe.

'I have not tell you best part of story,' said Lena. 'Why you tell me *hush*?' She chewed a fingernail. 'They take her back home,' Lena continued after a while. 'Her family think she have work in restaurant. Then they learn what happen to her. And the father take his shotgun – and he kill himself.'

Gabe looked at the food on the floor. 'You don't have to go back,' he said. 'Stay. Stay for as long as you like.'

She was quiet.

'You want to stay in London?'

Lena laid her head on her knees.

'I'll help you,' said Gabriel. He'd said it often enough. He would really do it. There was nothing he wouldn't do. 'I'll find Pasha for you. I'll help you both get jobs.'

Lena still said nothing. She rocked a little, hugging her knees.

Gabriel's own knees were hurting. He shifted his weight back on his heels. 'Hey,' he said, 'you're doing fine.'

'You know how they prepare new girls ready for working? You can guess?' She brushed his cheek with her fingers. 'Boris bring six men for my first night. This was party for them.'

Gabe got to his feet. 'Come on.' He took her hand. 'Let's watch some television. I'll clear this up in the morning.'

She let him lead her out of the kitchen. In the hallway she pulled back. 'I fight them,' she said.

'I know.' He squeezed her hand a little, trying to coax her through to the sitting room, thinking they'd be safe once the television was on.

'I kick and scream. I bite. I think they will not keep doing what they are doing to me when they see I am not whore.'

'Sweetheart. Please.'

She looked at him properly then, and it was with the contempt he deserved. 'This is not nice story for you?'

'I don't want you to upset yourself.'

But she had already receded, the blind look in her eyes once more. She spoke softly, wistfully, full of wonder at the mysteries of the universe.

'They laugh,' she said. 'This men. When I kick and cry. I think maybe they are crazy. They have lose their minds. But next day it happen also and also after that and then I start to think, this is normal. This is how things happen. Is me – I am crazy one and this is why they laugh. And then . . . then, I don't cry any more. I don't fight. And Boris he come, he say, good – you are ready now. And I – ' Lena smiled. 'I have want so much to see this world.'

They settled in front of the television and did not speak for a while. Gabe examined Lena's face. In the tricky reflected light her eyebrows were barely visible, two small thin scars arching across her brow. She pulled at her earrings. He said, 'Lena, those men were evil. You know that, don't you?'

She shrugged.

'Psychopaths. Crazies. Not you, them.'

She seemed not to hear him.

'And all the men who came to the flats, when you were . . . when you were working, they were evil too. But most men aren't like that.'

She kept her face turned to the screen.

'It must be hard for you to believe it, but most men are basically good.'

Lena, without turning, said, 'Like you, Gabriel? You are good?'

'I hope so,' he said, 'I'm not like those men who . . .'

'They are OK,' she said, 'most of them.'

'No,' he said.

'Yes.' She yawned. 'They are OK.'

'But what they . . .'

'Is one man who want for me to wear high shoe and walk on him. He is good customer. He never touch me. Never.'

Pervert, thought Gabriel, but he kept the thought to himself.

'Only one customer,' said Lena, 'is very bad.' She got up and switched off the television. She drifted over to the window and leaned, blackly silhouetted, against it.

Behind her the London night streamed by in a haze of headlamps, streetlights, neon signs and window lights.

'If I see this man,' said Lena. 'If I see this man, I kill him. This is how I promise myself.'

Gabriel always wanted Lena to talk to him. He wanted information. He would take the pieces of her, like a jigsaw puzzle, and arrange them, every fragment. But now that she was talking he wished that she would stop. The more she spoke, the further she drifted away from him. He did not wish to hear any more.

'He is . . . yes, I think,' said Lena, only a shadow against the window frame. 'I think he is evil, this man.'

'You'll never see him again,' said Gabe. 'Don't think about him now.'

'When I close my eyes, I see. Very ugly this man. Sit on my bed, push marriage ring round and round on finger.'

He looked around at the bland bedroom furniture seeking an anchor, a clue to the man who lived here and who would not touch this girl. A pine chest of drawers, a watercolour print, a bedside cabinet, a hard-back book waiting to be read. He trembled. Lena had shut her eyes. Close to tears, he sat on the edge of the bed and took hold of her feet. He appraised each toe, the pearly nails, each little knuckle, the delicate articulation of each joint. He slid his fingers around them and down her soles and rubbed gently on the heels, marvelling at how truly she was flesh and bone, his Lena, his ghostly girl. And the anklebones, they were real all right, the shinbones and the knees, and she raised her hips lightly so he could raise her dress. He worked slowly up her body, connecting every part of her, putting her back together again.

He smoked a cigarette in bed and Lena lay on her stomach with one hand trailing on the floor. Once, early on, she had put on a show, an old habit, pretending to enjoy the sex, but now she merely submitted to his claims. If it surprised her, his nightly examination, his intricate pawing that began with her feet, she did not show it. She was used to worse, he supposed. Another client fetish, better than others she had endured. After a certain point he could not stop himself. His desire was a foul creature that climbed on his back and wrapped its long arms around his neck. What did it want with him? He would cage it if he could. One day he would have the strength to kill it, for it was not part of him.

He stubbed the cigarette out in a saucer. Lena sat up and stretched, displaying her fatless rack of ribs.

'I find frame for photo of Pavel. You don't mind this?'

'Who's Pavel?' he said.

'Pavel. Pasha. My brother.' She opened the drawer next to the bed and took out a frame studded with beads of coloured glass. 'Is OK to put on table?'

'Yes, of course,' he said.

Lena held the frame on her knee and traced a finger across the glass. Gabe put his arm around her and studied Pasha too. If there was a family resemblance he couldn't see it. Pasha's head was almost square and his hair and eyes looked black.

Lena put two fingers to her lips, kissed them and transferred the kiss to the glass. A spark of warmth fired in her cold blue eyes and Gabriel understood what he should have seen at once: the man on whom she had bestowed a tender kiss was not her brother. Lena had a lover. This was the man whom Gabe had promised to find.

CHAPTER FIFTEEN

—⟋⟍—

STRIDING DOWN LOWER REGENT STREET, ON HIS WAY TO MEET ROLLY
and Fairweather, past sushi and burger bars, sandwich shops and
wholefood cafés, Gabriel felt a pang of hunger though he had, for a
change, eaten a reasonable lunch today. London wasn't the brains of
the country, as people said; it certainly wasn't the heart. London was
all belly, its looping, intestinal streets constantly at work, digesting,
absorbing, excreting, fuelling and refuelling, shaping the contours of
the land.

Where the road ran into Pall Mall, he looked up at the Crimean
War Memorial, cast in bronze out of the cannons captured at the siege
of Sebastopol. Charlie had told him that, when they strolled arm in
arm to the park one day. Most people (Gabe included himself) were
blind to the history around them. He crossed into Waterloo Place,
flanked on either side by the white stone and discreet grandeur of
clubbable London. How often had he passed through without sparing
a glance at the monuments? He checked his watch. Franklin, the Great
Arctic Navigator, he read, and his brave companions sacrificed their
lives in completing the discovery of the North West Passage in 1848.
The monument was erected by the unanimous vote of parliament. You
could feel the pride. Gabe passed to and fro between the Victorian
field marshals, noting their conquering stances, the manful sweep of
their coats, the way they held their swords. They had the look of
implacable confidence, of men who had turned the course of history,

and for whom it would never turn again. They held their heads high to the future and turned their feet out to the Empire. Here was John Fox Burgoyne, field marshal, and here John, first Lord Lawrence, Viceroy of India. Lord Clyde stood high above Britannia, who was seated on a lion, those twin symbols of the nation which now could only be viewed with an ironic smile. Gabe cast a final look over the square and the bright gold Britannia sailing high on the Athenaeum seemed to turn to him and wink.

He flew down the steps beneath the Duke of York's column, his feet hardly touching the ground, and along Horse Guards. It was a mild December afternoon and several small groups of tourists crunched over the gravel towards the Household Cavalry Museum. They looked to be hurrying and Gabe, who had never seen the Changing of the Guard, decided he might as well walk down Whitehall. He cut across and arrived in the courtyard as a fresh pair of Life Guards was marched out for inspection. In their red coats and white gloves, their spurred boots and spiked helmets, chin bands at lips and visors pressed over the eyes, they looked like toy soldiers, a re-enactment society, fakes. The tourists lapped it up with grins and digital cameras. This wasthe Britain they liked to see.

He hurried along the reassuringly wide sweep of Whitehall, a broad pair of shoulders on which the country could rest. London plane trees, with their camouflage trunks, lined the avenue, shedding their spiked little fruit. He passed the caged entrance to Downing Street, looked up at Big Ben, the scrubbed stone and moon face, and ducked through the underpass to emerge at the Houses of Parliament. Security, of course, was on high alert. Gabe walked past black railings, checkpoints, men with mirrors on sticks inspecting the undercarriages of cars, warning signs, ramps and barriers and policemen with machine guns. It all had to be done for security but it made the place look dangerous rather than safe, as if this were a siege situation, the hostage democracy itself.

Processed through the St Stephen's entrance, Gabe loitered by a marble statue of Walpole while he waited to be collected by a min-ion, but it was Fairweather, leather folder tucked under his arm, who charged across the hall.

'You've made it!' He offered congratulations as though Gabe had completed a solo Atlantic voyage. 'Admiring our first prime minister, I see. Lovely bit of marble. Can't help wondering,' he dropped his voice, 'what they'll do for the PM when he goes. Something a bit more modern, suit the medium to the message, a video installation perhaps?'

He hooted and pushed back his long blond fringe.

Gabe said, 'I've never been in here before.'

'Welcome to the asylum,' said Fairweather, leading the way. 'Would you like a tour? See the chamber? It's rather dull, I'm afraid. No, I don't blame you, to be honest it's better on the box. Well, they show the highlights, and the whole shebang looks more impressive. It's a bit of a disappointment, frankly, for visitors when they see this modest sort of public hall and, you know, I've watched them sitting up in the gallery and guess what they end up doing. Looking at the screens. And I don't blame them, no, it looks less dowdy somehow, more real than the thing itself.'

Fairweather talked on as he breezed down the cabinet-lined corridors, oozing congeniality, nodding left and right. Gabe tried to say that he would, in fact, like to see the debating chamber but found his attempts smothered in a blanket of ministerial charm. It occurred to Gabriel that he had underestimated this man, seeing only the amiable surface, which Fairweather used to great effect.

'Here we go,' said Fairweather, 'the Pugin room. Technically speaking, we're in the Lords, notice how the carpet changed from green to red, but we swapped it for some committee room years ago and they'll never get it back. Shall we have coffees or something stronger to celebrate? Rolly shouldn't be a minute. Someone will show him up.

'See that chap over there,' he said, after ordering a pot of coffee, 'chair of the Catering Sub-Committee. Minister for the interior, as he's commonly known.'

'It's how you met Rolly, isn't it?' said Gabe. 'Being on that committee.'

'It's all done in-house, you know, the catering,' said Fairweather. 'He came in on some consultancy gig. Can't so much as sell a sausage roll without a consultant these days.'

'And is it any good?'

'What, the food?' Fairweather grinned. 'Oh, for one of Bellamy's veal pies!'

'Should I take that as a no?'

The right honourable member leaned in close, as if a plot were about to be hatched. 'This *should* be the best place to eat in London. What chef wouldn't like to try his hand in here? I think' – he dropped his voice – 'I think we could be seeing some movement pretty soon on contracting out, and we're talking a turnover of four to five million as a starting point.' He leaned back. 'Anyway, first things first,' he continued, becoming hale and hearty again. 'Got to get up and running, establish the brand, as it were.'

'You've got the lease?' said Gabriel.

'Lucinda's signed,' said Fairweather, opening the folder. 'Place your paw print . . . just here.'

'Lucinda?' Gabe hadn't so much as met Fairweather's wife, and now he was going into business with her, it seemed.

'A formality. We are *allowed* to have business interests, as long as we register them, of course, but it keeps things simple this way.'

Gabe looked at Fairweather's rosy schoolboy cheeks, his expensive and casually rumpled suit, the air of self-assurance that enveloped him like cologne.

'It's tricky with your ministerial position, you mean.'

Fairweather sighed. 'I'm only one step up from a PPS, you know. And I get approaches – all these media offers – which I have to keep turning down. I've done one or two things before that seemed to go down rather well.' He fiddled modestly with his wedding band. 'But now I'm pretty much limited to the *Today* programme and *Question Time. Entre nous*, I've asked to be shuffled out.'

'You want to be demoted?'

'When the PM rearranges the paperclips. It's not a lack of loyalty, it's . . . well, I've decided it's my last term in Parliament and if I'm going to build up some outside interests . . .'

'Media work?'

'Oh, I don't know. I'm keeping my options open. There'll be the restaurant, of course. And it won't hurt the profile to do a bit of media stuff. But there'll be opportunities in business. I've made some contacts over the years.'

The waitress who brought the coffees, a skittery blonde with blacked-up eyes, made a meal of laying out the cups and saucers, the sugar and the cream. Fairweather practically rubbed his hands together, sizing her up like a parliamentary perk. She ventured little glances in return. Lucinda, remembered Gabe, spent most of her time at the constituency house.

'Ah, Mr Rawlins,' cried Fairweather, jumping up.

Rolly unbuttoned his coat and unwound his scarf. 'That girl who brought me up here says she's got an Oxford degree. Be better off as a bellboy, doing all that running around, least she'd get some tips.'

'Well, here it is,' said Fairweather, 'the final draft, the clean copy. Lucinda's signed and Gabe' – he pulled a pen from his suit – 'was about to borrow this.'

'Was I?' said Gabe. He could imagine Fairweather in a committee room, seamlessly moving the business along, taking words out of people's mouths or placing them there, quietly suffocating all opposition with his frank and pitiless charm.

'Let's get it over,' said Rolly, working through the next few minutes in silence. Fairweather, thought Gabe, liked to hide his intellect. He was clearly sharp as a knife, but the sharpest knives were always sheathed. Rolly was more like a grater, likely to graze your knuckles on contact, unlikely to inflict a mortal wound. *Thicko third son*, he'd once said to Gabe. *Proper dunce at school. Doctor and lawyer, the first two, and I went into trade. Someone called me flamboyant, this one time, I must have been wearing one of these shirts. And that was it. Hey presto –* flamboyant businessman. *I wasn't arguing. Made more money than the doctor and the lawyer put together. Shows what a thicko can do.*

'Seems to be in order,' he said now. Having signed he pushed the folder to Gabe, who added his name.

'A snifter,' proposed Fairweather, beaming. 'We must have a toast.' He'd bring the punters into the restaurant, thought Gabe, of that there was no doubt.

'So the money will go out of the account, what, Thursday, Friday? If you saw my cash flow you wouldn't be asking me to celebrate.'

Rolly wore another of his 'flamboyant' outfits. He'd taken his coat off to reveal a Hawaiian shirt.

'A stiffener, then,' said Fairweather.

'No time,' said Rolly. 'I only came over to sign and, oh yeah, I've got a proposal from an interior designer.' He handed Gabe an envelope.

'*Très bien*,' said Fairweather. 'But Lucinda's had a few ideas too. Somewhere in this folder . . .'

'You're taking the piss.'

'Oh, well, she's not a professional. Rather talented amateur, I'd say.'

'No, sorry, I don't work with amateurs. Look at young Gabriel here, rightly puzzled, scratching his head.'

Gabe slipped his hand beneath his thigh and trapped it there.

'Fine, fine. Take a look at the sketches, that's all I ask.'

'How about we get *my* wife to design the menus?' said Rolly. 'How about we get a Chinese Elvis for Monday nights, try and pull in the crowds?'

'OK, steady,' said Fairweather, smiling. 'Interior design happens to be a passion of hers.'

'I've seen plenty of mugs open restaurants with *passions*,' said Rolly. 'This operation's about money, it's not about dreams.' Gabriel nodded and Rolly closed the folder and slid it back over the table. 'Mind you,' he continued, 'what do people dream about? Money, mostly. Getting rich.'

'Yes, oh yes,' said Fairweather, 'everybody wants to live like a king.' He didn't appear the least bit put out by the knock-back, believing – most likely – he would get his way in the end.

'No they don't. They want to live like celebrities.' Rolly, on principle it seemed, disagreed whenever possible, even where the difference of opinion was wafer-thin.

'We want to live like celebrities,' said Fairweather, 'because we're worth it, as the ads say.'

Rolly's tropical shirt, Gabe noted, had garnered a certain amount of interest among the ash and charcoal suits. 'My son,' said Rolly, oblivious, 'he's seventeen. Guess what kind of car he wants. Expects me to buy it for him, of course. Teenagers. You been near one recently? Heard how they talk? I keep saying, Steven, we don't live in Kingston, Jamaica, this is Kingston KT1.'

'It's this footballers' wives society, isn't it?' said Fairweather. 'It does, I'm afraid to say, encourage greed.'

'Bullshit,' said Rolly, raising his fat pink hands. 'Greed is a fundamental of human nature. It's hard-wired.' In his own way, Rolly was quite as keen as Oona on taking people's lives out of their hands. Between God and genetics there seemed to be little room for manoeuvre, for a life you could call your own.

'Absolutely,' chimed Fairweather, 'and so easy for the advertisers to manipulate.'

'You politicians love to think you can change things by meddling. Biology is destiny, that's what you can't accept.'

'Keeps my feet on the ground,' said Fairweather to Gabe.

'You know there's a gene for generosity?' said Rolly. 'Put that in your social-engineering pipe and smoke it. Yeah, they've just found it, some researchers in Israel. Most of us are greedy, a few of us are generous – the ones with a rare variant in the AVPR1 gene. It's a mutation, an abnormality, like being born with a club foot, eleven fingers, three nipples – nothing you should blame yourself for.'

'Fascinating,' said Fairweather. 'But we'll never be able to understand all our impulses, don't you think?'

They batted on, back and forth, forgetting to draw Gabriel in. Gabe, quietly observing, saw afresh what a peculiar couple they made. It was touching, in a way.

'Sorry to butt in,' said Gabriel. 'I think we should go down to Alderney Street, finalize the design brief on-site.'

Rolly began negotiating his way back into his coat. 'I've got to run,' he said, though given his size and habitual gait he seemed unlikely to attempt it. 'You can have my input now – keep it cheap. My daughter's going to university, expects me to buy her a flat. Geraldine's having a new kitchen, maybe it's made of gold, wouldn't surprise me, you should see the cost. I wouldn't mind – ' He shook his head and blinked. 'I wouldn't mind if she knew how to cook.'

Fairweather and Gabriel traversed Victoria Gardens as, across the river skyline, the day gathered itself brightly in a pink and silver band and then promptly expired. They continued in the gloom along Millbank, past stolid, granite-faced buildings, on the walk from Westminster to Pimlico.

Gabe fired a Marlboro Light.

'Ah, I didn't know you . . .'

'Since I went up to Blantwistle,' said Gabe. 'Going to the old pubs with my sister, the old habits. Giving up again soon.'

'The evil weed,' said Fairweather vaguely. 'Now, Blantwistle. Blantwistle . . . haven't I had something across my desk recently? Name rings a bell.'

'In fact,' said Gabe, 'no time like the present.' He tossed the cigarette in the gutter and the rest of the pack in a bin.

'Ah, yes! There was something, a closure. Last mill standing – about to close its doors. Don't suppose it'll make the news – it used to, that sort of thing.'

'My dad worked in a mill,' said Gabriel. 'Worked in the same place all his life.'

'Really?' said Fairweather, his cheeks glowing with contentment as befitted, on this sharp dark evening, the owner of a cashmere overcoat and few self-doubts. 'How marvellous.'

'Must be Hortons,' said Gabe, 'the one that's closing.'

'Like to keep up with this sort of thing in the department. Though there's nothing we can do, of course.'

Gabe regretted throwing the cigarettes away. That had been rash. He rammed his hands into his pockets. 'Dad thinks the economy's going to pieces.' He laughed. 'He's watched that industry go down the pan. He doesn't understand about new jobs being created. If he doesn't see the factory, bricks and mortar, he can't understand.'

'We've a first-rate record on employment,' said Fairweather in his finest broadcast voice.

'Dad, the way he talks, it's like we're in the middle of a recession.'

'Bless him, no,' said Fairweather. 'The economy is very, very strong, as the chancellor keeps telling us.'

Gabriel glanced over, detecting, perhaps, an ironic note. Fairweather swept at his fringe although it was already blowing back in the wind.

'He says it's a house of cards. Dad, I mean.'

'It's difficult, isn't it, from where he's standing, not to see it that way?'

'What do *you* think, though?' It wasn't every day you could get official confirmation – from the lips of a member of Her Majesty's government – that your father was definitely, definitively, wrong.

'We all stand *somewhere*,' mused Fairweather.

Gabriel laughed. 'Are politicians born, or made?'

Fairweather hooted. 'We're biologically determined in the womb.'

'And you've avoided answering my question.'

'What's bred in the bone,' said Fairweather. 'Don't we go right here?' They turned on to a residential street. 'Spend too damn long talking to journalists,' he went on, dropping out of broadcast mode. 'Here's what I think,' he said, speaking quickly. 'There are two stories you can tell about the economy. You've only got to pick up a few newspapers, read some of the pundits – they all think they're being original, naturally, but there's only a couple of versions, slightly differently told. The first story will be the one your father prefers. The economy lacks substance – we've lost our manufacturing base, and the new industries don't compensate, as witnessed by our rather enormous trading deficit. In this narrative you bring the Germans into it. You say, look at them, with their Vorsprung durch Technik, all their cars and washing machines and their record trade surplus. You say, Japan, my God! Where are our Sonys and Panasonics, our Mitsubishis? Don't you know how much they're selling to China? You take a list of countries and tell pretty much the same tale. Pick a Scandinavian country, mention mobile phones. The States? Computers, aircraft, movies. You get the gist.' Fairweather spoke faster, impatient for the words to keep up with the thoughts. With his guard down, he'd let the easy-going manner slide. He'd lost the choirboy look. 'Then, what you do, you say the British economy is hollow, it's a reed blowing in the wind, singing a pretty tune. It's a wooden man who's hollow, and when he goes up in flames he's going to burn up pretty fast because there's nothing solid there. Bang on a bit about the City, and the housing market creating a lopsided economy, and property speculation fuelling consumer credit. Make it sound as combustible as you can. Imply the whole country's turned into a derivatives market, a billion and one trades a day, none of them real. Say we're one gigantic casino spinning speculators' money, while asset-stripping vultures shred company pension schemes and turn the few remaining factories into luxury flats and shopping malls.

'But there's another story, a different kind of reality, if you like. Tell it like this. Say the economy is booming because the economy is in good shape. Anyone who says otherwise is a masochist, an idiot, or downright envious. Say that we're into "sunrise" industries. Use the words "knowledge economy" and "creative economy". Throw in accountancy, insurance, advertising, banking; mention it's minds not muscles that are required, and don't forget to say we're producing more graduates than ever before. Imply that the new Gods of Commerce are easily insulted and if we fail to appease them daily they will vanish into the sky. Finish by saying that it's an actual fact that we're all better off than ever before.'

'OK,' said Gabe, 'you can give two different answers. I accept that. But which one do you believe?'

'You're asking the wrong question,' Fairweather shot back. 'The answer's no use if the question's wrong.'

'What would the right question be?'

'Can you ride it?' said Fairweather. 'Can you ride it, whatever it is? That's what you should be asking. It's what you should be asking yourself.'

'Make money, you mean? That's what you intend to do when you get out of politics?'

Fairweather didn't seem to hear him. They walked a little way in silence through the trim, deserted streets. Every time he walked through Pimlico in the evening, Gabriel had the same thought. Where did everyone go? They were residential streets without residents. Was there a curfew? Had everyone died? Were there any survivors who, when it finally opened, would eat in the restaurant?

'I think,' said Fairweather quietly, 'that private equity will be my thing.'

'I bet,' returned Gabe, 'that when you first joined the Labour Party, you never thought you'd end up . . . on the other side of the spectrum, I suppose.'

'That left-right dichotomy,' said Fairweather dismissively. 'No, that's totally broken down. Or you can be leftwing, so-called, and be as rich as you want, rich as you can get, anyway. You know, have the right books on your bookshelves, about poverty and globalization, and still shop at Prada – it's all about style. Look at these pop stars, the way they do it. It's not even considered hypocritical any more. No, I don't think I have a problem there. We're all entranced by money, that's the truth of it. Dazzled, if you like.' The longer he spoke the faster he spoke, and the faster he spoke the more precisely he spoke, the words cleanly and finely diced.

'Of course,' he went on, 'pop stars are small fry. They only *think* they run the world. And the ones who really do aren't quite so keen on publicity. I'll tell you . . .' He broke off for a moment to check a text. 'I'll tell you what's so difficult about being in office. You're right there with them, these turbo-capitalists, these Genghis Khans of the money markets, and you think, I'm supposed to be the one with the power. And what am I earning? Ninety thousand a year.

'And then, I've seen it with colleagues, they start to think, what's another ten thousand here or there? It's peanuts. Have you seen what those guys earn? And they get caught, like —' He named another minister. 'Fudging the second home allowance, claiming a few extra expenses, putting a family member on the payroll when they've never set foot in the House. Well, it's not much, they think. Nothing to get excited about.' Fairweather laughed, short and dry, not his usual honk. 'That's where their thinking is faulty. It's exactly *because* it's not much they get in trouble for it. These are amounts that people can under-stand and they're infuriated because *they* could do with another ten grand a year. And it may be out of their reach, but only just. Only just.

'But the Genghis Khans, they're a different story. People don't understand what they do. Neither do I, for that matter. Try saying "hedge fund" and watch people fall into a coma. More importantly, the amounts they earn are incomprehensible. When the numbers get so large they become meaningless, like the number of cells in the human body, or the distance between one galaxy and the next.'

'So people don't care?' said Gabe.

'It's disconnected. It's off the planet. May as well be happening on Mars.'

'But they're the wealth creators, aren't they? I mean for the economy, job creation, things like that.'

'Oh, we're supremely relaxed about it in government,' said Fairweather, a laid-back drag returning to his voice, 'supremely relaxed.' He came to a halt. 'Did we miss the turn?'

The two men turned round simultaneously, rotating one to the left and one to the right, and each continued on his trajectory so that they caught each other face to face in the middle of the street and stood there silent and frozen as if automatically locked-on to target, waiting out a few long moments before Fairweather engaged the manual over-ride. 'No, I think it's the next one,' he said, stepping back.

Gabriel could not move. In that instant he was filled with a dread so physical that he was at once paralysed and in fear of collapse. Fairweather was talking still, as if from a far distant place. Gabe wanted something to hang on to, something hard and real, so that this wave of fear would not sweep him clean away. It had already ripped out his stomach, an ice wind through his body, and he would cover the hole if only his hand would move. What was it? What was wrong with him? If he knew, if he could name it, then everything would be fine. Was this a dream? It must be. If not a dream then why not move, speak, laugh, cry? Anything to break this lockdown. He was sleeping, he was dreaming, there was nothing to be frightened of.

He was dreaming, he noted, almost coolly, in black and white, in shades of grey with an occasional splash of red. The brick of the Georgian terraces opposite was grey; the windowsills painted white and the railings shiny black. A woman appeared from behind a black front door dressed in a pillar-box coat. Two magpies tumbled together across the road, chased off by a black car. A red car would follow, he predicted, and sure enough, there it was. A black cat slunk behind the railings, with something in its mouth. It crept up the stairs and through a cat flap, after a little fussing, figuring out how to push the blackbird inside. The sage bushes in the smart planters quivered and the fragrance of the silver-grey leaves reached his nostrils, and he thought of what a wonderful herb it was, how underrated, and how he would never overlook it again.

'Chef,' said Fairweather. 'Chef?'

'I was just . . . I was . . .'

'Seen a ghost?'

'Thinking,' said Gabe. 'I was thinking . . .' The blood that had frozen in his body began to flow again.

Fairweather touched Gabe's arm. 'You know, I was thinking myself. I was thinking I've finally done it. I've literally bored someone rigid. Talked at you until you were stiff as a board.'

'No,' said Gabe. 'Oh, no. I was interested, I *am* interested, it's good to . . . I enjoy . . . sometimes, it's a low blood sugar thing, and if I was . . . if it seemed like I wasn't listening . . . no, oh no, it's not often that I get a chance . . . with work, and everything. No, I like . . .' They were walking along again. Gabe paused to try to pull a sentence together. They had been talking about the economy, about jobs, before he'd fazed out for a minute or two.

'Quite understandable,' said Fairweather, though even Gabe in his current state was capable of recognizing this as an untruth.

Gabriel breathed deeply. He told himself he felt completely fine again. It seemed to help. 'Wealth creation, we were just saying, all the new jobs that have opened up.'

'We politicians,' said Fairweather, reverting to his usual tone, a smooth blend of humility and utter self-belief. 'I'm afraid we do tend to love the sound of our own voices.'

'I wanted to hear your thoughts.'

'We have our own job creation scheme now, don't we?' said Fairweather. 'Eight employees at the start.'

Gabe looked at Fairweather. It was amazing, it really was, how he could flick some kind of switch and change. He had gone into full politician mode. It wasn't just his voice, it was everything; the way he held his body, the expression in his eyes, the attenuation of sharpness, like a sauce that has been thickened with butter and cream.

'And it's a gastronomic desert round here,' Fairweather continued. 'There's nowhere to go. There's a population that's not being served – it's why the streets are so quiet. Then there'll be the Westminster crowd.'

But everyone, thought Gabe, must do it. Wasn't he a different person when he was in the kitchen with Oona or Victor, or out with Charlie (don't think about her) or in Blantwistle with Dad? Gleeson always brought out the worst in him, and Lena, well . . . how could he begin to account for himself?

'Actually,' said Gabe, the words coming out more aggressively than he'd intended, 'I'm quite capable of discussing things on a broader level. I can get my head out of the cooking pot now and then.'

'Of course you can,' said Fairweather. He looked Gabe up and down and appeared to come to some kind of conclusion. 'Look, what do you want to know? It's a matter of interpretation. There is no gospel truth, off the record and between the two of us. There are more people in employment now than when we were elected. I guess that's indisputable; the rest is up for grabs.'

'Meaning?'

'Meaning what do you prefer to emphasize? I could say that the financial sector is thriving or I could say there's around a million white-collar drones inputting data and answering phones. Of course the Opposition would bang on about how many more foreigners we've got filling jobs in construction and agriculture and catering and how there's a pool of unemployed and virtually unemployable Brits.'

'There's a lot of xenophobia about,' said Gabe.

'Don't doubt it,' said Fairweather. 'Listen, what happened about that porter chap of yours in the end? The one who died? Did you find out any more about it? Was it one of those bonded labour situations, living in the cellars, desperate to pay off his debts?'

They were moving at a brisk pace down Alderney Street. Gabe could see the plate-glass window where the florists had once been and the restaurant would be soon. 'Not had the inquest yet. I suppose we'll find out more . . . What was that about bonded labour? What do you mean by that?'

'A form of slavery,' said Fairweather, 'for the twenty-first century. Taking away passports, debt bondage, threats of violence, that sort of thing. The gangmaster stuff you'll have read about in the newspapers. The pressure groups like to call it slavery, sounds more impressive, and we're really world class at that because we've gone so big on deregulation, you see.'

'But there are new laws,' said Gabe. 'After the Chinese cockle pickers thing.'

'The Gangmaster Licensing Act.' Fairweather stopped at the shopfront, put his hand to the glass and peered inside. 'You know, I think Lucinda's designs aren't bad. She's had an idea for the fascia I think could really work. You have a touching faith in government, by the way. The GLA set up an authority that is tiny and self-funding, it will hardly scratch the surface, but I guess as long as we don't have more mass drownings or other *spectaculars*, then nobody's really going to notice or mind. Nobody's in favour of rising food prices, you know.'

'I don't know about Yuri,' said Gabe. 'He came through an agency.'

Fairweather stood shoulder to shoulder on the pavement with Gabriel. The plate glass held their reflections, suspended in the dark like two souls lost in the fog. 'Shall we go inside?' said Fairweather, moving for the door. Lingering for a moment, Gabriel examined the figure in the window, the all-purpose jeans and anonymous zip-up jacket, and thought how bland he looked, how indistinct, like a featureless mannequin, every characteristic obliterated or obscured. He leaned forward to find a different angle, to get his face to show, and then the lights came on inside and he vanished and there was Fairweather beckoning him to go in.

Halfway through dinner service Gabriel had to send Damian home after he'd urinated in a bin full of peelings and lain down in the prep area with his flies open and his hat across his face. Gabe sniffed the glass from which Damian had been sipping all evening. He tasted the contents and spat the vodka out. Suleiman and Benny returned from their mission, having poured Damian into a black cab.

'Chef,' said Suleiman, peering up at Gabriel earnestly, 'I am thinking this boy is very much in need of help.'

'I know,' said Gabe. 'I'll sort something out.'

Suleiman nodded; he almost bowed. He was so deeply serious, as if he had every faith in Gabriel's words.

Victor swaggered up with his flies undone and a leek hanging out of his pants. 'Suleiman,' he said, 'Benny! Help me, please!'

'You're having a problem with this vegetable?' said Suleiman.

Benny attempted to lead Victor away from Gabe, saying, 'Now we have to get on with our work.'

'Oh, man,' groaned Victor, 'tuck me into my pants, you big, strong boys.'

Suleiman rocked anxiously on his feet, his little legs bent out. 'He very much likes to joke.'

Oona, on the pass, called an order. The kitchen was like a steam bath, several of the extractor hoods on the blink. Ivan had taken a knife and sliced air vents in his trousers and down the chest of his whites. Work went on at a furious pace, the boys shackled to their stations, without speaking or raising their heads, all except these three, this joker and the two who had stayed to protect him, both of them wringing their hands.

Gabe took a step towards Victor, who jumped away and dodged round the corner. Gabriel let him go.

'High spirits,' said Benny. 'This is something we cannot help in our youth.'

'Am I unreasonable?' asked Gabriel. 'Am I an unreasonable man?'

He walked round the kitchen without chivvying or prompting or tasting, simply observing his brigade at work. Nikolai's back was covered in sweat at the steam table, his face glowing red as his hair. A watery blister swelled on Ivan's thumb. Suleiman, beneath the little shrine he had erected to Ganesh, toiled devotedly, and Benny, taking on the additional burden of Damian's duties, concentrated on his activities with an uncomplaining hum.

Gabe stepped lightly in and out of the gangways, crossing and recrossing the kitchen, hovering momentarily behind each worker, his presence sufficient to fine-tune the performances, to turn elbows and wrists to full speed. Satisfied, or at least mollified, he joined Oona as a waitress returned from the dining room with an armful of plates on which the food had hardly been touched. The girl went past and crashed the plates down in the wash-up area and a porter began to scrape them off.

'Hang on,' said Gabe, intercepting the waitress, 'was there a complaint?'

The girl wiped her hands across her backside. 'No.'

'They weren't sending it back? They'd finished?'

The girl looked around, as if seeking someone to save her. 'Maybe they weren't hungry. I don't know. Do you want me to go and ask?'

'No.'

He began to watch the plates and dishes coming back, and to calculate the amount of food going to waste. He abandoned Oona and joined the porter, lifting the lid on the slop bin and taking a good look inside. This terrified the porter, who began to drop things on the floor.

Gabe drifted into the dining room, to the plush tinkle of laughter, the artful cascades of light, the smoky images flickering across the gilded mirrors. He took a seat at the bar, ignoring the heads that turned towards him, watching instead the play of water in the fountain across the room.

'Get you something, Chef?'

He told the barman no. He looked at the diners. He watched plates being served and plates being cleared. When he looked up at the ceiling he saw in one of the recesses a smattering of stars.

Returning to the kitchen he ran into Gleeson and Ivan, loitering in the passageway. Ivan, low-voiced, growled something to his co-conspirator, pushed his heel off the wall and turned without acknowledging Gabe.

'Dining-room inspection completed, Chef?' said Gleeson, so chirpy he practically sang. 'Think you'll find I run a tight ship.'

Gabriel loathed the sharp line of Gleeson's parting, the gloss of his hair, the too-snug fit of his trousers, the silky tie, the shine of his shoes, the snip of his tongue, the snaky look in his eyes. He loathed this man.

Without answering he moved on and went to his office. It was hotter than the kitchen in here. He pressed the down button on the air-conditioning, which appeared to have jammed. He banged the box with the side of his fist. Then he pressed the up button to see if it responded or if the whole thing had died. There was a beep and the vents began to blow hot air. Gabe wiped the back of his neck. Sweat trickled down his chest. He went out to the loading bay for a cigarette, from the packet he'd bought on his way back to the Imperial.

It was a clear cold night and he shivered, standing against a wall. He'd stop smoking when he wanted to; when he decided the time was right. Fuck, it was cold. He'd smoke in Ernie's shed.

When he pushed the door open he saw Ernie, unmistakable even in outline, lopsided and scrawny, sitting in the dark.

'How's it going, Ernie?'

'Oh aye,' said Ernie. 'According to plan.'

'Great.'

'How's it going wi' you?'

'Great,' repeated Gabriel. 'All going . . . according to plan. What is it you're doing? Why haven't you gone home?'

'Ah'm composing,' said Ernie. 'In ma head. Somewhere quiet and dark is all Ah need. Compose it in ma head before Ah write it down.'

Gabe took a final drag on his cigarette and put it out in a mug on Ernie's desk.

'Won't disturb you then.' He pulled the door behind him then pushed it open again. 'Ernie, come and see me first thing in the morning. There's something we've got to discuss.'

Before service there'd been no time to check the stock rooms. Gabe decided to do it now. In the basement, in the dry-goods store, running his hand along the shelf of pulses and beans, he remembered that first glimpse of Lena, the way she'd stood in the doorway, light from the naked bulb dripping dankly around her, the look she'd given him. She'd come to him. She had come to him. Keep that in mind. He didn't keep her locked in the flat. He hadn't stolen her identity. She wasn't in his debt. There was no debt bondage here. And anyway, he loved her. Why shouldn't he? Was there a law against that?

He loved Lena. He loved that stupid girl. Something, a little sound, bubbled from his lips. He wiped his eyes.

Dad had to meet her. She had to meet Jenny. She had to meet Dad before . . . and Gabe would tell him everything, he wouldn't cover anything up, because he wasn't ashamed of her. Be a man and tell the truth. Hands out of yer pockets. Stand up straight. Be a man. And tell it like it is.

He was ten years old, hands deep in the pockets of his Bedford cord flares, leaning against a locker in the tacklers' room sucking a Spangle, getting it proper thin and sharp, when Dad flamed through the door and set Gabe's cheeks alight.

'What the bloody hell were you playing at?'

'Me?' said Gabriel. 'What?'

'Get yer hands out of yer pockets.'

Gabe yanked his hands out.

'You cut them threads.'

'I never,' shouted Gabe. Thinking on his feet he added, 'What threads?'

'I should give you a bloody good hiding. Wasting my time like that.'

Dad's ears were a dangerous colour, his lips as thin as a wolf's. The tacklers on the benches looked up from their papers and their smokes. Mr Howarth coughed.

'What's 'e gone and done?'

'Got some bloody scissors and bloody snipped the warp on number twenty-five.'

Everyone laughed. What was so funny? They were laughing at him for being such a baby. They were laughing at Dad for showing himself up. It wasn't funny. Why didn't they shut it? What did it have to do with them?

'I never did,' yelled Gabe.

He got the blame for everything. Dad shouldn't have brought him in if he didn't have time for him. He'd disappeared for ages and left him standing by a loom. Gabe hadn't done *anything*, not for ages. The loom wasn't even on. There was nowt to do. Somebody (*they* weren't getting in trouble) had left them scissors lying around. He hadn't meant to do it and he'd only cut a bit.

'I know you did it,' said Dad. He was laughing now, to make it all of them against Gabe. 'I've just spent best part of an hour piecing together and them's not broken ends, they'd been cut. Let's hear the truth and no more said about it. Be a man. No waterworks. Tell it like it is.'

Gabe wanted to get the bus home. Dad said no. He said to shake hands. Gabe said no. Dad pretended like everything was back to normal (as if that could ever happen) and Gabe wished Dad was dead. He wanted to go home and see Mum.

Trailing after Dad round the weaving shed he shot lethal rays out of his eyes. Exterminate. Exterminate. Hadn't even said sorry. Laughing. How would *he* like it?

'Right,' said Dad, bending down, all casual, breathing over Gabe. 'This here's a dobby loom, one of the old 'uns, see the wooden shuttle, the picking stick, you've got the electric motor right there what powers it across.'

Gabe nodded with a high degree of sarcasm that was only wasted on Dad.

'I'll show you the Northrops. You coming or what?'

As if he had any choice.

'The newer sort, they've got the airjets and rapiers now. Know what they are?'

Gabriel couldn't care less.

'Northrop's been a big innovator, all these is Northrops what you see. This machine here's got a top speed of 260 picks per minute, meaning the rapier goes across that many times. Remember what I was saying? Aye, it takes the weft across, like the shuttle in the dobby loom. That's weaving. Weaves between the warp, like I said.'

Boring. Boring. Exterminate. Exterminate.

'Ten year ago, you'd have been looking at a simple battery here on't side of the machine, what contained the pirns. The bottom part of the pirn had an amount of weft, what's called a bunch, that was needed to go across three times.'

Who cared? When they got home Dad would say it was too late to play out. It wasn't fair. Jenny never got dragged in here.

Dad stroked the side of the loom like it was a wild horse, like he thought he was some kind of cowboy, going to break it in. 'Then this little beauty come along. The Unifill. See here, this is a winding head, and this here's the magazine.'

Honest to God, he wished Dad would drop down dead. He was rattling on just like a bloody loom.

'. . . specialist weaving, complex stuff they'll never be able to do abroad . . . insulation for electric cables what go under the sea . . .'

'Dad. Dad! Can I go home now? I feel sick. Me tummy hurts.'

Dad stopped talking. His mouth lay straight across his face like a ruler. He lowered his head to Gabe's. 'We've not got to the exciting bit yet. Don't you want to have a go on the Dacty machine? I'll let you punch out some cards.'

Gabe looked over the metal-and-fibre sea, to the horizon of the wall. There was no escape. 'OK,' he said.

'Good lad. Stick close, we're taking a tour of the jacquards first.'

Gabriel cricked his neck staring up at the yellow harnesses and stayed in that position like he was really, really amazed and couldn't stop looking at the machines. Dad droned on about the width of the beam and the harness and the reed having to be exactly equal and the warp going through the pirns and the healds lifting up the warp to make the pattern. And Gabe bet that Michael's dad never made him go to work with him. Michael's dad never made him do anything. His dad didn't even have a job. Michael was lucky. In his house they always had the TV on.

'Gabe, go back and wait for me in the tacklers' room.'

'What? Why, where you going? Can I go home?'

'Up there,' said Dad, pointing to the girders. 'I've got to get up there.'

'What you want to go up there for?'

Dad laughed. 'I've got to see to the jacquard.'

'How'd you reach it?'

'With a ladder, soft lad. Then I stand on the girder, like a bloody acrobat.'

Gabe kicked up a pile of lint with his toe and edged it across the floor. It started to roll up nice. By the time he got to the tacklers' room he had a wodge of it the size, if not exactly the shape, of a football. There was nobody in the room but him. He threw the lint ball in the air and caught it over and over until most of it was stuck to his T-shirt and cords and hardly any in his hands. He tried to dust himself off. He did handstands against the wall. Then he sat on the bench. He lay down on his tummy, had a coughing fit and fell asleep.

When he woke he reckoned Dad had gone and forgotten about

him because it was dark now and nobody had turned on the lights. Probably everyone had gone home and the whole mill was locked up and he'd have to stay there all night. Most boys his age would probably cry. Gabe wasn't even scared, wouldn't be even if all the lights had fused and he had to stay in the dark.

He got up, crossed the room and felt for the light switch. He flicked it and the lights came on. Rubbing his eyes he pulled open the door and for some weird reason he could hear the looms. He kicked along the short corridor towards the weaving shed where he'd left his dad. He'd forgot about the night shift. The mill stayed open all night.

'What time is it?' he asked somebody passing in the opposite direction.

'Nearly five.'

Was that all it was? But he'd been asleep for hours!

When he ran into the weaving shed he saw Dad lying on the floor beneath the girder, like he'd fallen off. Mr Howarth was crouching over him. Dad wasn't moving, and when Mr Howarth looked up Gabriel saw the panic in his face and decided Dad – what a bastard! – had gone ahead and died.

Mr Howarth started towards him but Gabriel ran out of the weaving shed, out through the cobbled courtyard and wrought-iron gates and struck out on his own for home.

He swung round at the touch on his shoulder, still holding the dried beans shelf with one hand.

Suleiman's clerkish face bobbed deferentially. 'Chef, excuse me for troubling, but you may wish to know – there is a fight.'

'Who?' said Gabe, though he knew the answer.

'Though my line of sight was partially obscured,' said Suleiman, 'I believe it is Victor and Ivan.'

CHAPTER SIXTEEN

—— *m* ——

MARCHING ON THE SPOT, SOME KIND OF VICTORY RITUAL, IVAN clinched Victor's head between his ribcage and bulging bicep. Gabriel pushed his way through the cooks. Ivan staggered forward as Victor's body, a flailing mess of arms and legs, was propelled out from behind a worktop. This did little to allay Gabe's expectation that, any moment now, the grill chef would grab a fistful of Victor's hair and dangle his head aloft.

Everyone had gathered round at a respectful distance. Fivers were changing hands. Benny, still at his station, close to the site of the action, folded white kitchen towels and stacked them neatly and quickly as if preparing emergency medical supplies. Suleiman, studious as ever, watched closely in case the subject should one day come up in an exam. Oona was speaking under her breath, no doubt offering prayers, and occasionally clucking out loud. It was time to put a stop to this show.

Gabriel, though, held back because a part of him, some mean streak he'd have sworn he didn't possess, was enjoying it, the raspberry red of Victor's face. At the very moment he was about to finally open his mouth Victor jerked himself free. Gabe waited to see what would happen. If he stayed quiet he might learn something about this feud.

Victor, the blood still in his face, charged at his opponent bellowing, head down like a bull. Ivan merely stepped aside. Victor ran into the desserts fridge with a clang. There was a catcall and a splatter of applause. Victor got back in the ring. He raised his fists this time. Ivan threw a punch that glanced off Victor's cheek; Victor answered with a kick to the balls. The look in Ivan's eyes made the spectators shuffle back a step or two.

Victor stood there panting, sweat dripping down his forehead. 'Cocksucker,' he said. 'Motherfucker. You're dead. You're dead. *You're fucking dead.*'

Ivan weighed his testicles. 'You fight like girl.'

'If you ever, ever speak about her again . . .' Victor leaned tightly into the words, shaking with juvenile passion. 'One word . . . I'm telling you, man, I'll kill you. You hear?'

Ivan, in his slashed clothes and bandanna, looked like a mutineer. All he was missing was a cutlass. He directed his bad ear towards Victor and cupped it delicately. It had turned a labial red. 'Hear?' he said. 'What?'

Victor hissed through his teeth.

'Girlfriend?' said Ivan. 'I say nothing. Nothing.' He made an obscene gesture with his mouth and tongue. 'She left you?'

Victor whirled round and snatched a knife from Benny's station, the broad blade glittering instantly, famously, in his hand. Brandishing the weapon, Victor let loose a blood-curdling scream that at long last set Gabe in motion. He reached Victor in a single bound, relieving him of the awful necessity of carrying this thing through. Victor let the knife drop.

'I should sack the both of you,' said Gabriel, steaming. 'I should kick you out right now. Consider this your last warning. Understand?'

'It was him . . .' Victor began.

' "He started it." Don't be such a child. Enough.' It wasn't the first fight Gabe had witnessed in the kitchen and it wouldn't be the last. It certainly wasn't the worst. In Brighton one of the commis, tiring of having his buttocks fondled daily, had taken a six-inch Excalibur filleting knife and stuck it deep in the sous-chef's arse. If Ivan and Victor's squabble was over a girl then Gabriel wasn't going to get into it, he'd leave it to burn itself out.

Service was all but over and so the clear-down began. Gleeson tried to seat a walk-in for ten a few minutes before the kitchen closed. Gabe still had the adrenalin pumping because it took scarcely a look to dissuade the restaurant manager from this plan. 'I see that's not to your liking,' said Gleeson, smiling the way he smiled at diners who ate at six thirty on a Saturday evening, dressed in their Sunday best.

Gabe went into his sticky cube. He took off his whites and sat in his T-shirt and checks going over the banqueting figures on the computer. The figures melted in the heat. Impossible to get a grip. He needed to draw up the shifts for the Christmas period. That would be easier. He looked out at the kitchen. Most people had gone home. He would go home for as long as he could over Christmas. Oona would have to come in every day. Too bad. What could he do? He could sit here feeling guilty about it, because guilt was what you consoled yourself with when something was out of your control. If you could change it then guilt became redundant because you could fix the problem, whatever it was. Guilt was only a booby prize.

He was drifting again. He couldn't remember going to the mill, after that day. God, Dad had pissed him off! And then he'd gone and fallen and broken his ribs. Dad was so invincible. Then he wasn't. It was hard to forgive him for that. But it was all in the past. He hadn't given it a thought in decades. He was getting to be like Nana, the mill, the past, more real to him than what was in front of his face.

'It OK if I get home?' said Oona, trundling in and wedging herself in the spare chair.

'You go,' said Gabe. 'I'm nearly finished here.'

'Finished off me own self, darlin',' said Oona, scraping off her shoes. She rubbed her feet together. It sounded like a dozen matches being struck at once. She leaned against the desk. Any moment now she would ask him if he fancied a nice cup of tea.

'Getting the Christmas rota finalized,' Gabe said briskly. 'I'll be up in Blantwistle, you know, with my father. You'll have to hold the fort.'

Oona picked up a pad and fanned herself. 'Course you will. Your father, God bless him and keep him. How is he?'

'Still dying,' said Gabe, perhaps a little too jauntily.

'Any time you need, you take it,' said Oona, her head at a sentimental tilt. 'Honly too happy to help.'

Gabe nodded. He looked back at his screen and tinkered

with the keyboard. After a short while Oona creaked to her feet.

'I split up with my girlfriend, with Charlie,' said Gabriel, his gaze still on the computer. 'She split up with me.'

He heard Oona rearranging herself on the chair. She would say, *it all turn out for the best*. She would say, *sometime a ting ain't meant to be*.

'That lovely girl?' said Oona.

'The very one,' said Gabe.

'You want her back?'

Gabe looked at Oona, her little sad smile, her plump cheeks bursting with concern. 'Of course I do,' he said, not knowing, not caring if he meant it, the conversation proceeding, as it must with Oona, in a series of platitudes.

'That is a problem, then.' This piercing insight provided all for free.

'Yeah,' said Gabe, 'that's right.'

'Mm'm,' said Oona, digging the heel of her hand into her bosom. 'A problem to be solved.'

'What's done is done.'

'Chef, if I know you . . .'

'Thank you, Oona.' Gabe jumped up and held the door. 'Thank you, it's getting late. Take a taxi if you want and put it on my expenses. See you in the morning. Goodnight. Did you put the requisition in with maintenance about the extractors? Oh, good. And the air-con's gone crazy again. Got to kick some arses in maintenance. No, don't fiddle with it now. Off you go, that's it, off you go, goodnight.'

Gabe took a fresh set of whites from the bottom drawer of the filing cabinet. Tying his apron he went out on the floor. The night porter drifted quickly and silently out of reach. Gabe got to work. He diced onions, carrots and celery. The mirepoix in this kitchen was never prepared properly. This was exactly the way it should be done. He heated some oil over a medium heat. There was always a burnt undertaste to the jus de veau lié because they coloured the meat and vegetables too quickly. Always in a rush. He put the veal and the mirepoix in the pot and adjusted the flame.

How long since he'd cooked from scratch like this? If he came up with one new dish every week before the restaurant opened, tested them in the dining room, and selected the best half-dozen . . .

He stirred the pot.

Suleiman came up from the locker room in his civvies heading for the exit but backed up when he saw Gabe.

'Chef,' he said, 'do you require help with anything?'

'No,' said Gabe, 'just cooking. You go on home.'

Suleiman bent briefly at the waist, nodding with his whole body. He turned to leave.

'Hang on,' called Gabe. 'I wanted to ask you something. Did you . . . is this something you always wanted to do? To cook?'

'Chef?'

'You know, when you were a kid? Did you decide this is what you'd do? Or did you sort of end up . . . I don't know.'

Suleiman in his smart cheap overcoat, woolly scarf tied at his neck, stood at attention. His hair clung in a slick black circle to his skull. 'It was decided. Most definitely. Of course.'

'You decided, that's right. When? How did you know?'

'Chef, something is wrong?'

'Why should it be? No, nothing. Taking an interest, that's all.'

'Padma Sheshadree Bala Bhavan Senior Secondary,' said Suleiman, drawing himself up to full height. 'In my home town of Chennai. Eleventh grade. It was decided in discussions with my father. He owns three teashops and he is very future-thinking regarding tourism in Tamil Nadu. After taking the CBSE matriculation, I attended the Sri Balaji College of Hotel Management and Catering Technology in Trichy where I received a Diploma in Hotel Management. It was a three-year course and equivalent to Bachelor of Science degree. Afterwards one year spent in Switzerland for purpose of gaining international experience and also first-rate cooking skills. Eighteen months to two years to be spent in UK for gaining first-hand knowledge of large-scale operation, banqueting function, and also improving English. On return to Chennai, these skills to be put to application in first instance through senior employment opportunity in major hotel chain. Thereafter my father and his associates will make significant investment for new resort and complex, with eye to western tourist market, in location to be later decided but most likely in

Kanchipuram, Kanniyakumari or Coimbatore.' He squinted anxiously at Gabriel to see if he'd passed the oral. His scarf, leavened by the heat, had fluffed up over his chin and lower lip. He tried to squash it down.

Gabe added tomato purée to the pan and leaned in to catch the rich sweet smell. 'Have you read *Larousse*?' he said. There was a lot he could teach this boy. 'Have you read Elizabeth David? She makes it all come alive. Read Brillat-Savarin, I recommend him. I don't know what for. Zola wrote about Les Halles and I read it when I was working in Paris and I can't remember exactly – but Zola, he's worth a look. Come to me, though, for recommendations. I can see you're serious and that's what I like about you.' He was babbling and he knew it. 'What about Balzac on gastronomy, oh yes, I was serious like you and I was always reading when I was your age. You get ideas, you see, inspiration, though mostly it's plain hard work. I read Hemingway on the subject of fried fish on the Seine.' There was a point he wanted to make. What was it? It was in his head, he could feel it pressing, but when he opened his mouth it stayed trapped and all these other words came out. 'Anyway, mustn't keep you.' He stopped talking and needlessly rattled the pan.

'I will try to procure these books,' said Suleiman. 'Which one should I start with?'

'Oh, you'll do just fine,' said Gabe. He added the veal stock. He'd use the jus for a chardonnay and leek sauce, and he had an idea to try a little fresh fennel instead of the usual mustard seeds.

He bent down to look in the fridge, deciding he'd take the first three ingredients on the top shelf as a starting point to make something surprising and fresh. When he was in Lyon they did it sometimes, the chef giving them all three items to be included and thirty minutes to come up with a new dish. The best one, if it was good enough, went on the menu for the day. It was fun, it kept all the lads competitive, and maybe he should do it tomorrow first thing when everyone arrived.

A fig, an avocado, a chilli. Gabe lined them up on a chopping board. He rubbed his hands.

Suleiman cleared his throat.

'Ah,' said Gabe, 'I thought you'd gone.'

'Should I go?' said Suleiman.

'Yes, yes. Go.'

Now, where was he? He'd thought of something good, it was form-ing, before Suleiman interrupted him.

What he should do was read more. He never had the time. When he worked abroad he'd lie on his bed between shifts with a book, if he couldn't get a girl. Cookery books, of course, but all sorts of stuff too, he liked books about the Second World War, scoured from second-hand stalls back home. Food writing. Anton – God, he hadn't thought of him in years! – Anton, in his intellectual phase, had lent him ele-gantly tattered volumes, which he'd inscribed 'ex-libris Anton Durlacher' on the title page with purple felt-tip pen. Novels. Whatever was left behind in the guest rooms, ghost stories, war stories, love stories, adventures on the Nile. He'd read them and enjoy them, mostly, even the love stories, but he could never remember them by the following week so it felt like something wasted, something lost.

Charlie, now she was someone who always had a book on the go. When they went on holiday he'd sit on the beach with a popular science book, learning about quarks or atoms, and she'd lie, all care-lessness and curves, across a sandy towel, saying why don't you read a novel, there's more truth in fiction than in fact.

In Lanzarote she'd made him read a book and he couldn't remem-ber the title, couldn't recall anything about it except that it featured a conman who had a job as a liftboy in a Paris hotel. What do you think, she kept on saying, isn't it brilliant? He said he liked it but that wasn't enough. It's not just a funny story about a conman, she said. This was news to him. So tell me, what? Oh, she said, can't you see it? Like it was his fault.

Gabriel de-seeded and sliced the chilli. He tasted a tiny sliver along with a slice of fig. Yes, something could work out.

He skimmed the stock.

But what was he doing? Why was he doing this? Had he forgotten what the restaurant would be? Classic French, precisely executed. Rognons de veau dijonnaise, poussin en cocotte Bonne Femme, tripes à la mode de Caen. Not dishes thrown together like a TV celebrity-chef challenge, like a trainee competition, like an anything-goes-with-chilli-and-balsamic school of cuisine.

Fuck it. God *damn*. He'd touched his eye. He hadn't washed his hands after slicing the chilli. Oh my God!

He gripped the worktop ledge.

How could he make such a stupid mistake?

Maybe, just maybe, he wasn't meant to be a chef.

He could have done anything. Could have been anything. Dad kept saying. You're a clever lad. Don't waste it, son. He should have stayed on at school. Should have gone to college, to university. Everything done and not done to spite his dad.

Jesus. Oh, Christ. He tried to rinse his eye at the sink, managed to make it worse because he still hadn't washed his hands. His hands. Wash his hands!

He soaped them carefully. His eyeball fit to burst, the pain drilling back in his brain.

Anyway, it wasn't true. He loved cooking. When you love something . . .

Nothing comes down to a day, to a moment. Life doesn't dangle by a thread.

He'd sided with Mum. That was natural, the way Dad treated her.

He dried his hands.

The pain was exquisite. Jesus. He'd had a shard of glass in his eyeball once, bounced up from a shattered plate, and that was less painful. If he had to choose – glass or chilli – he'd choose the glass.

She was wonderful. Dad never appreciated her. Even if she was ill that was no reason, no excuse. It was always an adventure being in her world. Running back from school to Astley Street, falling through the door into another dimension, never knowing what he'd find. One time he'd discovered her in the bedroom in a crinoline and she'd ragged her hair. Gave her a pincushion, knew she'd love it, a daisy in the middle, her favourite flower. They danced in the kitchen to anything that came on the radio, Val Doonican, the Beatles, the Stones. She'd whirled and whirled him until he was giddy. She could be over the top sometimes. You never knew with Mum which way it was going to go. It was a bit of a relief, probably, when Dad and Jen got home.

He'd made his own bed.

What angered him, really angered him, was how other people, less talented, had got ahead.

He was forty-two.

Other people got lucky breaks, they married money, they sold their souls to television, they got in league with footballers, they jumped on fads and trends.

Oh, sweet Lord! The fire in his eye was getting worse. He was going down in flames. Half-blind, he staggered to his office and crash-landed on his chair. Leaning back, legs extended, he gripped the arms, neck stretched, mouth open in a mighty soundless roar.

All he'd wanted, all he'd *ever* wanted, was his own place, nothing fancy, nothing flash. What was so hard about that? He should have done it long before now. At Guy Savoy he'd been the one. He was quickest, smartest, best. He got in earliest, stayed latest, worked on his day off. He charmed his way round the chefs, ate his way round the markets, and chewed up a million books.

At twenty-four he was there in a two-star in the middle of Paris and he kept his head.

But what about Le Chevalier? He hadn't been so sober then. Anton had called him from London. *Rapscallion, little rascal, mate. Fancy a whirligig around the wheel of fortune with your old comrade-in-arms?* Three months he'd been with Guy Savoy. It seemed like long enough. *They've made me general and I'll make you colonel. Bring your sash and your three-cornered hat and your ceremonial sword.* Twenty-four, he was, and Anton twenty-five. They'd take all comers. They took a shitload of drugs. Anton had finished with his intellectual phase. He was into action now. They played Jesus and Mary Chain in the kitchen, snorted coke off the cutting boards, and fucked the waitresses, when they were amenable, on the flour sacks. The food started off pretentious and nouvelle and went swiftly downhill from there. Nobody seemed to notice. The place was hot for a while. It ended predictably and badly and Anton – honour and valour deserting him – vanished, leaving Gabe with a cavernous hangover only partially induced by the sudden withdrawal of his evening cocaine wrap.

The truth was, no avoiding it, that this was what he was like:

weak-willed, unfocused, spineless. Unable to commit. It wasn't the only time that he had let things slide.

Everything was going to hell. Just look at him now. Fucking things up with Charlie, drinking and smoking in the locker room like a teenager, getting his rocks off with a—

He pulled himself up straight. His private life was a bit scrambled, but it hadn't knocked him off course. He was a steady sort of bloke.

Was he? He didn't think so a moment ago. At his core, though, he was . . . what? He couldn't think clearly, too much crowding in, too many notions, a sugar rush of thoughts.

You could make fantastic shapes out of sugar; he'd won a competition once. Spin it any way you wanted, all in the wrist action, make it look like anything.

Gabriel snapped forward on to the desk and laid his head on his arms. He hadn't been sleeping well. If he rolled his brow across his sleeve exerting a small amount of pressure it eased the pain in his eye. He concentrated on this and a few minutes later melted into a caramel sleep.

He woke around four thirty, brittle and thirsty, a crick in his neck. After drinking some water he went out of the kitchen and upstairs. Since he'd witnessed Gleeson and Ivan's assignation in one of the empty guest rooms he had been meaning to check it out. Now would be a good time, no fear of being disturbed.

The door was half open. The room was a standard double, the conversion not yet begun. It had the tinned-flower smell of polish and a lamp that had been left on. Gabe opened the wardrobe. He pulled out a drawer. There was nothing, no sign of life. The bed was made, the blinds pulled, the wastebasket empty, the sanitary tape was over the toilet, the toilet paper left with a folded end. Should he look under the bed? Perhaps he should hide under there and eavesdrop for a day or two. What did he expect? Contraband stacked in the shower? A corpse in the wardrobe?

He was about to leave when he noticed an envelope on the desk. It was the standard Imperial Hotel stationery left in every bedroom. But it was out of place, in the centre on its own. He carried on walking to the door but as he reached it he turned again. *Come on, Sherlock, investigate*. He picked up the envelope casually – too casually – and a waterfall of photographs cascaded to the floor.

Crouching, he gathered them quickly and at once his heart began to race. There was Charlie in her silver flapper dress, standing at the mike. Maggie, the Penguin Club waitress, staring dough-faced into the lens. Shots of tables, of punters, the backs of people's heads. A street shot showing the door. And here he was, with Ivan and Victor, Suleiman in the background, the night he took them all out. Somebody had taken a camera, couldn't remember who; it was innocent, completely innocuous, not evidence of some crime. He shuffled the pictures back into the envelope with clammy hands. Placing it carefully on the desk as he had found it, he headed back towards the exit, tiptoeing this time.

'Chef,' said Gleeson, hanging in the doorway fizzing, like a light bulb about to blow, 'what an unexpected pleasure this is.'

Gabe's arm shot up to the back of his head. 'Oh, hello, Stanley. Just passing, saw the lamp on . . .'

'Of course,' said Gleeson quickly. 'Me too, saw the light, naughty, naughty, wasteful, must pop in and switch it off.'

Gabriel checked his watch. 'Well.'

'Well, indeed. Will you do the honours or should I?'

'What's that?'

'The light,' said Gleeson. 'The *light*.'

'It's five o'clock in the morning,' said Gabe, 'I think we both know . . .'

Gleeson adjusted his cuffs. He cocked his head. 'Know?'

'Know . . .' said Gabe, 'that . . .' Hell. What did he know? 'It's the best time of day for catching up. No one else around.'

'Two of a kind,' said Gleeson, with a glutinous smile. His eyes flicked to the desk.

Branka, the housekeeping supervisor, snaked her head round the door. 'She's ready.'

Branka had all the right qualities for keeping her girls in order. When she passed down a corridor, checking up on them, she moved as if under sniper fire. She could probably catch bullets between those teeth.

'She's ready,' Branka repeated. 'Shall I bring her in?'

CHAPTER SEVENTEEN

—◊—

THE OFFICE DOOR BOUNCED OFF ERNIE'S NOSE AND BACK INTO Gabriel's hand. Ernie had been standing there in the dark. The night porter had switched off the lights and the breakfast crew had yet to arrive.

'Ernie,' said Gabe, 'sorry, if I'd thought there might be someone in here I'd have taken a bit more care.'

Ernie stood back to let Gabe through.

'Did it hurt?' said Gabe. He sat down while Ernie stayed standing.

'Ah'm OK,' said Ernie. He'd put a comb through his hair. His overalls looked as if they might have had contact with an iron. His socks were pulled up tight. He stood with a sheaf of goods-in dockets in his hands, twisting them around like a doffed cloth cap.

'Good,' said Gabriel, yawning. He waited. 'Is there something you wanted? I was about to go home.'

'You told me to come,' said Ernie, 'first thing in the morning, you said.'

'Oh,' said Gabe. 'Yes.' He'd meant his own 'first thing' which would be nine, or more like ten, not Ernie's which began at six, or even earlier today.

'Discuss something, you said.' Ernie, as usual, stared just past Gabe's right ear. Gabe had assumed this was because of some defect, a slight boss-eye, but as he looked at Ernie now, wondering if he should do the deed, he saw that he had been mistaken. Nor did it seem that

273

Ernie was simply avoiding all eye contact. Rather it struck Gabriel that the porter was looking directly at another person, another Gabe who stood at his shoulder, another version of himself.

He was so tired he'd started imagining things. He was in no state to deal with the Ernie issue. The physical stock and the computer records never tallied and Ernie should probably be let go, but now wasn't the time to do it, the 'discussion' would have to wait.

'Thing is, Ernie,' said Gabe. 'The thing is, I've forgotten what it was that I wanted to talk about. Sorry.'

Ernie extended his neck. 'Can't have been important, then. You'll think Ah'm daft. For a moment there Ah thought Ah was for the chop.'

When Ernie had gone Gabe decided to call Charlie. He had to warn her. He picked up the phone. Warn her about what? He hung up. Gleeson, wielding his deadly civility, had practically pushed him out of the room. 'Allow me, if you would, to undertake what needs to be done here.' Gabe hadn't put up a fight. And Branka, perhaps sensing landmines, had executed a quick and tactical retreat. There was nothing to tell Charlie. He'd found some photos. He'd got the creeps.

Who was ready? Why would Branka be bringing one of her girls to see Gleeson? Whatever Gleeson and Ivan and the housekeeping supervisor were up to was their business. Why should Gabriel do anything about it? It had nothing to do with him. Let Mr Maddox find another spy.

Unless it related in some way to Charlie. How could it? Perhaps if he told her, that would be sufficient. He wanted to speak to her anyway, didn't he? He'd better do it now or he would have it hanging over him, another item, another duty, another thing he hadn't done. He wrote 'Call Charlie' on the list he kept on his desk pad. He picked up the phone with his left hand and ticked off 'Call Charlie' with his right.

She answered on the third ring, heavy with sleep.

'It's Gabe. Look, I know it's early, sorry, but I have to tell you something.'

He heard her breathe.

'It may be nothing . . . you know, it might be best if I come round.'

'Gabriel,' said Charlie.

'Yes?' said Gabe, a chasm suddenly opening inside.

'Don't ring me again.'

The day clambered out of the trenches in its grey greatcoat. Gabe, in the back of a taxi, watched the flickering reel of buildings through half-closed eyes. The city at this hour belonged in an old war film. He opened his eyes properly and looked up at the few streaks of yellow, like mustard gas across the sky.

When he got home Lena was in the bath. She did not speak or move. He had, some time ago, stopped expecting any kind of acknowledgement when he returned.

'Sorry,' he said, 'about last night. I should have rung.' Some time in the early hours of the morning he had been cursed, condemned to keep apologizing to everyone for everything.

Lena shrugged, a mere ripple.

'I'm going to catch a few hours,' said Gabriel. He lowered the lid and sat on the toilet. 'Then I'll have to go back in.'

'I had dream,' said Lena. 'It was my town, Mazyr. And I walk through street naked and everyone look at me.'

'Tell me about your house, the house you grew up in.'

'After dream,' said Lena, 'no sleep.'

Her skin was nearly as clear as the water. If Gabe put his hand in the bath and stirred she would dissolve.

'Did it have a garden? How many bedrooms? What was the kitchen like?' Sometimes she'd feed him a bit of information. A phrase or two about a school, a friend, a pet. It brought them closer together, even if he had to suck it out of her, and it was a way of distracting Lena when she seemed likely to upset herself.

'How many bedrooms it have, your parents' house?' said Lena. She frequently picked up questions and flung them back like insults.

'When I was very young we had two. Those houses, they've demolished a lot of them, they're known as two-up two-down. They weren't so bad, really. Suppose you don't notice, anyway, when you're a child.' He groped his pockets for a cigarette. 'I'll smoke at the window,' he said, but stayed smoking on the toilet seat. If they could just talk, if she would just talk to him. Asking her questions, it wasn't productive; it was like trying to milk a cat.

'There was a toilet out in the yard,' said Gabriel. 'We had another one indoors, but the one outside we still used it sometimes and me and Jen we'd play tricks on each other.' He told her about the time his sister had caught a frog and left it in the lavatory bowl, the way you could climb up on the roof and dangle your face or (if you were careful) your arse over the small high glassless window, how he'd locked Jenny in once until after dark. Lena lay in the water carefully stroking her arm. 'She's great, Jenny, you should come and meet her. You'd like her. How about Pavel? Would we get on OK?'

Gabe passed lightly across the floor and sat on the edge of the bath. 'He's older than you, isn't he? What does he do? I mean, did he have a job?'

She looked at him sideways and looked down again. She wanted to talk about her brother, her lover, whoever he was, but Gabe saw she was afraid. If she began to speak perhaps she would give away too much.

'Tell me anything,' he said. 'Not about him. About you. Something you did at school, a little story, anything, what posters you had on your bedroom wall.'

She rested her cheek on her knees and looked through him. 'I don't know.'

'Please,' he said, pushing a strand of hair off her face. His hand hovered over her. He removed it.

'Is stupid,' said Lena. 'You – you are stupid.'

'Yes,' said Gabe. 'Maybe.'

He wanted to know her. But information was not the same as knowing. He could not enter her like data on a damn spreadsheet.

'What you have done to find Pasha?' said Lena. And then, answering her own question, 'Nothing.'

'That's where you're wrong,' said Gabriel. 'What do you think I was doing all night?'

That got her. She curled her toes.

'I went to Victoria, to the coach station, to that club you told me about . . .'

She actually looked in his eyes.

He shook his head. It was horrible, what she did to him. When he went home from school one time with Michael Harrison they rescued a bird from Michael's old tabby, prised it from between the cat's jaws, and it had only lost a couple of feathers, no blood or anything. Gabriel held the bird in his hands. The way its heart beat made him panic. He wanted to save it. He wanted it to die. They put it in a cardboard box in the airing cupboard and when they opened the box the next day the thing was dead. That shocked them. Besides being dead it looked healthy enough, it didn't look damaged at all.

'No,' said Lena. 'I don't believe.'

'It's no use,' said Gabe, 'I tried. It's not a little village, where you can just go ask around and find someone. It's London, for God's sake.'

She turned her face to the wall.

'Lena . . .' He brushed her shoulder with his fingertips. 'Lena, I think I know a way. What we'll do, we'll get a private investigator, I'll hire someone to find him.'

'No.'

'What do you mean, no? I will. A private investigator, a private eye – do you know what that is?'

'No.'

'A bit like a policeman . . . no, it's OK, not the police, a private eye won't tell the police anything, they only do what you pay them to do. And they find people. They know how.'

She ran the hot water. 'My Pasha, he want to see . . .' she paused to get her mouth around the words, '. . . Wembley Stadium. He say is home of football.'

'Good,' said Gabe. 'That's good. It could be useful. What you should do is write everything down. Anything that could be a clue. Places he might visit, his interests, that sort of thing. Start with the basics and then give all the information you can.' It would keep her busy. She needed something to do. 'I'll keep on looking in the meantime, then when we've got everything down on a sheet of paper I'll find a private eye, a good one, I'll pay for the best. We could probably get someone to start after Christmas, start straight away in the new year, it's not long until Christmas and then we'll crack it, we'll get the job done.'

She took a breath and slid under the water, the disturbance at the surface momentarily disjointing her limbs. Gabe held his breath too. If he could keep her until Christmas, that should be time enough. By then she might feel something. If Gabe could fall in love with Lena, it seemed only reasonable that she could fall in love with him too.

'OK,' said Lena, emerging. The hot water had put a red flush on her chest. 'You want have sex now. I come.' She made to get up.

'No,' said Gabe, pressing down on her shoulder. 'No, that's not what I want.' He was shaking with tiredness. 'It's not right. I don't want to. I need a few hours' sleep.'

He smiled at her and Lena nearly smiled back at him. Gabriel picked up the bar of soap. Gently, he lifted her foot and soaped it, massaged it, rubbing the suds between her toes. He knelt on the floor to get a better angle on her other foot. He worked in circular motions, half hypnotized by the slip-slide of his thumb. He took a sponge and, resting her foot by the tap, began to journey up her shin.

Lying in bed, he asked her about the client she had told him she wanted to kill. What he really wanted to know was why she did not hate the others. But that he could not ask.

'What did he do to you?'

Lena gnawed a ragged cuticle. It bled.

'Did he beat you, Lena? Did he?'

'Oh,' said Lena, wiping the blood on her arm. 'You like to hear about it? This is thing you like?'

'Of course not.' At other times she forced him to listen to stuff nobody wanted to hear and now this accusation. He could not win with her. 'I thought it might help you to talk things through. Not if you don't want to. I'm here, that's all I'm saying, if you want . . .'

'*I don't want talk,*' hissed Lena. She rolled on her side.

He shifted himself so slowly towards her it felt as if he had not moved but grown. He put down roots that twined around her, binding her to him. When he was almost asleep she said, 'One day he is coming and when he come to my room I see he is play with wedding ring and I say, "Oh, you are marry? You have wife?" Like this, I say, because I think maybe if wife come to his mind he will be better, he will not do this things to me. You see how stupid? You see how stupid I am?'

In his dream he wanders the catacombs, wafting through viscous violet light. He thinks he will never find the place. There is no point going on.

When he discovers the corpse he is so grateful that he falls to his knees. The food begins to pile up all around. He breaks a piece of cake. It is at his lips before he smells how bad it is. He picks up a pastry from a glazed gargantuan stack. A fat white maggot wags out at him. But here, over here, is his favourite chicken and it is fragrant, crisp, perfect. He tears off a drumstick and examines it closely, the lovely bubbled skin, the scent of garlic and herbs. He takes a bite and spits it out. When he looks again at the chicken he sees it is black with flies. He crawls back to the corpse and grabs the feet. A toe comes away in his fingers and he tosses it next to the drumstick on the ground.

In the two days since he found the photographs, Gabriel had rung Charlie five times. Once at home that same morning and four times on her mobile – calls that she did not answer, messages to which she did not respond. He would try one more time now, on his way to work, and leave it at that. While he was waiting to cross at Lollard Street a Mercedes pulled on to Kennington Road and a cyclist went flying over the bonnet, the bike still between his legs, twisting full circle before smacking down on the tarmac.

'Hello,' said Charlie.

The whole world stopped for a moment, poised, it seemed, to applaud this aerial ballet.

I saw someone killed, thought Gabriel. I saw someone killed on my way to work.

'Gabriel,' said Charlie.

People ran towards the cyclist. The driver got out of the Mercedes. In the queue of traffic that had built within seconds other drivers began to honk their horns.

The cyclist stood up. Three people led him to the kerb and sat him down.

'Charlie,' said Gabriel. 'Charlie, are you still there?'

He called again a couple of times standing at the bus stop. She didn't pick up.

When he got to the office he sat with his mobile, opened the contacts list, scrolled to Charlie and pressed the call button. The message service again. He repeated the process. He did it a third time. And a fourth. He kept going, working faster, cutting the line and redialling before the message service kicked in. Jumping up he opened the filing cabinet, threw in his phone and locked the drawer. He scratched his bald patch. He rubbed it. He scratched again. He put the cabinet key in the back pocket of his jeans. Good. All done. Then he turned round and looked straight at the phone that sat on his desk.

Grabbing a random file from his in-tray he decided to go and work in a quiet corner of the dining room. The trouble was it was too hot in his office. He could get heatstroke in here.

In the mornings Jacques served breakfast until eleven when the set-up for lunch began. It was around ten and the place was largely deserted, a few businessmen lingering over coffees and PDAs. So Gabe saw Fairweather immediately, pushing up his fringe like a schoolgirl, leaning over to his companion as if he were about to flirt with him. Fairweather, clearly endowed with acute peripheral vision, broke off and said, 'Ah, Chef!'

'Won't disturb you,' said Gabe.

'I think we were finished,' said Fairweather. 'Were we finished?' He stood up as he spoke so that his companion, a hungry-looking man with a jumper over his shirt and tie, had no choice but to agree.

'I'd run clean out of *bons mots* for him,' said Fairweather, as his companion withdrew. 'Sit down, sit down.'

'I'd forgotten we were meeting,' said Gabe.

'Oh, we weren't,' said Fairweather. 'I was meeting that chap for breakfast and I thought, why not the Imperial? Get out of Westminster for a change.'

'Colleague?' Gabriel scanned the dining room. No sign of Gleeson.

'Thing is,' said Fairweather, 'you meet a journalist for a chat and then there's something in the paper, some leak or scandal or other, and then the finger of suspicion points at you.'

'Can't be good for the career,' said Gabe. It was irritating even to have *thought* of Gleeson, as if Gabe couldn't do whatever he wanted. As if he shouldn't talk to anyone he chose, as if he should worry about being seen.

'Finger of suspicion,' said Fairweather ruminatively. 'Is that the correct phrase?'

It was Gleeson who should be worried. He was the one with something to hide.

'Anyway,' continued Fairweather, laughing, 'the trouble with a political career is that there's so much politics involved.'

'That's why you're getting out.'

'We'll see what happens at the next reshuffle. Resign in haste, repent at leisure, isn't that what they say?'

Gabriel lifted the vase of gerberas. Finally, fresh flowers as agreed. He rubbed a petal and then lifted the stem. He should have known it. Fakes.

He said, 'You're not asking to be shuffled out?'

'Possibly. I may. We shall see. Depends what I'm offered. There's been some talk. Certain positions are *very* difficult to turn down.'

'Keeping your options open.'

'Quintessentially British,' said Fairweather. 'Isn't that the British way?'

We used to know what it meant to be British. That was just Ted. 'Being open-minded, you mean?'

'Absolutely,' cried Fairweather. 'A core British value. Freedom, fairness, tolerance, plurality. Does one have to order a top-up of coffee or will it simply appear, do you think?'

Gabe lifted his chin to a waiter. He ordered a double espresso for himself. The anticipation of caffeine gave him an instant buzz. 'You're not on a husting,' he said.

'Think I'm giving you the party line?' Fairweather smiled. 'I mean it. Plurality. Our so-called British identity is like our economy, Gabriel, deregulated in the extreme. It's a marketplace of ideas and values and cultures and none of them are privileged over the rest. Each one finds its own level depending on supply and demand.' Fairweather had gone into rapid-fire mode. 'We talk about the multicultural model but it's really nothing more than laissez-faire. I think that's quite unique. Our national identity, in that way, is very distinct.'

'Isn't that the point about national identities,' said Gabriel, 'they're all different from each other?'

Fairweather raised an eyebrow. He paused a few moments, wondering, perhaps, if Gabriel were a worthy recipient of the intellectual bounty that he could, if he chose, distribute. 'It's a function of nation-building, naturally, to say "we're different from them". What's interesting, Gabriel, is the way in which the idea of Britishness is or has become essentially about a neutral, value-free identity. It's a non-identity, if you like. A vacuum.'

'I don't see it,' said Gabe. 'I don't feel like that.'

'I'm glad you don't,' said Fairweather. He pulled out his wallet though the coffee had not yet arrived. 'Now, it's been a pleasure as always. But I have got to dash.'

'Is it . . . do you find it worrying?'

Fairweather flourished a signature through the air and the waiter moved for the bill. 'No, I don't, as a matter of fact. Let's see, you could say, for instance, that the French are more decidedly . . . French in their identity. But why should that be a good thing? It depends what you prefer. We got the Beatles. They got Johnny Hallyday.'

'And we've got chicken tikka masala,' said Gabriel, 'and they've got decent food.'

'Dad, I'm not calling too late, am I?'

'I were up in the loft is all. Took me a bit of time to get down.'

'Should you be doing that? What if you fell?'

'I'll not fall. Don't tell yer sister, I've enough of a job with her as it is.'

'What were you doing?'

'Sorting things. It'll be less for you and Jen to do.'

'Dad . . .'

'Oh, I'm not doing it for you. There's a lifetime of memories up there.'

'A real museum.'

'Oh aye.'

'I'll go up with you when I come. I'll be home before Christmas, stay a few days.'

'Don't go spending yer money on me.'

'I won't.'

'Present enough to have you home.'

'OK.'

'Now, what do I get you?'

'Nothing.'

'Well, yer not having nothing. I'm not dead yet.'

'No . . . that's . . . I need socks. I could do with a new wallet. There's lots of things I need actually.'

'What about this wedding? You set the date?'

'Dad, you see, there's maybe a delay. We've decided, I mean, we've agreed to think about everything.'

'You've fell out.'

'Sort of. It's complicated. I'll tell you when I come home.'

'Thinking only gets you so far, Gabriel. Life carries on its own sweet way.'

'I keep thinking about Rileys. When you used to take me in. You remember? I skipped school once or twice.'

'Oh aye. I remember that.'

'I loved the Benninger room. When there was a complex job on, all the colours flying across.'

'Aye.'

'You said this thing about weaving. You said it's a bit like life. You've got the warp going one way, and it brings the pattern and the colour. And you've got to have the weft, the constant, which runs through everything. Dad . . . I . . . sometimes I think . . .'

'Is it that girl? That Lena? No, I've not forgot. Listen, son, you should know, threads break all the time. A decent weaver won't wait on a tackler. They'll fix it and get on.'

CHAPTER EIGHTEEN

—∽∽—

HE CRASHED SMACK–BANG OUT OF SLEEP AND LANDED IN BED ARSE side up. Gabriel lay with his head hanging off the mattress and his heart bursting out of his chest. He'd fought so hard to wake up, applied too much force, like ramming a locked door that suddenly opened and falling flat on his face. Still, he was glad to be out of it. The dream got worse and worse. Nightmares won't kill you. This one might, thought Gabe. He'd die of sleep deprivation. He'd die of a heart attack.

It was the morning of the inquest and Gabriel put on a suit before he left for the Westminster Coroner's Court. He sat in the wood-panelled room as the few witnesses gave their statements. Both he and Mr Maddox were called. After a brief adjournment, the coroner delivered his verdict: accidental death. The cause of death was to be recorded as a fractured cervical spine. No family members were present, though the inquest had been twice delayed to allow them to attend. Financial circumstances, explained the coroner, had not permitted them to travel. A representative of the Coroners' Courts Support Services would now read a statement on their behalf.

It was the usual stuff – loving husband, devoted father – a pro forma of life and death. Gabriel looked around the scattered few in the courtroom, the ambulance worker, the policeman. How difficult it was to pay attention. Maybe he would feel something, register some kind of emotion, if he weren't so utterly worn out.

Outside, on Horseferry Road, Mr Maddox punched Gabe's

shoulder. 'Result,' he said, as if the football scores were in. 'Come on, I'll give you a lift. Gareth can get in the back.'

With his permanent five o'clock shadow, the collar turned up on his big black coat, Maddox looked like the head of an organized crime family, a career in which he'd thrive.

'So that was it for Yuri. All over and done.' Gabe, abruptly furious, laid into a cigarette.

'Look like you slept in a ditch, Chef. Been burning the proverbial at both ends?'

'Don't give a toss, do you?' said Gabriel. 'So what if somebody died.'

'Listen to Mother Teresa. She's going to say a prayer.'

Mr James tittered obediently. He said, 'If we hurry you can make your two thirty. Shall we go?'

The way Mr Maddox was staring was like being punched in the face. Gabe took an involuntary step back.

'What?' said Maddox. 'What do you want me to do? Pass the collection plate?'

Gabriel shrugged. 'Why not? At the next board meeting. Industrial compensation, let's say.'

'No,' roared Mr Maddox. 'There's no question of it. No question at all. Didn't you hear what was said in court? There's no negligence charge here. If there was we'd fight it, they wouldn't get a bloody penny out of us.'

'As an act of charity, then,' said Gabe.

'I've got a better idea,' said Maddox. 'Why don't you consecrate the catacombs? Turn them into a bloody shrine. Right, Gareth, you still stood here? Well, go and bring the car round. Chef's decided to walk. He needs to clear his head.'

Lunch service the next day was funereal. Bomb scares at two Underground stations, miserable weather, the dwindling 'consumer confidence' he'd heard about on the radio news – Gabe was unsure how to apportion the blame. There'd been several cancellations for dinner and he bet there would be some no-shows and few walk-ins. It was a jittery day.

Gabriel, a bull in a bear market, sat with Nikolai between shifts in a pub off Shaftesbury Avenue. He wanted to talk about the dream. The dream was on a pillaging spree. It stole his nights. It didn't know when to stop.

Gabe sipped on a bottom-of-the-barrel musty pint. 'I keep having this dream – about Yuri.'

Nikolai was drinking lager from the bottle. He closed his eyes for a moment. What was that? Some kind of acknowledgement? A salute to the deceased? A mark of respect?

'Look at this table,' said Gabriel. 'It's filthy. One, two, three staff standing around behind the bar.' The pub was a tourist and out-of-towner hell hole, the kind that never expected to see you again and didn't give a shit. The food – 'trad pub grub' – was microwaved pies standing in a swill of cut-price baked beans, an inedible concoction, as a brace of American tourists were about to attest.

'It's a shame,' said Nikolai, with unnecessary gravitas.

Gabriel broke out in irritation. Nikolai, with his long white fingers and ginger hair, with his pretentious silence, with his ugly nose, with his judgemental claptrap, with his sloping shoulders, with his biding-my-time gaze. Nikolai! Why would Gabriel want to talk to him?

As quickly as it had flared up, the irritation died. Gabriel tried again. 'Thing is, with this dream, it's always the same. Starts off the same, any-way.' He filled Nikolai in, rounding up the details like bandits, driving them out of his territory.

'I see,' said Nikolai.

'Well?' said Gabe. 'Well,' he repeated. 'What do you think it means?'

Nikolai dispensed a cigarette to Gabriel, a prescription for all his ills. He shrugged. 'A dream is just a dream.'

'I know,' said Gabe. 'But I keep having it. That must mean something.' When he walked into this godawful pub he'd told himself it was quiet and close, that was why he'd chosen it. Truth was he didn't know where else to go. Now that Dusty's was closed and the Penguin might as well be. He used to know a dozen places. He used to know this town.

'A Freudian analyst,' said Nikolai, 'would tell you. You might not believe him though.'

'I don't need a shrink,' said Gabe. London was slipping away from him. The longer he lived here, the less familiar it became.

'No,' said Nikolai. 'Of course not.'

'Don't they just sit there?' said Gabriel. 'Sit there in silence while you talk. A bit like you, actually, Nikolai. Not a shrink, by any chance? Kitchen shrink, ha, ha.'

Nikolai condescended to laugh.

'Come on,' said Gabe, 'tell me something – why do they call you Doc? Are you a doctor, or what?'

'Once upon a time.'

'And?' said Gabe. 'So what's the story?'

'Things happened,' said Nikolai. 'My life changed.'

'If you'd rather not talk about it . . .' said Gabe.

'There's nothing to hide,' said Nikolai. 'I was a doctor in the Soviet Union. Then I was accused of being a spy and – ' He made a gesture of abdication with his cigarette. 'I had to leave.'

'Hang on,' said Gabe, 'when was this?'

'Gorbachev,' said Nikolai. 'Glasnost! Perestroika!' He spoke as if from the podium, with a rabble-rousing smile. 'The end of the Cold War! The end of history!'

'And you hadn't done anything? You'd done nothing wrong?'

'Of course I did something wrong.'

'Oh,' said Gabe, 'I see.'

'I was an obstetrician. I was investigating birth defects. There were many, of a particular kind, in our town. I did some studies of the river, the water supply, and found some interesting things about the chemicals dumped by the factory. This knowledge I made public. For this I was branded a spy. The factory supplied military parts, so I had exposed military secrets. So they said at my trial. I saw it reported, preferring – for reasons you will understand – to remain in hiding at that time. I was sentenced *in absentia* to fourteen years in jail.'

'This was under Gorbachev?'

'History did not end,' said Nikolai. 'It simply repeated itself.'

'And why . . .' said Gabriel. He wondered how to phrase the question.

'Why a kitchen knife? I have not held a scalpel for many years.'

'Why didn't you carry on practising? Take some more exams?'

'When I came here, I thought . . .' Nikolai shook his head. 'I got involved in . . . I spent too long . . .' He smiled and wagged a finger at Gabriel, as if he had nearly been caught out. 'Let us say *force of circumstance*, for want of a better phrase. It doesn't matter. I have accepted it. Let's call it destiny.'

Gabriel moved his elbow. It had glued itself to a sticky patch. *Destiny*, how grand, how grandiose! How typical of Nikolai. You had to think yourself special to feel destined for anything.

'You don't believe that. I mean, *do* you believe in that?'

'Believe in what?' said Nikolai.

'Destiny, fate, predestination – whatever you call it. A master plan from On High. That's rubbish, isn't it? What happens to choice, to free will?'

'There's no master plan,' said Nikolai. He took his time, laced his slender fingers, calculating no doubt that this pause would add weight to his delivery when it came. 'With that I agree,' Nikolai continued. 'But, as a man of reason and science I must disagree with your idea of free will. With that I cannot concur.'

'I take it you're joking,' said Gabe. Nikolai's hands were not chef's hands. They were not covered in old cuts and burns. He worked in the kitchen with surgical precision. Why should wounds be badges of pride?

'Or maybe I spent too long reading Schopenhauer,' said Nikolai.

'What? Who?'

'Seriously,' said Nikolai, 'let me ask you, let me find out what you believe. Do you believe, for example, that we are free to choose the most important things about our lives? To be born in the West in the twentieth century is the most enormous stroke of luck. After that, the parents we are given are the most significant factors to take into account. Would you not agree that the biggest events in our lives are things that happen to us, rather than things that we decide to do? And what of the present – our day-to-day conduct? Do we control even the basic functions? Can you wake when you want to? Sleep when you want to? Can you forget your dreams? Can you decide when to think, what to think about, when not to think at all?'

Nikolai took a hip flask from his pocket, swigged and passed it to Gabe.

'A little early for me,' said Gabe, 'but OK, thanks.' The vodka reminded him about Damian. He should do something about that boy. If he had the time. Anyway, Damian was a car crash waiting to happen. Probably not much he could do about that. He returned the flask. 'I get what you're saying,' he told Nikolai. 'But it's not the point. You miss the point.'

'Which is?' said Nikolai.

'It's obvious. I might not be able to fall asleep when I want, but when I'm awake I can decide what I do, when I do it, how I do it. That's free will. We make choices all the time. How we behave is up to us. For example, I can decide to behave decently – be good, in other words – or I can go the other way, be selfish and so on.'

'How we behave,' said Nikolai, drawing out the words, clearly pretending to think when actually he had prepared the lecture long ago. 'How we behave, you could say, is determined by our childhood, by the accidents of birth and parentage and what happened to us along the way. A particular childhood strips us of certain choices, propels us in certain directions.'

Michael Harrison, his childhood friend, slipped unbidden into Gabriel's mind. Not difficult to see, Gabe thought reluctantly, which way Michael was going to go. Then again, no, Michael was bright enough, Michael had probably made good.

'A psychoanalyst,' Nikolai went on – God, he could go on once he was on a roll – 'might disagree with your proposition. Freud's taught us that we need to examine a person's past in order to understand his behaviour today. If a person is not "good", is sadistic even, what has caused that person to be like that? Another person is unable to form stable relationships. Why? We can discover the reasons if we are so inclined.'

'Freud,' said Gabriel, 'has been thoroughly discredited.' He had no idea if this was true, but it sounded likely enough.

Nikolai screwed up his little mouse eyes as he lit another cigarette. 'Let's look at the question from another angle. You prefer a more scientific approach?'

'Yes.'

'Scientific, controlled experimentation, measurable results – proof, in other words?'

'I suppose,' said Gabe.

'Philosophers and therapists never give us proof. But when we see hard results, we go with the evidence, isn't that right?'

'We haven't got all day,' said Gabriel. He wasn't stupid. He could see what Nikolai was doing: leading him down a corridor, closing the doors of objection along the way. It was a salesman's trick.

'I will be brief. I'm thinking of a classic experiment conducted at Harvard University in the early nineties. Psychologists explored how students evaluate their teachers. A group of students were asked to rate lectures on the basis of a thirty-second video clip with no sound. The students agreed with each other about which teachers were most competent and professional, which possessed other good classroom qualities. All this after thirty seconds of viewing complete strangers.' Nikolai had another hit of vodka. He licked his colourless lips.

'And?' said Gabriel. 'So?'

'Not only did they agree with each other – the scores those students gave also accurately predicted the evaluations that the teachers received from their real students at the end of a full semester. The first group of students were, of course, acting on instinct; the second group – the real students – *believed* they were acting on reason, making logical choices, but it led them to the same place.'

'If that's the best you can come up with,' said Gabriel, 'that doesn't prove anything.'

'According to many cognitive scientists,' said Nikolai, 'we only think we act consciously because our inner voice is very good at construct-ing explanations for behaviour that is, in fact, unconsciously generated.'

Gabriel stretched. He scratched the back of his head, in a leisurely manner for a change, enjoying a good rub. If Nikolai wanted to waste his intelligence on justifying his own inertia, on why he shouldn't even bother trying to improve his own situation, then more fool Nikolai.

'You're talking about psychologists, right, those guys at Harvard? How many psychologists does it take to change a light bulb?'

'I could talk about neuroscience,' said Nikolai, 'I could talk about the half-second delay between the initiation of an action and the conscious decision to act, I could talk about all that but it might be too . . . unsettling.'

Gabe could imagine Nikolai in a political meeting, working the crowd, manipulating emotions, plying his rhetoric. Yes, he had probably been a troublemaker, Gabe could imagine it. But he wasn't pulling Gabriel's strings.

'We have to take responsibility.'

'For what?' said Nikolai.

'For ourselves, for each other, we can't retreat into that kind of . . . that kind of . . . playing with words.'

'Playing with words?' Nikolai smiled his bloodless smile. 'No, OK. Maybe this is why you dream of Yuri. You take some responsibility for what happened to him.'

'No,' said Gabe, 'what do you mean? How could that be my fault? It's not as if I said he could stay down there.'

'I did not say fault. I made a speculation about your feeling of responsibility – for the world in which we live, for the kind of world in which there will always be more Yuris, struggling to exist.'

'I didn't make the world,' said Gabriel, taking the hip flask. 'I just live in it. Same as you.'

On his way back in to work Gabriel stopped at Ernie's hut. Ernie and Oona, scrunched together over the computer, sprang apart. They looked at him.

'Nothing,' said Gabe, backing out again, 'never mind. Carry on.'

He glanced back through the window and saw Oona sucking madly on the end of her pen.

Gleeson was loitering in the passageway, speaking into his mobile phone. 'Victoria, same as usual,' he said, 'but the pick-up's going to be later . . . well, they'll just have to wait.' He turned and saw Gabriel, jabbed his first and second fingers at his eyes and then poked them in Gabe's direction: *I'm watching you.* He could fuck right off.

Gabe floated past him and went to the pastry kitchen to speak to Chef Albert. The place was in a mess, the bins full to overflowing, the Hobart mixer full of goo, the Carpigiani smeared with ice cream. Something was burning in the baker's oven, the Rondo had been left with a dangling pastry tongue, and there appeared to be a splatter of egg yolk up one wall. Chef Albert's muppet, piping meringue shells, was covered in flour, which also lay like a sifting of snow all over the floor.

Chef Albert leaned over a worktop examining a pair of breasts. 'Chef,' he cried. 'Look! Zis is a work of art, no?'

'What happened here?' said Gabriel.

Chef Albert closed his newspaper. He put his hands on his fat hips and tossed his head so that his toque sailed devilishly close to the wind. 'Spontaneity,' he said. 'Creativity. To make ze omelette, one must break many eggs.'

'Oh,' said Gabe. 'For a moment I thought someone had been throwing flour bombs.'

'Ha ha! Ha he ha he ha!' The pastry chef slapped his thigh. His hat slipped over one eye. When the convulsion had passed he straightened himself and the hat. 'Yes,' he said, 'zis is correct.'

'Right,' said Gabe, 'well, I'm sure you'll get it cleaned up. I wanted to speak to you about—'

'Psst,' said Chef Albert. 'I 'ave something.' He sidled into a corner, making cod-furtive gestures for Gabe to follow.

'Do you need to check the oven?' said Gabe.

'Later, later,' said Chef Albert. 'Excuse me, Chef, but I 'ave heard . . . about ze beautiful girlfriend, 'ow she . . .' He gripped Gabe's shoulders, pulled him close and administered a kiss to each cheek. 'You are suffering!'

'Not really,' said Gabe. He looked over at the assistant, busy piping meringue directly into his mouth.

'Yes,' said Chef Albert, his moustache trembling. 'Suffering!' He whisked a packet of pills from his top pocket. 'Ah,' he said, 'not zis. Although, maybe zis, also. You 'ave depression, *n'est-ce pas?*'

'No,' said Gabe. '*Non.*' He called to the assistant. 'Check that oven.'

Chef Albert shook a small brown bottle in Gabriel's face. 'Na ne na ne na,' he said, as if soothing a baby with a rattle. 'You decide – 'ow you say – to play ze field . . . ba boom!' He made a phallic symbol with fist and forearm. 'You make nice with ze girlfriend . . . ba ba boom! She begs you to stay.'

'Thanks,' said Gabriel, 'but no thanks.'

'Chef, I am fifty-two years old and my erection it lasts two, three hours. What a gift of life. You should see for yourself.'

'I appreciate the offer,' said Gabe.

Chef Albert tried to stuff the bottle in Gabriel's trouser pocket. The assistant opened the oven. Thick black smoke streamed out. The bottle fell on the floor and a cloud of white flour rose.

'Genuine Viagra,' cried Chef Albert, in his haste kicking the bottle beneath a counter. He got down on his hands and knees.

Gabriel got out of there, while the pastry chef crawled this way and that calling softly to his pills and the assistant leaped around with a fire extinguisher, coating the place in foam.

Sweating up a torrent in his office, Gabe couldn't settle to anything. His mind was too restless, and he needed to get a few things straight in his head. For example, was he heartbroken about Charlie or not? The answer seemed to be sometimes yes and sometimes no, which wasn't helpful in the least. Leave that one aside for now. What about Lena? Was he her knight in shining armour, or was he currently the last in a long list of men who had abused the poor girl? Being painfully honest with himself he had to say he did not know. Maybe the honest answer was both. Even his career, the path he'd followed, the straight line he thought he'd walked, was twisted and looped now he looked back on it, half hidden in the undergrowth.

He went out to the kitchen floor as dinner service was about to begin. Benny was dipping veal cutlets into flour and then egg wash and coating them in breadcrumbs. One tray was fully prepared and ready to go.

'Getting on OK?' said Gabriel.

'Yes, Chef,' said Benny.

'Do you . . . do you need any help?'

'No, Chef. Thank you.'

'I'll just do a few for you.'

'Yes, Chef.'

'Benny?'

Benny moved up the work surface to make room for Gabe. He

bowed his big head to his work. Gabriel stared at the silvery scar across his face.

'Benny, remember you told me about your friend, the little general?'

'Kono,' said Benny, the word resonating deep in the back of his throat.

'Yes, Kono. Where is he now?'

'I do not know.'

'When . . .' Gabe began. He didn't know quite what it was that he wanted to ask. 'When we went out for a drink that evening and you told me about him, about your friends, a bit about your life . . .'

'I remember. Alcohol makes me talk.' He accented the words so thickly you could stand a spoon up in them. 'Usually I don't touch it.'

'But the way you spoke was . . .' Benny's tales were so neat and ordered – compact, like Benny himself. 'I mean, you tell a good story,' he said.

'Thank you, Chef,' said Benny, drawing himself up as though Gabe had fixed a medal to his chest. 'But every refugee knows how to tell his story. For him, you understand, his story is a treasured possession. For true, it is the most important thing he owns.'

He left work early, taking a couple of the veal cutlets, which he fried for himself and Lena when he got home. After supper Lena sat at the kitchen table working on her 'brief' for the private eye, twisting alternately the pen top and her earrings. She wrote in Russian but still covered the paper with her arm whenever he approached. He kissed her on the forehead and went to get ready for bed. The earlier he went to bed, he had decided, the better he would sleep. It was overtiredness that ruined his nights.

He sat in bed with a book in his hands. He thought about Ted. He thought about Mum. He thought about catering college. Why did he quit school? He'd followed his interests, hadn't he, taken his interest in science in a practical direction. It all made sense.

What interest in science? A chemistry O-level. A notebook, written up at the Manchester Jarvis, while he was still a trainee, of his 'experiments' with grilled steak, listing times, temperatures, results, his keen observations regarding the Maillard reactions, the denaturing and coagulation of muscle protein. Gabriel started to feel his own coagulation, the blood thickening in his veins.

He opened the book again, *The Universe in a Nutshell*. He started to read. What did it matter, anyway, when he was just a speck – less than that, much less – on a planet orbiting a star in an outer arm of the Milky Way, one galaxy among billions and billions of galaxies, in a universe that is ever expanding, without boundaries in space or time.

His chest began to burn. He ignored it, turned the page and read about black holes.

He couldn't breathe. The only black hole he could comprehend was the one opening now before him. He shifted his legs carefully over the side of the bed and pushed his shoulders back, trying to expand his lungs. Oxygen, they needed more oxygen. Tingling in his hands and feet. Not enough oxygen. His blood was too thick. His heart couldn't push the blood. It was throwing itself against the inside of his ribs, getting all mashed up. He'd end up having a . . . heart attack. Christ, he was stupid. He tried to call out to Lena, but no sound came. His mobile was on the stand beside his bed, he grabbed for it and it fell to the floor. Gabriel fell too.

The pain in his chest and shoulder was searing. He managed to dial the number. He thought, this may be the last thing that I ever do.

'Emergency services.'

'Help,' said Gabriel. 'Help.'

CHAPTER NINETEEN

—ɱ—

THE MORNING SUN SCATTERED SUGAR HERE AND THERE ACROSS THE moors which stretched out ahead, white glowing spills among the russet tones of green and brown. Gabriel squinted into the distant cut and swathe. This gently sloping, ever-reaching land was filled with a vague kind of longing. The peaty ground was soft beneath his boots. The red winter bracken shouldered the wind.

It was Christmas Eve. They used to walk up to the tower on Christmas Eve and the whole of Blantwistle, it seemed, would be there, airing the children, the old folk, the dog.

'Where's everyone gone?' said Gabe.

Ted leaned two-handed on his walking stick. 'Shops. Shopping, I'll be bound.'

'We can stop here if you like.'

Gabriel had driven them up (raised Ted's old Rover from under her shroud) and parked in a lay-by. They'd walked scarcely a third of a mile.

'Give over wi' that fussing,' said Ted. But he stayed where he was.

Gabriel drifted off the path. He crossed some rocky ground. 'Back in a minute,' he called to Ted, and hoped the words weren't blown away.

It was all bracken. Where was the heather? When he was a boy there was bell heather here, and cross-leaved heath and of course there was ling – common heather – everywhere. In summer there'd be great thick purple carpets of the stuff. After they'd moved to Plodder Lane, they'd march out of the garden, him and Jen, across the cow fields, across Marsh End, over by Sleepwater Farm, and run on the moors. They'd not be missed until Dad got home. He'd take a stick to the nodding cotton-wool heads of the cotton grass. Jenny collected bilberries and tart little cloudberries and sometimes she found crow-berries, hard and black, and didn't eat them but drew with them on a rock. And there was lime-green sphagnum that sprang up when you pushed it down and the scattered yellow stars of the bog asphodel, and the sundew that ate insects, and if you were lucky you could lie on your belly in the soft and soggy ground and watch a butterfly slowly dissolving in the plant's red and yellow hairy mouth.

There was nothing now but coarse grass and ferns. Nothing to keep a boy here. When they were kids they'd spend a summer's day. If he came back in the summer maybe he'd find berries and flowers.

They'd always keep Twistle Tower in view because they knew the way home from there, and it was easy to get lost on the moors. There was a proper name for the tower but he couldn't remember it. He remembered pretending it was a space rocket, eighty-five feet of stone topped with a glass-domed cockpit. You could see Morecambe Bay from up there. You could see Blackpool Tower. You could see the Isle of Man. When the mist wasn't in, which it usually was. He'd smoked his first cigarette in the dank stairwell, French-kissed Catherine Dyer against the two-feet-thick stone wall, counted the eight sides, sixteen windows, ninety-two steps, one hundred and fifteen rivets in the viewing deck platform so many times he would take the numbers to his grave.

Sometimes Mum forgot they were playing in the back garden and went out and locked all the doors. There was always Twistle Tower and they'd go in out of the rain, though you could sit there a month and not get dry. If he planned ahead he'd take his binoculars and look for birds. In summer you'd see all sorts – curlews, skylarks, lapwings. They didn't interest him so much. Of course he liked the merlins, the buzzards and peregrines, the thrill of spotting a hen harrier or sparrow hawk. He'd seen a golden eagle once.

Today he'd not seen so much as a pipit, not heard the red grouse call go-back-go-back. In London he hardly saw a sparrow, a blackbird. From pigeons there was no escape.

Gabriel thought he should turn, find Ted, but the moor pulled him on a little further and a little further yet. He saw that there was heather here among the bracken and large stands up ahead. Now that he had stopped looking he saw the place was not so barren after all. Creeping dogwood in its purple winter foliage ran under his feet, and there was a clump of bog rosemary, here a juniper bush. He reached a track and looked down the spine of a shallow valley, the moors rising like soft gold wings, and the sun beat white-pale in the sky, sending flurries of light down on the hillsides and over the far clouds that started to roll in now, dark and low.

Gabe breathed deeply and gave himself to a single thought. *Yes, I am alive.*

Since he had called for the ambulance, over a week ago now, he kept thinking this same thing. By the time the paramedics arrived he had recovered, was only winded by the ordeal, the embarrassment, but they insisted on taking him in. The doctor ran an ECG. 'We see it pretty often,' he said. 'You'd be surprised. People always think they're the first person who's ever confused a blocked artery and a panic attack.'

It wasn't a heart attack but it still made him think. *I'm alive.* He could have a heart attack. People dropped down dead. If it could happen to anyone, it could happen to him. Why not? That he could, most certainly, die made him feel all the more definitely alive.

He closed his eyes for a moment to savour the wind on his face.

Lena hadn't come to the hospital but when he returned, though he told her everything was fine, she rested a hand on his chest and watched him. In the days that followed she kept watching him instead of the television and she even laughed a little whenever he made a joke.

Gabe found Ted by the dry-stone wall. A stray sheep pulled at a tuft of grass. Ted swung his walking stick in the red-brown brush.

'Here somewhere,' he said.

'What've you lost?'

Ted got down on his knees, the difficulty of the manoeuvre betrayed only by a tightening of the lips. 'This is it,' he said, pushing the vegetation back. 'Memorial stone.'

Gabe bent down to read the inscription. *Herbert Haydock, William Railton, Roger Wolstenholme.*

'What's this? Not buried here, are they?'

'Buried down by Kitty Fields. In t'cemetery. You not heard this story before?'

'Don't think so.'

Ted got up using his cane and Gabe for leverage. They leaned against the wall.

'I'd always a mind to tell,' said Ted. 'Mebbe I thought you were too young to hear when we came out them Sunday walks. And by the time you weren't too young . . . well.'

'Ghost story, is it?' said Gabe.

Ted shook his head. 'You read the papers, these days, look at the television, them reality programmes, all as they show is the worst of people.' He drew his lips into his mouth.

'Dad, are you telling the story or what? Not too young now, am I?'

'These three lads,' said Ted, 'they set off one Saturday afternoon from Sleepwater where one of them lived. It's thought they was headed for Duckworth Fold, though others says Higher Croft and that makes sense n'all because William's uncle lived at Higher Croft Farm. Anyway, it was winter and a snowstorm sets in, worst anyone could remember, and there's folks not long since passed what'd tell you the snow came up high as a bedroom window, and that were down in t'town. Up here, you can imagine it were whiteout. Whiteout.'

'When was this?' said Gabe.

'Nineteen twenty-one,' said Ted. 'Three lads. Herbert Haydock and William Railton, both sixteen years of age, best friends, so it's said. Roger Wolstenholme were Herbert's cousin. Only just ten, a little boy.'

'This where they died?'

'Found William in near reach of Rough Hall. Gone for help and almost made it, though you'd not see yer hand in front yer face. Few days before they found t'others. When there were a bit of a thaw. Drifts ten feet deep, mind. Easy enough to lose all direction when you can't see that tower. Herbert Haydock were over that direction, if I recall . . .' Ted waved his stick. 'About three hundred or so feet from his cousin. Froze to death, right enough. He's decided to try for help. Course he didn't get far – when they found him he's only got a thin jacket and shirt.'

'Not very sensible in a snowstorm.'

'Came up quick by all accounts. Weren't a storm when they set out. And he had a thick overcoat, Herbert, when they left. He's give it to the little un, wrapped it round, made his cousin comfortable as he could, up against this wall. Did right by him, you might say.'

'I would,' said Gabriel. He looked at Ted, watched the bob of his Adam's apple as he swallowed, the tightness in his cheeks. 'I would say.'

'We've to look sharp,' said Ted, moving, 'we want to miss the rain.'

'Bet it was quite a funeral,' said Gabe.

'So it's told,' said Ted. He looked at Gabe and then looked away as he spoke. 'You're a good lad, Gabriel. We've to say these things while there's time.' He nodded and walked away.

Gabriel trailed a short distance behind turning over the things he should say in return. *You're a good dad*, he decided, plain and simple. But he should have said it straight away. To say it now, it would sound false, as if he'd taken all this time to come up with it, as though it was something he had to force himself to say. The rain began to spot.

'Dad,' he called, 'what about Christmas pudding? Is Jenny bringing one tomorrow or should we stop at the shops?'

Ted and Nana dozed in their chairs in the afternoon while Gabriel, inert on the sofa, drugged by the television, the gas fire, the impossibility of truly living in a room stuffed with tinsel, old people and rubber plants, tried to make a plan to go into town for some last-minute presents. He was still alive, wasn't he? He could drag his sorry hide off the velour upholstery. He still had a pulse. Maybe. But he felt like someone, something, had sucked the marrow out of his bones.

Ted snored loudly, jerked half awake, and settled down again. When his father had answered the door yesterday evening Gabriel had almost cried out, confronted with a skull on a stick. After an hour or so his eyes had adjusted, the horror had gone, and a newly drawn father had emerged. He was like the old Ted, after all, only sharper and tighter and the soft sachets beneath his eyes were looser and rippled as he walked. But he ate his dinner and his breakfast, and with his appetite returned he would, Gabe thought, put on weight again. This morning he'd managed a walk. Perhaps Ted was in remission. Gabe hadn't found a way to ask but when Jenny came tomorrow she would fill him in.

Nana, her feet on the tapestry stool, was in bedsocks and a flowered garment that was possibly a dress, could be a nightie, and had much potential as an armchair cover. In her sleep she oozed from every visible orifice. Gabriel jacked himself up to the edge of the sofa, reached the tissue box on the occasional table, and was choosing between eyes, nose and mouth when Nana woke up and pulled a handkerchief from between the buttons on her chest. She wiped her nose.

'Is it washday?' said Nana. She moved her lips a while longer but didn't say anything else.

'I think so,' said Gabe.

'It's our Nancy's turn to lead the range. Don't forget I did it last week.'

'That's right. You did.'

'Aye, well,' sighed Nana. 'I don't mind a bit.' She drifted off in some opiate dream.

Gabriel changed channels. He found a news review of the year. They had some business types talking. 'Speaking personally,' said one, 'it's been a lean sort of year.'

Gabriel's stomach contracted. What if it was Dad who was right about the economy? Living in a dream world, he'd said. *How long can it go on?* If there was going to be a recession, the restaurant trade would be in the shit. All his savings – well, it was too late now.

'Hark at him,' said Nana, waking. She screwed up her face, achieving the seemingly impossible feat of multiplying her wrinkles. 'Wouldn't know the meaning of the word. Lean! He's no idea!'

She struggled to sit up, listing to one side and clinging to the chair arms as if being tossed on ocean waves. 'In't it shocking,' she cried. 'The waste! Is that our Gabriel? Is it? Well, they're not brought up right these days.' She pushed her lips around her face. 'Two bob a week, feeds a family of four does that. She were a champion cook, our mother. D'you remember, Gabe? Champion baker. We'd lick the bowls, you and me and Nancy. A sheep's head every week, and it's an economical cut and no mistake. Brains for Dad with a nice bit of bread and butter. Press the tongue for butties. Veg and barley in with the head and, ooh, it makes a lovely broth. Lovely, lovely . . . have I to be somewhere soon?'

'No, Nana, you're all right. You've got ages yet.'

But what did Dad know about economics? Fairweather knew, and he'd said the City was booming. Hadn't he? And the City led the way.

'It's my grandson,' said Nana, twinkling. 'He's getting married to a lovely girl.'

'I know,' said Gabe, putting his hand over hers. 'But not for a while.'

Nana touched the fragile blue-grey curls at her temples. She sank back in her chair.

They stared at the television. An anti-war demonstration in London. BRING THE TROOPS HOME NOW read one banner. UK OUT OF IRAQ said another.

'OUR BLOOD ON YOUR HANDS,' read Nana. 'These whatsits, Muslims, there's no understanding them, is there? I mean,' she said, her voice rising, 'we've took 'em in. We've give them a home.'

Gabriel looked at Ted. Still asleep.

Mug shots, terror plots, training camps, grainy videos.

Nana mopped her eye. 'What have *we* done to them? And we've to check under our beds every night. Not safe, none of us. Are we? Not safe in our own beds.'

The only thing Nana would find under her bed was a chamber pot. Maybe a Trebor mint. Our own worst enemies, Charlie had said. Worrying over nothing. That was what she meant. Something like that anyway.

The news review moved on to a celebrity package. WHAT'S HOT, WHAT'S NOT. WHO'S WED, WHO'S FLED. WHO'S MINTED, WHO'S SKINTED. Every five seconds a spinning tabloid headline.

'I've got to nip out,' said Gabe. He needed a cigarette, needed to get his shopping done. 'Will you be OK?'

'Course I'll be OK,' said Nana. 'I'm not ga-ga you know. Now what's all this? What they showing now? Why don't they just give over, these Muslims? Protesting this and protesting that.'

'No, it's a parade, Nana. An Eid festival, earlier this year, right here in Blantwistle. I think they've gone over to the local stations.'

'Look how they've blocked the road,' said Nana. 'There'll be no traffic down there today. It's dreadful, in't it? It is.' Nana clacked disapprovingly on her sweet. 'I was saying to Gladys only today, I said, Gladys, how is it these Pakistans take over all them houses, buy up the whole bloomin' street, and you know, they've not a mortgage between them, they club together, that's what, though how they get the money I do not know. And Gladys, well, I've known her all me life, and she says to me, Phyllis . . .' Nana's face trembled, her lips parted and closed. 'Phyllis . . .' Perhaps she had remembered that Gladys was dead, that there was, in fact, nothing they could have said to each other today. 'Ooh,' she said, taking refuge in the television. 'Ooh, look at all them children. They've *ever* so many, haven't they?' Nana looked at Gabe, anxious to know that this time she was speaking sense.

Gabe hesitated. She peered up at him as if from beneath the edge of a cliff. Would he stamp on her fingers or lend her a hand? 'Yes, Nana,' he said, 'that's right.'

Nana sighed. She was back on solid ground. 'No one can call me a racialist. I don't hold with any of that. But I tell you one thing I've noticed about the women. When they go shopping, know what they do, they squeeze all the fruit and all the vegetables. And then we've to buy what they've touched and left behind.'

The high street was strung with lights and garlanded with decorations. The wet pavements spooled colours into the drains. Pedestrians slapped this way and that under the influence of heavy bags or alcohol. A couple of squad cars stood by.

Our religious festival, thought Gabe.

'Merry Christmas, mate.' A man in a tracksuit and gold chain greeted Gabe. No reason, just friendly. You stopped expecting it when you'd been in London so long.

'Merry Christmas,' said Gabe. He smiled.

'Merry Christmas,' said the man to a woman almost entirely blotted out by a large black sheet, a black veil over her head.

The woman turned her face to the ground and quickened her step.

'And a happy New Year to you,' said the man, still amiable.

The woman didn't acknowledge him. She turned down a side street. Gabe paused to watch her beetle away, a black shell, a solid casing, broken only by the flick-flack of her heels.

Fuck you, he thought.

He didn't think that. No. He hadn't thought it, as such. He was thinking about the kind of reaction people might have. Like your foot flying up if the doctor hits a certain spot on your knee. A thought flying into your mind. Not his mind, but other people's. Well, it wasn't right, but you could understand sometimes.

The thing was, that woman – those women – they'd decided there was only one way to look at things. Black and white. *This is who I am. This is what I am.* Easy. All your answers, ready made. Not like the rest of us. We have to make it up as we go along. Maybe Fairweather had that right.

Fuck you for having what I don't.

No Whitsun Walks any longer, no Mothers' Union parade. Kids in shined shoes and new clothes, it still happened, but only for Eid. Large families, clubbing together, kinship and community . . . all the things that Nana missed most.

When Gabriel got back to Plodder Lane, Dad was in the kitchen making a shepherd's pie. The potatoes were on to boil. Dad was emptying a packet of mince into a frying pan with some chopped onions. Gabe would have recommended softening the onions and browning the meat separately.

'What can I do?' he said.

'Wouldn't say no to a brew.'

Gabriel filled the kettle. On the windowsill was a reindeer he'd made at primary school out of a toilet roll, pipe cleaners, lolly sticks and cotton wool. He gave it to Dad as a Christmas present and Dad brought it out every year.

Ted scattered some gravy granules into the pan and stirred the mixture vigorously. 'Stick a bit of hot water in here.'

Gabe poured some from the kettle.

'Nana likes it with a touch of ketchup cooked in.' Ted squeezed out a dollop, closed the lid, flicked it up again and added a dollop more. 'Look about right?' he said.

'Ah,' said Gabriel. 'About right, yes.'

'I've to break down these lumps,' said Ted. 'They clog her teeth.' He worked carefully, bending close to the stove.

This was what it was all about, thought Gabriel. All those cookery programmes and glossy magazines, the food porn. True, they'd never feature someone like Ted Lightfoot, cooking for someone like Nana, with ketchup and gravy granules. But this was what it was about, not filling a hole in a stomach but filling a hole in a life.

'Dad, I'm sorry I haven't been around more.'

'We manage. We don't do so bad.'

'I don't mean just now. I mean . . .'

'When yer mum were alive.'

Gabe scratched his head. 'Yes. No. All of it. Dad?'

Ted smiled. He wiped his hands on his butcher's apron. 'You got things to ask, son, I wouldn't put it off too long.'

'Do you . . . I've got this memory . . . Mum with the rag-and-bone man. He brought her home. I don't know. Do you remember? Do you know the time I mean?'

Ted reached in the cupboard. He was so thin he was painful to look at, sketched in a few brisk strokes. 'There it is,' he said. 'Flour. Spoonful for the thickening – Nana taught me how.'

Answer enough, thought Gabe. He said, 'When Mum was on the medication . . .' Should he say it? Where was the point in raking over old ground? 'She changed so much, it was like she lost her personality. Like she wasn't her any more.'

Ted took a fork and tested the potatoes. He drained them and the steam that rose from the colander for a moment obscured his face.

Gabe thought, no, he won't reply.

'I agree with you,' said Ted. 'In a way. Point is, she wanted it. She were tired. It were exhausting being her all the time.'

Ted clattered the pan into the sink. Gabe took over and did the mash. The rain tapped on the window. The lino squeaked under their feet.

It used to be Mum with Nana in the kitchen, the two of them cooking the tea. They clacked away like a pair of knitting needles, never lost for something to say. There must be a trick to it, a knack, which Gabe and Ted hadn't stumbled on yet.

'I'll fix those tiles behind the taps tomorrow,' said Gabriel.

'Christmas Day tomorrow,' said Ted.

'Oh yes.'

Ted moved slowly, gathering crockery for the table, a head of broccoli from the fridge. His brown slacks looked so empty it was difficult to imagine a pair of legs inside. He was shorter than he used to be.

'I heard about Hortons,' said Gabriel. 'Closing down.'

'Aye,' said Ted. 'That's right.'

'That's a shame,' said Gabe. 'Last of the mills.'

'Aye. Last one.'

Gabe opened an overhead cupboard to find the cooking salt. The handle pulled loose in his hand.

'Dad?' he said. 'That's bad, isn't it? Hortons going down.'

'Can be done cheaper elsewhere, Gabriel, that's all there is to it. Economics, in't it, when all's said and done.'

'They were good jobs, though,' said Gabe. 'The area needs good jobs like that.'

'Noisy, dirty places, is mills,' said Ted, with his hands in the washing-up bowl.

Why didn't he get his hands out of the soapsuds? Ted always ran his hands firmly over the nearest hard surface when he wanted to make a point.

'Steady employment though, wasn't it?' said Gabe. 'Not like this casual work Harley picks up.'

'It were on a cycle,' said Ted. 'Cotton industry . . . seen that many booms and busts . . . There was times . . .' His voice trailed away.

The back of Gabe's throat was scratchy. He coughed but it didn't clear. 'I remember the works outings,' he said, 'when we went to the panto, all of that. People doing stuff together, you know, something to be said for it.'

Ted dried his hands on his apron. The band of white hair around his bald head was longer and fluffier than Gabe had ever seen it, making it seem like even his skull had shrunk.

'Community,' said Ted, 'I suppose we had that. There were . . .'

'Go on, Dad. Go on.'

'Always another side to everything, that's the truth.' Ted spoke quietly. 'Community's good for those what's on the inside, but if there's some inside there's others what's out. I'm thinking of yer mother. Thinking of my Sally Anne.'

Gabriel went to bed early. The curtain seemed to stir, but it was only the play of the moonlight behind the thin fabric. He lay on his back, hands under his head, feeling pleasantly drowsy. He wasn't doing too bad. He'd recommend a heart attack (perhaps not a real one) to anyone. It was galvanizing. He'd got a lot done in the last week. Here, with Dad and Nana, of course he was a little more lethargic. But what could he expect? As soon as he walked into the sitting room he was half asleep from the ticking of the carriage clock, a little faint at the smell of polish and sherry and mints. But he'd talked to Dad, that was the important thing. Had a couple of long talks. Dad wasn't his old self. He kept hesitating. Gabe wished he'd go back to being sure of everything, though he'd never liked him that way.

He switched the lamp off. He turned on his side and flipped the pillow over to lay his cheek against the cool. Michael Harrison. Now what did happen to him? There was a kid you could point at, label, say he won't come to any good. But it was up to Michael in the end, wasn't it? Jenny said she'd ask around, someone would know. Tomorrow, he must remember: find out about Michael, and get the turkey in the oven by quarter past ten.

CHAPTER TWENTY

—◊—

THEY'D ENDED UP STUFFED AS USUAL. NONE OF THEM COULD MOVE quite yet. Gabe sat with the others at the dining-room table feeling bloated and flushed. He was warm and weary and irritated and congenial and bemused, bobbing gently in the soup of family. There was plastic holly and plastic mistletoe on the sideboard, a blanket and tablecloth over the table to preserve the mahogany, a double string of Christmas cards along the back wall. 'Twas ever thus.

Nana had swapped her Harvey's amontillado for her regular Yuletide bottle of Advocaat, which she cradled in her lap as she slept. On the shelf of her mighty bosom there had gathered bits of roast potato, carrots, peas, parsnip and pudding, altogether nearly enough for another lunch. Opposite her, Ted wore a paper crown and nursed a can of Boddington's, which he said was all that he could face today. They'd filled his plate anyway and it still sat there showing off his skeletal frame. Next to Ted was Jenny, with her fat arms and violent hair. They looked like an illustration in a children's book, the pair of them, some fable or morality tale. Round from Jenny was Harley, no, Bailey. It was difficult to tell the two apart. They'd dyed their hair crow-black, wore long choppy fringes, pencil-tight jeans, studded belts, lip rings and eyeliner. They seemed to have checked tea towels tied round their necks. Both stroked alcopop bottles with one hand and texted under the table with the other. Perhaps they were texting each other; perhaps texting was their vestigial communication skill.

During lunch Gabriel had tried unsuccessfully to engage them in conversation, though his interest, he had to admit, was more anthropological than avuncular. Bailey looked up now and – for a millisecond – made eye contact. She tugged her fringe over her face.

'I had a goth phase,' said Gabriel. 'When I was your age probably.'

Bailey twisted her narrow shoulders. 'I'd rather die,' she said, 'than be a goth. Seriously, I'd kill myself first.'

'Baaay-ley,' said Jenny.

Gabe smiled at Jenny to show she wasn't to bother. It hadn't been a bad lunch, he decided. The ingredients weren't of the best quality, the turkey unavoidably dry (it had been frozen), the vegetables over-cooked (for Nana's teeth), the gravy oversalted (by Jenny), the roast potatoes a little greasy (Dad's contribution), but Gabe's chestnut stuffing had turned out a treat, and the bread sauce was perfect and all in all he'd enjoyed it, cooking for the Lightfoot clan.

Harley put his phone on the table. He said, 'She's only emo 'cos she's gone and copied us.'

'You?' said Bailey. 'You? You're not even emo, you're a poser.' She risked a direct glance at Gabe. 'He only does it for the clothes and that.'

'*Baaay*-ley,' said Jenny.

Ted stood up and shuffled out of the room.

'What?' said Bailey. 'It's true. I've wrote poetry and that since I was, like, twelve. I've always been true emo.' She hugged her matchstick arms across her chest. 'Emo's what's in your heart, not what's on your back.'

'Poems?' said Gabe. 'What sort of poetry, Bailey?'

'Like about sad stuff, like pain, and how no one understands us and that.' She rocked a little in her chair, feeling the pain, presumably, of speaking to these old folk.

'Oh,' said Gabe. Then, 'Wow.'

Harley sniggered under his hair.

'Shut up,' said Bailey. 'Shutupshutupshutupshurrup.'

'*Bailey!*' said Jenny.

Bailey's lip ring quivered. Her marsupial eyes flashed. 'Harley's only emo because he likes getting off with other lads.'

Her brother picked the knife off his plate and pointed it at her. 'Since when was it, like, *emo* to be homophobic?'

'I'm not homophobic. I'm just saying. You're gay. End of.' But she went on, with a martyred whine, 'Stop accusing me of stuff what I've never ever said.'

'Hang on,' said Gabe. 'This emo thing – what's it got to do with getting off with other boys?'

His niece and nephew shrugged. Might as well ask why the earth was round.

'Sorry,' said Gabe, 'but it's not entirely obvious to me. Isn't it about music and clothes and . . .'

'Attitude,' said Harley. 'It's about—'

Bailey cut him off. 'Emo girls think it's hot when an emo boy kisses another emo boy. They do it for attention.'

'And to explore their sexuality?' said Gabe.

Bailey sighed. 'No. They do it to get girls.'

Gabriel looked at Jenny. Jenny burst out laughing. Shrieking, she flung her arms in the air triggering undulations down her stomach and up her chin. 'Kissing boys,' she said when she had caught her breath, 'well, I suppose it beats hitting them. Though it's one extreme to the other with you, Harley. What will you think of next?'

Nana woke and said, 'I'll just get these dishes done.' Gabe nabbed the bottle of Advocaat off her lap before she tried to stand up. Jenny wheeled the drinks trolley round and helped latch her on, precipitating a landslide of leftovers down her dress.

'Where's Dad gone?' said Jenny. 'I hope he's not washing up.'

'Stop interfering, Mum,' said Harley.

'Yeah,' said Bailey, 'he can wash up if he wants.'

Jenny looked ready to pop. 'Get this table cleared,' she said. '*You* do the washing. *You* do the drying. And if I find your granddad helping you're dead meat, both of you.'

They writhed like a couple of black adders, but they did as they were told and began to stack the plates.

Gabriel steered Nana through to the sitting room and just inside the doorway she took one hand off the trolley bar and placed it on Gabriel's arm.

'Ooh,' she said, sounding excited, looking around at the lit-up tree, the decorations on the windowsill, the tinsel over the hearth. 'Ooh,' she said, 'it looks like Christmas, doesn't it? It looks like Christmas in here.'

'That's right, Nana,' said Gabe. 'Shall we get you sat in your chair?'

He'd only just got her settled, lifted her feet up on the stool, when Mr Howarth came in with a sprig of mistletoe and kissed her smack on the lips.

'Now then, Phyllis,' he said, 'you've done me a power of good there.'

'Get away,' said Nana, two pink roses blooming in the white deserts of her cheeks. 'Go on, before my Albert catches you. Have your guts for garters, that he will.'

While the others watched television, Jenny and Gabriel sat in the dining room.

'Blimey,' said Jenny, rubbing her big round knees, 'I've ate that much.' She undid the broad white belt that had marked some notional boundary between her upper and lower halves. 'Mind you, I can afford to let myself go, now I've got a new fella.' She slapped her thigh.

'Good for you,' said Gabe. It was around Queen's Speech time. The light was fading, all the shapes in the room darkening now, except for Jenny's hair which seemed to be getting brighter. It was like watching the old black and white Grundig they had at Astley Street with the contrast turned right up.

'He's called Des,' said Jenny, 'he's pushing fifty, two grown-up kids, divorced. What else do you want to know?'

'Wasn't the last one called Des?'

'Den,' said Jenny. 'I was with him three years and I'd have thought you'd remember . . . never mind him, anyway. It's Des now. He's in sewage and I can't say that with a straight face. Nothing stinky, actually, manager's job over at the works, wears a suit and tie. Lord, I sound like Nana now. *My Des goes to work in a shirt and tie, which is more than I can say for some.* Well, he's nothing to set the world on fire, but he's . . .'

She pattered on like the rain. Gabe drank his coffee and waited it out.

'. . . and he's not a big drinker, and he's, you know, solid, and we're what you'd call compatible, and it's nice to have someone to settle down with in front of *Countdown*, who'll rub your feet and take turns at making a brew, and I know what I want when it comes to a man these days, because there's none of that nonsense, is there, when you get to our age . . .'

None of that nonsense, thought Gabe. She made it sound so easy. Why didn't he know what he wanted? Why didn't he want a cup of tea and *Countdown*? Why did he want Lena instead of compatibility?

'Anyhow,' said Jenny. 'Dad told me the wedding's off. Spill.'

'What did he say?'

'No gory details. I heard there's this other girl.'

'That's it really. I fucked up. Charlie's called it off.'

'Oh no you don't, mister. You don't get away that easy. Who is she, this girl? Not still seeing her, are you? And I can tell from the look on your face so don't bother answering that, but tell me everything else and you're not giving up on Charlie, tell me you're not, you're supposed to be marrying the woman, for God's sake.'

Gabe scratched the back of his head. He lowered his arm and tucked his hand inside his other armpit.

'You've to get rid of this other one first,' said Jenny, 'or you don't stand a chance. Know that, don't you? Know that?'

'It's complicated,' said Gabe.

'Course it is,' said Jen. 'Someone you work with, is it? That why you can't ditch her?'

'Someone from work. Yes. It is.'

'You silly sod. What, some pretty bit of stuff? Juicy young waitress? Don't be denying anything, Gabriel Lightfoot, I can read you like a book.'

'Not a waitress,' said Gabe. 'Younger, yes.'

'How old? Or should I say, how young?'

He saw Lena, standing sullen by the window, twisting her earrings, her fingers, her skinny shoulders. He saw her sitting, all angles and awkwardness, on the sofa with her feet pulled up and a sweater stretched over her knees. Christ, how old was she? Not much older than Harley and Bailey. Was she still a teenager? Was she?

He mumbled something.

'You what?' said Jenny. 'Oh, bugger, I've broke a nail.'

'She's . . . I don't know,' said Gabe.

'Come off it,' said Jenny. 'You dirty old man.'

'Early twenties,' said Gabriel. 'She's twenty-four.'

Jenny laughed. 'For a moment there, Gabe, I thought you were going to say eighteen.'

Gabe shook his head. 'Yeah, right.' He fiddled with his coffee cup, stuck a teaspoon in the sugar bowl, stirred, spilled some, brushed the sugar aside with his hand. He looked at Jenny, at her pretty eyes, the lovely oval of her face that floated so lightly above her bulging neck and chin. She seemed to be staring out of her body as if from a padded cell, saying, somebody cut me loose.

She narrowed her eyes. 'And you can stop that right now.'

'What?' said Gabe.

'You're giving me a look,' said Jenny, 'and I know what you're going to say.'

'What?'

'Don't give me that. "Where did the old Jenny go?" "Remember how it used to be?" Well, I'm sorry, but *I'm* not a teenager any more. I am what I am, Gabriel. I'm me.'

'What did I say? I didn't say anything.'

Jenny sucked on her inhaler. 'Allergies. Hear me? Hear me wheeze?'

'You should give up smoking,' said Gabe.

'I know. Wish I could. Bloomin' addict, I am.' She gasped at the inhaler. 'You given up again?'

'Smoke when I feel like it. Now and again.'

'Take it or leave it, can you, Gabe? My chest shouldn't sound like that, should it? I'm giving up, definitely. Doctor said I've to quit.'

'Don't want you getting ill.'

'I should put a light on. There, that's better. What are we like, sat in the dark? Who'd look after Dad and Nana? That what you mean?'

'He ate a lot yesterday,' said Gabe. 'I thought maybe he was in remission. But then, today . . .'

'I know,' said Jenny. 'I know.'

'Guess what Nana said when I took her through to the sitting room. She said, it looks like Christmas in here.'

Jenny laughed. 'Poor Nana,' she said. 'Found her a nice home, Gabriel. She can go in any time after mid-January.'

'Does she have to?'

'No,' said Jenny, tapping her box of Silk Cut, 'not if she can come and live with you.'

They smoked hanging out of the dining-room window. 'Look at the state of us,' said Jen. 'Me giving up and you not addicted at all.'

They giggled. Jenny took a long drag and looked beatific. She turned her face to him. 'So. How've you been? You know, Charlie, everything.'

'Oh, I'm OK. I guess. Not too bad. A bit up . . .'

'. . . and down.'

'Sometimes.'

'I bet you are. Then there's Dad, of course.'

'I don't know, Jen. There have been occasions when I've thought I'm not sort of coping. All the stress. Sometimes I'm kind of racing, pulling all-nighters, then I'm more or less . . .'

'. . . depressed . . .' she said, speaking over him.

'. . . depressed and it's hard to get anything done when you're feeling . . .'

'. . . feeling like that . . .'

'. . . but I'm OK, I'm basically . . .'

'. . . you're basically OK . . .'

'I had this thing, Jenny, I had a . . .'

'Did you, love?'

'Yes. A panic attack.'

'Oh yes, a panic attack.'

'And sometimes, you know, I'm just really, really down.'

Gabe flicked his fag butt on to the gravel.

'But you're OK.'

'I'm OK.' At least he'd felt OK until he started telling Jenny this stuff. He'd been OK yesterday, hadn't he?

'It's all understood much better these days.'

'What is?'

Jenny closed the window. 'And there's not the stigma any more. Lots of creative people have it. Always on telly, in't it, almost like they're showing off about it all.'

'I'm not saying . . . I'm not . . .'

'They do say it runs in families.'

'Jenny, I'm not bipolar. I've just been a bit . . .'

'. . . a bit depressed.'

'Will you stop doing that, for God's sake!'

'What?'

'Finishing my . . .'

'. . . sentences. Oh, there I go again, can't even help myself sometimes.'

'It's not the same. Not the same as Mum.'

'OK, Gabe. All right.'

They sat there on the windowsill. Leaning against the glass was colder than leaning out.

Jenny smoothed her hair. She said, 'Have you seen a doctor?'

'No.'

She said, 'I've never been one for pills.'

'I don't *need* any pills.'

'You know what?' she said. 'You're like those kids at school. *Your mum's in the loony bin.* Like I'm accusing you of something bad.'

'Who at school ever said that? I never heard that once.'

'Maybe not,' said Jenny, 'but I did. You were pretty handy with your fists.'

'I wouldn't mind another cigarette.'

'A little of what you fancy . . .'

'. . . does you good.'

'See, you're at it now.'

They opened the window again.

Gabriel watched the way Jenny held her cigarette. He could see Mum in her sometimes.

'Jenny,' he said, 'what about you? You happy? I mean, your life's OK?'

'Can't complain,' said Jenny. 'Well, I can. Who can't?' She laughed.

'Because I know you had plans, things you wanted to do with your life and then . . . other things got in the way.'

'Things?' said Jenny. 'You mean our Harley. He's not a thing, thank you very much, he's my son and your nephew, and he's never been *in the way*.'

'You know what I mean.'

'Not told you about my promotion, have I? Supervisor, me.'

'Great. Congratulations. That's really good.'

She pulled a face. 'Nah. It's not really good. It's still a chicken shed. But it's all right. You see, Gabe, you said I had things I wanted to do with my life, well, I never did. I wanted a house, I wanted a car, my own money, kids . . . not quite so soon, maybe. *You* were the one had something you wanted to do. Most of us, we just go along with things, take whatever comes.'

'Did I really want Michelin stars?'

'Like nobody's business. You were always so clear about everything.'

'I don't know, Jen, I don't know.'

'I'm telling you.'

'I've been thinking a lot and I look back and I see the way I've twisted things up in my mind. It's like the stars – I'd convinced myself I never wanted them. And then why did I want to cook in the first place? Sometimes I think I only did it to annoy the hell out of Dad.'

'Don't be so soft,' said Jenny. 'Oh, I've brought a lovely ham for our tea, but I've gone and left it in the car. I'll nip out in a sec.'

'And why did I want to annoy Dad? Because I didn't understand what was going on with Mum, and I thought he was, you know, mean to her. And I didn't understand anything, and everything I've done has been based on a total lack of understanding, because how can you really want something if you want it for all the wrong reasons? And I don't even want to think about it. It's like I've pulled a loose thread and the whole bloody jumper's unravelling now.'

Jenny stared at him. 'Gabriel,' she said slowly, 'will you just get over yourself.'

'OK,' said Gabe, 'OK.'

'I mean, we've enough on our plates with Dad and Nana. Does it matter, exactly why you wanted to be a chef?'

'No,' said Gabe. 'You're right.'

'Good,' said Jenny. 'Now I'll go and fetch that ham.'

At the doorway she stopped and rolled round on her heels. 'Found out about Michael Harrison for you. Trail goes cold about ten years ago, but last anyone's heard he's opened his own business over Ormskirk way and he's married with two kids.'

Gabe smiled. 'Thanks, Jenny. Thanks for finding out. Know what kind of business it is?'

'Tattoo parlour,' said Jenny. 'Bet he'd give you a big discount.'

As soon as he got into bed Gabe started making 'to do' lists in his head.

He fermented a couple of hours beneath the sheets and then he rose.

Ted, bent-backed at the kitchen table, did not hear him come in. The room was swaddled in darkness save for the bright casket of the desk lamp over Ted and his matchstick ships. Ted, absorbed, subsumed, made his devotions. Gabe stilled his breath, humbled for some reason that was quite beyond his reach.

His father, with his friar's hair, his mendicant face, his brown robe tied with a cord, gave himself to the task. Gabriel, in the shadows, longed for there to be light. What comfort could he take? Never, not one time, in forty-two years had he felt anything to be holy, never a glimmer, never a stir. Oh, dear God, he would be spiritual if he could. God save us. It was a talent he had always lacked.

Without looking up, Ted said, 'Can't sleep, son?'

Gabe shook his head. He went to the table and sat down.

'Look like you've seen a ghost.'

'I'm fine,' said Gabe. 'Well, I've got this problem. Something I'm trying to think through.'

'I'm listening.'

Gabriel told him about Gleeson and Ivan and their plotting. He got sidetracked on to Ivan and Victor's fights. He talked about Yuri and then about Nikolai. He even started telling stories about Oona and Ernie which made Ted chuckle so he told him a story about Chef Albert too. And then he went back to Gleeson and told about the photographs and what Branka, the housekeeping supervisor, had said.

Why was she bringing one of the maids to see Gleeson, who had nothing to do with them? And the more he thought about it, the more certain he was that there was some kind of link with the photos. Why were they there unless Gleeson had put them there? Who was he showing them to?

'What do you think I should do, Dad?' Gabe fiddled with a matchstick. It snapped in two.

Ted smiled. 'Never thought I'd see the day.'

'It's probably nothing,' said Gabe.

'My own son asking me for advice.'

'I might not take it.'

'Aye,' said Ted. 'You might not.'

'But what was he doing with them? Placed on the middle of the desk like that, with the lamp on, like it was set up for some kind of meeting. What's it all about?'

Ted glued a balustrade in place with a pair of tweezers. 'Wish I'd got old and wise, Gabriel, 'stead of just old. One thing I can tell you, looking back, I never worried about the right things. Like with yer mum, I worried that much – that I'd lose her because she'd lose her mind, or lose her to another man. And she goes and drops down dead. Well, you never think. You never in a million years.'

'I should stop fretting, you mean.'

'Some of us is made to worry, Gabe.' Ted wiped the tweezers clean. 'If I had my time again . . . but no, some things never change. I was sat here – before you come in – sat here worrying about the stupidest thing. I was thinking who'll have these ships, who'll want them? Jenny says they're full of dust and, you know, with her allergies. Harley and Bailey, they're not interested. Why should they be?'

'I'll take care of them, Dad.'

'What I'm saying is we fret on and it makes no difference. The time I've wasted. Worrying about this and that. What's coming to us pays no mind. Goes right along and comes. Like as not we don't see it coming because we've been looking the wrong way all t'time.'

CHAPTER TWENTY-ONE

—✳—

IN FEBRUARY THE BOILER BROKE. THE WATER FROZE IN THE PIPES. Gabriel called a plumber and stayed at home with Lena. They set up camp beneath the duvet.

If they could find a little planet somewhere, this size, they'd be just fine.

Beyond the corners of the duvet, and despite the progress they'd made, she eluded him still. Sometimes she would not speak. She bit her nails and burned. He told her that he loved her and she twisted, as if it were the most horrible thing she had ever heard. Sometimes, though, she gave him hope. She smiled. She seemed to like him. She told him he was a good man.

He could not hold her, that was the problem. She slipped through his fingers. Even her physical presence seemed doubtful to him, more will-o'-the-wisp than waif. Watching her cross the room was like a waking dream. If she disappeared into the wall he would not be surprised.

He had tried to pin her down. He said, 'How long did you spend in the flat in Edmonton?' She said, 'Why, what it is to you?'

If she didn't go up in a puff of smoke she could vanish simply by walking through the door and never coming back. It killed him. He died a little death every time he thought of it.

And he pieced her together nightly, assembling all he knew of her with his fingertips, working feverishly up from her toes. Everything that he knew about her and all that he might still learn, examining her heels, her insteps, her calves, her stomach, her arms, as if her body might offer up clues.

'What did he do to you?' he said one long restless night, asking about the 'client' who had hurt her.

She never told. She said he smoked and Gabriel examined her body for cigarette burns. He found none. He imagined worse. He thought about the man towering over her, doing unspeakable things. A married man. Probably he had kids. A pillar of the community, no doubt. Gabriel thought about killing him, imagined crushing his ugly face. He worked himself into a rage. 'For fuck's sake, tell me what he did,' he said, squeezing her arm. Images flashed through his mind. What sickness. But she would not help him. She rolled away. 'Lena,' he said, 'I'm sorry. It's just that you might feel better. If you get it off your chest.'

Oh, how he hated himself. He would never touch her, swore to it silently, looking at her back. He would kill this man. He would not touch Lena, not ever, not ever, but for this one final time. One more time, kissing her toes, one more time to make it right, and he was down on his knees and feeling blindly along her leg, and then the creature was on him and he could only do as he must though he knew he was not the piece of her that was missing, that however deep he inserted himself, he would not make her complete.

They had their setbacks, of course, but on the whole he felt they were gaining some ground.

He had decided that he loved her and he wanted little enough in return. When he felt guilty about the relationship he reminded himself that he had taken her in and given her a home. She came to him. If he grew angry at her he was careful to remember that she had been rude to him first. When he regretted scaring her about the world out-side his door he kept in mind that it had, indeed, been a dangerous place for her. It was all a trade. He played his part; she played hers. It pricked his conscience to lie to her about the private eye. But she had lied to him.

'Why does your brother have a different last name?' he had said, when she went through her notes with him so that he could write them up in English.

She picked her lip.

'Lena, is he your brother?' he said.

'Is my brother,' said Lena, twisting up.

'Why doesn't he have the same name?'

She shrugged. Eventually, she said, 'He have different father. Pasha is half-brother, OK?'

Gabriel smiled. 'Why didn't you say that in the first place?' He finished writing up the notes and when he got to work the next morning he took them out of his bag and dropped them in the bin.

This Pasha, this so-called brother with a lover's name, would take her away from him and he must not be found.

He was late for the end-of-month meeting with the building contractor at Alderney Street. When he arrived Rolly and Fairweather were there already, deep in discussions. The room had been freshly replastered and a decorator was painting the far wall white. Nothing of the florist shop remained, the building stripped back to its bare essentials, renouncing its former self. Gabriel shivered. He told himself he was ready for this.

He went through to the kitchen. The Rosinox stove tops had been installed. He ran a hand along and imagined how it would be.

'Nice of you to show, Chef.'

'Got a bit held up.'

Rolly slipped his thumbs under his braces. He eased them off his shoulders. 'Too bloody tight,' he said. 'Must have shrunk in the wash. Hope you're not turning into a prima donna, Chef, I've worked with too many of those.'

'Look,' said Gabriel, 'I'm sorry I was late.'

'No one's indispensable, you know.'

'Do we need to make a meal of it?'

Rolly blinked hard and fast, tapping out a message. *Don't take me for a fool because I dress like this.*

'It won't happen again,' said Gabe.

'Least you missed Lucinda,' said Rolly. 'That woman scares the hell out of me.'

They'd ended up with Fairweather's wife as interior designer. Fairweather had a gift for steaming ahead with his own ideas while all the time seeming to give way.

'Me too,' said Fairweather, coming in, 'and luckily the builders as well. Think they'll finish on time.'

'Less than three months to opening,' said Rolly. He belched. 'Stress and indigestion, very much linked. Need to order the crockery, six weeks or more lead time, often as not.'

'I'm on it,' said Gabe.

'Start poaching staff within the next month.'

'Yes.'

'We need to decide on a name. Haven't talked about that for a while.'

'I was thinking,' said Gabriel, 'that we could keep it simple, call it – maybe – Lightfoot's.'

'Oh yes,' said Fairweather, almost bouncing with enthusiasm, 'has a ring to it. I like it. *Magnifique.* Always adds a little something when the place is identified with the chef. Makes the cooking, the food, seem important, if you know what I mean.'

'It is important, I hope,' said Gabe.

'Excellent,' said Fairweather. 'All about communication. I do agree. The way you'll stamp yourself on this fine establishment, bring your personality to bear.'

'Fine,' said Rolly. 'Lightfoot's will do. Now, we'll use my usual PR outfit, they're quite good, well, they're a right shower, in fact, but all the other PR dollies are just as bad.'

'Exciting stuff,' said Fairweather. 'What will they do? Bash out a press release, line up interviews? I can just imagine it – Chef looking like some simmering culinary Heathcliff in the Sunday supplements.'

Rolly snorted. 'Or in the trade gazettes. See what strings you can pull with your media pals,' he said to Fairweather. He turned to Gabriel. 'I'll set up a meeting with Fleur, that's the publicity bird, and she'll ask you all the questions the journalists will ask you. You know, about your passion for food, how you got started, some stories about why you wanted to be a chef. Make it up if you have to, but make it sound good, OK?'

Gabe scratched his bald patch. It seemed to have doubled in size. Was he starting to look like a monk? 'Oh,' he said, with a half-laugh, 'that should be straightforward enough.'

'Terrific,' said Fairweather, 'that's the stuff! Newspapers love personal stories, love to find new characters. Hit them with everything you've got.'

'It's about the food really,' said Gabriel. 'Not about me.'

'You'll be a star,' said Fairweather. His mobile rang. 'Excuse me a moment,' he said, and wandered off.

Rolly said, 'I've got to go. Meetings.' But he looked reluctant to move. He leaned against the counter and rammed his fists in his pockets, perhaps as a sign of resistance, or perhaps to keep his trousers up now that his braces were down. 'Don't know why I do it,' he said. 'I mean, there's never a moment to enjoy.'

'Think we're committed now,' said Gabe.

'No one's trying to back out. Too late, anyway. That's not what I was saying. I was thinking about my life.'

He sucked saliva ruminatively through his teeth.

Gabe looked at his fat cheeks, his little eyes, his bright paisley shirt. Rolly looked sad in the saddest possible way, like a clown.

'I've been in this business a long time,' said Rolly, 'and I've built it up from scratch. We didn't have anything really, me and Geraldine, when we started out. Funny thing is, I think I was happier then.'

'Maybe you need new challenges,' said Gabe, 'like this place, for instance.'

'I've got two houses,' said Rolly. 'You've got to have your country pile. I've got a Jag and a Mercedes. I've put two kids through private school. I've got a stockbroker and investments.' He looked at Gabe and shrugged, as if bewildered by what it all meant. 'The building work's never finished, because Geraldine must have this and then that. The pile in the country is a bugger to maintain. The Jag got broken into, some bugger's dragged a key down the side of the Merc. You can't stop worrying. The kids still put out their hands. I had a bad night only this week because twenty grand's been wiped off some shares. I'm still up by five since a year ago so I sold, had done with it. Then I couldn't sleep. What if I've sold too early, what if I'm missing out?'

'You're doing all right for yourself,' said Gabriel. Rolly's sleepless nights sounded more reasonable, more productive, than his own.

'We started off in this little cottage in Twickenham. Think we were better off then. Didn't know, didn't realize, how much we didn't have. There's no end to it. It's like being on a merry-go-round and you want to get off and the ride won't end. You could jump but you don't want to risk it and it's the same bloody tune going on and on in your head.'

'You've got to think how much you've achieved,' said Gabe.

Rolly massaged his jowls. 'I said to Geraldine this morning – are you happier now or twenty years ago?'

'What did she say?'

'She said her therapist warned her to stay away from my negativity. I said, maybe I ought to warn your therapist to stay away from my money, she might catch something from it.'

Gabriel laughed. He said, 'Yeah, well, life's a bitch.'

'It's genetic, of course,' said Rolly, getting ready to go. 'Some people have an unfair advantage when it comes to happiness. And I envy people like you, Chef, because I don't know why I do what I do, I just do it. You're one lucky bastard if you can say you do it for love.'

Fairweather, still on the phone, strode purposefully up and down by the plate-glass window. He raised a finger to Gabriel to indicate he wouldn't be long. A blonde passed by outside and Fairweather swept at his fringe. The blonde looked back over her shoulder.

Fairweather had a wandering eye. Women seemed to like him too. Gabe supposed he was not bad-looking, a little short, but not short of apple-cheeked charm.

'Excellent,' said Fairweather, pocketing the phone. 'How marvellous,' he added, in equal parts emphatic and vague. 'My God, you *do* look tired.'

Gabriel put a cigarette between his lips.

'Didn't kick them?' said Fairweather. 'Never seen the appeal myself, but then I guess you don't if you never start.'

'You don't mind if I?' said Gabe, searching for his lighter.

'No, no,' said Fairweather. 'We all have our vices, don't we?'

'What's yours?'

'Ah, well, you know,' said Fairweather. 'Now, did you want to see me about something?'

'Remember you were asking me about Yuri, the porter, I mean. Well, I've been having . . . I've been thinking . . .' It was the dream. But he wouldn't tell Fairweather that. The dream must be for a reason. He had to figure it out, and then it would go away. Last time the food had buried him. He'd nearly suffocated, come up gasping for air. 'Well, Yuri was definitely an illegal, though he had a National Insurance number, don't ask me how because I've no idea. So do you think that means he would have been – what did you call it? – bonded labour, in debt to someone?'

'Inquest go off all right?' said Fairweather, encouragingly.

'Yes,' said Gabe, 'no problem. Accidental death.'

'Poor chap.'

'Do you think he could have been—'

'Does very little good now to speculate,' Fairweather interrupted. 'Who does it help?'

'I don't know,' said Gabriel. 'Maybe the agency should be prosecuted. If that's what they'd done to him.'

Fairweather checked his watch. 'Look,' he said, 'why go down that road?'

'But you said, in cases like this—'

Fairweather began speaking quickly. He crisped up. 'You can't equate the two things. A worker might enter illegally and then find work without facing a situation like that. Many do. Conversely, the majority of people identified as, technically speaking, trafficked have come to the country entirely legally.'

'Go on,' said Gabe. 'Explain.'

'All right. If you really want to know. What happens is, the traffickers use regular migration routes and work visas, but then charge fees for arranging work which put the workers into debt before they've even arrived in the UK. Sometimes their documents are removed, they're kept in poor housing and charged a fortune, charged for transport to and from work, and so on and so forth. Threats, abuse, all sorts of things. Don't forget that these people very often speak little English and they're not aware of their rights. Your porter, he could be a *victim*, should we say. Or he might not be. The fact that he was an illegal immigrant is neither here nor there.'

'But if he was . . .'

'What you've got to understand,' Fairweather fired away rapidly, as if he had thirty seconds in which to deliver a brief, 'is that even if it did happen to your guy, you're not going to change the world by making a fuss. It's too widespread for that. It's endemic, it's a structural problem. You get the odd media story but that's only the tip of the iceberg.'

'So why aren't you doing something about it?'

'The government? Even a Labour government? We're trying but it's not that simple. There's a private member's bill coming up about equal rights for agency workers, but for very complex reasons we've been unable to back it.'

'What reasons?' said Gabriel.

'Look, we have to think about what business wants as well, and what consumers demand. Even if the bill does go through, it won't be a panacea.'

'But it would be better than nothing.'

Fairweather made a dismissive gesture. 'Here's the real issue. There's a constant pressure to decrease costs. The old union model of labour is dead and gone. You've got longer and longer chains of sub-contracting and outsourcing, and employers want to buy labour as they buy other commodities – supplies which they can turn on and off as necessary without raising the unit price. So you see, if you want to be a crusader you've really got your work cut out. I'd drop it if I were you.'

'I want to drop it,' said Gabriel. He was so tired at this moment he thought he could sleep like a horse, standing up. 'I don't even want to think about it.'

'Well, you've said that your conscience is clean. That's what matters in the end.'

'I didn't say that.' His conscience *was* clean, but he'd say it if and when he wanted to.

'Didn't you?' said Fairweather, his demeanour changing, like he'd stepped out of the office and loosened his tie.

Was it his greatest political asset, this amiable vagueness, more useful than the sharpness contained within? It was largely impenetrable, it seemed non-threatening, and it swept you along.

'Didn't you?' repeated Fairweather. 'I'd rather thought you had. Maybe you should, you know. Have you heard of neuro-linguistic programming? Say something often enough, you start to believe it and lo, it shall come to pass. Let's say you feel guilty about something. Keep telling yourself you don't. It'll do the trick in the end.'

'Isn't that – I don't know – psychotic behaviour? If you tell yourself things that don't relate to reality.'

Fairweather's laugh echoed around the naked room. He put his arm across Gabriel's shoulder as they headed for the door. 'Lot of psychopaths in Westminster, then. Ha, ha, I should say. Goes with the territory.'

In his hot tight cell, his legs crammed under the desk, Gabriel sat thinking it wouldn't be any worse doing solitary in a Bangkok jail; and he was thinking, too, that his mind kept wandering and ought to be dragged back to the task in hand, whatever that was, when Oona, all bustle and creak, installed herself in the corner, cradling a towel-swaddled object in her lap.

Gabriel wanted her out of there. There wasn't enough oxygen for two. 'Oona,' he said, 'what's that you've got? A severed head?'

'Hooh,' said Oona, giving herself body and soul to her laugh.

'I'm in the middle of something, actually,' said Gabe.

Oona clucked and shook her head. '*Hal*ways busy.'

She took up too much space. When she sat somewhere it was like she'd put down roots, would stay until her children, her grandchildren, were grown. You expected to trip over her knitting or the babies that would crawl out from under her skirts.

'That's right,' said Gabe.

'Brought you someting,' said Oona, creasing her almond eyes. 'Look how thin you got!'

Gabe nodded. He wished she would go. He closed his eyes and wished her away.

'Hexhausted, too, m'mm.'

What did she think this was? Who did she think he was? A house-wife whose children were running her ragged, gossiping over the fence?

'Nice bitta stew and dumplin's, in a nice clay pot,' said Oona, 'thirty minutes at one hundred and eighty, darlin'. Know how it is when you only suppose be cooking for one. Easy to go without.'

Gabriel opened his eyes. He felt them bulge out of their sockets. Oona put the swaddled pot on his desk. On his papers, on his lists, on all his important stuff!

'Oona,' he said, choking with indignation.

She stood there making broody noises deep in her chest.

'I . . .' said Gabe. 'I . . .'

'Ho,' said Oona, 'don't need no tanks.' She folded her hands in front of her and began to move her lips silently.

What the hell did she think she was doing? Was she saying a prayer? He caught the last line as she shuffled off on leaden feet. God bless us and Amen.

He ran straight up to Human Resources and said that she had to go, he couldn't work with her any more. Gross misconduct, said the HR lady. Fill in this form. He sat and chewed his pen. What could he put? Praying while on duty? Offering unwanted casseroles? He'd already given her one formal warning. Couldn't he add another, for being late or something, and then that would be the end of it? The HR lady consulted her files. There's no record, she told him. Has to be a record or it doesn't count. He protested. He pleaded. The HR lady tapped her pen. Gabe, undefeated, suggested redundancy. The HR lady said no. Not unless it was in Mr James's 'restructure initiative'. Gabriel said thanks very much for your help. She smiled and said, any time, and about the goods-in porter, don't forget to deal with him.

During dinner service he prowled the kitchen. He watched the dish-washer stacking plates and scouring pans. This one was from Somalia. The other was from Sudan. Or maybe the other way round. The man wiped his hands on his overalls and hosed down the sink. He dragged a massive stockpot over, ran the water and started scrubbing, nearly up to his armpits, his head sunk low as if doing his best to hide. As a dish-washer it wasn't good to be noticed. The only time you were noticed was if you'd done something wrong, dropped a tray of glasses, or left some grime in a pot.

Gabriel drifted away to the heart of the kitchen.

'Jeez,' said Victor, wheeling. 'Didn't hear you come up. You're like a ghost or something, man.'

He watched his boys, Benny and Suleiman, busy at their stations. Nikolai, too old for this work, pressed a hand to the small of his back. Ivan stoked his fires.

A waitress came to say that a customer had a complaint and wanted to see the chef.

'About the food?' said Gabriel.

The waitress didn't know. She led him to the table and turned on her heel.

'Hello,' said Gabriel. 'How can I help you?'

'I've got a complaint,' said the man, 'I'm sorry to say.' He looked all right, shirt and chinos uniform, probably a corporate lawyer on a dress-down Friday, but not too full of himself.

'Sorry to hear it,' said Gabe. 'Hope I can put things right.'

'Take a look at my plate,' said the customer.

'You don't like the steak? Is it overcooked?'

'Steak's fine. But the plate. Look at it.'

The man's girlfriend pressed her fingers to her lips.

Gabriel leaned down and examined the plate. 'You'd like a different one?'

'See that,' said the man, pointing with his fork at a trace of some-thing on the rim, 'that's not been washed properly. That's a bit of old cack on there.'

The girlfriend smiled beneath her fingers. It seemed to egg him on.

'When you're paying well over ten quid for a main you might expect a garnish, but you don't expect it to be made of old cack.'

The girlfriend sniggered. The man leaned back swelling his chest, splaying his legs as if his balls had suddenly grown.

'I'll change your plate for you, sir,' said Gabriel. 'I'll get you a fresh steak as well.'

'I mean,' said the man, enjoying himself too much to stop, 'you're serving this lovely meal, and it's decorated with sick-up. Could you have a word with whoever's responsible?'

'OK, David,' said the girlfriend, her back stiffening, her eyes on Gabriel.

But the man was dining out now on the sound of his own voice. 'Is it too much to ask for a *clean* plate, for a bit of spit and polish? Is it? I mean, come on.'

'Certainly,' said Gabriel. 'I'll do it myself, right away.' With a flourish he removed the man's plate and raised it close to his mouth. He spat on the rim. 'There, sir, that's the spit. Now for the polish.' He gave it a vigorous wipe with his sleeve.

He returned the plate to the table and bowed. 'Enjoy your meal. *Bon appetit.*'

'Have you finally taken leave of your senses?' said Gleeson. He closed the door to Gabriel's cubicle and leaned against it as if Gabe might seek to escape.

Gabriel shrugged. 'What's it to you?'

'Have you gone mad? Are you crazy? Shall we get the straitjacket out?'

Gabe chewed a fingernail.

Gleeson adjusted his cuffs. 'Do you realize everyone saw? Do you know everyone was watching you?'

'So?' said Gabriel.

Gleeson quivered with bright-eyed righteousness. 'I had to sort out your little mess. It took quite a while to calm him down.'

'I didn't ask you to do anything.'

Gleeson continued to bristle then he dropped it, advancing with a conniving smile, dripping snake oil all over the floor. 'Shall we just say, in that case, that I've done you a favour. One gentleman to another, a good deed, a good turn that may deserve another, should you so choose, at some future date.'

'I don't think so,' said Gabe.

'I smoothed things over,' hissed Gleeson. 'I could have got you fired.'

'Sorry you missed that chance?'

Gleeson crackled with hostility. It hung around him like static. 'You are crazy,' he said. 'You've lost it. You're bloody mad.'

Gabriel jumped to his feet as Gleeson flowed out of the door. 'I see right through you,' he shouted. 'You're not a gentleman, you're totally . . .' he could barely get his words out, '. . . fucking . . . fake.'

Gleeson put his hands to his tailored hips and turned out a shiny shoe. 'Fake?' he said, in his most affected drawl. 'And what, pray, are you? A genuine what? Do tell.'

In the morning Gabriel went up to see Mr Maddox without an appointment. He knocked once and went in without waiting for a reply.

'Come in,' said Maddox, 'don't stand on ceremony. Why don't you come right in and make yourself at home?'

'I need to speak to you about something,' said Gabe.

Mr Maddox waved him over to the sofa in the corner of his office, and turned back to Mr James who waited by his desk like a school-boy in fear of the cane.

'Explain to me again, Gareth, why I have to get involved.'

'It's like this, Mr Maddox,' the deputy manager began.

'Problems,' said Maddox, rubbing his jaw, 'why do you always bring me problems? Can't you bring me a solution once in a while?'

'If I could just outline for you—'

'I don't want a bloody outline,' said Maddox. 'What will I do with an outline? Colour it in?'

Mr James smiled and said nothing. He lowered his head and his gaze.

'What do I employ you for?'

Mr James carried on smiling.

'Go on, remind me. Because it's not at all obvious.'

Gabriel pretended to look at a magazine on the coffee table, but kept watching Mr James. His smile was painful to see. It was the same way he always smiled and it was nervous, involuntary, like the twitch in Damian's right eye.

Mr Maddox passed his hairy fingers over his face. He lost interest. Didn't go for the kill.

'Go back to Marketing, Gareth. Say you've had a word with me. See if you can sort it out.'

Mr James went off clutching at his clipboard and his dignity.

Mr Maddox left his desk and took up the leather armchair opposite Gabe. It seemed to shrink as he sat down.

'I'm trying to curb it,' he said.

'What's that?'

Maddox rolled his head then grabbed it between his hands and twisted in either direction until his neck clicked. 'Came up the hard way, Chef. Old habits, you know.'

'Yes,' said Gabe. He'd come to talk about Gleeson and Ivan, the fact that they were using – still using, Gabe had kept intermittent watch – the guest room without authority.

'Back when,' said Maddox. His eyes went far away. They came round again. 'Respect, you see, was something you had to earn. Usually by beating the shit out of someone.'

Gabriel looked at Mr Maddox's brow. You could use it for hammering nails. Maddox had probably hammered a few heads with it in his time. Maybe it would be better not to say anything about Gleeson and Ivan at the moment, better to wait until he had a solution, or at least knew exactly what the problem was.

'Anyway, had a little lapse there with Gareth. I don't know.'

Gabe wondered what reason he could give for coming up and bursting in.

Mr Maddox, though, seemed in no hurry. He offered Gabriel a cigar. 'My grandfather,' he said, 'was in service, and my great-grandfather and his father before him, back and back. Servants, every one.' He paused for a while. 'What do you think of the smoke, by the way?'

'Good flavour,' said Gabe, 'red meat, roasted nuts.'

'Sometimes,' said Maddox, 'I think I'm still in their footsteps. Think I haven't put enough distance . . . inspecting bedsheets in the penthouse, a couple of hours ago. How's that for a chip on the shoulder? Impressive or what?'

'It was common enough, in those days,' said Gabriel, 'to be a servant. My family were all in the mill.'

'Interesting fact for you, Chef. As many people nowadays in service – cleaning, cooking, nannying, gardening – as there were in the 1860s. Progress, eh?'

The cigar was making Gabriel a little light-headed. He kept forgetting not to inhale. He nodded along.

'My granddaughter,' said Mr Maddox, 'she's ten years old. She said to me, Granddad, why are you angry all the time?' He stirred his feet and pulled at his trousers. 'Well, what could I say? I said, pickle, I'm not angry. I said, I've never been angry with you.'

'And? Did she believe you?'

'She's bright, you see,' said Maddox, 'she's top of the form.'

'Good for you,' said Gabriel. 'Good for her.'

'She's set up a swear box. Keeps the takings. Fucking raking it in.' He laughed unhappily. 'Now,' he said, 'what was it that you wanted to talk about?'

'Oh,' said Gabriel, 'I wanted to tell you that all-night room service is starting up this week. Benny's going to do the first shifts.'

He'd sort out Gleeson. He didn't need to take it up with Maddox. What he needed to do was act, force a confrontation, stop burying his head in the sand.

CHAPTER TWENTY-TWO

—ᴡ—

SPRING WAS COMING. IT WAS IN THE SNAP OF BLUE SKY BETWEEN THE
buildings, it was in the gently ruffled air, it was in the passers-by who
lifted hopeful faces to the light. Gabriel was reminded, as always, of the
ski season he'd worked in some wainscoted Tyrolean town. One
morning he'd woken and heard ticking, the rooftop snow counting
down the moments before it slid with a whoosh to the ground. When
he looked out of the window he saw in the spangled white garden a
miraculous little trapezium of green.

Cinnamon rolls, he thought, stepping lightly down the street from
the back entrance of the Imperial. Must have made a thousand in that
place. He could smell them still. He pulled up short on the pavement,
bobbing on a wave of nostalgia for a kitchen and colleagues he could
barely recall.

Across the road a demolition team in fluorescent vests flagged the
all-clear to the crane. A young woman click-clacking down the road
saw the builders and grew defensive. She folded her arms. The crew
took no notice. She glanced around.

The hoardings shook as the crane ground forward. A thin shout
went up. The unlovely houses gaped open, snaggle-toothed with doors
here and there. Gabriel watched the crane's arm swing. The wrecking
ball swept back, gathered itself in thought for a moment and then it
was on its way, a long and languorous journey filled with mild
encounters, remembered in ghostly white clouds.

The rucksack weighed cosily on Gabriel's shoulders, packed with food from the fridges and larders at work. He was going home after lunch service to spend the afternoon with Lena, and to cook a civilized meal. So many things to do. The important ones came first. You put in the foundations. You selected cornerstones. Last night he had been convulsed by thoughts of Gleeson, as if the straitjacket had been no mere taunt, as if he were bound and tied by rage. He'd struggled free. Gleeson was on his list. List upon list. Give the lists a structure, see how they stacked up, joined. See it, visualize it, hold it in your mind. Some tasks supported others, laid the groundwork, some ran together in an arch. It was like building a house. Let in light, generate heat, keep the rain off your head. It was a matter of architecture and food was no different, the molecular structures, the way you ordered a plate, you had to build, and when you organized a kitchen, pulled together a team, you had to see the architecture, have a blueprint, keep it tight and strong.

Before he turned the corner Gabriel looked back at the site. As he watched, a wall collapsed in slow motion with a vague, protesting sigh.

The flat was empty when he got home. Lena must have gone to the shop. He waited for fifteen minutes and then he rang her mobile. He left a message and made a cup of tea. He went down to look for her. He tried her mobile again.

He stood by the long sitting-room window and every moment expected her to come into view. Then he grew superstitious and thought she would not come as long as he stayed there. Sitting on the sofa he stroked his knees and waited for the sound of the key in the door.

She would come exactly at the point he had stopped thinking about her. That was how these things always were. She might have gone to the cinema. She had done that once or twice and told him about it. He had encouraged her.

He jumped up and went to the bedroom and flung open the wardrobe doors. All the dresses he had bought her were there. To be sure he opened the drawers.

Back in the sitting room he paced steadily. The more he looked at the furniture the less familiar it felt. The hard green sofa belonged in a waiting room, the black chaise was hideous, the lacquered shelves were empty and the white-cube coffee table was pretentious beyond belief. Who would want to live here? Who could call this place a home?

There was a sound in the corridor. He ran outside. Across the hall his neighbour fumbled with his key.

'Oh, sorry,' said Gabriel, 'I was expecting someone.'

'Hi,' said the neighbour, smiling absently. He went into his flat.

It was typical, thought Gabriel. That was how selfish people were. Wouldn't exchange a few words. Wouldn't give you the time of day. Those neighbours, whenever he saw them, they didn't even break their stride. *Hi* and that was it. Gabe hadn't done much better, he admitted, but at least it was in his mind to invite them over, he'd been on the point of doing it, nearly asked them round for dinner when he'd first moved in.

He resumed his pacing. The fact was things had gone downhill. When he was growing up it wasn't like this at all. In those days people took an interest. They rallied round. They knew your name, at least. Now nobody had the time. They didn't keep an eye out for any-one. If he went over and knocked on the door and said, *have you seen her?* they would smile politely and say, *who?*

Gabriel chewed on his fingernail. He smoked a cigarette. He looked out of the window, which put the jinx back again. He had to stay away.

He found himself standing in the kitchen, turning the tap on and off. The rucksack was on the counter. He hadn't unpacked it yet.

When he had a son he would say to him, *when I was growing up*, and the boy would think to himself, *that was the last century, the last millennium*. He'd take the boy to work sometimes, if he wanted to come.

Where was Lena? Stop worrying. Without money, how far would she get?

What would he show the boy at work? Would the boy have been proud of him yesterday? Well, there were pressures, too complicated for a child to understand.

It was nearly seven o'clock. Where was she? If she didn't come by seven she wasn't coming. That was clear enough.

When he used to go to Rileys with Dad it was different. He preached loyalty, honesty, respect, as if those things were woven into the fabric of his work. But now it wasn't like that. The world was a different place.

It was seven. This could not go on. He seized a knife, the devil's own blade, and plunged it into the solid beech worktop with all his God-given strength. The black handle shivered as he retreated, issuing a silent plea. *If you're out there, if you can hear me, let me not be mad.*

He opened a bottle of wine and forced himself to sit on the sofa with the television on. He was OK. He was rational. Lena was probably at the cinema. She wouldn't expect him back until after ten. If she could see one film then why not two, a double bill? Everyone got wound up once in a while. It hardly made them insane. Gleeson . . . why should he even think about anything that viper had to say? Jenny . . . well, Jenny, bless her, had got hold of the wrong end of the stick. She said it runs in families. But he wasn't Mum. He didn't go on crazy spending sprees. He didn't run off with the milkman. No, his life was still his own.

He shifted uncomfortably, tried a cushion behind his head, removed it, put his feet on the coffee table and then down again. He swung his legs on to the sofa and stared up at the ceiling.

What if his life were a series of blunders based on misreadings, on misconceptions, on a series of childish mistakes? If he made choices without understanding, what kind of choosing was that? It was like some madman, believing himself the King of Spain, carefully deciding if he should wage war on France, or if it should be Brazil. Working out his options in his padded cell, weighing and deliberating, playing with his own shit.

When he looked back it seemed to him . . . no, wait, better not to look. Things were better the way he used to remember them.

If he'd listened to Dad, he would have gone to university. One thing followed on from another. You didn't walk a path, you got on a train and the stations were few and far between.

What happened between you and Dad? You couldn't reach a finger into your past and touch something and say, *there, that's it, right there.* There were too many reasons, too many ways of looking, thinking, remembering. Ah, yes! What was important was not what happened but how you remembered it. It was Dad who told him that. You're so right, Dad. Dad, do you know how true that is?

Gabriel rose from the sofa and resumed his pacing. Now all he had to do was choose the right way to remember. It was clearly up to him. Although, having said that, it wasn't so easy to put thoughts out of your mind. What he needed, no, what he needed was an adjudicator, someone who knew him, who knew what he was really like. A friend, you see, a friend could say impartially, *oh, you were always destined, you were cut out, there'd be no stopping you.* Someone with faith in him.

He had friends. He'd call one now. Of course he had friends. Did he? But what he needed was a witness. Someone who knew what made him. Someone who would stand up and say it. *Yes, I vouch for this man.*

When Jenny picked up the phone she was still speaking to someone at the other end.

'Jen,' said Gabe, 'it's me.'

'Oh, Gabe,' said Jenny, 'hang on a minute.'

Gabriel heard raised voices, followed by a muffled bang.

'Like World War Three in here,' said Jenny. 'Bailey's grounded, but she's just walked out the door and I said to her, Bailey, don't even think about it because there'll be hell to pay and she looked at me like . . . yeah, go on then, and off she goes and Harley, don't get me started . . .'

Gabe smiled. 'What's he done now?'

'He's only gone and . . . no, don't get me started. I'll tell you when you come up because I've the ironing to do tonight. You coming up, Gabe? Dad's not doing so good.'

'I will,' said Gabriel. 'Soon.'

'Don't leave it too long.'

'Jenny,' said Gabe, 'I was thinking about when we were kids.'

'You saying I'm too strict with mine?'

'No,' said Gabe. 'I was just thinking when we'd go down and play by the railway track . . .'

'Which definitely wasn't allowed.'

What could he say to make her understand? Jenny had worries of her own. 'Those summer days, they went on for ever. Remember how long they were?'

'I get it,' said Jenny, 'we were no angels, never home on time. But Harley and Bailey, they think they're grown-ups, think they can do whatever they like, and I suppose they're right but not under my roof is what I tell them, there's lines you cannot cross. Gabe, when do you think you'll come?'

'Soon,' said Gabriel. 'Next week or the week after, whenever I can get away.'

'Good. I best get on,' said Jenny, distracted, 'nice to hear your voice.'

'Yours too,' said Gabe, trying to keep the misery out of his. A deep hole opened inside him, a big black space. Everything he tried to hold on to was sucked into the vacuum and he stayed empty, this hollow at his core.

'Well,' said Jenny.

'Wait! Michael Harrison's tattoo parlour, do you know the name of it? Thought I might try to track him down, sink a couple of pints, you know, for old times' sake.'

'Be easy enough to find him,' said Jenny, 'but you might have to make do with a brew. Bev heard it off Mrs Tisdale who got it off Sandra Sharples who's going out with—'

'Jenny!'

'Keep your hair on, Gabe. Plenty of time, he's not going nowhere. He's in Warrington, got eight years for assaulting a police officer, aggravated something or other and GBH.'

'But you said . . .'

'I know, but that was ages ago. So anyway, looks like you won't be going for that pint.'

'What happened? What went . . .'

'. . . wrong? I don't know. But, tell the truth, I'm not surprised. I mean, I was shocked, of course, it's terrible, but when you think what his dad was like. It was the drink, probably, for both of them. Alcoholic, you know.'

'Such a . . .'

'. . . shame, and he was such a bonny lad,' she said, sighing, as if this was what was lost. 'Don't suppose you'd have that much in common, though, not after all this time. Even if he weren't banged up.'

'No,' said Gabriel. 'Probably not.'

'Right,' said Jenny, 'we'll expect you soon.'

'That's right.' He cast about desperately for a way to keep Jenny talking. It was like fishing in a dried-up well, he couldn't dredge anything up. Oh, there was that time, Jenny would love this, at the top of Twistle Tower and Bev was there . . . or was it Jackie? It'd come back to him if he closed his eyes.

'I'll tell Dad,' said Jenny, 'but you better call him too. See you, Gabe. Bye-bye, then. Cheerio for now.'

When she saw him at the kitchen table, Lena started. She put a hand to her chest. 'It's you,' she said, and smiled.

'Yes,' said Gabriel, 'who else? Who else would it be?'

'I make tea,' said Lena. 'You want I make for you?'

'I mean,' said Gabe, 'you wouldn't be expecting anyone, any visitors? Nothing like that.'

She was filling the kettle and humming her tuneless hum. 'I have hear,' she said, laughing, twisting her cat-like back, 'I have hear something funny today.'

She spoke and he listened and he thought he had seen this before; it wasn't happening, it was something remembered, yes, it had been just like this. There was music, that's right, she'd put the radio on and she was swaying and giggling, even dancing a few pretty steps. Such simple things fill a heart. Telling him how a man had been locked in a public toilet for two days. He laughed because she laughed, and her hair which she had plaited swung behind her shoulders and she had a bright dress on.

What happened now? Did he go to her? Did he take her in his arms?

'Where did you hear it?' he heard himself say.

Lena looked in the breadbin. 'I make toast.'

'Who told you? Lena, who?'

'Is news,' she said.

He got up and moved closer. His shadow fell across her.

'You don't watch the news. You don't read newspapers. Where did you go today?'

She turned away from him. 'I go out.'

'Yes. Where? Where did you go? Look at me, Lena. I said, where.'

She whipped round. 'Why you ask like this?'

The scene went bad from here, as he remembered. What could he do? He felt sick. He was sweating. All he had to do was keep his mouth closed.

'It's a reasonable question,' he said.

'You keep me here like . . . like prison. Like animal in cage.'

He could see what he was doing wrong. He looked at himself with a mixture of pity and disgust. What a sap. What a fool. Would he never learn?

'Do I lock you in? Do I beat you?' He should know better than to shout. He did know better. But here we go again. 'Don't I give you everything you ask for and more?'

'You promise,' said Lena, attacking her fingernail, 'but you don't give.'

'What?' he said, the poor fool. 'What don't I give?'

'You say you look for Pasha. You say you pay someone. But I don't believe.'

The idiot stood with his hands on his hips, attempting to be affronted by the idea. Anyone could see what he was like. Wake up and smell the coffee, buddy boy.

'I can prove to you . . .'

'You say you give me money. How long I wait for it?'

He was watching her twist the end of her plait around her finger. He was looking into her glazed blue eyes, trying to make them focus on him. He was thinking a thousand thoughts and none of them was right.

'I didn't find that money. Nikolai took it and sent it to Yuri's family. It was Yuri's all along, wasn't it, the money wasn't yours.'

Oh no, no. Stop looking. Don't hear any more.

'I have earn that money. *I have earn it.* Here, with you, is not for free. Why you don't pay me? Pay me what you owe.'

He took Nikolai down to dry goods to help with the stock check. The shelves laddered up each wall, bustling with bottles and boxes, jars and packets, containers and cans, shouty labels, eye-test print, cloudy canisters, glinting glass, nasty tin. The floor, an obstacle course of sacks and cardboard cartons, begrudged Gabe's presence, always trying to trip him up. It was a madman's bunker down here. And still they would order more.

'Fava beans, haricot beans,' said Gabriel. 'Arborio rice.' He watched Nikolai writing on his prescription pad. 'Tell me something,' he said. 'Are you happy? Being a commis, it's not what you expected to do.'

Nikolai made a gesture of indifference with his hands.

'I suppose,' continued Gabe, 'a lot of people aren't.'

Nikolai nodded, still assessing the patient, perhaps.

'I mean,' said Gabe, 'even if they're rich and successful and all the rest, they feel unhappy, they get depressed.' Last night he'd smoked cigarette after cigarette, walking round the block. Lena could not feel anything, was incapable. It was that client who had made her like this. If he ever saw the man he would kill him with his bare hands.

'It's normal,' said Nikolai.

'I don't mean me. I'm all right. On the whole.' Gabe, staring at a hessian sack, wished he could curl up on it and sleep. But if he went to sleep he would have the dream he didn't want to have.

'In my home town,' said Nikolai, his long white fingers caressing the pen, 'when I was a boy we had a Happiness Day Parade. Everyone had to go. We mocked it, of course. We were ordered to be happy and so, to be subversive, we went out of our way to be miserable, and nothing could have made us happier than this forbidden misery.'

'Did you have to march through the town?'

'With banners,' said Nikolai. He paused. He was preparing to give his diagnosis, Gabe could tell by the look on his face. 'Crude ideology, easy to laugh at it. Yours is more sophisticated and so dominant that it has been internalized and it works much better that way. Unhappiness is normal but if we are unhappy we think that we have failed. Every day in this country is a Happiness Day Parade, but we don't march shoulder to shoulder, each must march alone.'

Gabe sat down on a packing crate. 'You know, if I could get a good night's sleep I'd be happy. I'd be ecstatic, in fact. It's this bloody dream.'

'The dream,' said Nikolai. 'You told me.'

Why didn't he say anything? Why did he look like he knew more than he chose to say? 'What does it mean?' Gabriel burst out. 'It must mean something. It's doing my head in.'

'The interpretation of dreams,' said Nikolai, 'a subject close to Freud's heart. Personally I find this part of his work less satisfactory, and I know you are not a big fan of his. There are people who claim to read dreams much as they read tea leaves or palms.'

'Why do I keep having it? Over and over again. It might mean,' he said, wildly, 'something significant, like Yuri's death was no accident. It might mean that the dream won't stop until the killer is caught.'

Nikolai looked at him with his rodent eyes. 'You mean,' he said, in his precise little way, 'that Yuri's ghost is haunting you?'

'No, of course not, no. Christ. It's just the same thing, over and over, so I'm down here in the catacombs somewhere and there's this horrible light, it . . . it beats, sort of pulses like a heart or something, and it's kind of pulling me along. Or sometimes it's chasing me, I don't know, and I think it's going to – it sounds stupid – *drown* me. And, anyway, I always end up in the same place, with Yuri's body and – did I tell you about this? I told you – I have to kind of crawl around and examine it and then there's the food . . .'

'The food. Do you eat it?'

'Yes. No. I used to but now it's full of maggots and stuff. Or maybe it's not rotten any more, I don't eat it, I just try to stop it burying me alive.'

'So the dream doesn't stay the same, it changes.'

'Sort of, but basically it's the same.'

'I see,' said Nikolai. 'And this light you mention, what happens when you stop by Yuri's body, does it catch up with you?'

Gabe scratched his head two-handed. His elbows flapped. 'No, there's no light then.'

'So how do you see the body? How do you examine it?'

'It's not dark, it's normal, you know, I don't know, it doesn't all make sense, it's a dream.'

343

'But you want to find meaning in this thing which doesn't make sense?'

Gabriel laughed. 'Think I'm losing it. Can't get a grip on myself. Never mind. Let's get on. What's up at the top there? I can't see. Is that where the flour is?'

Nikolai stood on tiptoe on a twenty-litre drum of Frymax. 'Dried fruits, sugars, nuts.' He turned round. 'But what is this self you are losing? You mean a kind of soul?'

It was pointless, thought Gabe, to have these conversations with Nikolai. He wouldn't allow himself to be sucked in. 'I only mean what ordinary people mean when they talk about themselves.'

'Ah,' said Nikolai, 'but that's going round in circles.'

Gabriel raised his hand as if to ward Nikolai off. 'It's pretty obvious to everybody. Everybody except you.'

'Scientifically speaking . . .'

'Oh, stuff your scientific speaking,' Gabriel barked. Nikolai said he was a doctor. A likely story. You don't go around believing every story you hear.

'I understand,' said Nikolai gently. 'After all, it seems that we are biologically programmed to have what we might call a sense of self.'

Look at him, thought Gabriel, standing on his soap box, his oil can, about to address a meeting. He wasn't a scientist, he was a politician, always trying for another convert. He looked like he lived in a cellar, like he'd never seen the light of day, a little albino revolutionary stirring it up from underground. 'Oh, whatever,' he said.

They continued with the stock check. Gabe kept looking at Nikolai. They counted bottles and tins. Nikolai found mouse droppings at the back of a shelf.

'No,' said Gabe. 'No, those are old. That problem's been sorted out. OK?'

'OK,' said Nikolai.

They carried on.

'Know what your problem is,' said Gabriel.

Nikolai waited patiently.

'No, I can't be bothered to tell you.'

They worked on, calling product names and numbers, sliding boxes and hefting sacks.

'I'll tell you what your problem is,' said Gabe. 'You go on about science, you think you know everything, but you don't know about people at all.'

'My ex-wife would agree with you.'

'Science tells us this, science tells us that,' said Gabe, his voice rising, 'we're machines, we have no free will. Well, bloody science doesn't tell me anything about how I bloody well feel.' And that, he decided, had always been his problem. As a chef as much as anything. His marvellous scientific approach. He'd even given Oona a lecture on the molecular structure of custard. For God's sake! Who needed to know that? What you needed to know, standing there stirring, was exactly how it felt as it was all about to thicken.

'Perhaps you're right,' said Nikolai, remaining damnably calm.

'Go on,' Gabe urged, 'go on, talk, don't treat me like an idiot.'

'Perhaps,' said Nikolai slowly, 'it would be interesting to look at it from another point of view. Leave science aside. Let's say you are read-ing a novel, and this novel is about a man's life. It begins with his childhood and follows him through various events until, maybe, a crisis somewhere in middle age.'

Nikolai paused and Gabriel instantly became incensed. 'Well,' he cried, 'get on with it. Don't make a speech. Just talk.'

'All right. Let's say it is a decent novel and you believe in this character, you begin to understand him. Now, as you read, the character is always making decisions, choices, about his life, think-ing, vacillating, about which way he will go.'

'Yes! Exactly! That's how it is. That's how people are.'

Nikolai gazed out steadily from beneath his combustible stack of hair. 'But if we have got to know him, his make-up, his circumstances, then we know how he will act. It is these books which take on authority, inevitability, because we feel they are true to life. The protagonist cannot be otherwise, cannot do otherwise, and yet he is condemned to behave – as we all must – as if he were free.'

'Oh, bullshit,' said Gabriel hotly. 'How boring is that? How boring is a book without twists and turns? What about characters who act on impulse, without any reason, without even knowing why they're doing something?'

'Of course. That too,' said Nikolai, soothingly. 'But if they are controlled by impulse and act without reason, that is also an argument against the existence of free will.'

'That's only . . .' said Gabriel. Nikolai thought he was so clever and see where his cleverness got him. A commis, no more, no less. Gabe would explain to him clearly how false his argument was. 'What you don't . . .' he began again and faltered. His mind whirred like an electric whisk, beating in an empty bowl. He had to speak. 'It's you who goes round in circles. You twist everything to fit one idea. You think you're proving something but it's just your opinion, your belief. For God's sake, you're like a true believer,' he said, shaking with anger. 'It's like a religion with you.'

When he'd finished the stock-take, Gabriel told Suleiman to come outside with him for a moment. He needed a cigarette.

Suleiman peered and squinted, the consternation caused by this irregularity.

'Relax,' said Gabriel. 'You're not being had up in court.'

Suleiman wrung his toque between his hands. 'Oh no, Chef, it is most pleasant to enter a conversation with you.'

'I wanted . . . er . . . to see how everything is going. Making progress? All OK?'

'It is the appraisal?' said Suleiman, looking like a man who has left his briefcase on the train.

'That kind of thing,' said Gabe. 'I'm very impressed, I should tell you, very impressed by your focus, your attitude. I'll be setting up my own place – you have to keep that secret for now – and I could certainly find a position for you. It'd be a promotion. Would that suit you?'

Suleiman rocked on his crooked legs. 'Thank you for these kind words. May I have a little time to consider your offer, please?'

'Yes, yes,' said Gabriel expansively, his back against the cold yard wall, his face turned to the sun. 'Think and we'll talk again. See if it fits in with your plans. I haven't forgotten, how you've got it all worked out.'

'It is my father's influence,' said Suleiman smiling. When he smiled he did so vigorously, as if it were a form of exercise undertaken for the good of his health.

'Jolly good. And what about . . . tell me, is it just your career you have mapped out or do you have plans for . . . wife, kids, all the other stuff?'

'Most certainly,' said Suleiman. 'It would be utmost negligence to leave these things to chance.'

Gabriel nodded. He enjoyed his cigarette.

'My parents are presently selecting a number of girls,' continued Suleiman, 'from good families, of course.'

'And then you'll choose the one you like best.'

'Subject to compatibility screening, when that has been carried out.'

'But you can't know if you're compatible unless you spend some time together. Your presence will be required.'

'Eventually,' conceded Suleiman. 'But not in the first phase. First our charts must be matched.'

'Oh, how does that work?'

'Astrological charts. It is exceedingly most important, otherwise a correct decision cannot be made.'

'Really? Like a marriage horoscope?'

'Based on birth stars of the boy and the girl. It is an ancient science, very complex, and it reveals much detail. For instance, the presence of a certain alignment, the Dina Koota agreement, ensures that the husband and wife will remain healthy and free from diseases. The Ganam and also the Yoni Kootas will determine sexual compatibility, and if Rajju is in present alignment it bestows the girl living happily with the husband for a long time.'

Gabriel lit another cigarette. It made him cough and it made his eyes run. 'But do you,' he said between splutters, 'believe all that?'

'No one in my family,' said Suleiman, earnestly, 'has ever got divorced. Maybe as modern men we should not believe what is written in the stars. But as a way of making bride selection it does appear to work as well as any system you have here.'

The tube train pulled into Russell Square before he realized what he'd done. He'd got on the wrong line. How could that have happened?

Going in completely the wrong direction when he'd done this journey so many times. He made a dash for the doors and they closed in his face. At King's Cross he studied the underground map as if he'd never seen it before. No point going back now, he could get the Hammersmith and City or the Circle to Edgware Road. He stared at the map, all the connections and intersections, you could know every detail and still have no idea about London at street level, still be lost in the real world. When he'd first lived here he used to get the tube between Covent Garden and Leicester Square.

He turned to face the platform and saw a little black mouse on the tracks, running brave and scared. He saw a Chinese ancient with a plaited beard, a couple kissing, a girl with a bandaged knee, and a man carrying a silver birdcage. The train rumbled in the distance, they stepped forward, all those gathered here, and a mighty wind blew from the tunnel mouth as if God himself were about to speak.

Gabe sat in solemn and vacant contemplation, and it was only when he arrived at Edgware Road that he hesitated, and then decided to press on. At the sound of Charlie's voice on the intercom he nearly ran away.

'Hello,' said Charlie. 'Yes?'

'It's Gabriel. Can I come up?'

She buzzed him in and when he reached her front door it was open. He screwed his eyes up for a moment, trying to squeeze his brain, to get it working again. He went inside.

Charlie stood in the sitting room with one hand on her hip, lovely as a summer's day.

'I . . .' said Gabriel. 'I brought you some flowers. I left them on the train.'

'Hello, stranger,' said Charlie. 'Won't you sit down?'

'I know you don't want to see me. And I don't blame you.'

'Guess what I did today. Spent the morning in a school.' Charlie swung out her desk chair and sat on it the wrong way round, hugging her arms across the back.

'Did you? That's great. Going in for this teaching business, then?'

'It was so noisy. My ears are ringing still.'

Gabriel laughed. He glanced around at the porthole window, the sloping ceiling, the framed film posters, the vase of tulips, the patch-work quilt that draped the sofa, all the brilliant clutter of the room. He said, 'Is it OK if I take my coat off?'

Charlie looked at him with her jade-green eyes. 'You are funny. Would I ask you to sit and then order you to keep your coat on?'

'I've missed you.'

She looked away, took a breath, looked at him again. 'Same here.'

'Charlie . . .' His heart wept and sang.

'I mean,' she said, in a rush, 'we can still be friends, can't we? After all this time. There's a friendship to be salvaged, I think.'

'I didn't think you'd want to see me. You didn't return my calls.'

She swept her hair from behind her neck and pulled it forward over one shoulder and that sweet, familiar gesture nearly brought him to tears.

'That was ages ago,' she said. 'You haven't called me for ages. I kept expecting you to ring or show up here.' She smiled. 'You know, come round and apologize, grovel for all you're worth.'

'The number of times I've thought . . .'

Charlie came over to the sofa. She sat sideways on the arm with her feet on the cushion next to him. She wore a cream skirt with a nipped-in waist and a dark cashmere vest and she looked sensational. She looked like the girl he'd been trying half his life to find.

'So,' she said, 'if I may be so bold, what finally brings you here?'

'God, I've missed you and I'm so, so sorry, and if we could be friends,' he gabbled, 'that's . . . that's so wonderful and I am sorry, really sorry, for . . . and I'm incredibly sorry, I am.'

'Go on,' said Charlie, laughing, poking his leg with her foot. 'Go on, grovel, more.'

He looked at her, engorged with emotion, his mouth and tongue thick with it. 'Tell me how you are, Charlie. How are you?'

She pressed her hands on to her thighs, lifting her shoulders. 'Oh, the usual, still worrying about Darfur, the polar ice caps, the wrinkles round my eyes.'

'All the trouble hotspots of the world,' said Gabriel. 'Look at this, I'm going bald.' He turned his head.

'We're not getting any younger, are we?'

Gabe spread his hands. 'I come to you for help and what do I get? You're supposed to say, no, that bald patch is not visible to the human eye.'

Charlie grew serious. 'Why now, Gabe? Why come now? Help with what?'

'There is something,' said Gabriel. He told her about Gleeson, and Ivan and the housekeeping supervisor, and how he'd found the photos on the desk. 'I don't know what's going on but there's something not right and whatever it is, they're still at it, still using that room. You're the only person I can talk to, Charlie, and it's you and the Penguin Club in those photographs, I thought you had a right to know.'

Charlie thought for a while. 'When was all this?' she said.

'Before Christmas.'

'And you thought I had a right to know . . . but you didn't tell me until now.'

'I called. I left messages.'

'OK. And it's happened again? You've seen the same thing, the same set-up?'

'Well, they're more careful now but I know they're still using that room.'

'I see.'

'Charlie?'

'Gabe, have you considered that you might be imagining things? It doesn't seem like anything to me. You don't like Gleeson, do you? You *want* to make it seem sinister.'

'If you don't believe me . . .' said Gabe, 'I thought you'd be the one person I could talk to about this.'

'Stop chewing your fingernails,' said Charlie, suddenly irritable. 'Have you been sleeping properly? You look tired.'

Gabe put his head in his hands. He groaned. 'Things have been tough, to be honest.'

'Oh, Gabe, your father. I didn't ask.'

'Lost a lot of weight, not eating properly, but battling on as people say. We went for a walk at Christmas. But Charlie, it's not been easy, one way or another, I've been having a hard time.'

'Poor Gabriel,' said Charlie, in a tone he couldn't gauge. The clock struck the hour and she got up and went over to it, a piece of kitsch she'd picked up in a flea market in Camden Town. 'The man and woman don't come out any more. They seem to be stuck.' She opened a little door and fiddled about, wound the hands on to the next hour. The clock struck again. 'Well and truly bust.'

'As a matter of fact,' said Gabriel, 'I've hardly slept in weeks.'

'I don't know why we're avoiding the subject,' said Charlie. 'Don't know why I'm avoiding it.'

'I could have a look at that clock for you.'

'I guess I'm going to have to ask you straight out.'

'I remember when you bought that.'

'What happened to the girl? Lena, wasn't it? What happened to her?'

'It's good that we can talk, Charlie, that we can be friends again. You know, whatever does happen, you'll always be able to turn to me.'

'Did something happen, Gabriel? Gabriel, what did you do?'

'Nothing. I didn't do anything, she's fine, I'm still . . . taking care of her.'

Charlie chewed it over. She put her hands on her hips. 'Taking *care* of her?'

'Did you think I'd done something to Lena? Come on, you know me better than that.'

'She's still with you.'

If anyone could understand, it would be Charlie. If he could explain to her. 'Last night,' he said, 'Lena said a truly terrible thing to me. Well, it was in the middle of a big row, I suppose.' He gave a short laugh. 'She may only be young but she can give as good as she gets.'

Charlie opened her mouth and struck a note that could break a glass.

'What?' cried Gabriel, leaping up. 'What is it?'

'As good as she gets?' screamed Charlie. She picked a magazine off an artful stack and hurled it at his head.

'I'm sorry,' said Gabe, ducking, 'I thought it was all over with us. I didn't think you'd have me back.'

'Have you back? Are you crazy?' She tossed her head.

'Look, if I knew you'd be so upset . . .' He ran his tongue over parched lips. He ran out of words. A minute ago he'd been full, brimming, bursting at the seams. And now, from nowhere, this drought, this dry canyon.

'And you come round here looking for sympathy? *I'm having a hard time.* You want me to feel sorry for *you?*'

A desert wind blew inside him; it blew the dust and the tumble-weed. Trembling, he stretched out his hand. 'But you said . . . we can salvage a friendship. You said so, you said, you did.'

She sagged and she looked at him, not unkindly, and the scorching wind in his belly quieted down. 'Go away, Gabriel,' she said sadly. 'Go away now. You're on your own.'

CHAPTER TWENTY-THREE

—m—

DRIFTING ALONG THE ROAD AWAY FROM CHARLIE'S, HARDLY KNOWING which way he was going, Gabriel continually troubled his mobile, trying to raise his old life. He got three answering services, two 'number unobtainables', and one wife who said she hadn't seen the bastard in six months. Nathan Tyler picked up on the second ring.

'Gabriel Lightfoot! You little fucker. And about time too.'

'Nathan,' croaked Gabe. He cleared his throat. 'Hello, mate. Fancy a drink?'

'Always.'

'Great. Where are you now?'

'On a beach in Thailand getting massaged by two teenage whores. Where d'you think I fucking am?'

'Guess you're at work.'

'You're a fucking genius. Listen, I've got to go home after the shift or Lisa's gonna have my balls. Now the baby's come, you know . . .'

'Hey,' said Gabe, 'I'm really . . . boy or girl?'

'Boy called Sam. Got Lisa's nose and the biggest baby-boy cock you've ever seen,' said Nathan, with unmistakable pride.

'Congratulations,' said Gabriel. The way it came out sounded strangled, ungenerous. He tried again. 'That's great.'

'I know,' said Nathan. 'What you doing next Thursday? My night off, gonna scale the walls.'

'I'll call you,' said Gabe.

'You little fucker,' said Nathan affectionately. 'You say that, but you won't.'

It was around five thirty when Gabriel got back to the Imperial. He worked prep with Benny and Suleiman. For dinner service he put Oona on the pass and cooked with his brigade, with all his boys. He held the line all evening and didn't shirk the clean-down. Afterwards he went to his office and stirred some papers around. He wasn't going home tonight, he was staying to stake out the room. But now he had hours and hours and they draped around him like a necklace of shrunken skulls. He wouldn't see Lena tonight. He wouldn't call. Last night when she . . . but what did it matter, anyway?

In the lift, ascending to the top floor, he looked at himself in the bronze-toned mirrored wall. He held the brass rail and leaned his head against the glass, which steamed up and took out his face. The doors slid discreetly aside. Gabriel floated down the vanilla corridor of penthouses and master suites. The silence was cloying and the air trembled, the whole place fallen into a swoon of luxury. Not a single soul came past. He descended one floor, traced the length and breadth of the hotel and fell into checking each room for a strip of light beneath the door. A woman went by in stockinged feet, coat slung over her shoulders, dangling a pair of high heels by their straps. Gabriel shivered. Only déjà vu, but he hated this sense of a life already lived. He roamed on, descending and ascending, padding softly along in the anaesthetizing blandness, bowing his head in reciprocal acknowledgement as the lift doors curtseyed open to him.

When he finally gravitated to the kitchen, he saw Benny standing at the counter reading a book.

'Benny? It's four a.m.'

'Yes, Chef,' said Benny. 'It is very quiet now. Most of the orders were coming between one and two.'

'Oh,' said Gabriel, 'of course.'

'You don't mind, Chef,' said Benny, 'if I undertake some studies while I am waiting?'

'It's fine. I wasn't checking up on you.'

'I appreciate,' said Benny, his accent flowering the word with many syllables, 'your support on this first night of room service.'

'Wanted to, ah, make sure you were OK.'

'Thank you, Chef.'

Benny spoke with such good grace Gabriel felt chastened for having forgotten all about it. He picked up the book. 'What are you studying? Accountancy?'

'I hope to qualify. But it will take many years.'

'How do you find the time? You'll have to stop working double shifts.'

'But then I will not be able to afford the fees for the course.' Benny chuckled from deep down in his belly.

Was he going to study and work day and night? Gabriel looked at Benny's small, neat frame. How could it contain such reserves?

All of a sudden and with tremendous force it struck Gabe that he had misunderstood everything about Benny. Benny was no mere victim, of war and poverty and fate. That he had made it this far, across continents, could be no accident. Here was a man who had hewn his own life, out of the most difficult material, out of granite, and with only a blunt penknife.

'Chef, are you OK?'

'What? Yes, of course, I'll let you get on. You can get back to your studying.'

Benny waited politely. After a while he said, 'Excuse me, but is it possible for me to have my book back again?'

Gabriel released the book, which had somehow become clasped to his heart. Benny searched for his place, running his finger up and down the text.

Gabe thought about Benny's story, the one he refused to tell. *There was fighting and I ran away.* He thought about Kono, the little general who needed the encouragement of the knife. He looked at the scar, five inches long, across Benny's face.

The room-service phone began to ring.

'Kono?' said Gabriel.

Benny looked at him with his sad yellow eyes. He picked up the phone. 'Good evening, room service,' he said. 'Benny speaking. How may I help you?'

Gabriel must have nodded off on his feet on the stakeout, wedged in the first-floor alcove. Branka, about to sink her teeth into a chambermaid, knocked on the door and Gleeson's forked tongue replied. 'Yes, yes.'

Branka gave the girl a quick shove in the small of her back. They went in together and Gabriel's heart began to accelerate. He made up his mind to march in there and get cooking, slap the steak right on the flame. But as he moved away from the wall there was Ivan, with his bandanna pulled over his cauliflower ear and menace in the swing of his arms, and Gabriel shrank back. When the door had closed behind Ivan, Gabriel tiptoed across the hall. He pressed his ear to the wood but could not hear anything except the sound of his own breath. It would be stupid to go in now, three against one, better to wait until later and catch Gleeson on his own and off guard.

For the next three hours he fried up paperwork at his desk until, around eight thirty, Ernie scuttled in ducking his head.

'The very man,' said Gabe. 'Good.' If he let Ernie go this morning that would be one less thing waiting to be done.

'Ah want to let you know,' said Ernie, 'Ah've been brushing up ma skills.'

'Always useful, Ernie, to make yourself more marketable. Would you like to sit down?'

'It's Oona,' said Ernie, still standing. His toes pointed in, his hair stuck out and his trousers skimmed the tops of his socks. He wasn't so much employed as in day care.

'What's Oona?' said Gabe.

'Taught me to use the computer,' said Ernie. 'Ah've nae problem now.'

'The thing is, Ernie . . .' said Gabriel. But maybe it was true. When he'd done the stock-take with Nikolai, all the records matched up. 'I mean, can you do it all by yourself? Filing orders, tracking them, booking everything in?'

Ernie's head bobbed loosely. 'Chef,' he said, 'you'd let me know if . . . if Ah was for the can?'

Gabe looked at Ernie and saw that he had his fingers crossed like a kid. 'Job's safe, Ernie,' he said, 'as long as I'm here I'll make sure.'

'Ach,' said Ernie. 'Thanks.'

'How's it going with the poems, Ernie? The cards? How's it going with the business targets and everything?'

Ernie smiled serenely at the top of the filing cabinet. 'It was going quite badly, actually, Ah was missing every target, you know. But Ah've fixed it OK now.'

'Have you? How'd you manage that?'

'Simple,' said Ernie. 'Changed the figures so they matched. Matched the forecasts with what Ah'd sold. Revision, it's called, like *re-vision*, to see again.'

'Brilliant,' said Gabriel, 'you just changed what you wanted to happen, the plan, to fit what's really happened.'

'Ach,' said Ernie, modestly. 'Aye. Exactly right.'

A couple of minutes later Maddox entered in his usual manner, like this was a bust.

'Was that Ernie out there? Thought you were supposed to be putting him out of his misery.'

'Had a review with Ernie,' said Gabriel. 'He's doing OK. Had some training and he's fine.'

'Didn't I tell you . . .' Maddox suddenly halted the baton charge. He moved a stack of Gabriel's papers and sat down carefully on the edge of his desk. 'Never mind.'

'I know he's been on courses before,' said Gabriel, 'but I don't think they suited him. I arranged some one-to-one tuition this time.'

Maddox waved the matter away. 'I've been thinking,' he said, slowly, 'that I'm getting on a bit. And there's nothing more ridiculous in our society than an angry old man.'

'I definitely want to keep Ernie on.'

'It's a young man's game,' said Maddox. 'Be angry while you're young, Chef, that's my advice.'

'Do you want me to . . .'

Maddox talked over him. 'I don't want to be on my deathbed and all the family's grouped round, and there I am, Daddy, Great-uncle

Brian, Granddad, calling the doctor a bloody fool and telling the priest he's a prick.'

'So it's fine then?' said Gabriel.

'What? Oh, Ernie, yes.' Maddox shifted his weight. 'What did I come down here for?' He picked up the stapler and fired staples over the floor. 'Sorry, must stop doing that. Right, the event on Saturday night, you know half the PanCont board will be there. We need to run it through.'

They moved into a discussion and Maddox gave his instructions with great civility. Gabe found it disconcerting. It was like swimming in the warm shallows, knowing that close by the ocean floor shelved steeply and the dark waters ran suddenly cold. And Gabriel was so tired he could hardly see straight. He wished Mr Maddox would go. If he could have a little nap he'd be fine. He hadn't slept a wink in two days.

As soon as he was alone, Gabriel lowered the blind in his cubicle and closed the door. He sank down in his chair, legs stretching under his desk. His entire body heaved in gratitude as he lost himself to sleep.

The sweet oblivion didn't last long enough. The dream grabbed him and pulled him down and as he was reaching a hand out to the body he woke with a sob and a whiplash neck.

He flew out to the kitchen and shouted, 'Where is he? Why isn't he here?'

Victor, setting up his station, performed a drum roll with two wooden spoons. 'Who, Chef? Who?'

'Nikolai,' said Gabriel, trying to calm himself. 'Where?'

'In the locker room getting changed,' said Victor. 'What's the . . .'

But Gabriel was already at the basement door. He tore down the stairs.

Nikolai sat on a bench buttoning his whites.

'You've got to tell me,' said Gabriel. He pushed a locker door, which banged shut and flew open again. 'I can't sleep. I need to sleep.'

'What is it,' said Nikolai, lacing his delicate fingers, 'that you need from me? I am no longer a doctor, I cannot prescribe any pills.'

Gabriel hovered back and forth between the chipped enamel wash-basin and the black plastic bin. 'This dream, you know all about it, I've told you, and you don't say anything. What is it? What the fuck is it? What does it mean? It's got to stop, I'm telling you, because I have had enough.'

'Ah,' said Nikolai. 'You still believe it has . . . significance.' He inserted the word like a rectal probe.

'Damn it, damn it,' cried Gabe, hopping about. 'I don't know. You knew him. He was your friend. Don't you care? You must know something, you must have an idea, a hunch, anything.'

Nikolai unlaced his shoes. He slipped his work clogs on. 'Such as?'

Gabriel drew close to Nikolai. 'Maybe he was killed.' He was panting. His mouth was hanging wide. 'Maybe . . . how about this, there's a clue. The clue is in the dream, you see, somewhere in my subconscious I know something but it's buried and I can only find it by . . . digging. It's in the food. Or . . .' He held up a wavering finger. 'Or, the clue is on the body and that's why I have to keep looking very, very closely, so *disgusting*, I can see the hairs on his toes . . . But then, no, how would we . . . where is he buried? Even if I . . . can he be dug up?' He broke off and slumped against a locker, groaning. 'Oh, it's too revolting. And then there might have been . . . someone else, someone living in the basement with Yuri, I don't know, I'm not saying, you have to understand . . .' He burbled on without the faintest idea of what he was trying to say.

'Chef,' said Nikolai. He put his shoes in a locker, turned the key and put it in his pocket, everything he had to do was so clear, so easy. 'Chef, there was a post mortem, there was an inquest. They didn't find anything wrong. Yuri's death was an accident.'

'I know,' howled Gabriel. 'But the dream!'

Nikolai shrugged. 'These things we cannot control.' He put on his toque and went to the door.

Gabriel was still gripped by the conviction that Nikolai knew why he had the dream; it was a faith that went beyond reason, was without explanation, and defied all logic. He knew it in his bones. He wanted to seize Nikolai by the shoulders and shake it out of him. But it was Gabriel who shook as he put a hand on Nikolai's arm and breathed, 'For God's sake, tell me why.'

Nikolai smiled gently. 'OK, I'll tell you.'

The words coursed through Gabriel's body.

'You think it has some significance. You want to know what that is. Am I correct?'

'Yes,' murmured Gabriel, 'yes.'

'The significance of Yuri's death,' said Nikolai, 'is that it is in-significant. That is why it is so troubling. That is why you dream.' He freed his arm from Gabriel's grasp. 'But this is only my interpretation and, of course, the dream belongs to you. Naturally, you may interpret it any way you wish.'

The last person he wanted to see right now was Oona and sure enough there she was, all plump-armed and broody, smiling at him with her hearthside eyes.

'Oh, what is it now?' he said, as if she'd been bothering him all morning.

'Been looking h'all over,' said Oona, laughing.

'Well, you couldn't have looked very hard. I was in the locker room.' Why couldn't she laugh like a normal person? Why did she have to laugh like that? What was funny, anyway, about finding him here in the kitchen? The kitchen was where you'd expect to find a chef.

'About Saturday,' said Oona. 'Had a few ideas. Pretty good ones, hoo-hoo.'

Her laughter enraged him. It had no range. If you wanted to laugh after praising yourself you did it in the appropriate manner, with a knowing smile. Oona's cosmic laugh was plain wrong for every occasion. She never got it right. 'Leave Saturday to me, Oona,' he said. The event was too important to let her fuck it up.

'Won't take a little minute,' said Oona, licking her finger and flick-ing pages in her file. 'We can go through them now.' She backed her rump on to the big sack of dirty linen that was directly behind her and settled down to hatch an egg.

Gabriel looked around at his crew. Lunch service was about to start. He didn't have time for this. 'No,' he said, 'we can't.'

Oona laughed again. 'Don't make me get up, Chef. Got nice an' comfy here.'

'Right,' shouted Gabriel. 'That's it! Another warning. Second formal warning for you.'

Oona pressed her hand deep into her bosom. 'Warnin'?' she said. 'What for, darlin'? Why?'

Gabriel tore at his hair. 'Laughing,' he said, striding up and down, 'inappropriately. Inappropriate laughter. I'll take it to Human Resources this time. It's on my list. You're on my list, Oona, there's no escape.' He continued to pace.

Oona got up and patted her chest as if inviting him to snuggle down on it. 'Let's get you in your office,' she said, 'and have a nice cuppa tea.'

'Look at that,' said Gabriel, as she took his arm. 'Look at Damian! What time is it? Not even twelve and he's drinking.' He snatched his arm away from Oona and sprinted around the counters. 'Not in my kitchen,' he said, almost hollering, 'you don't get drunk in my kitchen. Not here, not on my time.'

Damian backed away from him, twitching and chewing on his tongue like a newborn calf. 'It's w-water,' he stuttered.

'Water?' roared Gabriel. 'Water?' He picked up the glass. 'Is that what it is?'

Oona waddled in front of Damian. 'Oh, bless him, poor ting, not drinking any more, m'mm.'

Damian's gormless face peered over Oona's shoulder. Gabriel raised the glass to his lips. He lowered it again and swept round. 'Everyone looking?' The kitchen had stopped work. Suleiman, Ivan, Victor, Nikolai and the rest stared back at him. 'Everyone looking?' repeated Gabriel. 'Oona, you got that boy under your wing? He's not drinking? This is not vodka? I don't know anything?'

Nobody spoke. An extractor hood gasped and wheezed. A big slug of vodka, thought Gabriel, was exactly what he needed, hell, it was what he deserved. He took a swig. Water. He pressed the glass into Oona's hand.

'The boy having a few troubles,' said Oona. 'Few troubles at home. Got him a bitta counselling and . . .'

But Gabe wasn't listening. He was watching Ivan staring down Victor and miming slitting his neck.

'Come with me,' called Gabriel, motioning to Victor. 'Yes, you, it's your lucky day. Come on. Jump to it.'

He stayed so hard on Victor's heels he almost pushed him down the stairs. 'In there. No, no, there. And yes, I'm closing the door.'

They stood in the meat locker. Victor's head was positioned between the two hanging halves of a suckling pig.

'This time,' said Gabriel, picking up a big beef shank and swinging it like a truncheon, 'I'm getting some answers. I'm getting some answers from you.'

'Tough guy,' said Victor, his right leg vibrating anxiously. 'Think you scare me?'

'We'll see,' said Gabriel. It was Victor who would tell him what was going on with Ivan and Gleeson. Victor knew. He hadn't fallen out with Ivan just over some girl.

'Man,' said Victor. 'This is bullshit.'

'What is it with you and Ivan? Did he cut you out of some deal? Some sordid little thing you had going with Gleeson?' Gabriel knew when a steak was done. He didn't need to work it out. He didn't time it. He just knew.

'You gonna hit me with that bone?' Victor sniggered.

'Maybe,' said Gabriel, whacking it hard against a metal surface.

Victor squealed something about harassment and lawsuits.

'Still watching all those cop movies?' said Gabe. He moved in close to Victor, close enough to see the pimples nesting in his eyebrows.

'Man . . .' said Victor.

Victor was the weak link. He was the one who would talk. That was why Ivan kept threatening him. Gabriel threw the shank aside. 'You think Ivan's your worst nightmare? I can protect you from Ivan. But who's going to protect you from me?'

'In Moldova . . .' began Victor.

'Fuck Moldova.' Time to cut the steak. 'You're in London now.' Gabe seized the sides of suckling pig and swung them against Victor's head. He squeezed the halves together with his forearms, crunching them on to Victor's cheekbones. Only his nose poked out. The nose went red, then purple. It pitted with white. Victor re-enacted the animal's last, piteous sounds.

'Are you going to talk?' said Gabriel. He was dizzy from squeezing so long, all the air pressed out of him.

A muffled yes escaped from the pig. Gabriel let go. Victor crumpled to the ground as if Gabriel had been dangling him by his head. Gabe squatted next to him. 'Go on.'

Victor rubbed his face with his sleeves. He spat and rubbed his mouth. 'Stinks.'

'What else can I do to encourage you?'

Victor sat up, propped against a shelf of vacuum-packed duck breasts. 'Ivan, that motherfucker,' he said. He dug in his pocket and pulled out a small bottle of cologne. He sniffed it like smelling salts.

'What did he do?'

'He gets girls from the hotel. He gets them and sells them on.'

'Yes,' said Gabriel. 'Girls from the hotel.'

'Cleaners. The maids. New ones coming in, so no one knows them, no one misses them.' Victor touched his cheeks. 'Have you marked me? Did you mark my face?'

Gabriel shook his head.

'The restaurant manager,' said Victor, 'he shows them photos. He says, you can earn more money there, working in this bar as a waitress or a dancer, whatever the story is. If they want to dance he shows them photos of dancers. If they want to sing he shows them, look, you can sing like her. *I got that job for this girl.*'

Yes, thought Gabriel, that would appeal to Gleeson, to use Charlie's photograph like that. It would give him a kick. When had he started to use it? Right away after the staff night out? Or later, when they had begun their slide into warfare?

'And then?' he said. 'What happens?' He knew how this story would go now, but he wanted to hear Victor tell it.

'In his smart suit, telling lies.'

'Yes, Gleeson, a good frontman, they'd believe him. They'd be scared of Ivan. And then?'

'That woman who's in charge of housekeeping? I don't know her name . . .'

'Branka.'

'Looks like one mean dude. If you saw her in a movie it'd be when they'd just checked into a hostel and the receptionist comes through the wall with a chainsaw. She'd be the receptionist, yeah.'

'Yeah,' said Gabe. 'Go on.'

'She brings them in. Selects them nice and fresh. Knows who's legal and illegal, who's desperate for money, who's got friends here who'd give a shit if they go AWOL, you checking me?'

'Yeah, yeah,' said Gabe. 'And then what? What happens next?'

'I'm not scared of that motherfucker,' said Victor, jutting his chin. 'I'll tell the whole fucking world.'

'Start with me,' said Gabe.

'Ivan, like, introduces them to the club, the bar, the whatever, that's the line. He takes them, he sells them like meat, man, two dollars a kilo.'

'He pimps them himself or he sells them to a pimp?'

Victor picked up his hat, stood and straightened himself. He ran a hand through his hair to make it stand up in cocky rows. 'How should I know? I told you what I know.'

'Well, you seem to know a lot,' said Gabriel. 'Were you in on it? Were you?' Gabriel sprang to his feet. He punched a beef loin that lolled on a hook.

'Fuck you, man.'

'What makes you so sure, then?'

'They picked the wrong girl. My friend from back home, but she didn't tell no one she knew me. Two days before, one of the other maids told her she was taking this new job, waitressing, Ivan arranged it and the money was very good. Then they brought my friend and talked to her early in the morning, they said look at this great opportunity but you have to go now, today.'

'So she didn't have time to think.'

'Yeah, but my friend she came and talked to me and I said, no, let me check it out first. I went to this place, this club, and – guess what – they weren't hiring, they didn't know Gleeson or Ivan.'

'And the first girl? The one who took the job?'

Victor clicked his fingers. 'Gone. Like that.'

'What about your friend? Is she here? Can I talk to her? Would she talk to me?'

'You think she hung around here? Jeez.' Victor had recovered his self-esteem. He measured up his reflection in a glass case, coming on to himself.

'It's all speculation,' said Gabriel, drifting between carcasses. 'We don't know anything.'

'Think about it,' said Victor. 'It's a beautiful system. You've got a ready-made supply of girls. None of that business about getting them away from home, smuggling them, all that shit. Less hassle, less expense, feed them through, get paid. Who's gonna care?'

'But there's no proof,' said Gabriel, shivering, finally feeling how cold it was.

Victor opened the door of the walk-in. 'Like I told you before. First time you brought me in for interrogation.'

'What?'

'You're better off not knowing. So why'd you even ask?'

He hunted Gleeson down to a meeting room in the marketing suite. He told the others to get out.

'Oh dear,' said Gleeson, smirking, 'have we forgotten our medication today?'

Gabriel kicked Pierre's chair. 'Go on. Clear off.' The bar manager stood up and clenched his fists.

The marketing executives drew breath audibly.

Gleeson, smiling tightly, said, 'I think the sentiment that Chef is trying to express is, would you excuse us, please?'

When they were alone, Gabriel prowled the length of the table and back again.

'Well,' said Gleeson, adjusting his cuffs, 'I don't mean to pry, but what is all this about?'

'I know,' said Gabe.

Gleeson cocked his head. 'Know?'

'I know everything,' said Gabe fervently, extending his fingertips to the ceiling.

'And might I enquire as to the nature of this enlightenment? Is it Damascene?'

'I know about the photographs. I know what you do with them.'

Gleeson straightened his papers. 'Much as I'd love to play this parlour game . . .'

He was about to get to his feet but in a bound Gabriel reached him and pushed him back into his chair. Gabriel swung the chair round and held the arms, trapping Gleeson, staring into his pale blue eyes.

'Do you deny it?' said Gabriel. 'Do you?'

'I neither confirm nor deny. I have no idea what you're talking about. Neither, I suspect, do you.'

Gabriel could see nothing in Gleeson's eyes except the sparkle of self-righteousness. It flowed through the iris like a cleaning fluid, scouring out everything else.

'I know about the girls. I've seen you. Branka brings them. For fuck's sake, I've seen.'

Gleeson began to hiss. 'You are in my *personal space*.'

Gabriel leaned in closer. He smelt fabric conditioner, hair dye and fear. 'I know what Ivan does with them. I know where you're spending the next ten years.'

Gleeson raised his foot and kicked Gabriel's knee so that the chair went spinning back on its wheels. He slithered out of his seat. 'I've had enough of this.'

'But it's you, you evil fuck, you persuade them to go with him.'

'If you ever, ever . . .' Gleeson sprayed the words like poison over the room. He stopped, pulled back his top lip in a sneer and shook his head. 'You are, quite clearly, mad.' He laughed. 'Oh dear, oh dear.'

'I'm going to . . .'

'Do go on. You're going to what?'

Gabriel's jaw became locked.

'You don't know anything,' said Gleeson, coolly. 'Perhaps you've been hallucinating, it's quite possible.'

'I'm going to . . . I'm going to . . .' Gabriel's arm jerked. He struck the table again and again. His other arm flew up to the back of his head. His whole body trembled and bucked with exertion, trying to halt his flailing arms.

'As I was saying,' said Gleeson, blowing a speck of dust from his sleeve, 'I've had quite enough of your insane insinuations. And while the substance of your allegations remains, it must be said, somewhat hazy, they are, of course, entirely slanderous. Should you take it upon yourself to repeat them, I shall be forced to complain most vociferously to the management, although I will naturally cite the mitigating circumstances of your deteriorating mental health.'

Gabriel finally wrenched his arms out of their contortions and immediately held tightly on to one with the other so that he was more or less hugging himself.

Gleeson flicked his tongue around his lips. 'Since you don't seem to know, Chef, what it is that you're going to do, permit me to make a suggestion. Take some time off, have a little break, check yourself into a clinic. You may not have noticed, but you appear to be having some sort of ghastly nervous breakdown.'

CHAPTER TWENTY-FOUR

—ııı—

BACK IN HIS OFFICE, WITH THE DOOR CLOSED AND THE BLIND STILL lowered, Gabriel skimmed from corner to corner, failing to find purchase anywhere.

Gleeson thought he was so clever, trying to turn the tables like that, threatening him with . . . with something which was no longer clear in Gabriel's mind, and which seemed, in consequence, all the more terrible. Gabriel raged silently.

Yes, he was furious. Who in their right mind wouldn't be? It was an outrage, the situation with the air-conditioning. Why hadn't it been fixed? He was under enough stress as it was. He would not blame Lena, although of course she . . . He took off his chef's coat and slung it on the chair. He missed Charlie so much, their relationship was dead and he'd had no time to grieve. But it was Gleeson, that bastard, don't get distracted, Gleeson was the one. Gleeson would get what was coming to him. It was much too hot. He stripped off his T-shirt. Gleeson could threaten whatever he liked. Gabriel did not even care. He floated above it all because he was leaving this place soon.

He'd promised Rolly a revised spreadsheet now that the final building costs were in. There was a fuck of a lot to do and he'd get down to it right away. Was it Wednesday today? The PanCont charity gala was on Saturday night and he'd barely begun to make plans. He took his trousers off and sat down.

Now he was ready to work. He opened up the spreadsheet. His

mobile rang. He saw from the screen it was Jenny but he would have to call her back later or he'd never get anything done.

Lightfoot's would be the place to go. He'd have his own place, finally. Nothing better than making a place your own, chef patron, stamp your own personality, just like Fairweather said.

He whittled at the figures. That was realistic. Or maybe not. Who knew? Who could tell? What was his personality, anyway? And if he didn't know what it was, how could he stamp it anywhere?

But he was wasting time. He jumped up, away from his desk, almost falling over in his haste. He had to get to the pastry kitchen, had to see Chef Albert and brief him about the gala now, this instant, straight away.

'*Bienvenu*,' said Chef Albert, wrapping an arm around Gabriel's shoulders. 'No formalities – *bravo*! We are all friends, *n'est-ce pas*?'

'Listen,' said Gabriel, urgently. It appeared to be bedlam in here. He might have to sort it out himself. He picked up a tray of choux pastry puffs and began tipping them into the bin.

'Sit down,' said Chef Albert, positioning a stool and pushing Gabriel down on to it. 'Sit down, my friend. You are tired, no?'

Gabriel admitted as much with a sigh.

'Energy drink,' said Chef Albert, handing Gabe a can. He opened another for himself. 'Gives you wings, like zis.' He flapped his elbows and ran around in a tight circle. 'Heh, heh, don't drink more than three. Four at the most. If you are very sleepy have another one or two.'

Albert's assistant giggled behind his hand.

Chef Albert brandished a rolling pin. 'In ze anus,' he promised gleefully.

The assistant retreated behind a barricade of ciabatta rolls and sourdough baguettes.

Chef Albert pulled up another stool and sat with Gabriel at the marble counter. 'I too feel zis exhaustion,' he declared. 'My new girlfriend, she is thirty years old. *Mon dieu!*'

Gabriel finished his drink. Chef Albert handed him another can. At these close quarters Chef Albert's skin was biscuity, his nose was iced with pink, and his eyes, which once had been deep and sorrowful, were only two burnt currants embedded in his head.

'Well, I'm sure,' said Gabriel. 'But I'm not here to talk about that. I'm here to talk about food.'

'Our first love,' cried Chef Albert. 'We will talk of nothing else. My *maman*, God rest 'er soul, was from Dordogne and she 'ave teach me what she love – confit, truffle, fois gras. And my *papa*, God rest 'is soul, was from Brittany, and from 'im I 'ave learn about ze seafood. One time we went to the river and – zis will make you laugh – ' He slapped the counter and laughed helplessly.

'What we need . . .' began Gabriel.

'Yes, yes,' roared Chef Albert. 'What we need – to relax, to laugh . . . You are always welcome in my kitchen. One time we went to the river . . .' He broke off as the assistant approached, a question on his lips. 'Get back!' shouted Chef Albert, waving his arms. 'Men are talking. Go back.'

'I was twenty-three and twenty-four,' he continued, 'when I was in military service in Africa. Two years in Ivory Coast and Senegal. I 'ave learn so much. In Senegal, they 'ave a dish with rice and vegetables and fried fish, and you eat from a big pot on the floor and you roll your sleeve, like zis, and when ze oil runs down to ze elbow it is – ' He smacked his lips. 'Perfect. And – zis is very funny – one day zey gave me some hot chilli chutney and I 'ave dip a prawn and – *incroyable* – like fire on my tongue and this mama comes . . .' He broke off once more to throw a wholegrain roll at the assistant who again had wandered too close. 'She says, I 'elp you, and we went to ze coconut tree and then . . . but you need another drink.' He jumped up. When he sat back down he began another story, about Corsica, which he did not complete before moving off into another anecdote.

The assistant looked on from a safe distance. Every time Gabriel glanced over he caught him staring. Gabriel frowned back.

For another twenty minutes he sat there half listening to Chef Albert's half-told tales. He drank another two cans. At the back of his mind there was a notion, increasingly dim, that he had come here to discuss something in particular. When his legs finally stirred themselves and he stood up he tried once more to rake up what that particular matter might be. He could not remember but about this he felt no sense of failure. On the contrary, his load was lightened, as if he had accomplished something. If anyone was going bonkers around here it was not Gabriel, it was Chef Albert.

'We are free spirits, no?' cried Chef Albert, grabbing Gabriel as he rose.

Gabriel, at the clammy feel of the hand on his skin, looked down.

'*Liberté, égalité, nudité,*' shouted Chef Albert, removing his white coat as Gabriel, in his socks and boxer shorts, padded swiftly out of range.

The main kitchen, between shifts, was deserted and Gabriel made it back to his cubicle without being seen. He dressed himself. At least he wasn't sweating now. At least he had cooled down. In fact it had been a good idea to sit chilling in pastry for a while. Was he ever one for following petty conventions? No, he had always gone his own way. He scratched the back of his head with both hands. He scratched until it hurt. He looked at his fingernails. They were covered in blood.

Damn it, why was everything turning against him? Why? What had he done to deserve it? He hadn't done anything. He was a good man. Basically, in his heart, where it counted, he was good. All he had ever done in his entire life was work hard, stay on the straight and narrow, and be as decent as he could. Well, fuck it, fuck them, and fuck it all. Gabriel leaned against the wall so that his arm was trapped. He felt the blood trickle down the back of his neck.

He worked himself into the space between the filing cabinet and the wall. This was a good place to think. Ha! He was resourceful. He was resilient. He was disciplined. He'd show everyone.

Strength of character, that was what it took. He had it, and in spades. He stared at the cracked plaster in the corner. Pins and needles in his arms.

Was he disciplined? Was he resourceful? What evidence did he have?

He pushed his weight on to the filing cabinet until it budged a millimetre or two.

If there were one, just one way he'd describe himself, it would be thoughtful. He never rushed into things.

Although with Lena, he had to admit, events had overtaken him.

Something surged and sucked back inside him, like a tide that was going out. He needed to know now, and he needed to know urgently, what he was. He grabbed at words. Fair. He was fair, oh yes, everyone said so, everyone knew it. He was fair and he was reasonable. That was him. A perfect description. Above all, he was a reasonable man. Maybe not this morning with Oona, no, that was out of character. He wasn't really like that.

What he was . . . though it was hard to think with the pain in his arm and the pain in his head . . . he was really . . . to everyone close to him . . . and he included . . . the main thing about him . . . loyal . . . oh, damn it . . . fun, funny . . . for Christ's sake . . . he knew what he was.

He was empty. The tide was far from shore.

For a few minutes he hung his head, his legs felt loose, and the only thing keeping him upright was being wedged between the filing cabinet and the wall.

What am I? he thought. What am I? The question pinged round and round plaintively until, firing faster and faster, it took on a sharper edge. What am I? What am I? A nobody? A nothing? A zero? Am I a hollow man? He was angry. He was furious. He backed out of the hole into which he had forced himself. He rubbed his arms to get the circulation started again.

Gabriel paced the office floor. What was he? Was he a man without qualities? A man about whom nothing could be said? No, he was somebody. He knew who he was.

He had cooked in a two-star restaurant in Paris. At the age of only twenty-four he had run a London restaurant with a friend. He had cooked in Austria, in Switzerland, in Brighton and Lyon. He had worked at the Savoy. He was somebody. He pulled up the blind and sat at his desk to survey his domain. He was somebody. He lacked only the right words. With a shaking hand he pressed the message button on the telephone. He listened and then played it again and once again. *You are through to the office of Gabriel Lightfoot, executive chef of the Imperial Hotel.*

'That's me,' said Gabe, out loud. 'That's my telephone, this is my office and that is me.'

The next moment he was seized by a new idea. It seemed to enter not so much his mind as his body, making him jump up and run out.

He couldn't describe himself. He couldn't see his own face. He would have to ask someone else.

'Suleiman,' he said, panting with excitement. 'Suleiman, if you had to describe me in three words, what would you say?'

Suleiman peered anxiously over the top of his imaginary spectacles. 'Chef, could you please repeat the question?'

'Three words. Describe me. First three things that come into your head.'

Suleiman looked aghast. 'Without preparation—' he began.

Gabriel had already moved on to Benny. 'OK, listen, this is not a trick question and you can say whatever you like. How would you describe me in only three words?'

'Only three words?' said Benny.

Gabe nodded eagerly. 'Yes, brilliant, you've got the idea. Good man.'

'I would say, tall.' He looked Gabe slowly up and down. 'Tall. White. Male.'

'No,' moaned Gabriel. He collapsed against the worktop.

'Chef?'

Gabriel sprang to life. 'Never mind.' He raced for the door. Only Charlie could help him. He had to see her now.

Twice, over the intercom, she told him to go away. 'Please,' he begged, 'I'll only stay two minutes. If you ever loved me . . . please.'

'Oh, you're really something,' she said, and buzzed him in.

He tried to embrace her in the doorway but Charlie dodged him, backed up quickly and inserted herself in a chair.

'Thank you for seeing me,' he said, trying to calm himself. He hovered on the rug.

'It better be good.'

'I have to talk to you, Charlie, you have to talk to me, there's no one else . . .' He bit his tongue to stop it babbling. He needed to anchor himself to something. He darted to the table and held it by two corners. If he let go he might float up to the ceiling like a helium balloon.

'What's that on your collar? Are you bleeding?' said Charlie, half getting up. 'Why have you come in your work clothes?'

'It's nothing, it's nothing,' said Gabriel. 'It's a scratch.' He glanced at the dark streaks on his fingers, the cakes of blood beneath his nails.

Charlie crossed her legs. She held herself so stiffly that her back became concave. 'Well? Let's hear it, whatever it is.'

'Darling . . .' said Gabriel.

'If you think . . .'

'No, no, let me explain. You're the one who really knows me. That's the reason I've come here. I know you won't . . . I know we can't . . . All I want is for you to tell me. And I'm the one who knows you too.' He was appalled by his burbling but still he carried on. 'We had some good times, do you remember? I remember. I haven't forgotten anything. When you broke a heel — that was our first date — and I had to . . .'

'Gabe! I'm going out soon. What do you want? What do you want me to tell you? That it's over? It is.'

'I know,' groaned Gabriel. 'You don't have to tell me that.' He let go of the table and began to drift around the room. 'Oh, for God's sake, Charlie, it's a mess. It's all a mess. What's happened to me?'

Charlie folded her arms. With her legs still crossed, she tucked a foot around the ankle of the other leg. The more Gabriel talked the tighter she wrapped herself away from him.

But he could not stop. 'You asked me why I became a chef. Do you remember? You do, I know you do — you see, I know you. I know how you are. Every look. That one too. What was I saying? Oh yes. By the way, am I talking too much? I won't keep talking. I'll sit down and then I'll ask . . . it's the only reason I came and it won't take two minutes, I promise you. Why a chef? I can't sit. Do you mind if I walk?' He walked and talked.

Abruptly, he stopped pacing and whipped round to face her. Charlie had grabbed a cushion and squeezed it to her chest. Her voice wavered slightly as she spoke. 'Gabriel, will you please calm down. Sit down and take some nice, deep breaths.'

'Charlie,' he cried, springing to her side. 'Don't worry. I'm fine. I'm sorry, I must look a mess. Should I wash my hands? Is there blood on my face? No? It's OK, I won't touch you. Now, look at me!' He took some deep breaths. 'I'm calm. I'm normal. I'm fine.'

Charlie put the cushion behind her back. She uncoiled a bit. 'Your father, what were you talking about? You were speaking so fast I couldn't . . . is he all right?'

'Oh yes,' he said, reassuringly. 'Dad's perfectly all right. Apart from the cancer. Apart from that. Now, where was I?' He took up his pacing again. His fingers were digging into the back of his head. The pain was stopping him thinking properly. 'I know,' he said, quickly patting his pockets, 'I'll have a cigarette. You don't mind. Otherwise, I keep scratching, you see. It's a little trick I've learned.' He smoked and weaved in and out of the furniture. Suddenly he saw everything clearly. Yes, he could face up to it now. 'All my life, Charlie, I've been drifting. I have. That's my problem. I'm owning up.' His voice rose as if in ecstasy. 'Drifting – from town to town, from job to job. Yes, from girl to girl. Don't . . . don't look at me like that. Can't you understand? My mother scared me. It's true. A boy never recovers. It's all . . . you never get away from . . .'

'Stop,' cried Charlie, getting up. She placed her hands fiercely on her hips. 'I've heard enough. You come round here and make excuses, the most pathetic excuses, blaming your mother – how do you think you'll get away with that? You cheat on me, you have a . . . I don't know what . . . with a . . . with some poor girl who . . . and you come round here and *explain* that it's all your mother's fault, and I'm supposed to . . . what? *I was scared of my mother* as if . . . bullshit, Gabriel, it's the first I've heard of it.'

'I wasn't scared of her,' said Gabriel, tapping ash into a vase. 'She scared me. Don't you see the difference? No, you can't throw me out. Close the door. Close it. I'll close it. Shit, sorry, mind my cigarette. Are you OK?' He trailed her like a shadow as she flitted around the room. His left arm began to jerk up. He stood still for a moment to light another cigarette. He held it in his left hand and smoked alternately from left and right. 'I'm getting to the point now, Charlie. I'm coming right to it.' Oh, she was lovely. He loved the way she tossed her hair. He should get on his knees. He should kiss her feet.

'What are you doing?' said Charlie. 'Why are you smoking, anyway?

You're dropping ash all over the place. Gabe, I want you to leave.'

'I will,' said Gabriel, passionately. 'I'll do whatever you want.'

'You shouldn't smoke.'

'It's a free country, isn't it? It's my choice.'

'It's an addiction. What kind of choice is that? Oh, I don't even want to argue with you. I just want you to go.'

'I'm not addicted,' said Gabe.

'You're smoking two cigarettes.'

'Because I want to,' declared Gabriel, lighting a third from the butt of his first. 'Now, will you tell me – and then I'll leave, for ever if you like. You don't want me to leave for ever, do you, Charlie? You don't mean that.'

'Tell you what?' said Charlie. She stood behind the sofa. He stood in front of it with his knees pressed into the seat. She looked down at his hands as if they held two smoking guns.

'Tell me what I'm like. Describe me. In as many words as you want.'

Charlie opened her mouth. She shook her head. She uttered a word he could not make out.

'Bit louder,' said Gabriel, trembling in anticipation. 'I couldn't hear.'

'Unbelievable,' said Charlie, loud and clear. 'You are fucking unbelievable.'

'Yes?' said Gabriel. 'Really? In what way?'

'You want me to talk about you?' shouted Charlie. 'It's all about you? You want me to tell you what you're like?'

'You're the one who knows me.' He could scarcely breathe but he pulled on one cigarette and then the next. In a moment she would tell him. Charlie, who knew him best.

'No,' she yelled. 'I won't do it. I'm not going to stand here and talk about you. I'm not interested. I don't care.'

'Oh, please,' said Gabriel with great ardour. 'I'll never ask you for anything else. All I'm asking for is a few words.'

'I'll tell you what you're like, then,' cried Charlie. 'You're selfish. You're the most selfish person I've ever met.'

'Oh, thank you,' said Gabriel, almost crying with relief. 'Selfish, I see, I'm sure you're right, not the best quality but still . . . and what else? Anything else you can think of? Anything at all?'

'Self-obsessed, pig-headed . . .' said Charlie. She began to count off on her fingers. Her eyes flashed. Her nostrils flared. She looked quite crazy but Gabriel didn't mind in the least. '. . . insensitive, unfeeling, stubborn, stupid, selfish, selfish pig!'

Gabriel sank on to his knees on the sofa. He tried to hold her but she escaped. 'I want to thank you,' he gasped, 'for your honesty, for speaking so freely. I want to thank you for . . . knowing me.'

Charlie crumpled into a chair. She shrank inside her clothes. 'Oh, Gabriel, I don't know you. I don't know you any more.'

Somehow he was in the street, and by some means he was moving although he seemed to make no contact with the ground. Perhaps he was being blown along like a paper bag. He didn't know where he was. Buildings, pavement, tarmac and then buildings again. What would it matter if he went on for ever this way? And was he moving or was it the street that moved? It seemed to flow around him. It seemed to pass through him.

He was sure now that he had stopped. He shivered. It was dark and cold. For a time he stood there and marvelled at the miracle of his own body, so true to itself, so fully occupied with shivering. The next moment an enormous jolt passed through him, as if he had received an electric shock. He began to run. His feet slapped the pavement so hard he could feel it in his teeth.

He ran and ran, every muscle, sinew, nerve ending on red alert. He could feel everything. He felt the marrow bubble in his bones. Only minutes ago he had been nothing, an empty husk, and now this. A million things were happening inside him, a frenzy of activity, dilations and contractions and connections, circuits made and lost, pumping and pounding, absorbing, excreting, reacting, every bit of him living and living from the skin of his fingertips to the very depth of his bowels.

And still there was more. He was crammed with fragments, memories, images, songs hurtling through his brain, a picture of his mother singing, a premonition it would rain, an advertising slogan – *the ride of a lifetime*, a snatch of conversation on a loop, Jenny riding a bike, Nana's clacking teeth. He kept on running. He was getting warm. He looked up at lighted windows, at streetlamps and neon signs. The lights streamed into him and he into them. The cars streaked, the buildings blurred, fuzzy people went by. And he wasn't whole, he was part of it, or it was part of him. He was in the blood-stream of the city that was in his blood. And he was growing hot, too hot, and he was only a molecule, a protein speck in the city and his bonds were beginning to break. At a certain temperature a globular protein will begin to uncoil. The basic science of cooking. He ran though his legs were shaking now. Heat a molecule and it vibrates more and more, and if the vibrations are strong enough a protein will shake itself free of its internal bonds. He remembered, he still knew this stuff. It was called denaturing.

He looked up behind him, head between his knees, trying to catch his breath. Upside down he read a street sign – Holloway Road. Oona lived here, somewhere close, this very area, maybe he would see her, she might get off that bus that was pulling up. He straightened and jogged over to the bus stop. The people queuing kindly moved out of his way but she was not there. Disembarking passengers stepped around him carefully. How considerate they were. He would wait here, take a seat in the shelter and rest. Oona would surely come. It wasn't a sign he had seen – it was a *sign*. How could it be a co-incidence? He hadn't meant to come here and yet here was where he was. As if some hand had guided him to this very place. Oona was the person he needed. Oona would put him right. Dear, sweet Oona. She would take him home with her. She would make him a cup of tea. His eyes filled. He rocked to and fro.

He shifted up to make space for a woman with heavy shopping bags but she didn't notice and walked to the kerb and set the bags down.

Over the road, in the window of a pizza parlour, a word flashed on and off – DELIVERY. He watched the buses come and go. There were signs everywhere. In the windows, above doors, on the walls. They were pasted on the sides of buses, painted on taxi rumps. They were in the leaflets and newspapers that flowered from the pavements. They were lettered on to the bins. They sprouted at junctions, splashed along hoardings, and shouted out from the billboards. Open, closed, no turning, three reasons why, no hot ash, deep discount, beauty, best value, fried chicken, free. Gabriel closed his eyes. Where was Oona? Why didn't she come?

He smelt the acid smell of old urine, the hard burnt smell of the road. Brakes flared, someone erupted, a radio blazed from a car. Gabriel burst into action. He had to get out of here before the whole place went up in flames.

For a long and unknown time he drifted and dissolved from one street into the next. The traffic began to drain, and the walls sucked people in. Lights flicked off, shutters closed. Gabriel was pulled along. He saw a man in surgical scrubs dry-heaving in a doorway. A tramp passed by holding a can of Special Brew and a mobile phone. A woman cycled on the pavement, a book tucked into the back of her skirt. Gabriel tried to get his bearings. He looked around. That was a train station. Where were the signs when you needed them?

A man approached. His face was round and waxy, like a church candle. 'How long have you been on the streets?'

'Oh,' said Gabe, 'I don't know. I lost track.'

The man smiled with infinite kindness. 'Yes,' he said, 'it's difficult, isn't it?'

'I don't know where I am.'

'Don't know if you're coming or going. Have you eaten tonight?'

'No.'

The man nodded. He seemed to understand everything. 'Do you want to come with me, and we'll get you sorted out?'

At last, thought Gabe. He began to shake. 'Yes. Where will we go?'

'Start with some food, shall we, and take it from there.'

Gabe reached out to the man and stumbled. He almost fell on his saviour. 'Where shall we go? I know a lot of places. I'm a chef, and I know . . .'

'Chef, were you?' said the man, retreating a little. 'Tell me all about it as we're walking. Soup van's parked around the back. Where are you going? Hey! Aren't you coming with me? We can find you a bed for the night.'

Gabriel stood on the bridge and looked down at the slick black water. The bloated city fizzed all around. He opened his mouth and let out a low moan. He looked up at the sky that seemed to hold, not stars, but the weak reflected lights of the never-ending earth. If Oona were here she would pray for him. He would pray for himself if he knew how. He fell to his knees and bowed his head to the railings. He dug deep, he squeezed, he wrung, he couldn't do it, he couldn't manage, he didn't have, he wasn't given, he'd never been blessed, and it was only tears that came. Oh, the pity of it. The pity. He lifted his head, he threw it back, have pity, have mercy, let us pray. *And now these three remain: faith, hope and love. And the greatest of these is love.* Oh, dear Lord, why do you not hear me? Why do you not help me? Why do you not exist?

CHAPTER TWENTY-FIVE

—◊—

HE IS IN THE CATACOMBS, DRIFTING, AND WHEN HE COMES TO THE place the body is not there. He looks into the other rooms as he floats down every corridor. Only one room remains, and when he opens the door it is filled with dazzling white light.

'Hello,' he calls. 'Hello?'

'Oh, there you are,' says his mother. She reaches out a hand from the far side of the room and takes a step towards him, the collar of her swingy white coat turned up, her earrings snagging on it. 'Oh, there you are. I've been looking all over for you.'

'Mum,' he says, squinting into the brightness. 'I'm sorry, Mum.'

'That's not why I've come,' she says.

'Is this . . . are we in . . . ?' He cannot see clearly. 'Are those wings on your back?'

'Don't be silly, Gabriel Lightfoot,' she says, laughing, 'and get yourself ready. Get your dressing gown on.' She turns on her heel, and calls out to him before she is swallowed up by the light. 'Ever seen a shooting star? Hurry up, Gabe! Don't miss it. Be quick. Don't miss it this time.'

He woke and sat up on the sofa. The sun licked a broad stripe down the sitting room from the casement window to the door. For a few moments he struggled to remember what had happened and why he had slept in his clothes. He blinked in the primrose light and rubbed his eyes, unfurling from his sleep. He had found his way home, walked the long night through, the dark edges of the sky beginning to crumple by the time he climbed the stairs. At most he'd had a couple of hours asleep. Some instinct had saved him. Something deep within delivered him home. Through all the tiredness, it shone in him now.

He crept into the bedroom and watched Lena sleeping. Usually he felt like a thief when he watched her, even if she was awake. But now, he knew, he would never take anything from her again. He would only give. She had not believed him when he said that he loved her. Well, she had been right. But he loved her now, pure and true. If he had loved before it was only blue flicker and red crackle, not this still white heart of the flame. She turned on her back. Love lifted him off his feet. He loved Lena as he should. He had it in him. He loved Charlie and always had. He loved Dad and he loved Nana and Jenny and Harley and Bailey and it was inexhaustible, inextinguishable, this love of his. He looked around at the blandly furnished bedroom and saw its potential. All it lacked was some photographs, some flowers, a few touches to bring it to life. Even a room needed love.

He went to the kitchen and checked the time. Nearly eight o'clock. He filled the coffee machine.

All night he had walked and thought. He had worked things out, he had come to realize, had come to understand . . . No, what he had done was suffer. If there was light in him now it wasn't because he'd screwed the bulbs in, it was the light of suffering. It had changed him and he had woken – it should be no surprise – to a new and better self.

He was glad of it. He wouldn't miss the old Gabe, that miser, counting his love like money, hoarding and rationing, seeking out bargains. With Lena he was always calculating who did what for whom in a trade that was never fair or free. All that careful accounting to make sure he got his share. What did he want from her anyway? What did he deserve?

He recalled with shame the many times he had shaken her down for information, sifting through her story for flaws and inconsistencies, marking them down as lies, every lie a debit chit. He had understood nothing.

'Why?' she would say, when he asked if it was the Bulgarian girl she had lived with first or the Ukrainian and whether it had been for six months or three. 'Why? What is difference to you?'

He wanted to believe her story. It had to have order and neatness. It had to be credible.

But life had not been reasonable to Lena. Life was random and cruel. And why should she, to please him, try to make sense out of it?

He wondered if the changes inside him would be reflected on his face. Was love visible? He went to the bathroom to wash and smiled serenely to himself. He wanted to see what others would see.

He almost reeled back but held on to the sink and lowered his eyes to the plughole. It wasn't possible. There had to be some mistake. He tried again. Again the image confronted him. A lunatic stared out of the mirror with red-rimmed eyes. His skin was grey, unshaven and flaked. He had a cut on his forehead and a green and purple bruise on his cheek. There was a wild look about him, his hair standing in tufts and clumps as if he had been pulling it out. His chef's jacket was stained with blood and other unidentified substances. He looked like a man on the run – an escapee from the asylum in a stolen white coat, a pathetic attempt at disguise.

Gabriel took a deep breath. It's what's inside that's important. Everyone knew that. But he ran the hot water, stripped for the baptism, shaved his face and brushed his teeth. He arranged his hair as best he could. Then he tiptoed into the bedroom and assigned himself a new identity with a red sweatshirt and a clean pair of jeans.

Lena had kicked the covers off. She sprawled across the bed like a homicide. Tenderness welled in Gabriel, and a new feeling grew in him. The fact that he had met Lena held great importance. It was meant to be. The feeling nurtured itself; it grew and thrived. Their meeting had been momentous. It had changed their lives. It was not some hapless and shoddy encounter. He would make sure of that. He touched his fingers to his lips.

Although minutes ago he had been certain that life was random and beyond control he was in no doubt at this moment that everything happened for a reason. He was meant to help Lena and help her he finally would. Lena was not insignificant. He would not let all that had happened be meaningless.

He would begin by emptying his bank accounts. There wasn't much left after putting the sixty thousand in . . . Never mind. The point was to make a start. He fizzed around the flat gathering his wallet, watch, keys, chequebooks and, in an inspired move, the passbook for a long-fallow Post Office savings account. He was fired by a sense of purpose. There was so much you could do if you opened your heart. And it wasn't just Lena – he would seize every chance.

All the limits he had placed, all the walls he had built! Let them come crashing down. He would not cut himself off any more. He would be involved. He would live. What would he do? Everything! He would go out there and do it now. He was ready and he would begin right away with random acts of kindness and senseless acts of love. Was that a song? He had heard it somewhere, something like it, and it was beautiful. There's beauty. There's beauty if you take the time to look. But he was wasting time and he would go now, descend into the world and see what he could do.

Immediately an opportunity presented itself. The front door of the opposite flat stood open and it could not be more obvious.

'Hello,' he called. He popped his head round the door. 'Hello,' he said again with great warmth as he stepped inside the sitting room. 'Isn't it a beautiful day?'

That was an excellent start. He was managing to keep himself calm although he was bursting with good will and energy. He didn't want to startle his neighbours. He would ease into conversation.

'Uh,' said the woman. 'Hi.' She stopped in her tracks in the middle of the room.

'I'm Gabe, your neighbour. It's silly, isn't it, I don't even know your name.'

'Sarah. As you can see . . .'

'Sarah, that's lovely, and your husband is – or your boyfriend?'

'Down at the van.' She seemed a little nervous. She pushed her hair behind her ears. 'Be up in a moment, though. Can I . . . Can I help you?'

Gabriel observed her keenly. Before today he had noticed nothing about her. About thirty, dark brown hair, that was all he could have said. Now he saw everything – athletic shoulders, strong hands, a scattering of freckles, a crooked incisor, the wrinkle at the bridge of her nose that made her look as if she were reading the small print.

'Can I help you?' she said again.

'Oh no,' said Gabriel. 'If anything, I'm here to . . . but let's start with a little chat. Getting-to-know-you type thing. What is it that you do? Is it advertising? You look like . . . something in the media? Aha! I'm getting warm. Television? Is that it?'

She took a step backwards. 'I'm sorry,' she said, 'but as you can see we're rather busy. We're moving out today.'

Gabriel looked around. To his astonishment, the room, which a moment ago had appeared perfectly normal, was a wasteland – a couple of chairs and a few cardboard boxes remained. He scratched his head. It seemed impossible. He was so alert, so . . . so . . . ah, there were two shelves that had been missed. He would pack the items for her. He would load the boxes on the van. 'What a shame!' he cried, bounding over. 'But let me help.' He grabbed some books and put them in an open box. He shoved in some papers and files.

'Excuse me,' said Sarah. 'What do you think you're doing?'

'It's nothing,' panted Gabe, working feverishly. 'Glad to help.'

'Don't touch them. Please! Stop it! You've muddled my papers. I was keeping those things . . . Oh God, now you've broken that. Leave it alone. No, leave it all. I'll pick it up.' She stooped to retrieve the jewellery box. The lid had cracked. As she came up, Gabriel's arm, unbidden, went off and ricocheted off her head.

'Oh my God, oh my God,' she shrieked. Her voice had become so shrill it set him twitching and jerking again.

He lowered his head to hers. 'I think if we could speak quietly, whisper like this, then it'll all be fine. Let me take a look at that for you. Do you have any ice?'

'Get away!'

'Oh, such a shame you're leaving,' he said, flooding with neighbourliness. 'Where you going to? Not too far, I hope. I mean, we could still meet up, couldn't we?'

Sarah was trying to say something, but all that emerged from her mouth was a dab of foamy spit.

'Still hurting?' said Gabriel. 'Poor thing. Sure you don't want me to take a look?'

She was probably quite shy. Right from the moment he'd come in, he'd noticed how hard it was for her to communicate. No wonder they'd remained strangers until now. The fault had lain with him.

Sarah pulled out her mobile phone. She found her voice. 'I'm calling the police,' she said, a little hysterically. 'I'll have you arrested if you don't get out of here.'

It was certainly harder than he had imagined. By mid-afternoon he had been shouted at, sworn at, spat at, kicked and generally abused. Worst of all, a little girl had burst into tears. But he felt OK. The light had not gone out. For the first time in his life he could honestly say that at no time during the day had he walked by on the other side.

He had been to the bank and the Post Office and had the money in his pockets – £8,570 and some change. He ran upstairs to the flat, his trainers barely skimming the wooden treads.

Lena, dressed in her mourning clothes, was sitting on the edge of the bed, her hands tucked under her thighs.

He stood in front of her, only shaking very slightly. 'Hey,' he said gently. 'Guess where I've been. Guess what I've been doing.'

She lifted her face and looked right through him. 'I don't care,' she said.

'I know,' he said. 'Why should you? But look – I've brought you this.' He pulled the envelopes out of his jeans and his sweatshirt and laid them on her lap.

'What it is?' said Lena, still sitting on her hands.

'Have a little look,' he pleaded. 'Go on, open them.'

Lena pulled her hands free. She picked up the first envelope, felt the wad of notes, and slid a finger under the seal. Quickly she moved to the second envelope and the third. She put the envelopes on the bed, picked up the first again and pulled the money out. She began to count. After a few seconds she broke off. 'My money,' she said.

He assured her it was so.

She carried on counting, began on the second envelope then

quickly measured it against the first. 'How much?' she said. 'How much money for me?'

'All of it,' said Gabriel. He pulled up the chair and sat opposite her. 'Tchh,' she said.

'Eight thousand, five hundred and seventy pounds,' he declared. 'Everything I have. Well, there's seven pounds something in my pocket but that's all.'

Lena twisted her earrings. She looked angry. The tendons in her neck ridged up.

'Lena,' said Gabriel, urgently, 'it's not a joke. I'm serious. I want you to have it. I wish it was more.' The phone rang in the kitchen. He left it to the answering machine.

'What . . . what I have to do?'

'Nothing. You don't have to do anything. It's yours. You can do . . . anything you like. I'll help you get a flat, find a job . . .'

'Tchh,' she hissed at him. The blood raced to her cheeks.

When he looked at her now he marvelled at how wonderfully real she was, because so many times he had had the feeling she was only something out of his dark imaginings.

'I've let you down,' he said. 'Forgive me. But you can trust me, honestly.' From somewhere in the sitting room his mobile cried out in alarm.

'You find flat and job?' said Lena. 'Like you find Pasha for me.'

'Sorry, I'm sorry,' he mumbled.

She stayed quiet and after a while he looked up at her. He looked at this young woman, red-cheeked and white-knuckled with defiance, and he was truly crushed. What had he done? How could he ask for forgiveness when it was the last thing he deserved?

How, oh, how had it happened? Why had he not behaved – as he knew from the very start – the way he should? He had given free rein to his impulses, turned his desires into needs and his needs into obsessions, all in the service of – what exactly? Himself, of course. Me, myself and I. It was as though he had some monster lurking inside him, some great and greedy ever-feeding beast, some half-blind animal enraged by an old wound, some troll beneath the bridge, a narrow and boundless figment, his certified and monstrous self.

He thought that he had woken to a new and better Gabe. Who was he kidding? No, he had not slain the beast. He had patched its wounds. And now he was – *forgive me* – asking Lena to do the same.

Gabriel held his head in his hands. He sobbed and was ashamed.

'Is OK,' said Lena. 'No need for cry.'

He could not stop. He felt her hand on his shoulder as if she wanted to comfort him. He tried to dry his eyes so he could look at her and tell her on the level that it was all right, that she had every right to despise him, that she did not have to pretend.

'Lena,' he said, still choking. 'I know that you . . .'

He looked into those eyes where he had so often looked and seen nothing, as if they were milky with cataracts. They were clear, bright blue. And he saw in them pity. He saw compassion. Wasn't that a kind of love? He was more afraid of it than of her hate. Despite everything . . . in spite of it all . . . love was what remained. Gabriel could not speak. He bowed his head.

'Gabriel,' said Lena, delivering a chaste kiss on his crown, 'like the angel.'

He heard her gathering the envelopes and slipping out of the room.

A little while later, Gabriel called Oona and told her that he'd gone home with a migraine yesterday, that it had taken until now to clear and that he was on his way. As soon as he left the building he turned round and went back up to the flat. There was something he had forgotten. If only he could remember what it was. Stupidly, he checked all the rings on the cooker were off. It was pointless but nevertheless soothing. Lena sat circling ads in her newly bought copy of *Loot*.

'These flatshares,' said Gabriel, 'it'd be better if I came with you to check them out. You never know what . . .' He couldn't finish the sentence. The hypocrisy made him sick.

Lena hardly looked up. 'Yes, is better,' she said.

He went to the newsagents and bought a packet of fags, which left him with less than the two pounds he needed for the bus. At some point last night he must have lost his travel pass. He thought briefly about borrowing some cash from Lena. *Trust me*, he had said, *the money's yours*. He would have to walk.

He crossed Westminster Bridge against the flow of office workers in the midst of their daily exodus. To get to work he needed to go north along Whitehall and then up Haymarket. Instead he walked south-west down Victoria Street and turned left on Buckingham Palace Road. When he reached the coach station he stood outside at the crossroads looking up at the white deco building, then over at the construction works, the row of turquoise Portakabins, and the stone colonnade that fronted the shopping mall. What was he doing here?

He entered the building and drifted aimlessly for a while. He looked overhead at the signs as if they might provide a clue. Arrivals, Gates 2–20, Toilets, Bureau de Change, Continental Check-in, Left Luggage, Refreshments. He sat down by Gate 12, which was for the coach to Harrogate. A large African family, their luggage packed in laundry bags, squabbled among themselves in French, two Arab men argued over tickets with an inspector, a couple of Asian porters, on a break, ate rice from Tupperware. Gabriel had taken out his cigarettes before he saw the notice – NO SMOKING, *ZGODNIE Z PRAWEM*.

Gabriel moved on, looking for somewhere to smoke. He paused by the timetable that was fixed to the wall. Who was it that wanted to get the National Express to Port Talbot at 03.35? Or the Megabus to Sheffield leaving at 04.05, or the 03.20 to Bridgend?

He found a café and spent a pound on a cup of tea. He smoked a cigarette and then another. A tramp asked for change and Gabriel emptied what was left in his pocket. He needed to ring Jenny back. It had probably been her calling earlier on. He looked through his ruck-sack but all he had packed was a fresh set of whites, must have left his mobile at home. As soon as he got to the Imperial he would call.

After an hour or so the waiter tried to clear his mug. Gabriel held on to it. Another waiter came on shift but left Gabe alone. Gabriel watched the drift of the terminus. As it grew later the travellers began to change. There were fewer families and more young men, many in dirty work clothes.

Eventually Gabriel got up and went to sit on one of the grey metal seats that served the gates. It was the middle of dinner service and he should have been standing at the pass. But his long night of walking had caught up with him and every muscle hurt. His legs were stiff.

He'd sit a while longer yet. A peak-capped official passed by swinging a bunch of keys on a chain. On the opposite bench an elderly gentleman in brogues and spectacles read a catalogue of antique maps. Next to him a group of Eastern European workers solemnly passed round a pornographic magazine. The station grew busier as evening turned into night. Some people had to sit on their bags and the air became humid.

Still, Gabriel could not move. What was he doing? Once upon a time he had told Lena that he had been here to search for her brother. Was this the reason he had come? A part of him believed it, a part of him did not, and some other bit didn't wish to consider the matter at all. It was as if he were divided into three selves. The first self wanted to go back in time and set a few things right, the second laughed at the absurdity of this idea, and the third's only and ardent wish was for the other two selves to go away.

Finally, when the smell of cheap food and tinned beer had saturated his skin, when the grind and squeal of the coaches slinging into the slip road had set his ears jingling, when he could taste on his tongue not only his own tiredness but that of the travellers, he shook himself down and left. Outside he watched a procession of coaches, white, orange, green and blue. He glanced back down the side street. The first thing he saw was an Imperial Hotel minibus, stopped at a pedestrian crossing. The crest and lettering had worn away or been removed but the outlines remained so that the words were clearly legible. The bus moved on, turned off at the first right and parked outside a restaurant. Gabriel followed along.

A group of around twenty people, mostly young and male, with meagre baggage and wary faces, tested the edges of the pavement with shuffling feet. They made unlikely hotel guests. Gabriel put his hood up. He leaned against a wall and watched. The driver got down from the bus and spoke in some Slavic language. He began to count heads. He had to be picking up cleaners to take them for a shift at the hotel, though Gabriel at this moment couldn't think why they should have their luggage with them.

The driver didn't seem satisfied. He went back on the bus and emerged again with a sheet of paper, perhaps some kind of list. Gabriel pushed off from the wall and shuffled into the mix. A man, one of the older ones, began to cough as if he would bring up a lung. A woman looked over her shoulder at Gabe and when he began to smile at her she flinched and looked quickly away. Gabe strafed the gathering, darting looks here and there. Casually, he turned round and there through the crowd he saw him, Lena's brother or lover. Pavel. Pasha.

Gabe tipped his head to the purple sky as if to acknowledge an answered prayer. He felt no jealousy and for that, if for nothing else, he was deeply grateful. He risked another glance at Pasha to make sure he wasn't mistaken. The square head, the purplish lips, it had to be him. The driver had started the head count again. Gabriel stayed in line. He'd get a ride up to the Imperial and talk to Pasha there in private. It would only cause a commotion if he tried to explain himself here.

The group began to board. Gabe stepped up and took a place at the back. For a few minutes he watched the splattered lights of the city rush towards him as hushed conversation pattered down like rain, and then he succumbed to the hum of the engine, the well-worn air, the roll and rattle of the seat. He closed his eyes.

CHAPTER TWENTY-SIX

THE HEADLIGHTS SHIVERED OVER HEDGEROWS AND GABRIEL, AT THE back of the bus, shivered too. The harder he tried to stare out of the window the more his own reflection got in the way. He wiped his hand across the glass and then turned his head to look at his fellow passengers. Of the three seats at the back, one was taken by Gabriel, another by bags and the third by the man who had been coughing as they lined up. He wore a black and red anorak which rode up over his face, and the sleeves had eaten his hands. From the angle at which he leaned into the corner, Gabriel judged him asleep. Several others were also slumped but most seemed intent on scrutinizing the dark world beyond the glass, quietly taking leave of each new section of road.

They weren't in London but where they were or how much time had passed, Gabriel did not know. He could see the back of Pasha's head, packed in a black beanie hat, towards the front of the bus. The seat next to him was occupied, much to Gabe's relief. He was going to talk to Pasha but thank God there was no possibility of doing it now. He needed some time to think. Pasha would ask a hundred questions and Gabe wanted his answers prepared.

SWAFFHAM, said the road sign, 5 MILES. What the hell was an Imperial Hotel minibus doing in Norfolk? Gabriel's stomach clenched. He didn't belong on this bus, with these people, he wasn't one of them. He wanted to shout to the driver to stop and let him off but forced himself to stay quiet. He hummed a tune in his head, some nursery rhyme, and it calmed him. It was all OK, no one had kidnapped him, and there was a reason why he was here even if he did not know exactly where he was. He couldn't get off in the middle of nowhere, in the middle of the night, with no money and no phone. For now he'd go along with everything, find out what was going on, and in the morning it would all be different when he told them who he was. For a while he stared at the back of Pasha's head, and then he dozed again.

He was woken either by the smell of manure or the epileptic fits and starts of the motor as the bus stalled its way down the dirt track. In the pallid dark he saw a dog chasing down a moonbeam across a stubbled field. The bus pulled into a yard in front of a long row of animal sheds. Leaving the headlights on and the motor running, the driver got off and closed the doors behind him. Inside the bus there was a general shifting and stirring, the sound of things not being said. Gabriel pressed his face against the window and got a better look at the sheds, which now appeared more like army barracks, flat-roofed, metal-shuttered, purposeful, comfortless. On a line strung between building and tree the defeated washing hung like a warning, echoed in the scrawling cracks of the plasterwork, a fate written into the dead shape of things.

From somewhere out of the gloom a second man joined the driver and they entered through one of the three doors. Light leaked from behind the shutters, voices were raised, shouts went up, something or other crashed down. Gabriel gripped his rucksack as if his life were contained in it. He watched as the men emerged from the low chamber and stood uncertainly in the yard. They formed a ragged line. They were tall and wiry, dark, unshaven, foreign, Afghans or Kurds, and the contents poked out of their hastily packed bags. They stood in silence. One of them ran over to the washing line and began to stuff the clothes into a plastic sack. The others remained in the glare of the headlights as if facing a firing squad.

Gabe tried to exchange glances with his fellow passengers but no one, it seemed, would look at anyone else for fear of confirming what they saw. The Afghans' small stores of resistance had been spent and

393

now they were resigned. Gabriel felt the same way. There was nothing for it but to see how this played itself out. Even if he spoke, would anyone understand? If they understood, would they listen? If they listened, would they care? In the kitchen, he spoke and others obeyed. But if he got up and started talking now, what difference would it make?

The driver returned to open the bus doors and shout instructions. Gabriel followed the others and got down. He listened carefully while the second man shouted more orders as if he might glean something from the intonation, might hear some meaning in the foreign words. Again, he had no option but to fall in with the rest, forming a single line for another headcount. It was as if he had slipped into another dimension. One ride on a bus and he had left the known world behind.

He was too weary anyway, and in the morning, once he'd spoken to Pasha, he would get out of here.

They filed into the barracks and squashed into what seemed to be some sort of kitchen, although there was also a mattress on the floor. Gabriel looked over his shoulder as he entered and saw the Afghans in a blur of light, being sucked into the bus.

The kitchen smelt so strongly of onions and burnt oil and bodies that it made his eyes begin to smart. There was a two-ring hob in the corner, a microwave with a blackened door, a sink full of pots and pans, dirty plates and open cereal packets on the surfaces and, squatting under the window, a chest freezer spattered with rust spots. Gabriel looked at the only two women, their pinched faces and large red hands, standing close together, guarding each other's space. Gabe's back-seat companion leaned on a rickety table and succumbed to a coughing fit, making a horrible clacking sound as if shaken to his very bones. There were lines beneath his eyes, thick and black, tattoos of fatigue. The supervisor began to speak. Although nobody said anything he seemed to get angry, his bald red head burning up. He clapped his hands.

At this signal, one man simply dropped down and lay on the mattress but the others began to disperse into the corridor and divide up among the rooms. Gabriel didn't see where Pasha went so he followed the coughing man.

A naked light bulb lit the room, which rightly belonged in the dark. The place was fetid. There were two metal-framed single beds, one made of soft cheap pine, and a fold-out camp bed. A mattress leaned against the wall, a tall cupboard with broken hinges stood in a corner, and a camping fridge masqueraded as a kind of bedside cabinet. Despite the signs of habitation it seemed unlikely that any life form would flourish here, except perhaps the mould that bloomed in large patches along the walls.

Gabriel ended up with the camp bed and was grateful that he'd avoided the mattress, which was now wedged into the small space left on the floor and would have to be vacated if anyone wanted to open the door. He took off his sweatshirt but kept his jeans and socks and T-shirt on and climbed under the still-warm sheet. Lying on his stomach he watched a silverfish swim across the carpet. The light went off.

For a while he tried to put together a story for Pasha, but he didn't know how much to tell or how it should be told. He passed a couple of turbulent hours, unsure if he was awake or asleep, unable to distinguish between reality and dream: a barking dog, a sob, an owl screech, a looming human shape, a crushing weight on his legs, tiny creatures scratching his face. When the light came on again he was glad to crawl out of bed. He queued for the bathroom and in the kitchen ate a slice of thin white bread out of the pack that was passed around. Someone gave him a mug of black tea. Within half an hour, he calculated, he'd be on his way, while these poor sods dug potatoes or sweated in polytunnels, picking lettuces for supermarket shelves.

Outside, once more they lined up. The supervisor passed down the ranks ticking off names and filling in details. Gabriel couldn't see Pasha, but he had to be here somewhere. The moment he spotted Pasha, he would go and talk to him and then he would leave straight away, take Lena's brother or lover back with him if he would go. Now that it was daylight he was beginning to see clearly again. It was stupid of him to have waited the entire night to approach Pasha. It would be easy. All he had to do was give him Lena's mobile number and she could tell him whatever she wanted to. Gabe couldn't tell her story for her. It was up to Lena what she told.

Gabriel scanned the line again and thankfully saw him this time. *At last*, he thought, *I have done something. I have done something for her.* His heart began to race. He slipped out of position and moved down close to Pasha, who immediately looked furious as if telling Gabe to back off. Hoping to draw him discreetly aside, Gabriel put a hand on Pasha's arm. In a somehow threatening gesture, Pasha removed his hat.

Was it Pasha? Gabriel was no longer sure. 'Lena,' he said. 'She's looking for you. I can take you to her.'

The man swore at him with his eyes. Had he even understood what Gabriel had said?

'Lena. You know her? Lena. She's a friend of mine.'

The name seemed to make no impact. The man spat on the ground. Gabriel shuffled past and went to the end of the line.

He looked at a row of silver birches, pretending not to know that everyone was looking at him. Though he stood up straight, inside he was collapsing. He had just about had enough. He could never do anything right. Whatever he tried to do it turned out some other way. He had tried to do something for Lena, but it was hopeless. He was wrong, wrong about everything, from the moment he woke to the moment he fell asleep, and the rest of the time as well. Over and over, he berated himself until all the words became meaningless and he was unable to latch on to a single thought, unable to comprehend a single thing, as if all that he had known had been taken away from him, the whole world revealed as a lie.

The supervisor, at last, reached Gabriel. 'Im'ia?' he said.

Gabe shook his head.

'Im'ia!' demanded the supervisor. 'Nazwisko?'

Gabe watched some men disgorge from the far end of the barracks, six workers who had escaped eviction last night. He envied the sense of purpose with which they climbed into the back of an open truck.

The supervisor poked Gabe in the chest with a pen. Gabriel shrugged. Everything he did would be wrong so he wouldn't do anything. The supervisor said something under his breath, crossed the yard and returned with another man who wore a waxed green jacket, green wellies, his hair in a sharp side parting and a look of sparkling contempt in his eyes. If Gabe had seen him a few minutes earlier he would have sworn that he recognized him from somewhere, but now he had given up making judgements like that.

'So,' said the man, while the supervisor bobbed around deferentially, 'this the one?'

'Yes,' said the supervisor, his accent so heavy it clattered on the flag-stones, 'he don't say nothing.'

The boss – although Gabriel wished to judge nothing he could not help himself – put out his hand for the clipboard. 'So this one doesn't know who he is.' Briefly, he checked the papers and then gave a tight, smug smile. 'Only one name left on here, Tymon, my friend. What do I pay you for, eh?'

Tymon tried to shred Gabriel with a glare.

'Danilo Hetman?' said the boss, turning away.

Gabriel said nothing.

Tymon divided the group into threes and fours and put Gabe together with the coughing man who introduced himself as Olek, and the two women who remained tight-lipped. They walked out past the silver birches and a sign reading Nut Tree Farm, past a tumbledown cottage with brambles growing out of glassless windows, and over a fern-matted stream. The fields stretched to the ends of the earth. Tymon handed out gardening forks. He reached down and dug out a bunch of spring onions and knocked off the earth against the tines, complet-ing the operation in quick, disparaging movements as if this were the easiest work in the world. He looked at the group with one clear message: what are you waiting for?

The women rapidly arranged themselves either side of the next long green row and, squatting on their haunches, began to break the soil. Gabriel finally opened his mouth. Before he could speak, Olek nudged him in the ribs and then bent down to work. Tymon turned to leave and Gabriel, knowing this had gone on long enough, stepped forward as well, but Olek banged his ankle with his fork in a way that made him stop at once.

Gabriel stooped and turned over a clod of thick black earth and shook some onions free. He looked at Olek, working further down the row, at how hooded and bruised his eyes appeared. It was touching that Olek, a total stranger, had tried to help him, preventing him from getting into trouble by stepping out of line.

Gabe swept his hand across the emerald-green onion blades and watched how firmly they sprang back into place. He inhaled the mineral richness of the soil and the vivid succulence of the plants. A breeze tickled the back of his neck. The sun shone weakly in a near-cloudless sky. All the way to the horizon, the fields waved mild and bright. Gabriel set to work.

Tymon drove up in a battered white truck and unloaded a stack of blue plastic crates, which Olek distributed among the group. Gabriel knelt down to gather his onions and lay them carefully in the first box. He stayed on his knees to dig, trying to disperse the pains that had congregated in his back and shoulders. The damp spread quickly along the legs of his jeans, dark patches reaching up his thighs. He stabbed and twisted with the fork and loosened the next clump of onions. He brushed the soil off with his hand, admiring the pearly skin and delicate curling roots. He fell into a rhythm, pushing, pulling, turning, brushing, his body leading the way, his mind merely following. One time he looked up and saw a curlew, its long brown trunk and the two white bars across its wings, circling overhead, but otherwise he was fully absorbed, his knees sinking into the earth as if he had put down roots of his own. The first crate filled and he began to pack another. As he worked he listened intently to the soft thwack of metal into the soil, cushioned in the stillness all around. He watched a centipede ripple up the handle of his fork, a mighty little military parade, and with one finger laid it tenderly on the ground. He carried on.

When Olek tapped him on the shoulder and by a simple gesture said it was time for a break, Gabriel was astonished to see that the women had filled four boxes each and Olek was on his fifth, while Gabe had managed only two. All his joints protested as he struggled to his feet. They sat on upturned crates and knocked the soil off their hands. The others had brought knapsacks with bread and cheese and water. Gabe's mouth filled with saliva. His stomach howled. He walked a little way off and lit a cigarette, not wanting to embarrass the others with his need.

The cigarette tasted foul and he put it out. He didn't feel like smoking today.

Olek came up beside him. 'Ukrayinets?'

Gabriel shook his head.

'Polyak?' Olek coughed and took a packet of tobacco from his pocket. The tips of his fingers were thick and slightly flattened. 'Serb? Rosiyanyn?' He found his papers and began to roll.

Gabriel smiled apologetically. 'English.'

Olek started. 'English?'

'Yes.'

Olek shrugged and looked into the distance as if they had come out here to admire the view. 'OK,' he said. After a couple of moments he reached into the inside pocket of his anorak and took out two plain biscuits which he offered without comment.

'Thanks,' said Gabriel. He ate them casually, trying to conceal his hunger. 'Here,' he said, holding out his pack of cigarettes. 'I don't want them. You can have them if you like.'

Olek nodded and took the cigarettes. 'Must working,' he said, as Tymon drove by with the window down and his angry head sticking out.

At first Gabriel thought that he would not be able to bend his back sufficiently to continue. He managed to get to his knees but then seized up. The pain made him bite on his tongue. He clawed at the earth with his hands. He poured all that he had left, his entire being, into pulling up the next bunch and when he succeeded he felt a great sense of accomplishment, as if he had delivered not a handful of salad onions but something of great worth. He ignored the pain by focusing on the rough wooden handle of the fork when he picked it up, the way the tines glinted when the earth slid off, the crisp boldness of the green shoots, the coy lustre of the bulbs. He worked and scarcely looked up for there was so much to see where he knelt, a hundred shades of black in the peat. It was as if until now he had seen the world only in a blur, in fat brushstrokes, unable to distinguish the details. He watched a beetle walk officiously over the back of his hand, he crumbled the soil with his fingertips, he watched the waves of muscular contraction that propelled a worm, shortening and lengthening, across the furrow. He felt the cool touch of the wind on his face, he felt the breath enter and leave his body, he felt alive.

He worked on, noticing everything and asking no questions so that there was only the flow of one moment into the next and it came to his mind that he had never done this before. All his life had been spent in planning, asking what came next, or looking back at what had already been, so that the present, that infinitesimal slice of now, between a future that never arrives and a past always out of reach, was only a dim possibility, as if life could never be truly lived. He observed the thought but then, instead of filling his head with voices, with arguments for and against, he rubbed the sap from a green shoot between his fingers and filled his lungs with air.

That night he slept like a king in a four-poster bed, undisturbed by dreams. When he woke, though he could smell his own body and when he stretched his arms and rubbed his eyes he could see the dirt beneath his nails, he was relaxed and fresh. Instead of queuing for the squalid bathroom he went outside to urinate in the field and listen to the birdsong. Gabe's mind was pleasurably blank. He felt like hugging himself, like a child who has run away out of the back door, immeasurably content to escape from his parents' latest row. He would have to go home at some point, but he would not go quite yet.

Some of the young men kicked a football in the yard and one used a bucket of water for a wash. Olek sat on a wooden bench in his over-sized anorak, tossing a coin. Gabe sat down next to him.

Olek spun the coin, caught it, and slapped it on the back of his hand with his other hand covering it. He nodded to Gabe.

'Heads,' said Gabriel.

Olek removed his hand. He smiled, showing his brown teeth. He tossed again.

'Heads,' said Gabriel.

Olek revealed the coin, and then threw it in the air.

'Heads.'

They both laughed this time.

Olek tossed and slapped the coin down on the bench, keeping it concealed. 'What is chance,' he said, 'for to be heads?'

Gabriel considered. 'Luck's got to break. Had three in a row, so I reckon the chance of it being heads now is . . . one in ten, one in a hundred, I don't know.'

Olek shook his head. 'No, chance is one in two. Fifty-fifty. Only two possibility. Every time chance is same.'

A van drove into the yard and Olek picked up the coin. He stood up and said, 'Food.'

The driver opened the van's back doors and a group gathered round, buying bread, packet ham, cereal, milk.

'When do we get paid?'

Olek coughed and lit up one of Gabriel's cigarettes. He held up two fingers of his other hand.

'Two days? The end of today?'

Olek shook his head.

'Two weeks?'

'Normal, yes.'

'Christ,' said Gabe. 'And how much? How much do we get?'

Olek pulled a face. 'How many box you fill?'

'Well, how much for a box?'

'Many expense,' said Olek, 'we must paying transport, house, tax – sorry for my English.'

'Transport?' said Gabriel. 'That old minibus?'

'Yes.'

'How much for rent?'

Olek shrugged and the dark rings around his eyes seemed to get darker still. 'Saying thirty, but possible charging more.'

'I've only got a camp bed.'

'Yes. Van will go. We must buying now. Later, tomorrow, buying from shop, more better, more cheap food.'

'I'm OK,' said Gabriel. 'I don't need anything.'

Olek bent down as if to tie his shoelace. He took a five-pound note out of his sock and pushed it into Gabriel's hand. 'When you getting money you pay.'

Gabriel went to the van with Olek and bought a pack of rolls, crackers, cheese and toothpaste. After breakfast they walked out to the onion field together, the two women trailing behind. Gabriel asked a few questions and Olek, in halting English, told him a little about himself. He was from the Ukraine, used to work in the accounts department of the telephone company, but had lost his job. He came to England hoping to save enough money to start his own business when he returned. The first job he had been promised failed to materialize. He found work on a construction site but when he took time off after an injury someone else took his place. Then he worked in a meat-processing plant somewhere in the north, and when his pay packet came after two sixty-five-hour weeks there was only forty-four pounds in it. He had not been told about the £150 'arrangement' fee. He made a fuss and was thrown out and for a while he dossed down in a park. Now his only ambition was to scrape together enough money to afford the journey home.

'God, that's really tough.'

'Same everybody,' said Olek. 'Nobody choosing this job.'

'That's true,' said Gabriel. 'Guess I kind of drifted into it myself.'

They started where they had left off the previous afternoon and worked in silence, punctuated only by Olek's coughing fits which were more frequent than yesterday. When he coughed he shrank inside his anorak as if it were eating him bit by bit. But when he stopped he sniffed and cleared his throat and nodded to Gabriel to show that he was fine. For the first few minutes a nagging voice in Gabriel's head told him he should not be here. He didn't listen to it and focused on pulling the onions from the ground as cleanly as he could. The minutes passed into hours and, chained by his fork to this patch of earth, he felt remarkably free, as if he were burying his burdens one by one.

Only a couple of days ago he had been convulsed with worry about who he thought he was. Was he this way or that? What did people think of him? It made him smile to himself. What did it matter? He wasn't Danilo Hetman. He wasn't Gabriel Lightfoot. He wasn't any-body, he was just a man, digging in the soil. He let it all go and sank into a deep warm pool of calm. All those anxious days chasing his tail, scheming, scheduling, plotting, moving restlessly from one care to the next, justifying, reasoning, arguing with himself, all the tension and contradiction, the endless search to get whatever it was he wanted, although he did not know what that was. He exhaled long and hard and let go of everything. He didn't need it any more.

When he looked up he saw a rabbit, shiny fur and liquid limbs, shimmer up the next row. It peeked over its shoulder at him, shook its cotton tail and ran away. The clouds pleated softly across the sky. Green chased green down the fields and a lone weeping ash tree at the boundary trailed its tresses close to the ground. Gabriel dug on. He pulled up a weed with a small yellow flower and examined the tiny stamen. Mum used to say, when she went into the garden and it was growing wild and out of control, no matter how many weeds you pull up, there'll always be more.

He worked, and while he was absorbed he was surprised to find a new self growing in the space that he had cleared, and it had no voice or thought, and he sensed it rather than knew it, and it didn't ring in his ears, and it did not divide him but made him, for the first time, whole. And for the first time in his life he felt that he was connected to the earth, to the trees and sky, and that there was a prayer in him, not words to be offered up, but a life to be led. He thought, *this cannot be true, I am only imagining things.* He thought, *I will wake up tomorrow and everything will be as it was.* But it was only his mind turning things over, as minds, of course, will do. Thoughts, like buses, would come and go, and he would watch them, standing well back from the kerb.

Olek had received instructions from Tymon that they were to return to the barracks for lunch because in the afternoon they were needed in a field at the far side, to finish clearing another crop. As they walked, a series of random reflections entered Gabriel's head. He remembered a suit he had left at the dry cleaners in January and wondered if it would still be there. He thought that he must join a gym and take regular exercise. It seemed that he had stopped scratching his head and he pondered whether, now that he had noticed this, he would start doing it again. A baby rabbit – did he have this right? – was called a kit. An image of Oona floated into his mind; she was laughing her cosmic laugh and showing her gold tooth, but it didn't irritate him. He thought about Charlie. He had messed things up with her and now it was hopeless, beyond repair, and he received this thought without agitation, he accepted it, so that instead of remaining, as it had done so many times before, as a kind of oscillation in his brain, it quickly flowed away.

'How long will it take you to save up?' he asked Olek, as they jumped across the little stream.

Olek began to reply but was overcome by another bout of coughing. When he had recovered he seemed to have forgotten the question. He lit a cigarette.

'Should you be smoking?' said Gabriel. 'I mean, with a cough like that.'

'No,' said Olek, taking another drag.

He told Gabriel about a woman he had met in London when he worked on the building site. When he had been laid up with a leg injury he had lost touch, but before he went home again he intended to stop off in London to see if he could find her.

'Big place, London,' said Gabriel. 'If you don't have her address or anything, running into her would be . . . a big coincidence.'

'Not good chances,' said Olek. 'But must asking question. Sorry for my English.'

'No . . . listen, thanks for that money.'

'Twenty-two persons coming here on bus with you,' said Olek, observing Gabriel with his bloodhound eyes to see if he was following. 'What is chance for two this persons sharing same birthday?'

'So out of the twenty-three of us who arrived, two of us having the same birthday? I don't know how to work it out but it doesn't seem very likely. Three hundred and sixty-five days in a year so the odds are stacked against. The probability is going to be . . . five, six, seven per cent.'

'Over fifty per cent,' said Olek. 'With fifty-seven persons or more, probability of ninety-nine per cent – almost it is certain.'

'Really?' said Gabe. 'Are you sure?'

'Yes,' said Olek, 'I am knowing. Maths degree, Donetsk University.'

'Amazing.'

'Chance,' said Olek, gravely, 'many often not how you think should be.'

They sat on the bench outside the barracks, eating salty crackers and hunks of plastic-tasting cheese. Tymon was in the yard, sorting workers into the backs of two trucks.

Gabe thought about Ted, making shepherd's pie for Nana. He thought about the last time he went to Rileys and Ted standing in the weaving shed spreading his hands firmly over a stopped loom. *Remember, lad, the important thing . . .*

A young man ran up to Tymon, shouting and waving an envelope. Tymon yelled back at him.

The man pulled a piece of paper from the envelope and waved it in Tymon's face. Tymon swatted it to the ground.

'What's going on?' said Gabriel.

Olek shrugged. 'He saying something wrong with payslip, only a hundred pounds for two weeks.'

He was more boy than man, Gabriel saw when he looked carefully, young enough to think that being right meant that you would win.

The shouting continued. Tymon flapped his arms as if to wave the boy away like a stray dog.

'What are they saying?' said Gabriel. 'What's happening?'

'Tymon telling him go if you not liking here, and boy say but they taking his passport.'

'What are—'

'Shush,' said Olek, 'for listening.'

Gabriel sat quiet and still, trying to find a calm space within.

'OK,' said Olek, 'Tymon saying, this boy illegal now, can't working nowhere.'

'Why have they got his passport?'

'For register – work legally.'

'But they didn't do it?'

'No. Now time has passed.'

'Bastards,' said Gabe.

'Yes.'

They thought they could get away with it, because they thought that nobody here was in a position to stand up for this boy. Gabriel tried to let this thought wash over him. He tried to let it go. The last thing he wanted was to lose the peace that he had found.

The shouting continued. Olek offered Gabe a slice of bread.

'It's not right,' said Gabriel. 'Someone should stop them.'

'Yes.'

But the thing was, you drove yourself crazy if you didn't accept the world for what it was.

'Someone needs to go over there and stick a rocket up Tymon's arse.'

'Yes,' said Olek. 'Who?'

It had to be Gabriel. There was no one else. He knew he had to act and at the same time he knew it was only his ego telling him that. Who was he? He was nobody. There was nothing he could do.

The boy remonstrated furiously with Tymon, who suddenly grabbed his arm and twisted it behind his back. Gabriel jumped up and ran over.

'Let go,' he yelled. 'Let the boy go, right now!'

Both Tymon and the boy started, and curious expressions spread over their faces, as if Gabriel had spoken in Japanese.

Tymon dropped the boy's arm. For a couple of moments he stared at Gabe in bemusement. 'English?' he said, at last.

'What you're doing is illegal,' said Gabriel. 'You're infringing this boy's rights.' He tried desperately to remember what Fairweather had told him about this kind of practice and the names of any laws he could throw out that would sound frightening. He settled for saying, 'You might like to know, I'm friends with a government minister. He'll be very interested to hear about this.'

Tymon looked at Gabe's unshaven chin, then down at his muddy trainers and jeans. 'You,' he said, his voice and face sharp with contempt, 'you wait there. I bring Mr Gleeson.'

An alarm went off in Gabriel's head, so loud he could barely hear his own thoughts. Way back, when he'd first started at the Imperial, Gleeson had told him that he grew up on a Norfolk farm. When Gabe had recognized that man – why didn't he trust his own instincts? –

he'd been absolutely right. It must be Gleeson's father, no, *think*, think properly, his brother, more like. And . . . and . . . there was something else . . . what? The minivan. Hadn't he overheard Gleeson once, talking on the phone about a pick-up at Victoria?

But it was none of his business. Oh, why hadn't he kept his mouth shut? Just when he had found a refuge, some peace and quiet at last. He would let it go, let the whole thing go. Think about something else. He had to ring Jenny, don't forget. Ah, there was Dad, big strong hands, *Remember, lad, the important thing . . .*

Tymon strode around the corner with Mr Gleeson in his wake.

'What's your name?' said Mr Gleeson, marching up, and Gabe could see he was poised between fear and anger and preparing to combine the two.

Gabriel hesitated. If he chose, he could back down and act dumb. But he wasn't the kind of person to . . . or was he?

Gabe stood up straighter. 'My name is Gabriel Lightfoot,' he said, 'and I demand you pay this man. What is he owed?'

Mr Gleeson looked at Tymon, the boy and Gabe. Indignation set fire to his eyes. 'What are you?' he said. 'Who are you? What are you doing on my property?'

'And give him his passport back,' said Gabriel. 'Do it now.'

Mr Gleeson looked around the yard as if he expected to be ambushed. 'Who do you work for?'

'I'm currently employed by you.'

Mr Gleeson half lowered his eyelids so that he looked like a reptile basking in the sun. Languidly, he moved away from Gabriel and towards Tymon. In the flick of a tongue he issued a rapid instruction, and Tymon and another henchman, whom Gabe had failed to notice, grabbed him by the arms.

'Search him,' said Mr Gleeson. 'Take his notebook and tape recorder. Son of a bitch!'

Gabriel stood impassively while the two men went through his pockets. They came up empty.

'I'm not a reporter,' said Gabe.

'I'm losing patience,' said Mr Gleeson. 'I have a business – a legitimate business – to run. I'll ask you one more time. Who are you?'

'And I'll tell you one more time – pay that boy.'

Mr Gleeson came up close and looked Gabriel up and down. He smelt just like his brother, of aftershave and righteousness.

'Not a reporter?' He grabbed Gabriel's hands and scrutinized the dirt beneath his nails, the old burns and scars and calluses, the webbing between two fingers where a wound had healed badly. 'No, so I see. A bloody fruitcake.'

'Listen,' said Gabriel, 'I know a lot of people and you could get in a lot of trouble. One of my good friends is in the government, he's a minister, and one word to him about what I've seen . . .'

Mr Gleeson burst out laughing. He slapped Gabriel on the shoulder as if they were sharing a marvellous joke. The henchman joined in the laughter and took the opportunity to give Gabe a friendly shove.

Tymon came out of the barracks, carrying Gabriel's rucksack. He opened it and, without looking inside, tipped Gabe's whites and the rest of the contents on the ground.

Mr Gleeson stood with his hands planted on his corduroy hips, and stamped one wellington boot on his green and pleasant land. 'Do we have any vacancies, Tymon, for a chef? No? I didn't think so. Right, you – get out of here. Run, before I set the dogs on you. Go on, run!'

It took the rest of the day, walking and hitching, to get back to London. When he reached the outskirts of the city he went into an Underground station and hurdled the barriers. Eight thirty when he walked into the kitchen, and it was in full battledress, trays on every surface, the prep area overflowing. Victor nudged Suleiman when he saw Gabriel and within a few seconds everyone had looked up and stopped work.

An unnatural silence pressed down.

'*All* right, O-K,' crooned Oona, bustling over. 'Betta get on with tings.' She led Gabriel into his office and closed the door.

'Something happening tonight, Oona? Event?'

'Yes, yes, yes,' said Oona. She made it sound like a lullaby. 'PanCont Charity Gala. Not to worry, 's all under control.'

'Oh my God,' said Gabriel. 'Has Maddox been doing his nut?'

'Ho, no,' said Oona. 'Told him you ring in sick. Benny, Suleiman and Nikolai been working extra shifts.'

'I'm sorry, Oona.'

She crinkled her almond eyes. 'Look like you need a rest. Why don't you—'

'I've got to see Gleeson,' said Gabe. 'Do you know where he is?'

'Seen him go down to the lockers, but—'

'I can't explain things now,' said Gabriel, 'there isn't time. Could you make sure the petits fours don't come out of the pastry kitchen until it's nearly time to serve. They start melting otherwise, and last time half of them stuck to the trays. Right, I'll go and see Gleeson and then I'll go upstairs and check on . . . oh well, I suppose I'd better get changed first. Any clean whites in the locker room? You know, I don't think our laundry service is really all that good. Maybe we should think about—'

Oona cut in. 'Chef, me an' the boys got everyting covered. You go on home.'

Gabriel looked at Oona's neat clipped ears, her large square bosom, the matronly way she filled his little sickbay. A lump rose in his throat. 'Don't know what I'd do, Oona,' he said, 'without my executive sous-chef.'

Gleeson was in the locker room changing his tie. Still facing the mirror, he drawled, 'Look what the cat's dragged in. Where have you been?'

Gabriel rubbed his chin. 'Nut Tree Farm.'

The restaurant manager froze and unfroze in two rapid frames. He adjusted the knot at his collar. 'OK, let's go along with this fiction for a moment. What were you doing there?'

'Picking spring onions,' said Gabriel. 'For two days.'

Gleeson turned round so smartly that his heels clicked together. 'How amusing,' he said, raising one eyebrow.

'I met your brother. He looks a lot like you.'

'Dear, oh dear, what a state! There are hygiene regulations in a kitchen, you know.'

'I apologize,' said Gabriel, 'for my appearance, but the facilities at Nut Tree Farm are a little limited.'

Gleeson bowed. 'Well, it's been fascinating, as usual, to talk to you. You're so . . . imaginative!' He stalked towards the door. 'By the way, have you managed to find a psychiatrist yet?'

'Don't you want to hear what happened?' said Gabriel. 'I think you should know.'

Gleeson hovered by the doorway. His tongue darted out and ran quickly over his lips. 'Speak, if you wish, and I'll listen, and we'll call it a talking cure.'

'Your brother threw me out.'

'You do surprise me. Can't imagine why.'

'I raised an objection to the way a worker was being treated, an Eastern European – I'm not sure which country he was from.'

Gleeson tutted. 'If you're going to make something up, make it good. Add some details, make it concrete.'

'Apologies once more for the messy presentation,' said Gabriel, peaceably. 'Anyway, as I was saying, this lad wasn't paid what he was owed, and your brother and his thugs had taken his passport, supposedly to get him legally registered. And now they're telling him that they didn't do it, and . . .' He talked on without rancour, feeling only the inevitability of the situation, as if he were only a note being played in someone else's melody. '. . . and he's stayed too long without permission in the country so he can't go to the authorities, so that he's at your brother's mercy . . . and mercy may be one of the qualities your brother happens to lack.'

'This is all very droll,' said Gleeson, polishing a cufflink with his thumb, 'but it may have escaped your notice that this is one of our busiest nights of the year. I only popped down here to change my tie, it had a spot on it. In any case, even supposing anything you say bore the slightest resemblance to reality, why are you telling me?'

Gabriel shrugged. He glanced down at his mud-caked shoes and clothes. How had it come to this? It all went back to Yuri. If Yuri hadn't been drinking that night, if he had dried his feet properly after his shower, if he had fallen a couple of inches further forward or to the side and woken up with a sore head, then Gabriel would never have seen Lena in the doorway, looking at him like that, and one thing would not have led to another. He would have travelled in a different direction. But Yuri was the first link in a tightly coiled chain thrown suddenly overboard, and there was no way to stop it unravelling. Yuri could have dried his feet. But he didn't. It was all random and utterly inevitable. Gabriel saw it both ways, and between these two ways of seeing he felt not the slightest contradiction.

'I don't know,' said Gabriel. 'Giving you fair warning, I guess. That kind of intimidation, you know, it amounts to forced labour, a kind of slavery. Your brother could end up in jail.'

'Oh, for God's sake! A bunch of lies and fairy tales.'

'No,' said Gabe, some heat entering his voice, 'I know what I saw. And I know about the girls as well.'

Gleeson laughed. 'Whatever that's supposed to mean. But what are you waiting for? Off you go to the police. You must have plenty of witnesses to corroborate your little daydream.'

Who would come forward? By the time he had left Nut Tree Farm it looked like the boy was the only person he had managed to scare. Perhaps Olek would be prepared to speak out. But the last time he did that he ended up sleeping rough.

'I won't let it go,' said Gabriel. 'And what about the hotel minibus? That's stolen property, you can't get out of that.'

'What stolen . . . oh, that old bus. We bought it, you loon. Why don't you go and check? You know, I'm starting to feel rather sorry for you.'

Gabriel walked past Gleeson, who, throughout the conversation, had shimmied about the room as if engaged in a fencing match.

'I've said what I had to say,' he told him. 'And I'm going now.'

Gleeson dashed across to the door and began hissing. 'You sanctimonious little arsehole. What gives you the right? Passing judgement on everyone else. People want work, we employ them, it's called giving people what they want. There's a market price, it's called commerce, that's how everything works. Why don't you just get over it? Get real, Chef. Start accepting how things are.'

'What if I don't like how they are?'

'Oh, grow up!' Gleeson yelled at Gabriel's departing back. 'You arsehole! Those workers come through an agency. What about you? What about your own kitchen? Where are your porters from? Are your hands clean? Are they?'

Up in the ballroom, amid a swirl of fancy dresses and penguin suits, the charity auction was in full flow. Although the place was crowded, Gabriel made his way through easily. People stood quickly aside for him. He spotted Maddox talking to a man with an important beard. The man kept raking it with two fingers as if there was much wisdom to be gleaned from it.

'Come on, ladies and gentlemen,' called the auctioneer. 'I know that's not the best you can do. Remember it's for a fantastic cause. Our charity tonight, I'll remind you once more, is the Helping Hands Foundation, and all the money raised will be going to help poor farmers in Africa. Now do I hear one thousand five hundred? One thousand five, I am bid. One thousand six, anybody? Thank you, sir. One thousand eight hundred pounds?'

The item in question, being held up by a scandalous blonde, was a pair of knickers, autographed, and previously worn, by a mega-league pop star.

Gabriel hung back in an alcove, waiting for an opportunity to approach Maddox. He looked around at the men, all dressed in black and white, a collective statement of certainty, no room for shades of grey. The women, with glossy hair and hoisted breasts, fiddled with jewellery that seemed to strobe under the lights. The knots of people standing closest to him drifted steadily away. Discreetly, Gabriel sniffed his sweatshirt. He didn't smell too bad.

He had a better line of sight anyway, to Maddox, and just beyond him he could see Rolly and Fairweather now. Fairweather was laughing and chatting to a young woman in a backless dress. He touched his hand briefly to the ridge of her spine.

'Two thousand three,' said the auctioneer. 'Do I hear two and a half?'

Mr Maddox clocked Gabriel. He threw him a look like a left hook. 'Wait there,' he mouthed.

Gabriel nodded, understanding Maddox's desire to avoid introducing him as executive chef to a member of the PanCont board.

Fairweather, with his finely honed self-deprecating smile, swept back his long blond fringe.

Gabriel, starting to feel a little dizzy, leaned on the edge of the alcove. His head was light, but there was a weight in his stomach and the room began to grow dim. He kept watching Fairweather.

The moment grew inexorably nearer, and though it had not happened yet, it was as good as done.

'One pair of black and red panties, as worn on the Sugar Daddy world tour and signed by the legend herself, going for three thousand one hundred . . . and I'm bid three thousand two.'

As if at the end of a dark tunnel, Gabriel saw Fairweather laugh and twist his wedding band, turning it around his ring finger.

Fairweather, such a way with the ladies, such a way of making them blush! How did he live with himself?

But hadn't he explained to Gabriel the way of dealing with guilt? *Say something often enough, you start to believe it. Let's say you feel guilty about something. Keep telling yourself you don't. It'll do the trick in the end.*

Gabriel looked for a way out, but the doors slammed all around.

'A good cause, ladies and gentlemen, a fantastic cause. Who'll give me three seven fifty?'

Lot of psychopaths in Westminster. Ha, ha, I should say.

Gabriel floated towards Fairweather, he couldn't feel his feet on the ground, couldn't feel anything except the lead in his belly, and the weight in his fists.

'For the poor farmers of Africa, I am hearing four thousand pounds, for these super-sexy panties, signed and worn by a bona fide superstar.'

In the dim outer circle of his vision, Gabe could see Mr Maddox, he could see Rolly eating a canapé from a stick, but they looked like ghosts to him. Fairweather, flesh and blood, flushed and carnal, spotlit in the centre, raised a hand and smiled.

'Going once . . .'

Gabriel raised his own hand, still shaped into a fist. 'What did you do to her?' He drew the fist back.

'Going twice . . .'

He let it fly.

'Sold to the gentleman in the—'

The room imploded in a volley of gasps. Fairweather didn't go down at the first blow, just swayed on his feet with a stunned expression and a great deal of blood pouring from his nose. 'Who?' he said. Gabriel pounded him again so he had him on the floor and got him by the ears and banged his head against the boards and tried to knee him in the groin and pressed his thumbs into his throat and didn't know how he could stop, and then submitted easily to the hands that pulled him off.

Although Mr Maddox and Rolly were standing in front of him and shouting, Gabriel could not hear them, because of the general din. All that punching had left him feeling battered, and a member of hotel security had him in a bear hug from behind. The room grew quieter, as the delayed recognition set in that it might be unseemly to show such excitement at a brawl.

'What the hell? What the hell?' shouted Mr Maddox, disabled by anger.

Rolly dropped to his knees and tended to Fairweather, who was rolling his head from side to side. Fairweather gave a feeble groan.

'Someone get an ambulance,' said Rolly, losing control of his emotions and spraying spittle all over his friend.

Fairweather tried to sit up. 'Oh God,' he moaned. 'I'm OK, nothing broken, no ambulance. We don't want press on this,' he added, before slumping down again.

'Cancel the ambulance,' said Rolly, looking up with reddened eyes. 'You're finished, it's over,' he said to Gabriel. 'I don't even want to hear . . . get yourself a lawyer, if you can afford one, because if you think I'm giving you your money back . . .' He tailed off, overcome, and began to dab at Fairweather with his handkerchief.

Maddox, unable to give full vent before the audience, was turning green and purple, like a head of sprouting broccoli.

'I never – I say *never* – want to set eyes on you again. You go out the back door, don't stop to collect your stuff, don't come back again.'

He turned his back, but then turned round and succumbed to another rant.

'You think you'll get another job in this industry? You think you'll ever work . . .'

Gabriel tuned him out. He looked at Fairweather, sitting up and sipping a glass of water, ministered to from all sides.

He'd had to do it, hadn't he? For Lena's sake. He'd done it for her. *If I see this man I will kill him.* Well, he'd done his best.

A five-strong coterie helped Fairweather to his feet. One of his eyes was beginning to close up, his nose was still dripping, but he adjusted his hair, nevertheless, with a certain panache. He looked at Gabriel almost shyly, the mixture of hurt and bafflement heightened by the lopsided swelling on his face.

Gabriel grew uneasy. Something wasn't right. A plague of doubt spread through him. He opened his mouth but failed to say anything. Where would he begin?

'No,' bellowed Mr Maddox. 'You don't speak. Just get out of here.'

He was frogmarched down the back stairs and then through the kitchen to get to the back exit. He could feel the brigade, all his boys, watching him but he didn't look at them, though he counted, automatically, the dockets fluttering above the pass.

Oona planted herself, rock solid, in front of the door, interrupting the eviction.

'Oona,' said Gabriel, 'it's . . . erm . . . what . . .'

'News travel fast,' said Oona. 'I already heard.'

'Not my finest hour. Not my best day.'

'Tomorrow be better, you see.'

'Well, I guess this is goodbye.'

'You need anyting, you call me.'

'Thanks . . . erm . . . Oona, I have to tell you, because you should know . . . I tried to get you fired.'

'I know,' said Oona. 'News travel fast.'

'Sorry,' he whispered.

''S OK,' she whispered back. 'You not been yourself lately.' She smiled at him and her eyes and her gold tooth twinkled. 'Lord bless you and keep you,' she said.

Gabriel swallowed hard. He sought release of one arm and the security man was good enough to grant this wish. Gabriel, moving slowly, with infinite tenderness, unhooked the diamanté hairclips from Oona's white coat and slid them into her hair.

'Thank you,' he said.

As he was bundled out of the door, he looked back and saw that all his crew had gathered at the nearest station, Victor, Nikolai, Suleiman, Benny, Albert and his assistant, Damian and the rest, only Ivan missing.

'Six dockets up, six tables waiting. Back to work,' he called.

'Yes, Chef,' they cried as one.

She was gone, of course, had left no note, all the drawers she had taken over cleared. Gabriel went into the kitchen, without switching on the light. He stared at the answering machine, the red number blinking at him. Eventually, he pressed play.

'Gabe, I think you best come home,' said Jenny. 'Dad's not doing so good. OK, call me, I'll try your mobile as well.'

'Gabe, could you call me? It's Jenny, by the way.'

'Where are you, Gabe? Dad's had to go in, he's—'

Gabriel hit fast forward. He found the last message.

'This is Jennifer Lightfoot calling on Saturday at 10am. Dad passed away at 9.15, and if anyone else picks up this message, please inform Gabriel Lightfoot that he's to come home straight away.'

CHAPTER TWENTY-SEVEN

—◊—

GABRIEL WAS A FEW MINUTES EARLY FOR HIS APPOINTMENT WITH THE manager of the Greenglades Nursing Home. He was shown into a small reception room which gave on to the landscaped grounds. Beneath the window, set between gravel walkways, a few woody lavenders, etiolated rosemary bushes and ornamental thyme made up the 'aromatherapy garden' which he had seen described in the brochure. Beyond this, however, running a long arc down the gentle slope of lawn, camellias in unrestrained bloom provided an alternative tonic. The lawn gave way to a flower garden, itself fringed by a wood, so that the incarcerated had at least the consolation of a pleasant enough outlook.

Gabe stood in front of the fireplace and examined the painting that hung above the mantelpiece. It was a still life. It showed two apples and a brown and white feather laid on a velvet cloth on a table placed by a window. Although the picture was not, Gabriel assumed, of the highest artistic value, and was cheap enough to reside at Greenglades, and though it could not be said to have a photographic reality, and though he suspected it of not being 'good', he was drawn to look at it, and could see the ripeness of the velvet, reckon the bursting crispness of the apples, and the feather had a certain quality which he had never before observed, just as the painted window offered something which he had failed to notice at all when looking through the real one: the texture, the tone, the way the light fell, the very glassness of the glass.

'Mr Lightfoot?' The woman had the warmly bulldozing manner of Matron and, at her hip, a bunch of warder's keys. 'Mrs Givens,' she continued, extending a hand. 'Manager, for my sins. Shall we start with a walk round?'

'Ah,' said Gabe.

'See you were admiring our painting. Favourite with our guests as well,' she told him, leading the way. 'Sometimes we sit them in here if they get a bit . . . agitated. Calms them. Seems to. I find that interesting, because if I sat them down with a couple of pieces of fruit and a feather . . . well, I don't think it'd have the same effect. Right, here we are, offices to your left, kitchen off to your right, downstairs cloakrooms, physio suite, we'll stick our head round the door.' She moved briskly along. Gabriel, who had visited Nana a couple of times already, wasn't in need of a tour, but he had wanted to meet Mrs Givens, to know what kind of person was in charge. He let her speed on.

'Recreation room,' said Mrs Givens. Although there were two card tables and a cupboard with board games stacked on top, the only recreation being pursued was the television, which seemed always to be on and was tuned to a cookery programme. But the room, like the rest of Greenglades, was clean and airy, and didn't smell, as Gabriel had feared before his first visit, even remotely of cat food and pee.

'Very nice,' said Gabriel.

'Bingo at eleven thirty,' said Mrs Givens, 'watercolours at three.'

They went to the lounge, where most of the inmates were installed and where the television was a constant companion and boon. Several of the residents, however, were unable to watch, due to the severe curvature of their spines. They appeared to be trapped in a permanent search for something of great importance and minute dimensions lost in the folds of their laps. A couple of the more alert old ladies looked at Gabriel with winning smiles, unsure if they were meant to recognize him, but prepared (if not physically then at least in spirit) to rise to the occasion should he turn out to be a grandson or even husband.

'Hello, Mrs Dawson, how are we today? Ready for another round of whist, tea time? She won ninety matchsticks off me the other day. Any questions? Shall we take a peep at the dining room?'

Mrs Givens moved remarkably quickly on her short, stout legs.

Gabriel lengthened his stride to keep up. She clearly liked to remain on the go and Gabe did not blame her; if you sat too long in this place you would be reminded that every room in it, whatever its labelled purpose, was actually a waiting room.

'What's for lunch?'

'Chicken curry,' said Mrs Givens, 'spotted dick and custard, or ice cream.'

'I'm not sure Nana likes curry,' said Gabe.

'If they don't like curry, they can have coronation chicken with rice.' She smiled at him.

'Great,' said Gabe. 'And the coronation chicken, would that be the curry with sultanas thrown in?'

'No flies on you,' said Mrs Givens. 'But you'd be surprised the difference it makes. Now, she's in her room, knows you're coming, least we told her you were,' she continued, knocking at the door and opening it in one continuous movement. 'Mrs Higson, it's your Gabriel here. My door's always open, Mr Lightfoot, to discuss any concerns you might have. We had a few teething problems, it's not unusual with our guests, but I'd say, on the whole, that she's settled down quite well.'

Nana, in her smart knitted navy suit and best white blouse, sat by the window, a faraway look in her eyes. Backlit by the sun, her hair appeared not quite attached to her head, but hovered around it in a soft gold halo. Her hands gripped the armrests of her chair as if it might magically fly her away, as if it were a wishing chair, which in a sense it was, as good a place as any to sit and dream.

She wrenched her attention to Gabriel. 'Hello,' she cried with anxious gaiety. 'Have you come to fetch me home?'

He kissed the parchment of her cheek. 'Hello, Nana, I've brought you some magazines.' He placed them on the bed and sat down next to them.

'I'm going home today,' she said, pursing her lips, divulging, despite her better judgement, this confidential news. 'I've been in three weeks – is it four? – and Doctor says I'm good and ready, yes, I'm healed up nice. Now what was it, just remind me, I've been in for? My hip, was it? Ooh, it's a big operation, but I've not done so bad, have I?'

'Doing really well, Nana,' said Gabe.

'Ted'll fetch me home,' said Nana. 'But if you don't mind, young man, we'll need a hand with the bags.'

'Lovely garden you've got here,' said Gabe. 'Why don't we go out for a little walk?'

'Ooh,' said Nana, scrunching her shoulders, 'it *is* lovely. Lovely, lovely. And a lovely sunny day.'

She gave a tremulous smile, putting her all into it.

Gabriel placed his hand over hers.

She sighed. 'Sad, though, isn't it?'

'It's OK,' said Gabe. 'We're OK.'

'That's right,' she said.

She began to weep silently, fat tears sliding down her face. Gabriel curled his fingers under her palm. Her sadness was too general and too deep to be consoled, so he did not say anything. Though it was without proper reason it did not seem unreasonable for her to cry. Gabriel squeezed her hand gently. He felt the warm rush through his own body that meant he was close to tears, and for the first time since he was six years old and had broken a piece of her best china and been scolded and then forgiven, he cried with his nana. And it was the first time in his adult life that he had cried so openly, without even a trace of shame.

'You'll set me off, you will,' said Jenny, tripping in on her pointed heels.

She sat the other side of Nana and rubbed her other hand.

'All these moaning minnies,' grumbled Nana, reclaiming both her hands. 'There's enough here already, that's the truth.'

Jenny laughed, although the tears had welled. 'Now I've brought some more photo albums, Nana. Beautiful photo I found of you and Mrs Haddock on Blackpool Pier, well she wasn't Mrs back then, can't be more than sixteen . . . Look, you've got identical dresses, never mind best friends, could be twins, couldn't you?'

Nana, with the album propped on her lap, ran a finger across the photograph as if reading an invisible text. 'That's me, that's Gladys,' she explained. 'Blackpool – you can see the tower there. Ooh, I do look

420

vexed! Look here, young man. That's Gladys, that one, oh, what a minx, she's gone and copied my dress.'

They spent an hour with Nana, looking at old photographs, and when she dozed off in her chair Jenny eased a pillow behind her head and they went to sit outside. They found a bench in a sheltered part of the flower garden, surrounded by china-blue hydrangeas and white roses, just coming into bud. Jenny lit a cigarette. 'Good you've given up,' she said. 'I definitely am, but not the best time to try, is it?'

'No,' said Gabe, 'give it a while.'

For a few minutes they sat together, listening to birdsong and the river flow of traffic on the road that lay not far away but out of sight. Since he had returned to Blantwistle six days ago, he had talked endlessly to Jenny about what had happened to him, a little manically at first, but more calmly with each passing day and each retelling. He had told her about Gleeson and Ivan and their dirty secret. He had told about Oona, and the way that he had behaved to her. He had done his best to explain about Lena without turning his explanation into an excuse. And about Charlie. It wasn't easy, but he had tried to piece the story together, without leaving anything out, including his breakdown and how he had thrown away both his job and the new restaurant along with the punches he had thrown at Fairweather on that Saturday night.

When he reached that part she had burst out, 'Oh Gabe, what were you on? I mean, you couldn't have done a better job of cocking things up if you'd tried.'

'I did an excellent job of it,' said Gabe.

Jenny giggled. 'You really did. First rate. So this bloke twiddles his wedding ring and that's why you bash him. Hardly the only one, is he? Loads of men do that.'

'At the time . . .' He broke off, and then laughed. 'It seemed like I had to do it. Stupid. It was spectacular, though.'

'Making a spectacle of yourself, as Nana would say.'

But mostly he had talked seriously and she listened without seeming to pass judgement, accepting his apologies, only asking, from time to time, 'And are you OK now? Are you sure you're OK?'

'What I can't get my head around,' said Gabriel now, at last breaking the silence, 'is where is Nana? I mean, physically she's in her chair. But where's the person, the Nana that we knew?'

'Did I tell you?' said Jenny. 'You know she's got a Zimmer frame now and she doesn't like it, well, the other day she only went and nicked the tea trolley, rattling off down the corridor. And one of the carers says, "Come on now, Phyllis, you know better than that," and Nana puts on her poshest voice and says, "I've a grandson twice your age, I'll have you know, and it's not Phyllis, thank you very much, it's Mrs Higson to you." And away she goes, tea sloshing everywhere, biscuits flying off!'

Gabriel smiled and shook his head. 'Nana! I met Mrs Givens today and she said there were a few . . . what did she call them . . . teething problems, you think that's what she meant?'

'Shouldn't think so. It was a bit tricky, first few days, getting her used to it. There were a few *incidents*. I thought they'd kick her out, honest to God! Apparently she's made a few of them cry. Well, she can be a bit rude, you know. And she goes quite a clip on that Zimmer, and she barged past another old lady on a frame in the corridor, nearly knocked her down.'

'Sounds like Nana.'

'I know,' said Jenny. 'Still Nana in there somewhere.'

It was a fine April day, fresh and sunny as a bowl of lemons. Jenny took off her coat and laid it on the bench. She looked thinner though she assured Gabriel she hadn't lost a single ounce. She was dressed, as she had been all week, entirely in black, effective for both slimming and mourning. Combined with her high, pointy boots and the band of dark roots which now striped her peroxide hair, she looked part punk survivor, part dominatrix. Gabriel much preferred the new outfit to her work blouses in their pastel shades.

'You're quiet today,' he said. 'All week, in fact.'

'You normally think I talk too much.'

'I've never said that.'

Jenny narrowed her eyes at him.

'Honestly, Jen,' he said, with such lack of conviction that they both got a fit of giggles.

'Not that I've been able to get a word in edgeways,' said Jenny, finally.

'Sorry for . . . you know.'

'Don't be daft.'

'I haven't told you the latest. Oona called earlier today.'

'Which one is . . . oh yeah, I know, go on.'

'Ivan, my grill man – he's been arrested, and charged with trafficking.'

'Wow,' said Jenny. 'So it's all true, what what's-his-name told you.'

'Victor. Looks like it. We'll see.'

'What about the restaurant manager? Gleeson, wasn't it?'

'He's disappeared, and so has Branka, who ran Housekeeping. Police are looking for them.'

Jenny whistled. 'Must have been a long conversation you had this morning. Took about five days to tell me.'

'No,' said Gabriel. 'I didn't get into it all. And Victor had told her what he knew so she pretty much had the picture.'

'What's Oona going to do? She's not got you or Gleeson . . . and with the restaurant to run.'

'Oona will do what she's always done,' said Gabriel. 'Oona will cope.'

'They'll want to talk to you,' said Jenny. 'The police.'

'Expect I'll hear from them soon. Jenny – do you think I should tell them about all that stuff on the farm?'

Jenny crossed her legs and stabbed him fondly in the shins with the tip of her boot. 'Course you should! Why? You're not thinking you can't be bothered, are you?'

'It's not that. But what happens to all those workers if they lose their jobs, get deported even?'

'It's not right, though,' said Jenny. 'You know that.'

Gabriel sighed.

'Anyway,' said Jenny, 'maybe the police will go to the farm, looking for Gleeson. Maybe it won't all be in your hands.'

'Maybe,' said Gabriel. 'Shall we walk for a bit?'

★

They meandered through the garden, past white columbines and fox-gloves and a thicket of the same type of lilies as they had laid yesterday on Ted's coffin.

'I don't understand,' said Jenny, 'why you're giving up so easy on the restaurant. Explain to that bloke – you know, way you explained to me. It'll be embarrassing, I give you that.'

'Fairweather might shake hands and forget it. But Rolly never would. Even when I missed a meeting he'd do his nut, say I was a liability, and this was . . . this was something else.'

'Get your money back, Gabe,' said Jenny. 'You can't give up – sixty thousand! – that money's yours.'

'I don't know. I'd have to get a lawyer. Rolly's ended up in court with partners before, and he's always won.'

'That's robbery!'

'I don't even have money to pay a lawyer.'

'When we've sold Dad's house . . .'

'But the fees for this place . . .'

'Yes, Greenglades isn't cheap,' said Jenny, 'and Nana, though she's officially been ill since 1972, will probably outlive us all.'

They walked up to the lawn. Two blackbirds flew down, their yellow eye-rings and orange bills flashing against black plumage. With courtly demeanour, they bowed to each other before commencing the duel. The birds ran at each other, and though the fight was short and, to the undiscerning eye, inconclusive, the matter appeared to be settled. The victor rose to his perch in a thorny bush and sang a low melody, and the vanquished ducked his tail and then flew away.

'What about you?' said Gabriel. 'How's your work? Will you go back next week, d'you think?'

'I've got to,' said Jenny. 'Don't want to lose me job. Though there's these rumours going round – might lose it anyway.'

'You're kidding – what?'

'Not just me. Whole place might close. They're looking at an Indian call centre, apparently.'

'We'll set up a fish and chip shop, then. People still eat fish and chips, don't they?'

'They do. But we'd have to sell kebabs as well.' Jenny stopped and puffed out her cheeks. 'God, will you slow down? These boots are killing me! And I've really got to lose weight, I'm sinking into the lawn every blinkin' step I take. How did I get this fat, Gabriel? I never even noticed, you know, it all creeps up, and remember when I was seventeen, how thin I was back then? And look at me now!'

'You're looking good,' said Gabriel. 'I was just thinking that when we were sitting down.'

'Sod off,' said Jenny.

'I mean it. I like you in black, I like those boots, I particularly like the black stripe down the top of your head.'

Jenny hit him on the shoulder. 'Watch it,' she said. 'You're not the only Lightfoot can throw a punch, you know.' She looked pleased. 'And you're not so bad yourself.'

'I'm going bald.'

'Where?'

Gabe touched the patch.

'Can't see it. Not with all those curls.' She reached up and felt his skull. 'What, that? Honestly. Anyway, if the call centre closes and we can't afford a chip shop, I've got something else up me sleeve.'

'Wondered what you kept up there,' said Gabriel, tickling her on the arm.

'Mum, Gabriel's teasing me!'

'So,' said Gabe. 'What?'

'Know Rileys?' She smiled to acknowledge that the question wasn't strictly necessary and quickly went on. 'Well, they're opening up a new bit – Weaver's Time Tunnel, it's called, and it's, like, this sort of museum, heritage centre, they say, explaining all about the old days, going back to the Spinning Jenny and the first looms and all that stuff, right up to the nineties, I think. And, anyhow, they're wanting people, tour guides sort of thing, and I thought I might enjoy it, you know, give me a chance to talk.'

'Great,' said Gabe, 'that's great.' For a second he wondered what Ted would think, before he realized his mistake.

'What I need is a holiday,' said Jenny. 'We really want a few days away but I'm not keen on leaving the kids, though Harley's of age, as he keeps reminding me, and Bailey should be old enough. I wouldn't be easy, though, leaving them. I'd not be easy in my mind.'

'Few days away with Des sounds like a good idea,' said Gabriel. 'How about if a highly responsible and reliable uncle spends some overdue time with his nephew and niece?'

Jenny patted his back and pressed around his shoulder blades.

'Well, I am unemployed,' said Gabriel, 'so I'm not sure I deserve all that patting, but thanks, nice to be appreciated.'

'Just checking something,' said Jenny.

'What?'

'For a minute there, Gabe, I thought you might be sprouting wings.'

Jenny drove him back to Plodder Lane and said she'd come in but not stop long. They went into the porch and Gabriel pulled up the blind, which, for reasons lost to history, was always lowered when the house was empty and raised when someone returned. He picked the post off the doormat and stacked it on the vegetable rack which had long served as the porch's shelving system, and once inside the hallway, hung the door key on the hook. Although Jenny had offered to put him up, he had been staying in the house all week, sleeping whenever he wasn't talking to Jenny, though occasionally he had found himself with duster in hand, doing a slow but thorough round of housework. The house, which had seemed so dead with Dad and Nana in it, insisted on living now that they were gone, a quiet but irrepressible life that Gabriel could not help but witness when he wiped over Nana's drinks trolley or lifted Ted's retirement carriage clock to dust. He saw it now when he sat down on the sofa and looked at Ted's armchair, the permanent hollow in the seat cushion, the worn fabric of the arms at the two exact places on which Ted would spread his hands.

Jenny fell into Nana's wingback chair which she seemed naturally to inhabit now on her visits. 'Well, I'll love you and leave you,' she said, but put her feet up on the stool and seemed unlikely to go anywhere.

'Are you absolutely sure you don't want to stay with us?' she said. 'It's no bother, there's plenty of room, well, there isn't, of course, but we'll make some.'

'Thanks. I'm OK here. I've settled in.'

Jenny's eyes were bright. She sniffed and rubbed her nose. 'Oh, I hate leaving Nana. I hate it every time I come away.'

'But she needs full-time care, Jenny, and you've got to work.'

'I know.'

'I liked Mrs Givens. She was good with the residents – she won't be calling Nana Phyllis.'

'No. It's the best place, I looked at quite a few. It's just that . . . I feel I'm not doing right.'

Gabriel looked at the row of cards on the mantelpiece. Last time he had been here there had been Christmas cards. Now the cards all said *In deepest sympathy* or *Sorry for your loss*. 'You've done right by her,' he said. 'You've always done right by everyone.'

Jenny held herself together by a smile. 'What you going to do, Gabe? All your plans . . .'

'Ah, well.' He shrugged and laughed. 'Make a new one. I'll be fine.'

She looked at him closely. 'You'd tell me if you weren't.'

'Of course.'

'Promise me you'll see a doctor if . . .'

'I will,' he said, not blaming her for her scepticism. He was a little sceptical himself. 'I promise.'

'There's a load of boxes in the loft still want sorting out. Dad made a start and I've done a bit, but . . . it takes ages because you keep stopping and looking at things and thinking . . . oh, I found a pin-cushion, by the way, made it at primary school and gave it to Mum, done in these big cross-stitches, daisy shape, gave it her for Mother's Day, I think, and that's what I was meaning – you find something like that and then go off in a bit of a dream.'

'No, that pincushion,' said Gabriel, 'I think I . . .'

'What?'

'Nothing. No, nothing. It's nice that she . . .'

'. . . kept it. I know. I was really pleased.'

They were quiet for a while.

'Don't know what to do with half the stuff, that's the problem. Don't want to keep it, don't want to throw it out. What about Dad's ships, Gabe? What'll I do with them?'

'I'll have them.'

'There's quite a few.'

'I'll find room. My flat's pretty empty.'

'With Lena gone. Think she'll ever be in touch?'

Gabriel shook his head. 'Jenny, I don't know what you must think of me, hearing all of that.'

Jenny put her feet down, sat up and rapped him on the knee with her knuckles. 'I'd give you a hard time, Gabriel Lightfoot, if you hadn't already done it yourself. Only reason I'm not – you've made a right thorough job of it.'

'I'd like to think she'd call if she needed . . . but realistically, no, she won't.'

Jenny rearranged the black folds of her new svengali garb. 'There's someone who might be calling you, though. Spoke to Charlie last night.'

'You spoke to Charlie? You rang her? How did you get her number? What did she say?'

'Remembered the name of the place where she sings, you told me, and Harley looked it up on the internet.'

'You called her at the Penguin? What did she say?'

'She sounded lovely,' said Jenny. 'Told her about Dad, of course, that's why I rang, thought she should know.'

'But what did she say?'

'Said she'd call you. Said she'd do it today.'

'She won't,' said Gabriel. 'Why should she? She won't call.'

Jenny sighed. She made as if to get up but then sank back in the chair. 'It was a nice service, wasn't it?'

They'd had this conversation several times today. It had become a kind of litany.

'Yes. It was very nice.'

'Everyone came.'

'Lot of people.'

'Good turnout.'

There was something he'd been wanting to ask her. 'Did . . . did Dad want it in the church . . . did you . . . ?'

'Talk about it, yes. He did.'

'But he didn't go. Not since we were little, dragged us to Sunday School anyway, I can't remember when.'

'No,' said Jenny. 'Gabe – did you pray?'

'Sort of.'

'Me too. Do you believe?'

'No. Do you?'

'No.'

'I don't believe,' said Gabriel. 'But I have faith, if you know what I mean.'

'What in?'

'I don't know. Life. Carrying on, I suppose.'

'Yes.'

'Jenny, I know I've been a bit wrapped up in myself recently, but . . .'

'Oh, I wouldn't say that,' interrupted Jenny.

'No, I have.'

'I wouldn't say recently.' She gave him a sideways look. 'I'd say about the last thirty years.' She giggled and then gave way to a screech, and she laughed so hard she threw up her hands and slapped them down on her thighs, riding a roller coaster, and Gabriel joined her and they sat and laughed like little children with tears pouring down their cheeks.

Gabriel waved Jenny off as she reversed out of the drive, and then went into the kitchen. He opened the fridge. Aside from the clingfilm-wrapped sandwiches left over from yesterday's funeral tea, there wasn't much in it, a couple of chicken breasts, some salami, a jar of pesto, a few tomatoes. He gathered all the vegetables from the basket and assembled them on a cutting board. He laid out the contents of the fridge, and lined up some tins which he took from the cupboard. He thought a bit. He felt like cooking, but he didn't know what to make. Not the most promising of ingredients but give him a minute and he'd come up with an idea. Yes, he thought, having a glimmer, he could make something out of this.

His mobile rang. 'Charlie,' he said, 'I didn't tell her to call you. She got your number off the internet.'

'I'm glad she did. Gabriel, I'm really sorry. Sorry to hear about your dad.'

'Thanks,' said Gabe. 'It was a lovely funeral.'

'I'm sorry I never met him.'

'I'm sorry too.'

It was his turn to speak but Gabriel couldn't. He squeezed his eyes closed.

'Gabriel,' said Charlie, 'how are you? I've been so worried about you.'

'About me?'

'Yes, you, you twit. You were behaving like a lunatic the last time you came round.'

Gabriel saw Charlie as clearly as if she were standing next to him, the curve of her hip, the roll of her shoulder, the way her green eyes danced over his face. 'Think I blew a gasket or something. Sorry.'

'I've got a spare fuse in the drawer.'

'Charlie . . .'

'Look, when you're back, maybe we should get together for lunch.'

'I'd love that.'

'Only lunch, Gabriel. Only lunch.'

'A dry crust is fine for me.'

He felt the touch of her breath down the phone.

'What I'm saying, Gabriel, is don't go getting your hopes up.'

'Oh, I won't. I promise. I'll try not to,' he said, in all earnestness and with a great deal of hope in his heart.

ACKNOWLEDGEMENTS

I am grateful to the following authors, whose work has informed my own: Peter Barham, *The Science of Cooking*, Springer, 2000; Hervé This, *Molecular Gastronomy*, Columbia University Press, 2006; Robert L. Wolke, *What Einstein Told His Cook*, Norton, 2002; Jo Swinnerton (ed.), *The Cook's Companion*, Robson, 2004; Mark Kurlansky, *Choice Cuts*, Jonathan Cape, 2002; Anthony Bourdain, *Kitchen Confidential*, Bloomsbury, 2000; A. Wynne, *Textiles*, Macmillan, 1997; J. E. McIntyre and P. N. Daniels (eds), *Textile Terms and Definitions*, The Textile Institute, 1997; Caroline Moorehead, *Human Cargo*, Chatto & Windus, 2005; Rose George, *A Life Removed*, Penguin, 2004; Larry Elliott and Dan Atkinson, *Fantasy Island*, Constable, 2007; Joseph Rowntree Foundation (Gary Craig, Aline Gaus, Mick Wilkinson, Klara Skrivankova, Aidan McQuade), *Contemporary Slavery in the UK: Overview and Key Issues*, 2007; Klara Skrivankova, *Trafficking for Forced Labour: UK Country Report*, Anti-Slavery International, 2006; Nalini Ambady and Robert Rosenthal, 'Half a Minute: Predicting teacher evaluations from thin slices of nonverbal behaviour and physical attractiveness', *Journal of Personality and Social Psychology*, 1993; Eliot Deutsch, *Advaita Vedanta: A Philosophical Reconstruction*, East-West Center Press, 1969; Galen Strawson, *Freedom and Belief*, OUP, 1987; John Gray, *Straw Dogs*, Granta Books, 2002; Richard Sennett, *Respect*, Allen Lane, 2003, and *The Corrosion of Character*, Norton, 1998; and Zygmunt Bauman, *The Individualized Society*, Polity Press, 2001.